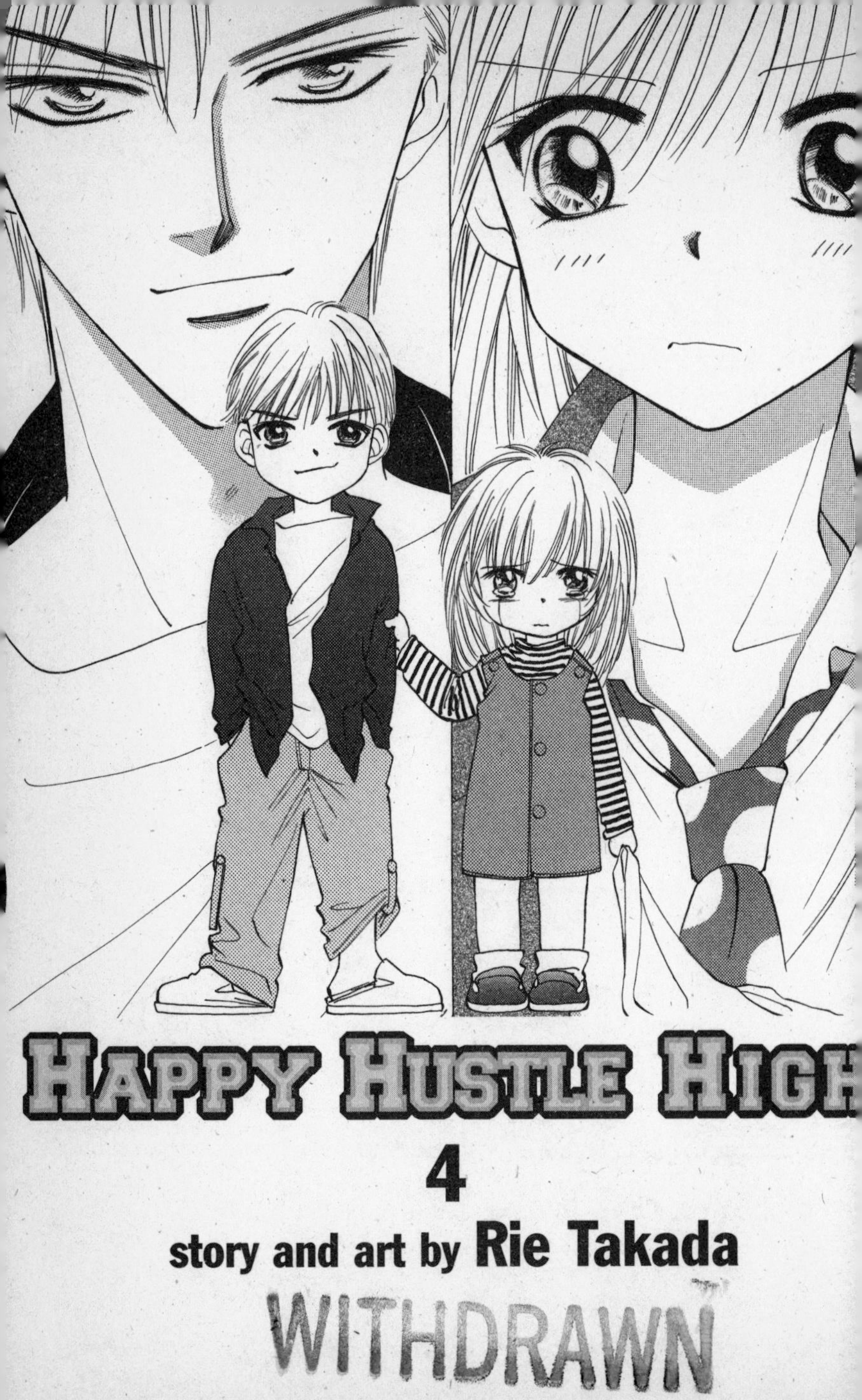

HAPPY HUSTLE HIGH

4

story and art by Rie Takada

CHARACTER

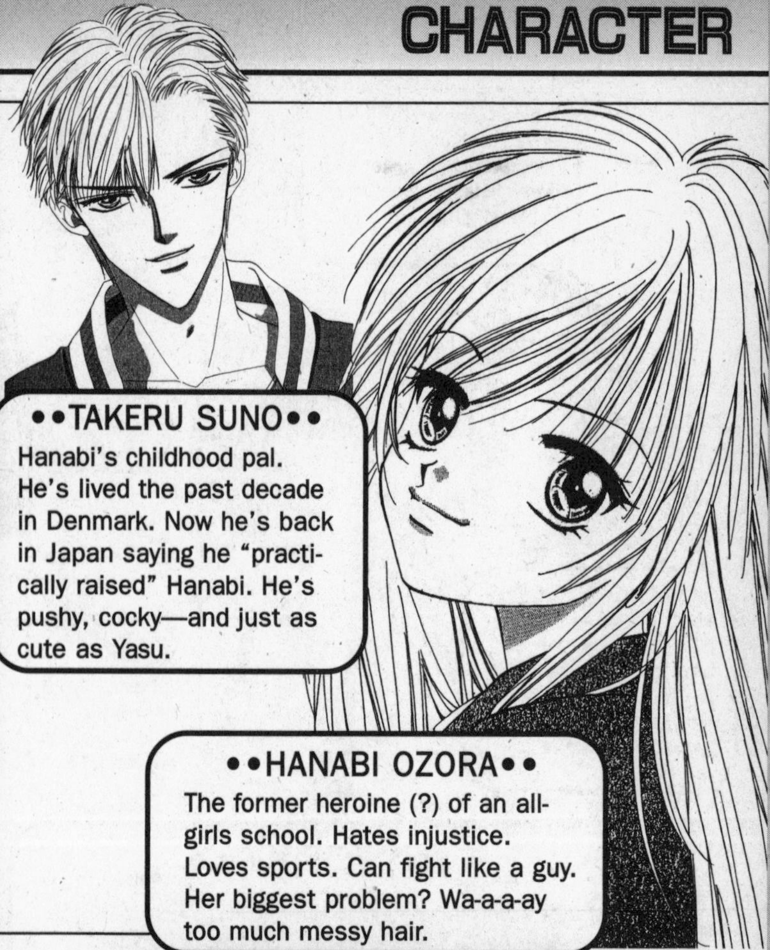

••TAKERU SUNO••

Hanabi's childhood pal. He's lived the past decade in Denmark. Now he's back in Japan saying he "practically raised" Hanabi. He's pushy, cocky—and just as cute as Yasu.

••HANABI OZORA••

The former heroine (?) of an all-girls school. Hates injustice. Loves sports. Can fight like a guy. Her biggest problem? Wa-a-a-ay too much messy hair.

HAPPY HUSTLE HIGH

Vol.4

CHARACTERS

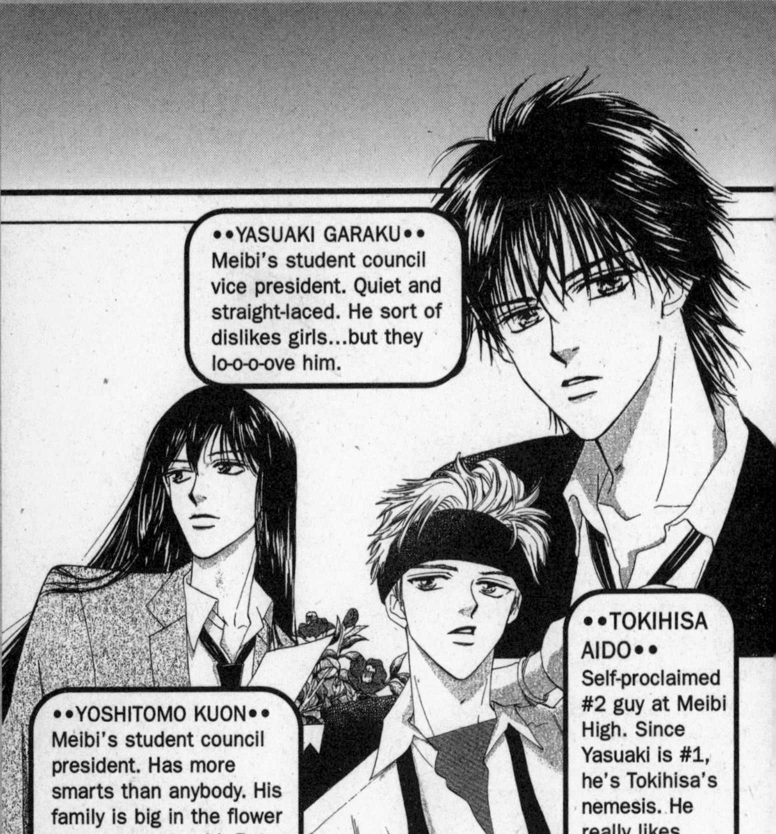
••YASUAKI GARAKU•• Meibi's student council vice president. Quiet and straight-laced. He sort of dislikes girls...but they lo-o-o-ove him.
••TOKIHISA AIDO•• Self-proclaimed #2 guy at Meibi High. Since Yasuaki is #1, he's Tokihisa's nemesis. He really likes Hanabi, but has stopped chasing her.
••YOSHITOMO KUON•• Meibi's student council president. Has more smarts than anybody. His family is big in the flower arrangement world. But behind his handsome exterior...

•••STORY•••

One day, an ordinary all-girls school merges with Meibi High, a very elite all-boys school. Hanabi, a popular tomboy, is the girls' rep on a student council full of hot guys. To her surprise, she starts dating Yasuaki, who seems cold but is actually very nice! True love ain't easy, and now the happy couple has one big problem: Takeru Suno, Hanabi's childhood pal. After ten years away, Take suddenly reappears—and declares war on Yasuaki! Who will Hanabi choose?

HAPPY HUSTLE HIGH

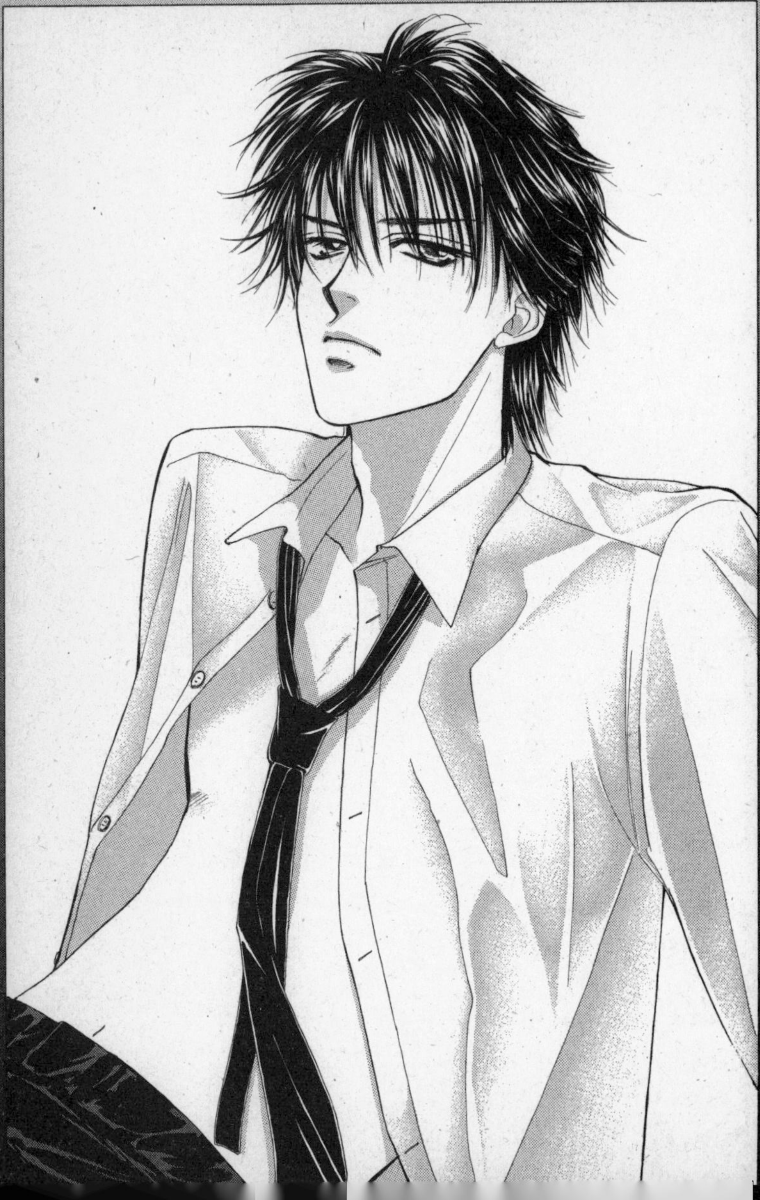

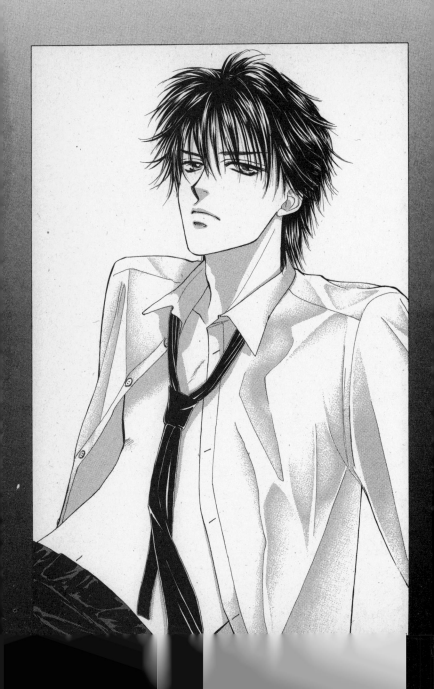

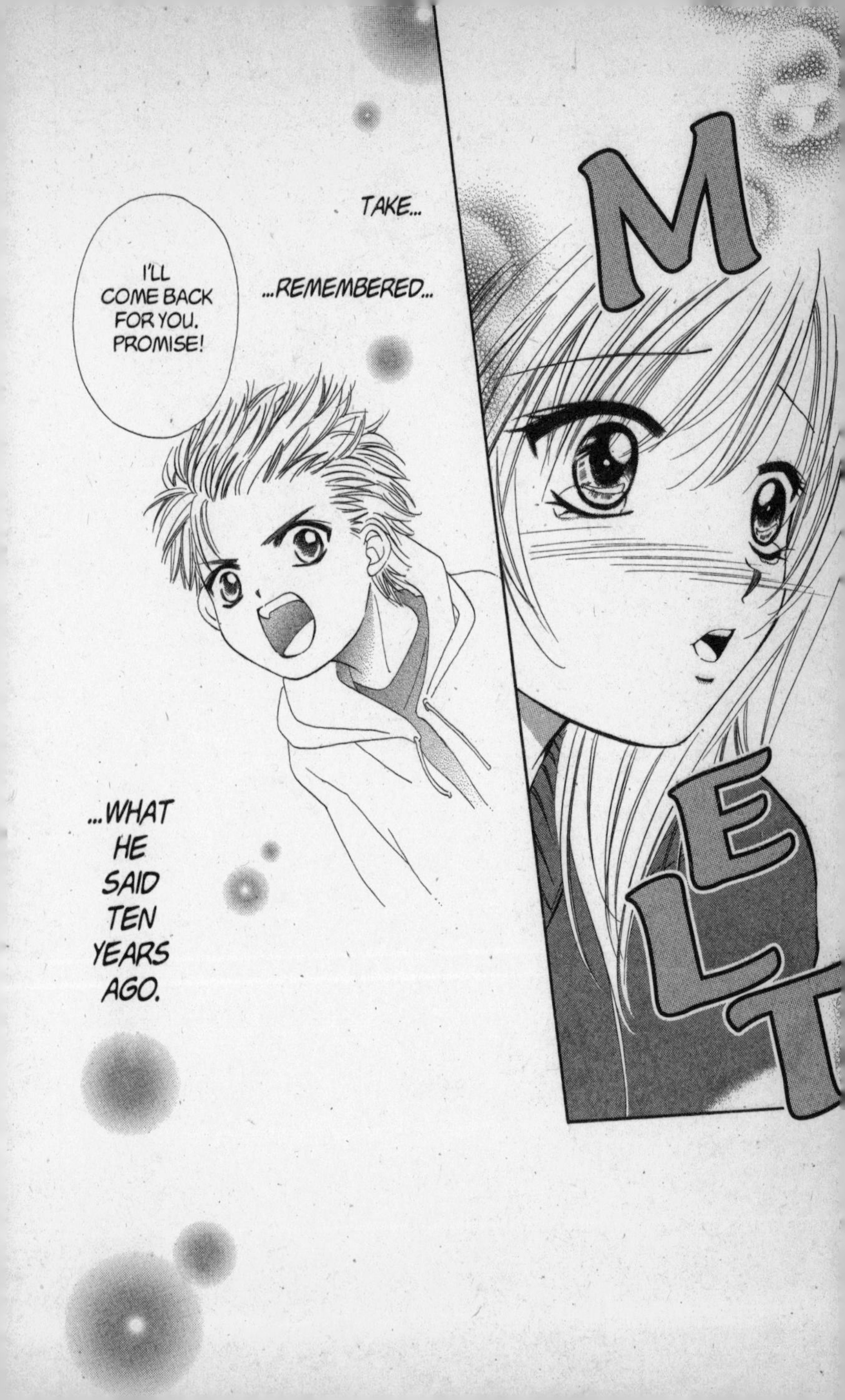
MELT
TAKE...
...REMEMBERED...
I'LL COME BACK FOR YOU. PROMISE!
...WHAT HE SAID TEN YEARS AGO.

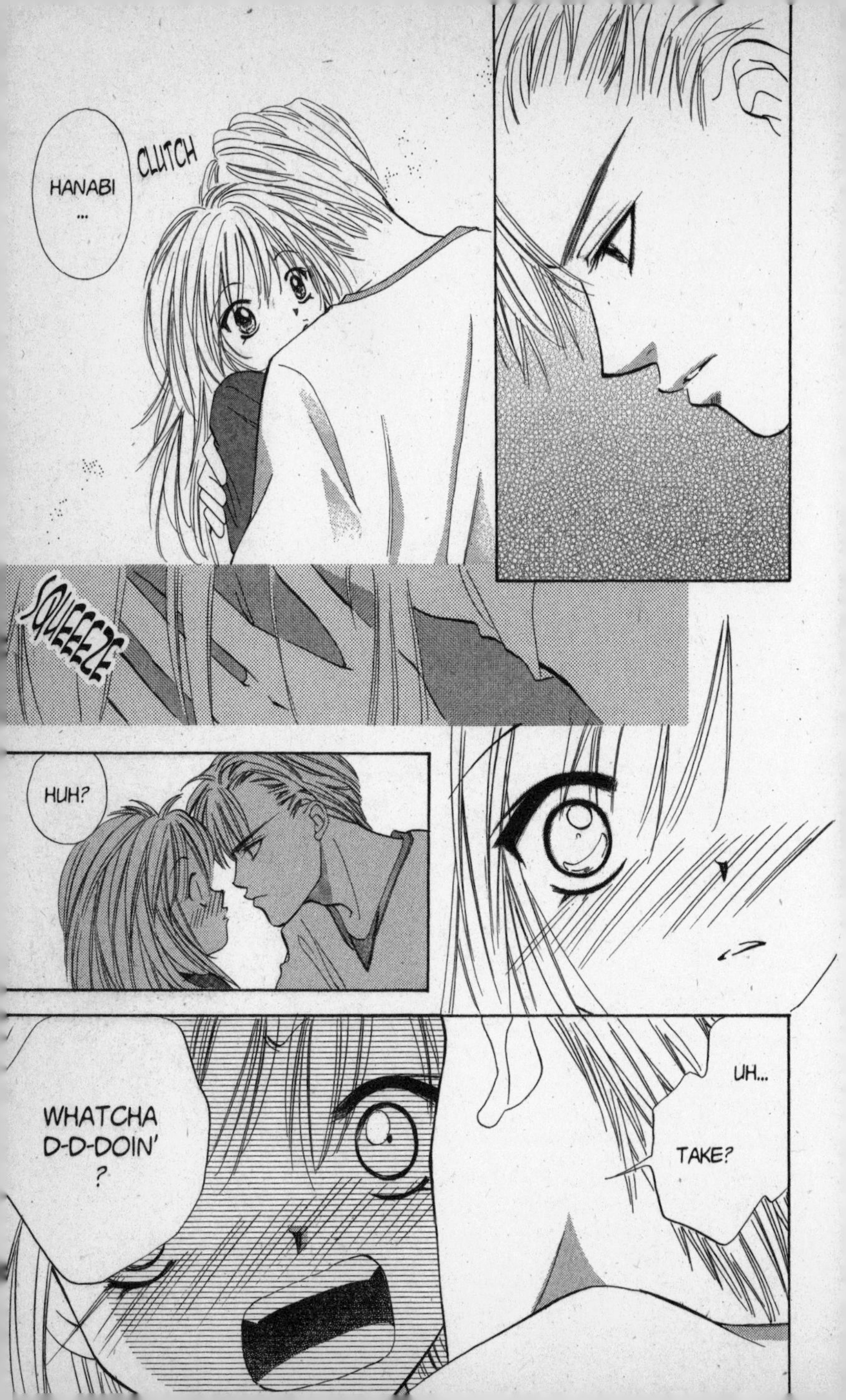
HANABI ...
CLUTCH
SQUEEEEZE
HUH?
UH...
TAKE?
WHATCHA D-D-DOIN' ?

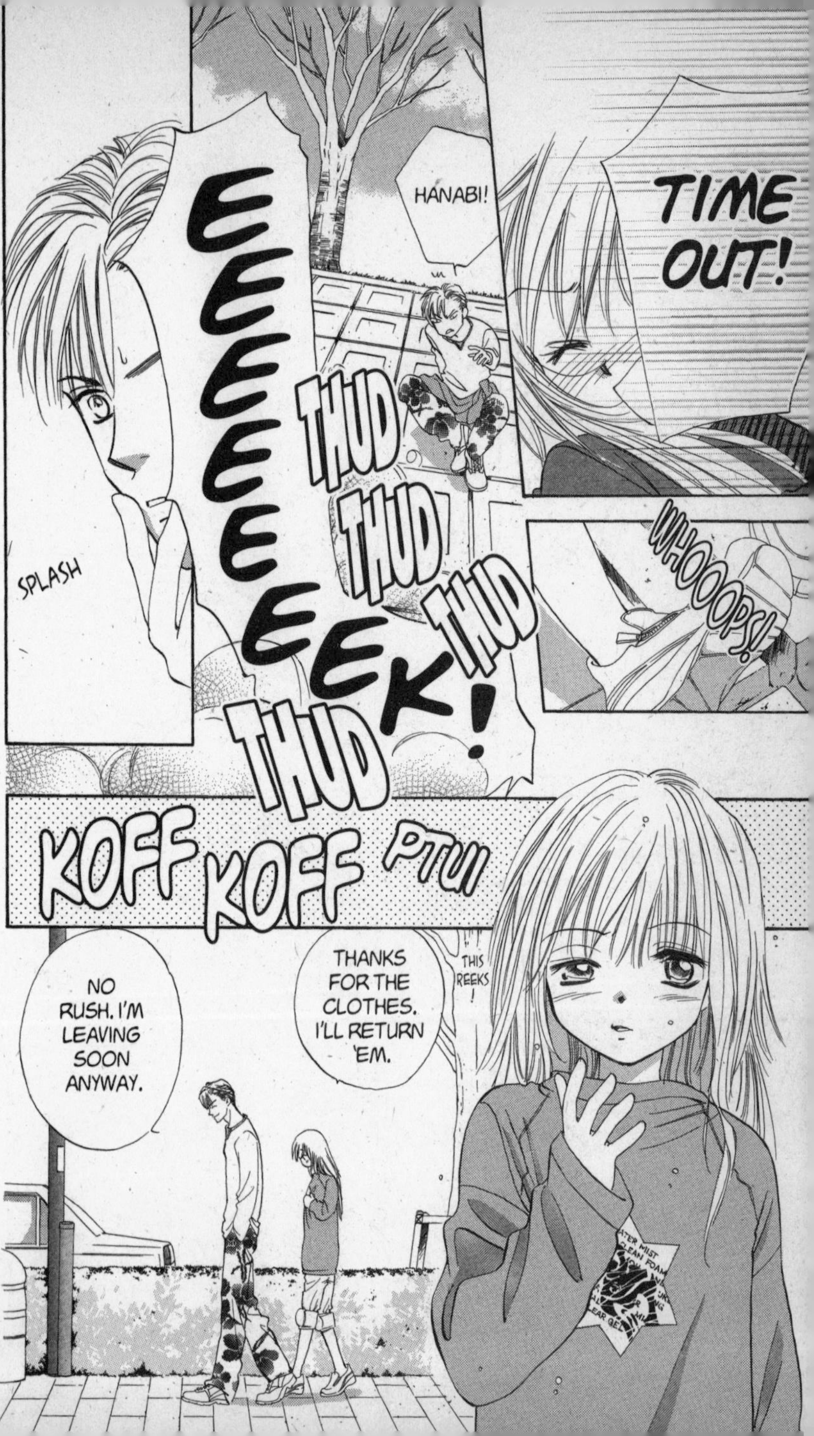
TIME OUT!
WHOOOPS!
HANABI!
EEEEEEEK!
THUD THUD THUD THUD
SPLASH
KOFF KOFF PTUI
THIS REEKS!
THANKS FOR THE CLOTHES. I'LL RETURN 'EM.
NO RUSH. I'M LEAVING SOON ANYWAY.

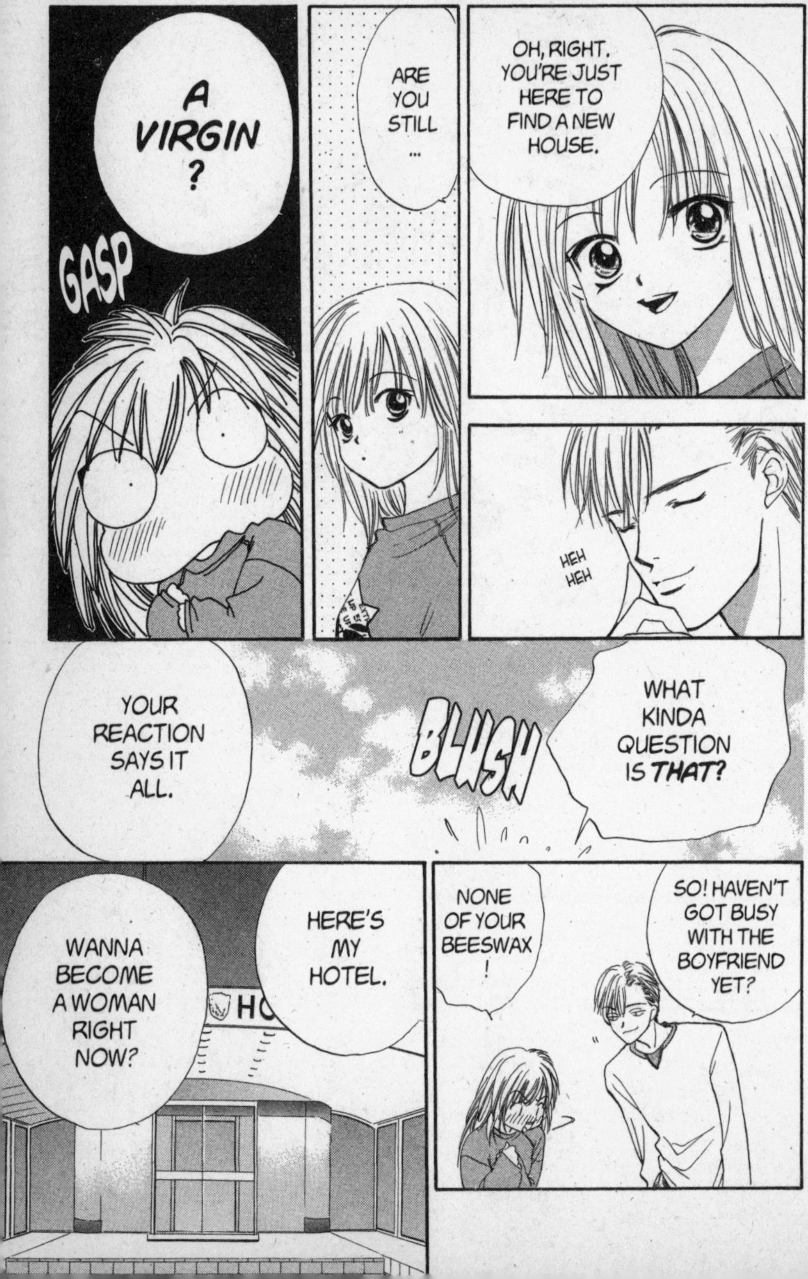
OH, RIGHT. YOU'RE JUST HERE TO FIND A NEW HOUSE.
HEH HEH
ARE YOU STILL ...
A VIRGIN ?
GASP
WHAT KINDA QUESTION IS *THAT?*
BLUSH
YOUR REACTION SAYS IT ALL.
SO! HAVEN'T GOT BUSY WITH THE BOYFRIEND YET?
NONE OF YOUR BEESWAX !
HERE'S MY HOTEL.
WANNA BECOME A WOMAN RIGHT NOW?

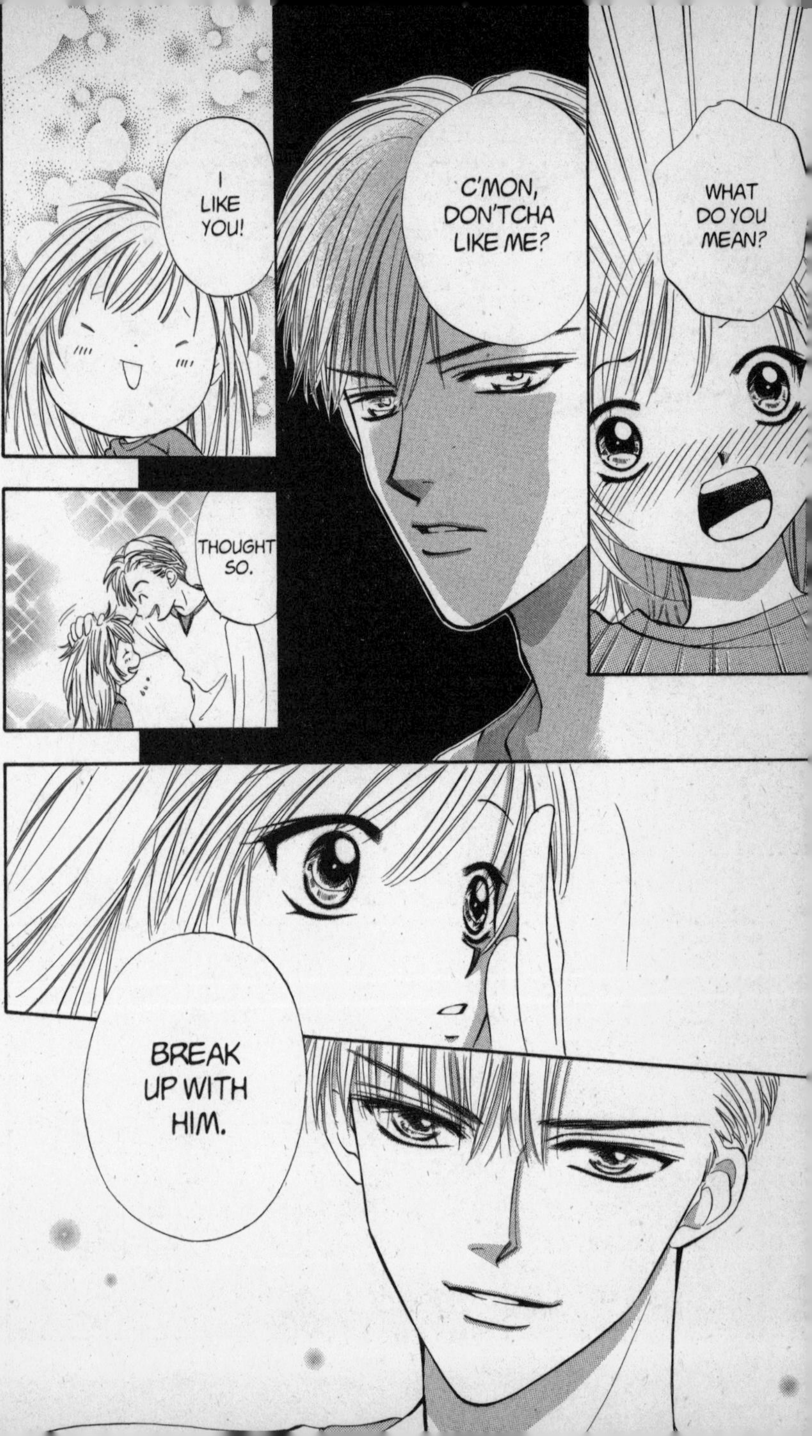
WHAT DO YOU MEAN?
C'MON, DON'TCHA LIKE ME?
I LIKE YOU!
THOUGHT SO.
BREAK UP WITH HIM.

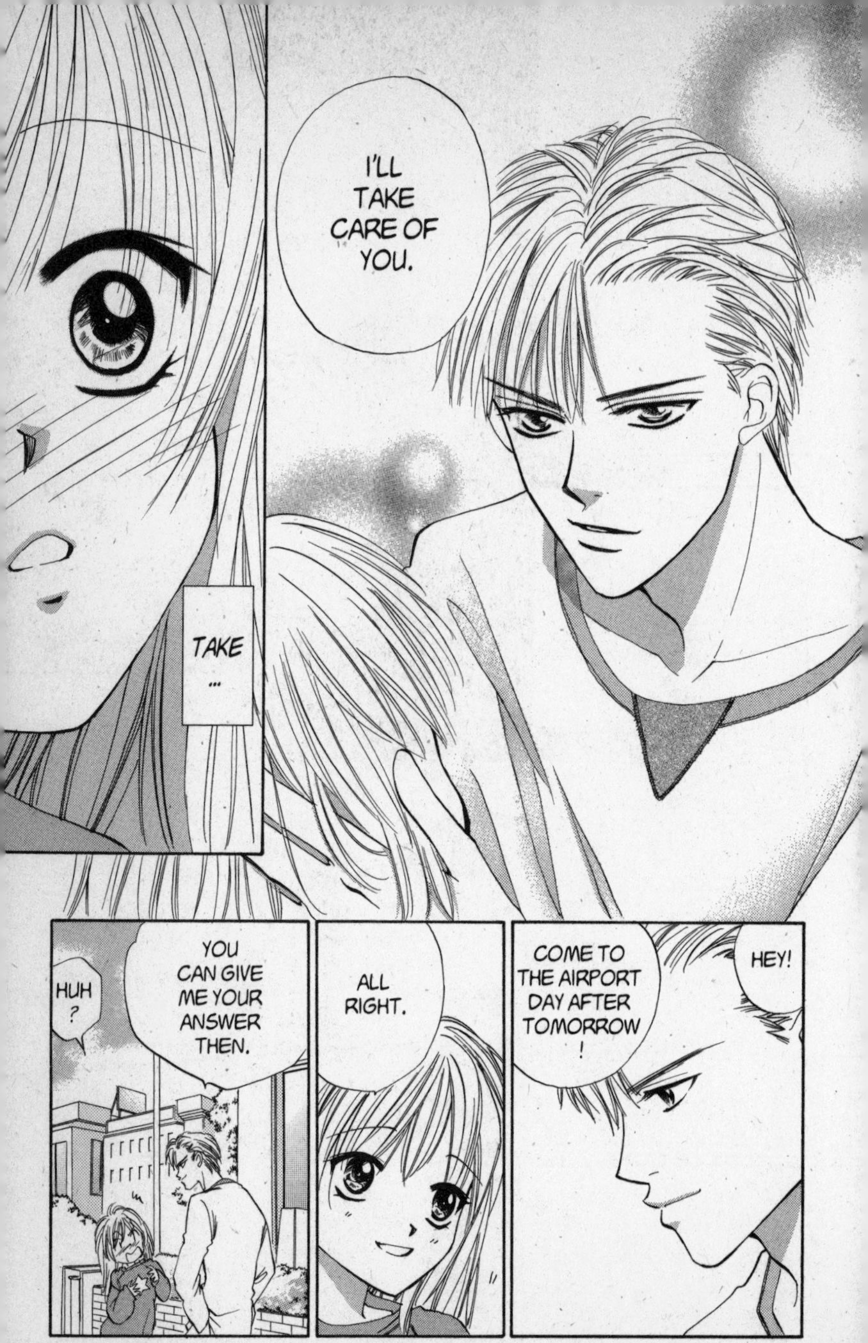
I'LL TAKE CARE OF YOU.
TAKE ...
HEY!
COME TO THE AIRPORT DAY AFTER TOMORROW!
ALL RIGHT.
YOU CAN GIVE ME YOUR ANSWER THEN.
HUH?

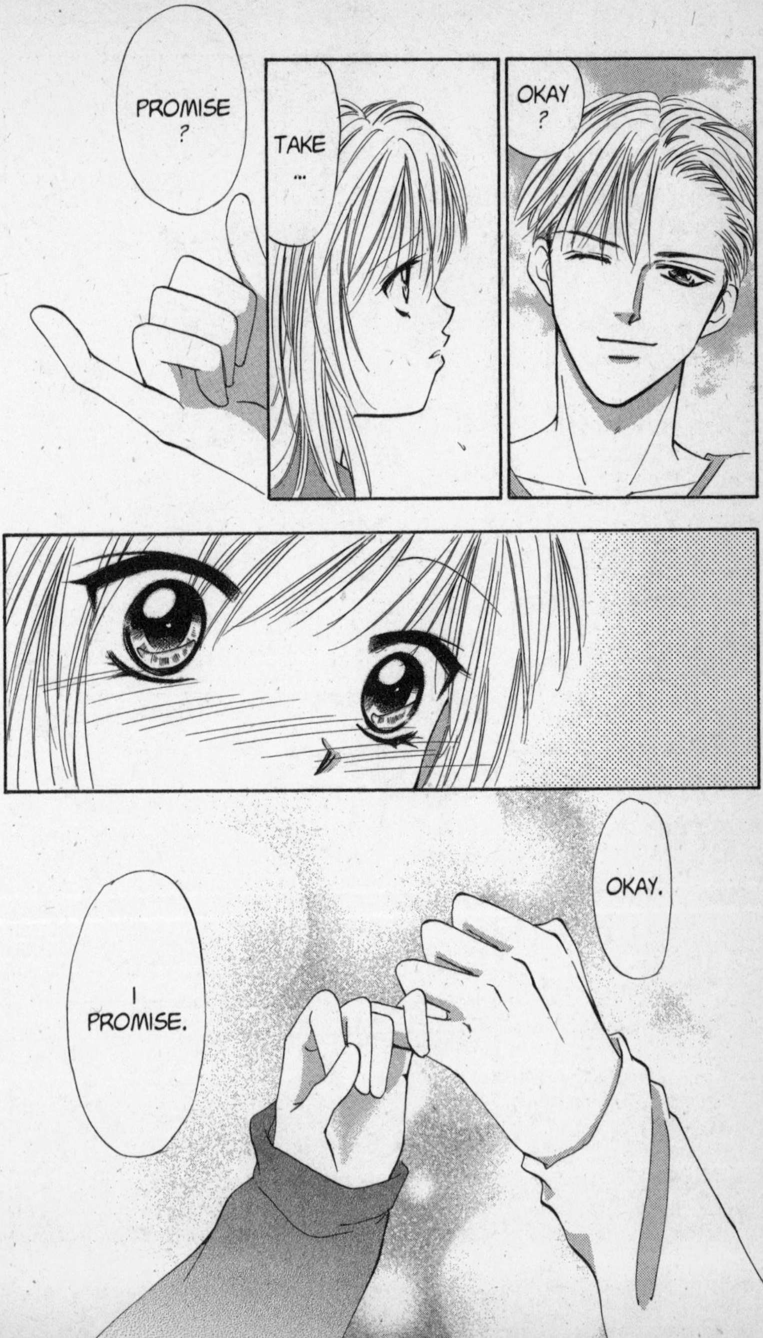
OKAY ?
TAKE ...
PROMISE ?
OKAY.
I PROMISE.

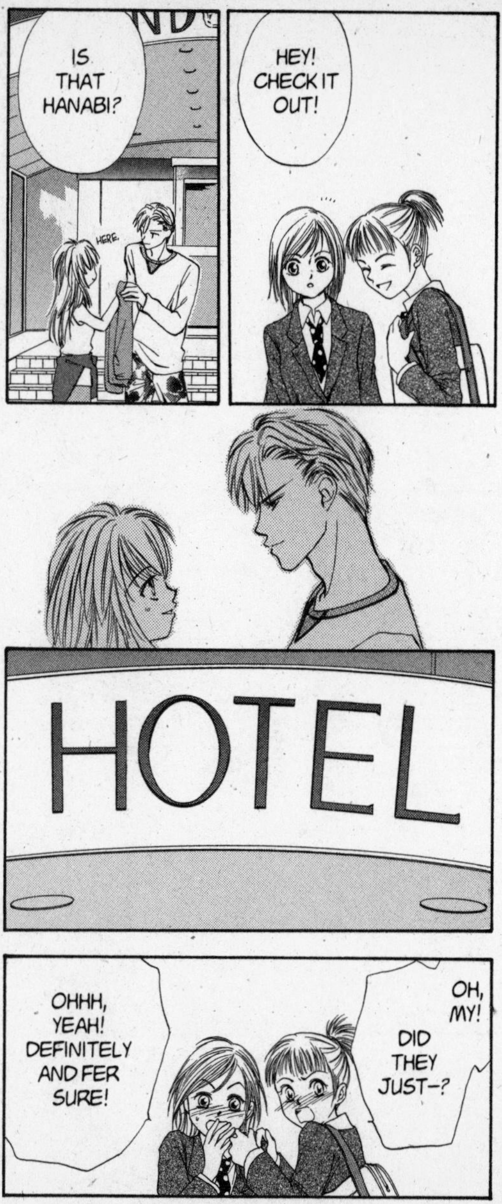
HEY! CHECK IT OUT!
....
IS THAT HANABI?
HERE.
HOTEL
OH, MY!
DID THEY JUST-?
OHHH, YEAH! DEFINITELY AND FER SURE!

GREETINGS + THE TUGBOAT

HELLO! I USUALLY PUT PICTURES OR ANSWERS TO QUESTIONS HERE. THIS TIME I HAVE A REQUEST!

A WHILE BACK, IN ANOTHER MAGAZINE, I WROTE ABOUT MY SEARCH FOR "THE TUGBOAT," A JAPANESE CHILDREN'S BOOK. MANY READERS PROMISED TO LOOK FOR IT. THANKS SO MUCH! UNFORTUNATELY, THAT OLD BOOK IS REALLY HARD TO FIND.

IT HAD A PINK COVER, I THINK...

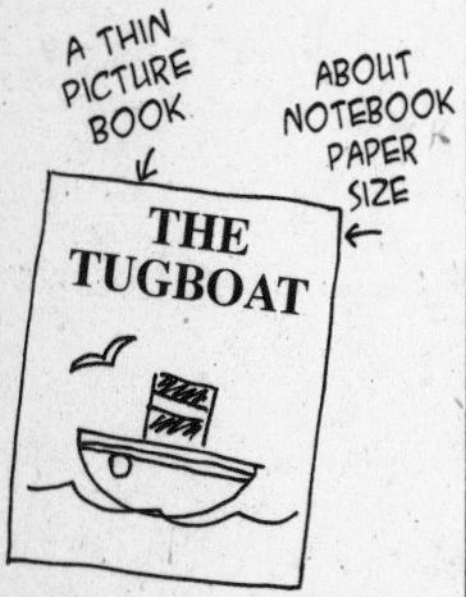
A THIN PICTURE BOOK
ABOUT NOTEBOOK PAPER SIZE
THE TUGBOAT

THE LITTLE TUGBOAT WAS DIRTY BUT WORKED HARD IN THE HARBOR. I WAS ABOUT FIVE WHEN I READ IT. HOPE TO AGAIN SOON!

-RIE TAKADA

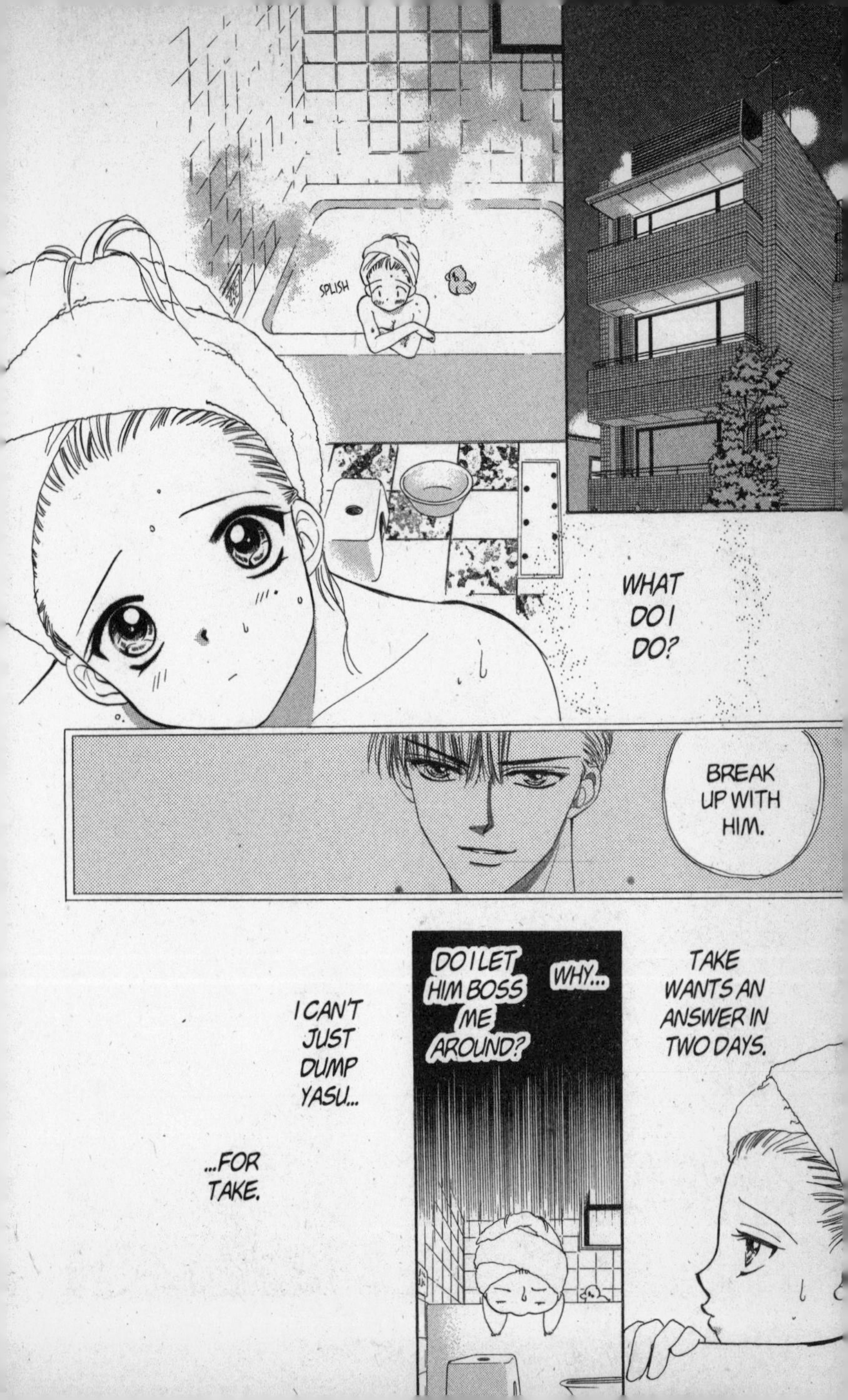
SPLISH
WHAT DO I DO?
BREAK UP WITH HIM.
TAKE WANTS AN ANSWER IN TWO DAYS.
WHY...
DO I LET HIM BOSS ME AROUND?
I CAN'T JUST DUMP YASU...
...FOR TAKE.

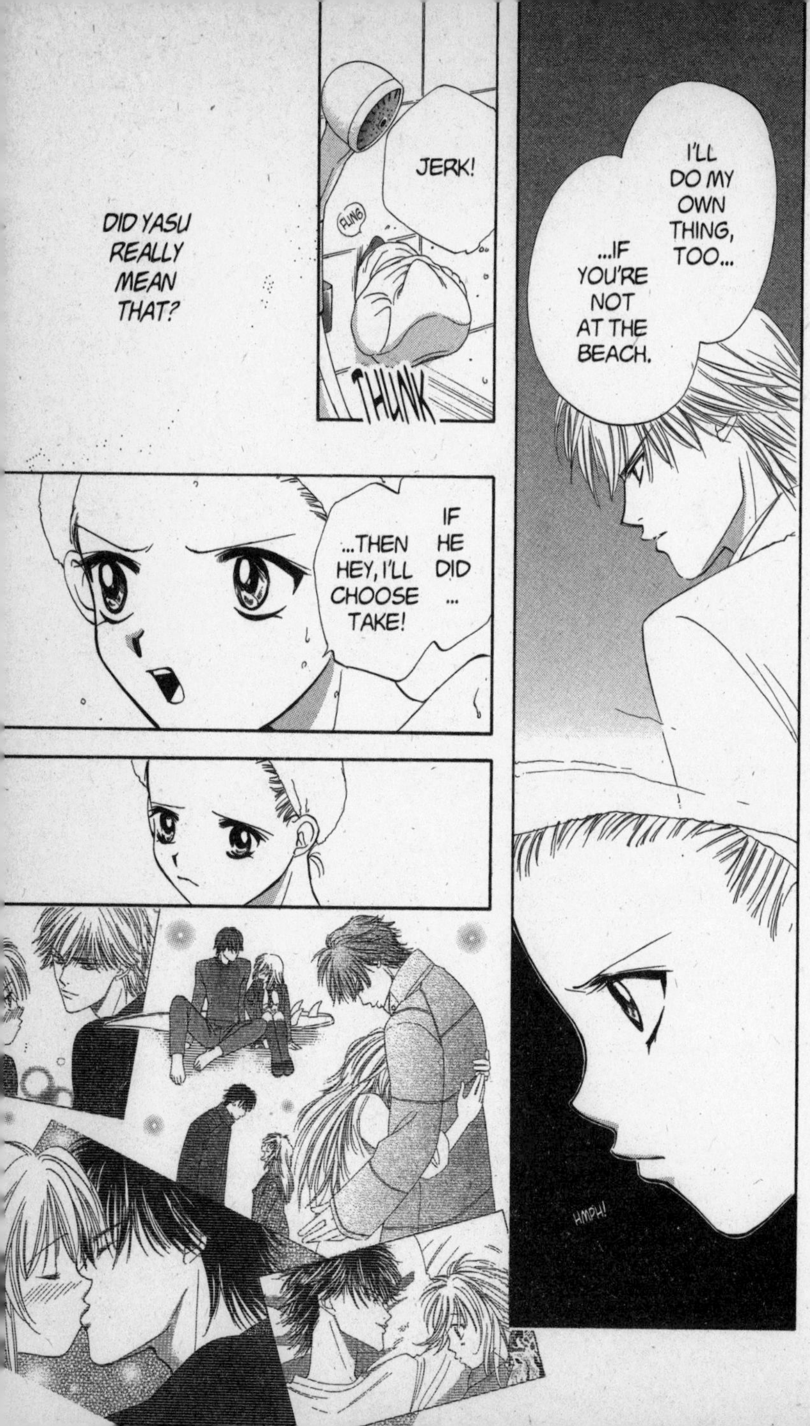
I'LL DO MY OWN THING, TOO...
...IF YOU'RE NOT AT THE BEACH.
HMPH!
JERK!
FLING
THUNK
DID YASU REALLY MEAN THAT?
IF HE DID...
...THEN HEY, I'LL CHOOSE TAKE!

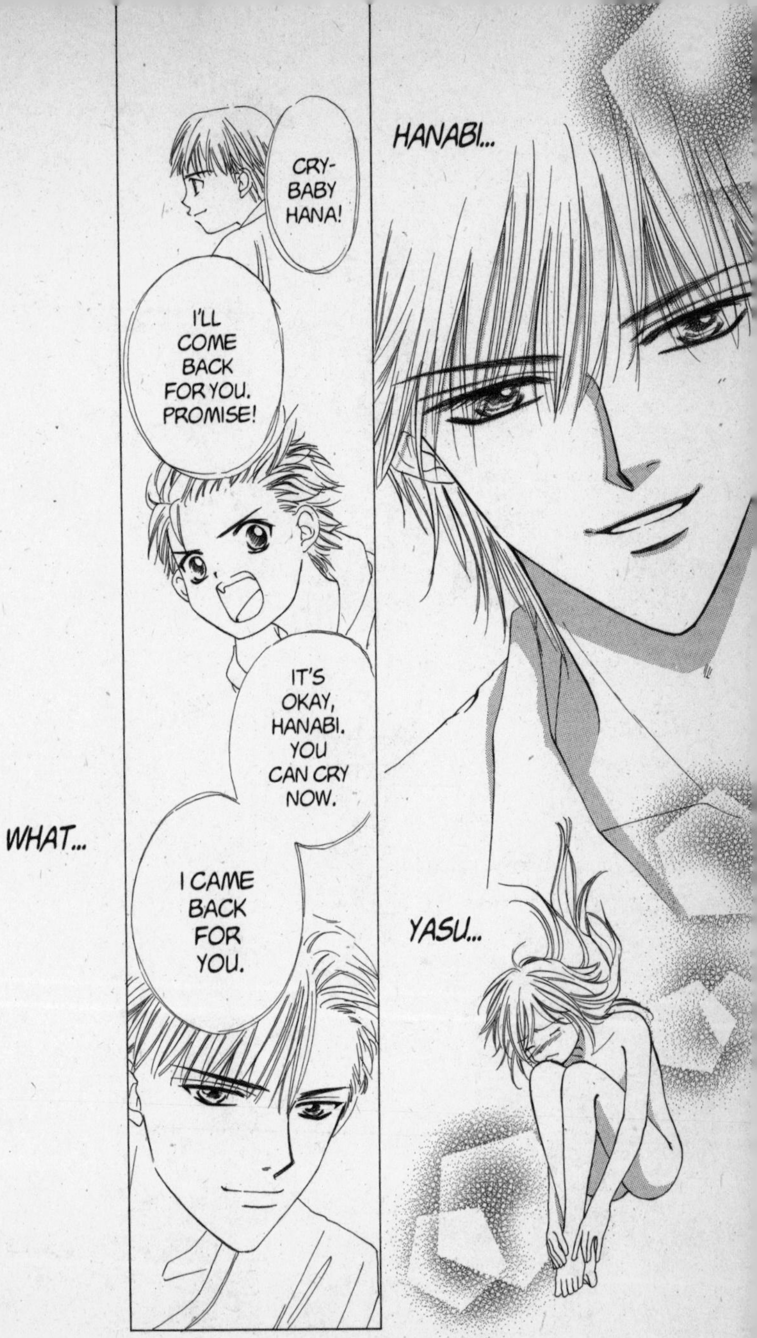
HANABI...
YASU...
CRY-BABY HANA!
I'LL COME BACK FOR YOU. PROMISE!
IT'S OKAY, HANABI. YOU CAN CRY NOW.
I CAME BACK FOR YOU.
WHAT...

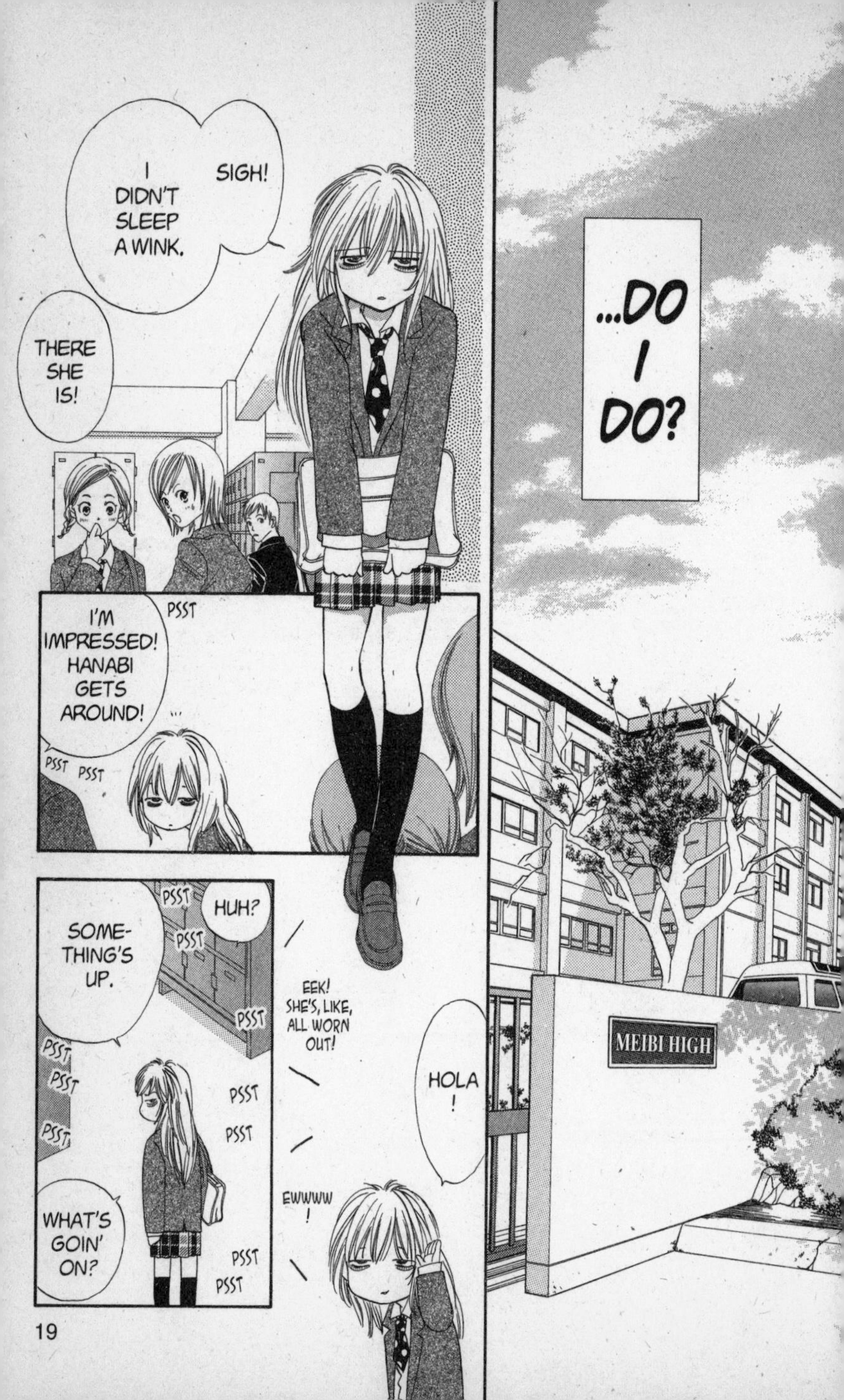
...DO I DO?
MEIBI HIGH
SIGH!
I DIDN'T SLEEP A WINK.
THERE SHE IS!
PSST
I'M IMPRESSED! HANABI GETS AROUND!
...
PSST PSST
HOLA!
EEK! SHE'S, LIKE, ALL WORN OUT!
EWWWW!
HUH?
SOME-THING'S UP.
PSST
PSST
PSST
PSST
PSST
PSST
PSST
PSST
WHAT'S GOIN' ON?
PSST
PSST

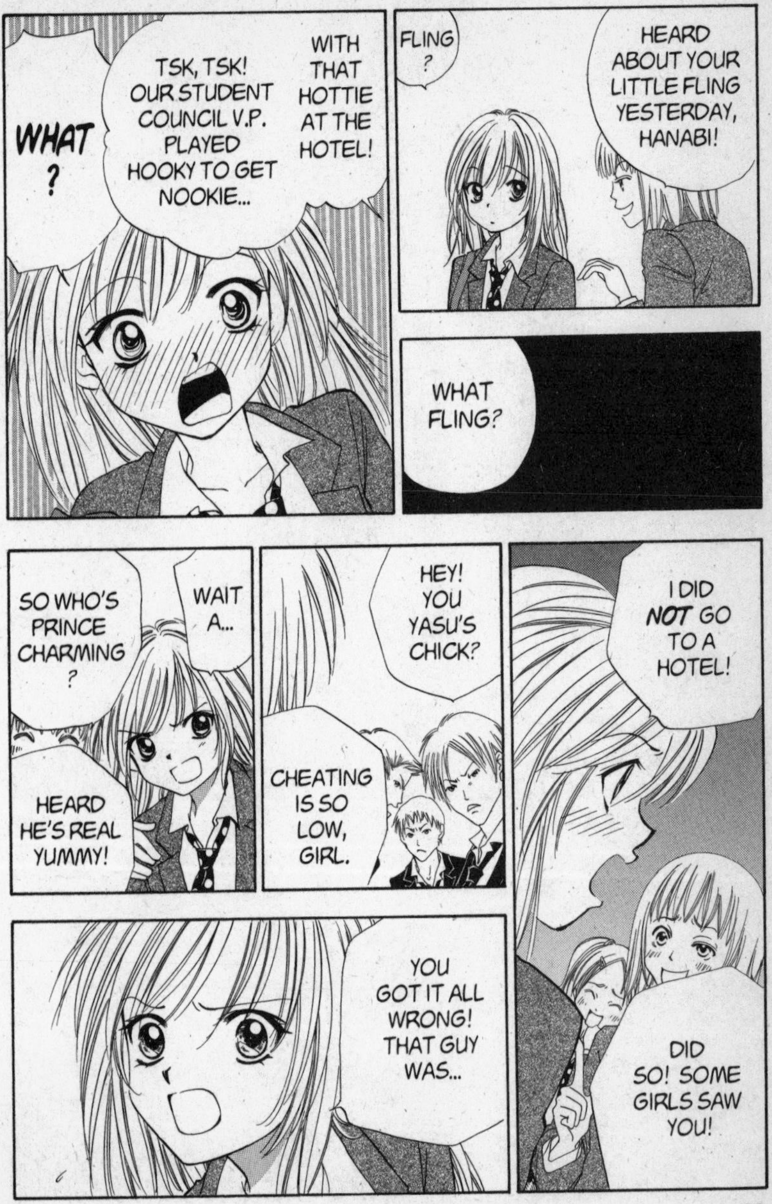
HEARD ABOUT YOUR LITTLE FLING YESTERDAY, HANABI!
FLING?
WHAT FLING?
TSK, TSK! OUR STUDENT COUNCIL V.P. PLAYED HOOKY TO GET NOOKIE...
WITH THAT HOTTIE AT THE HOTEL!
WHAT?
I DID **NOT** GO TO A HOTEL!
DID SO! SOME GIRLS SAW YOU!
HEY! YOU YASU'S CHICK?
CHEATING IS SO LOW, GIRL.
WAIT A...
SO WHO'S PRINCE CHARMING?
HEARD HE'S REAL YUMMY!
YOU GOT IT ALL WRONG! THAT GUY WAS...

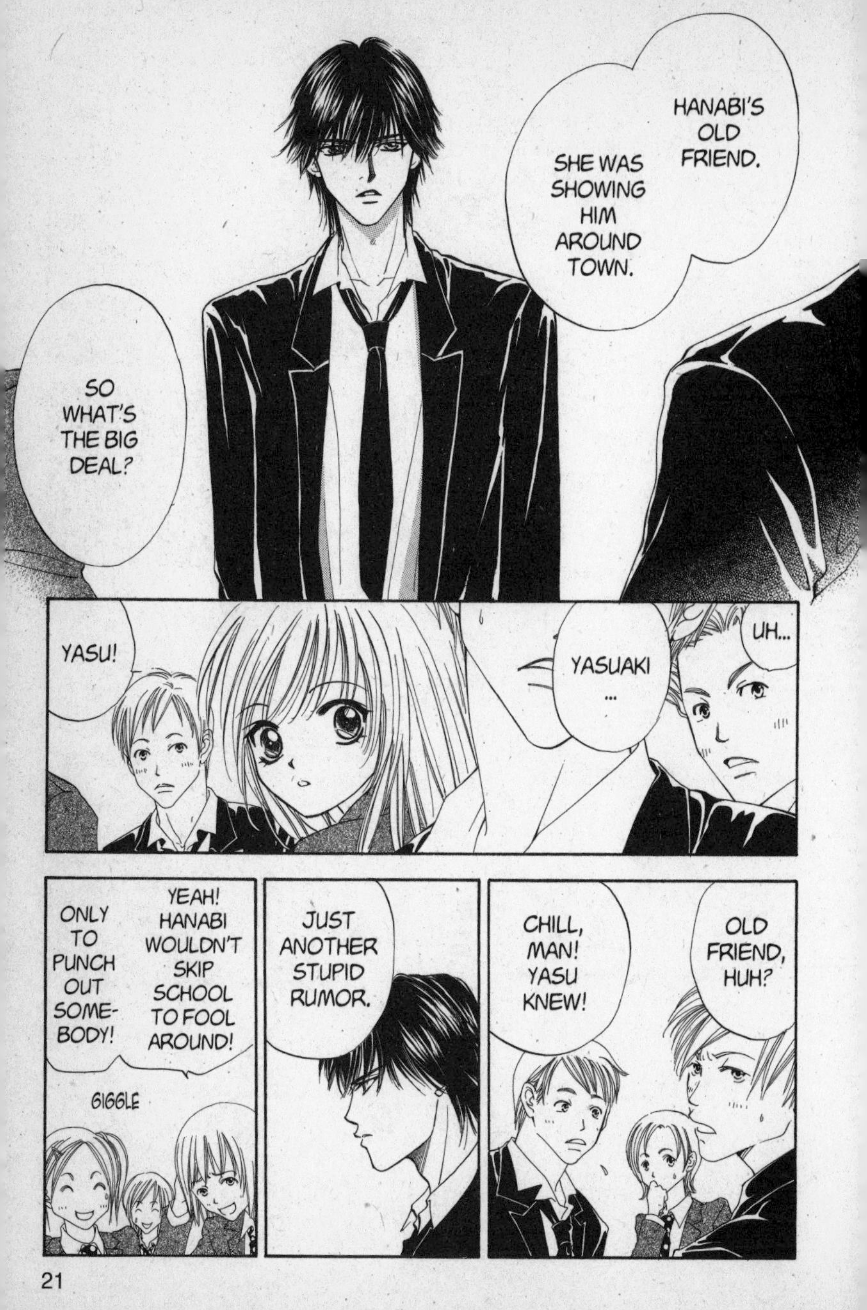
HANABI'S OLD FRIEND.
SHE WAS SHOWING HIM AROUND TOWN.
SO WHAT'S THE BIG DEAL?
UH...
YASUAKI ...
YASU!
OLD FRIEND, HUH?
CHILL, MAN! YASU KNEW!
JUST ANOTHER STUPID RUMOR.
YEAH! HANABI WOULDN'T SKIP SCHOOL TO FOOL AROUND!
ONLY TO PUNCH OUT SOME-BODY!
GIGGLE

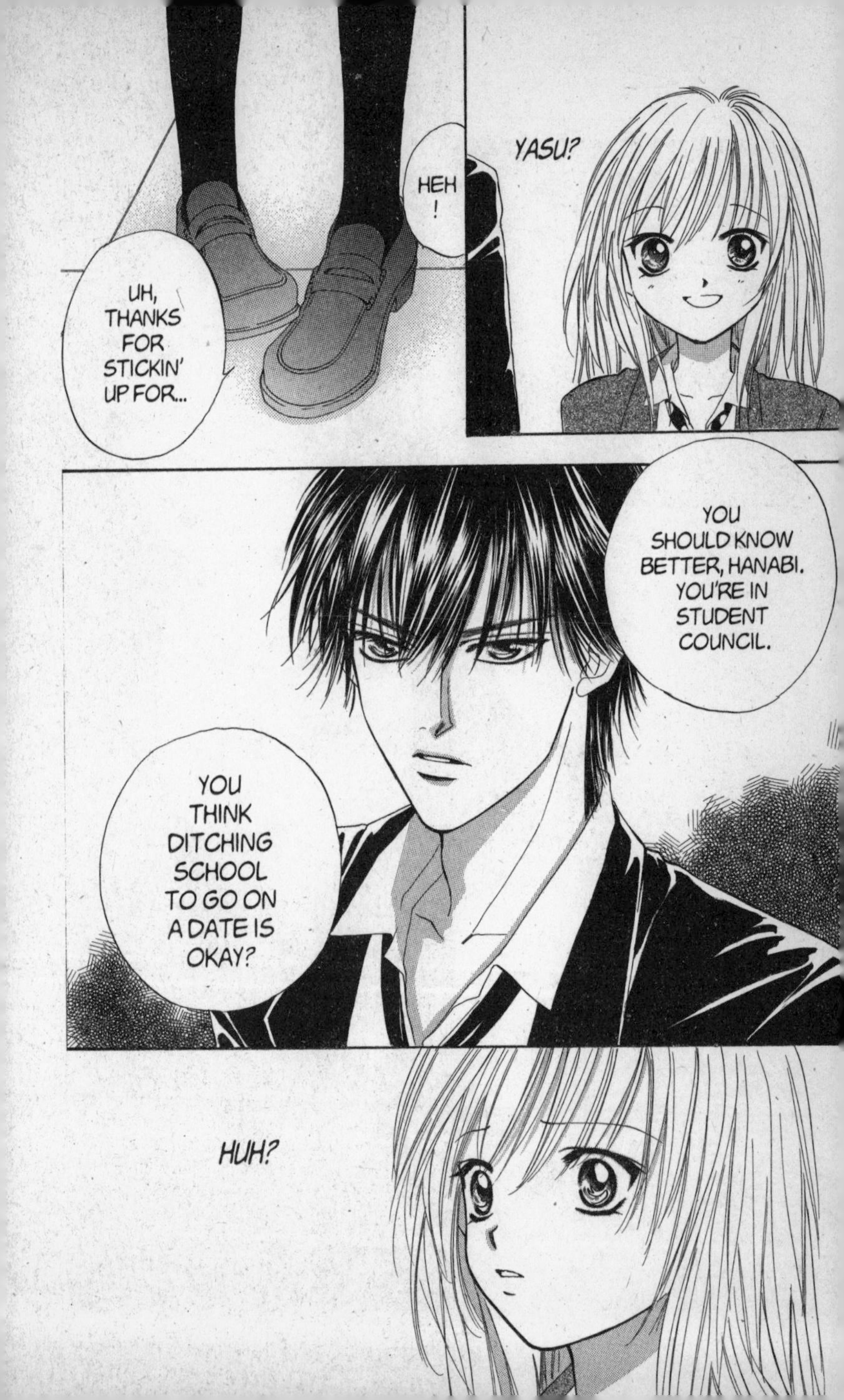
YASU?
HEH!
UH, THANKS FOR STICKIN' UP FOR...
YOU SHOULD KNOW BETTER, HANABI. YOU'RE IN STUDENT COUNCIL.
YOU THINK DITCHING SCHOOL TO GO ON A DATE IS OKAY?
HUH?

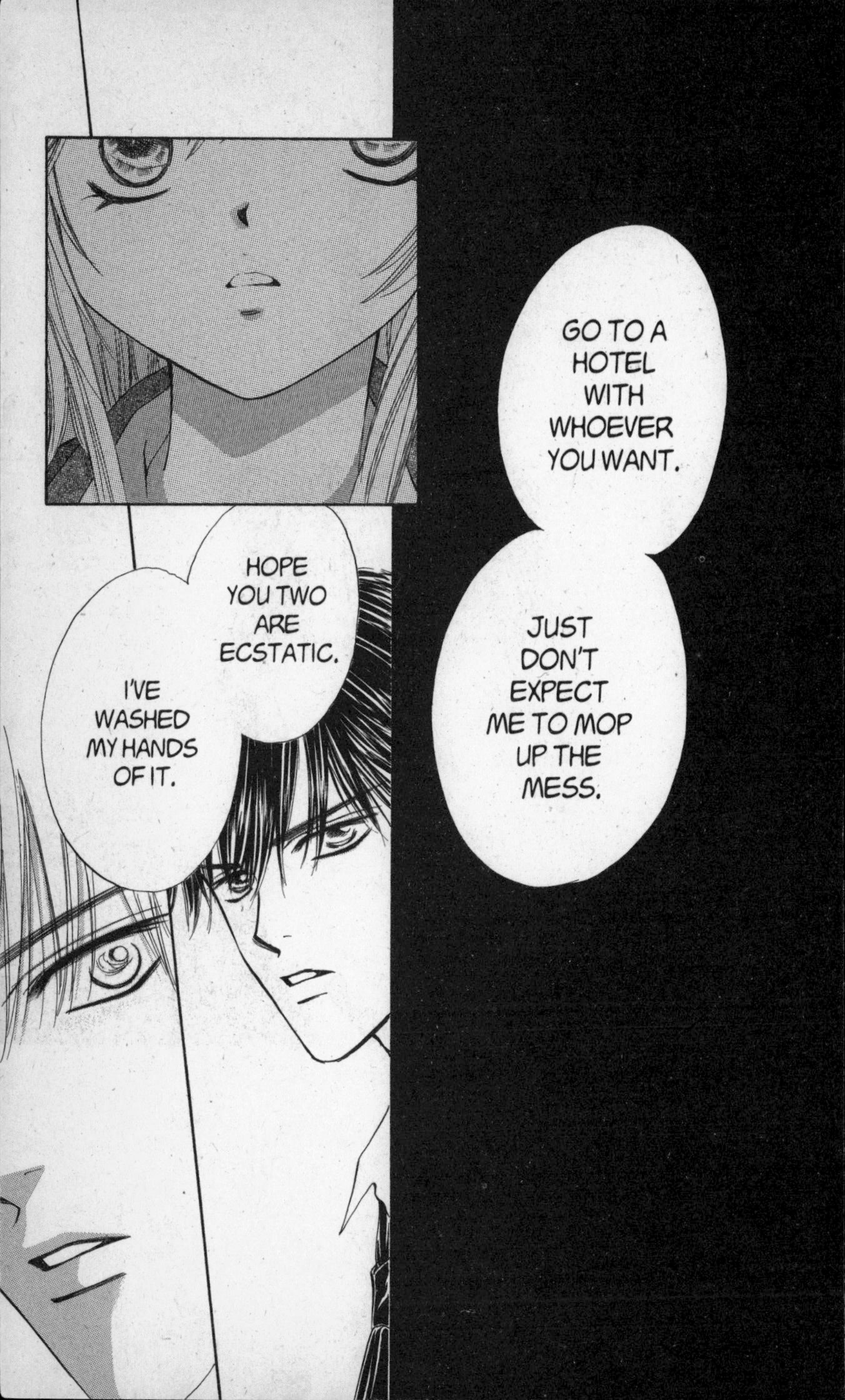
GO TO A HOTEL WITH WHOEVER YOU WANT.
JUST DON'T EXPECT ME TO MOP UP THE MESS.
HOPE YOU TWO ARE ECSTATIC.
I'VE WASHED MY HANDS OF IT.

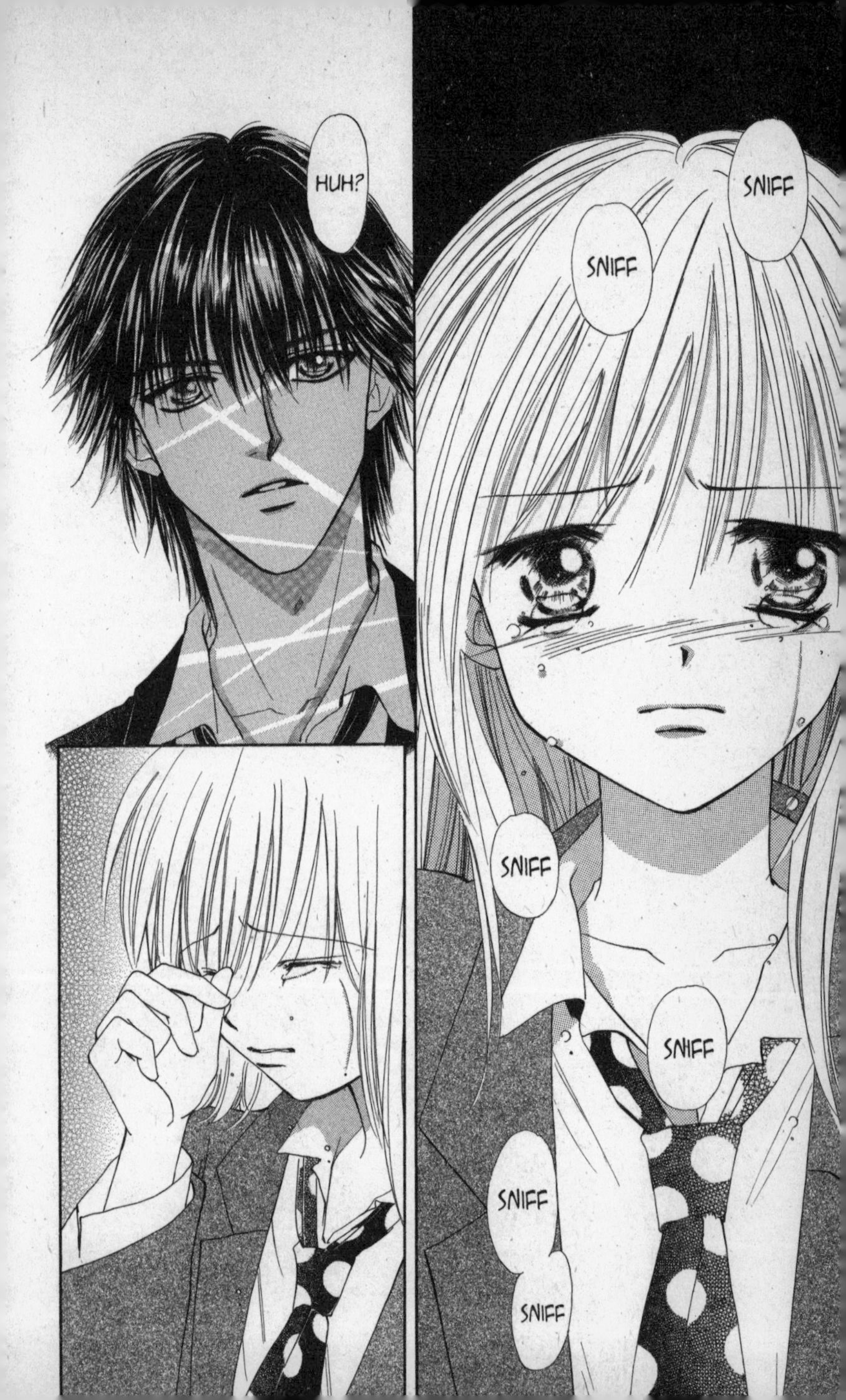
SNIFF
SNIFF
SNIFF
SNIFF
SNIFF
SNIFF
HUH?

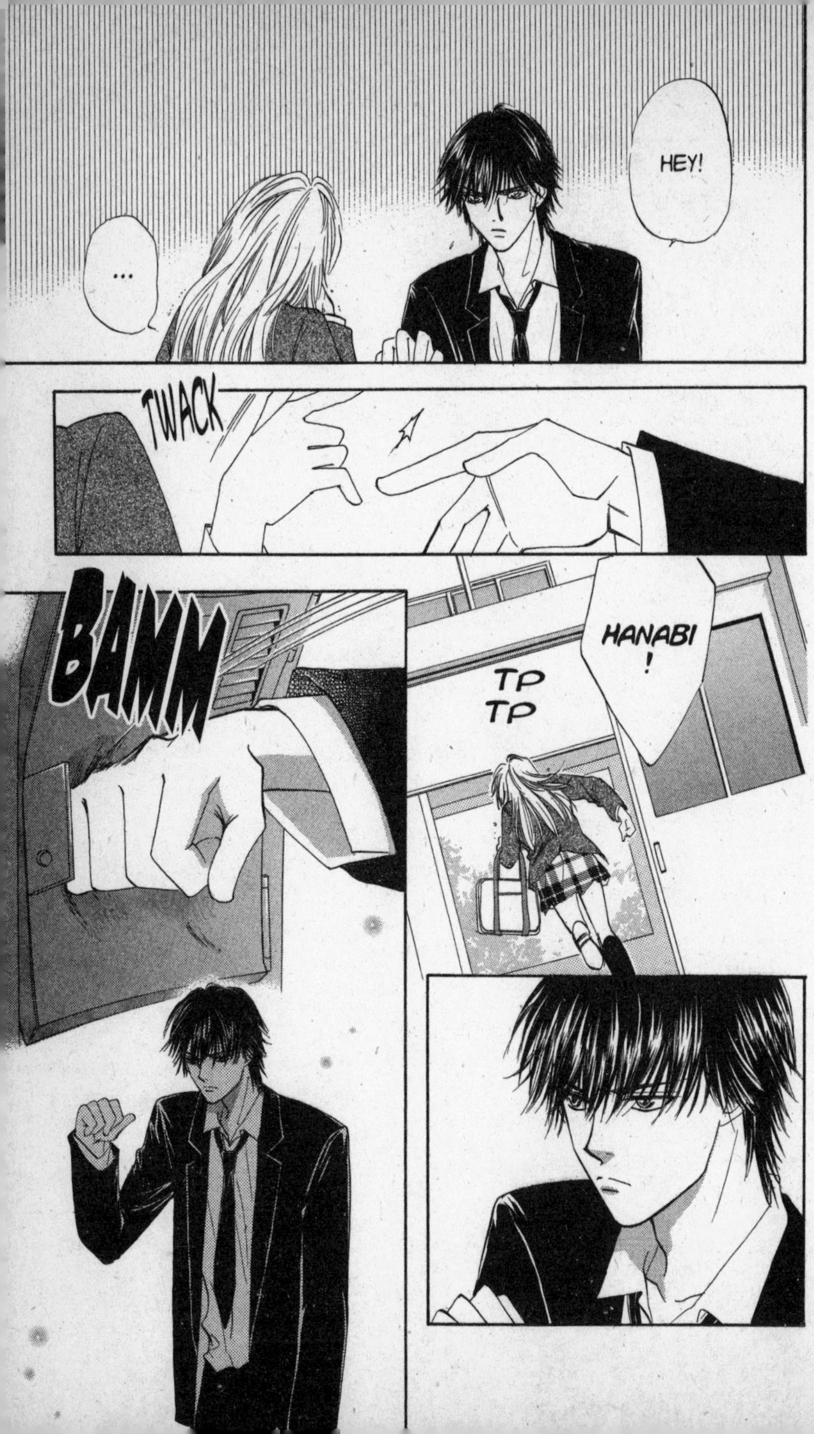
HEY!
...
TWACK
HANABI!
TP TP
BAMM

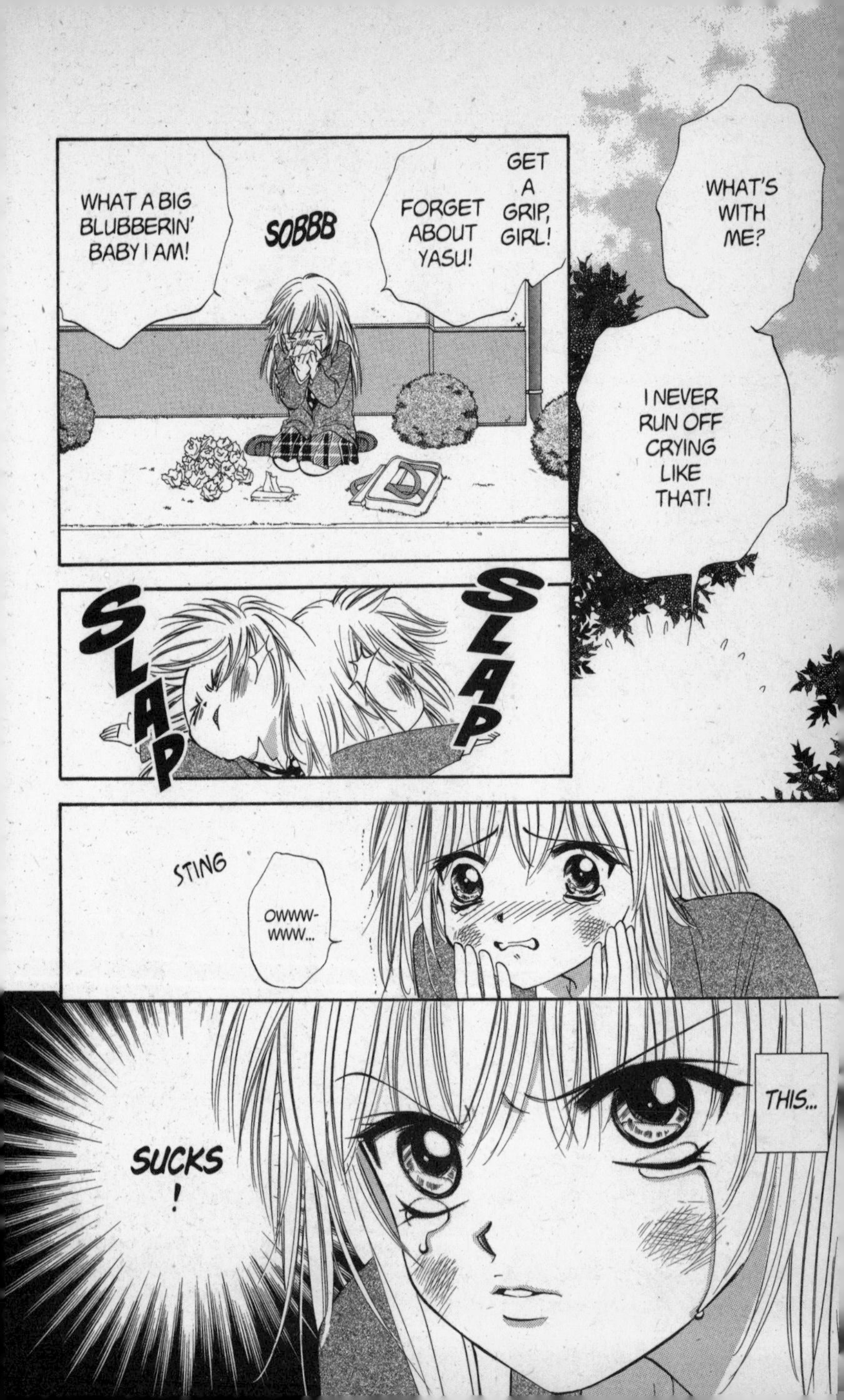

WHAT'S WITH ME?
I NEVER RUN OFF CRYING LIKE THAT!
GET A GRIP, GIRL!
FORGET ABOUT YASU!
SOBBB
WHAT A BIG BLUBBERIN' BABY I AM!
SLAP
SLAP
OWWW-WWW...
STING
THIS...
SUCKS!

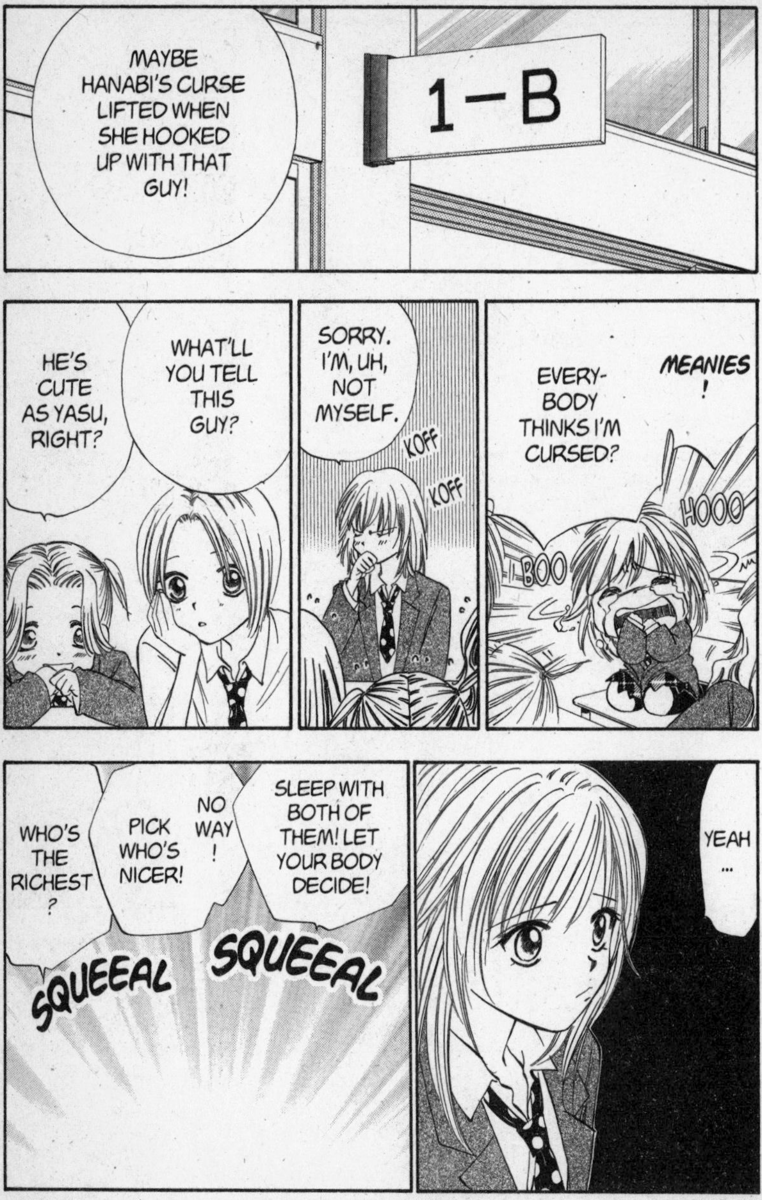
1-B
MAYBE HANABI'S CURSE LIFTED WHEN SHE HOOKED UP WITH THAT GUY!
MEANIES!
EVERY-BODY THINKS I'M CURSED?
HOOO
BOO
SORRY. I'M, UH, NOT MYSELF.
KOFF
KOFF
WHAT'LL YOU TELL THIS GUY?
HE'S CUTE AS YASU, RIGHT?
YEAH ...
SLEEP WITH BOTH OF THEM! LET YOUR BODY DECIDE!
NO WAY!
PICK WHO'S NICER!
WHO'S THE RICHEST?
SQUEEEAL
SQUEEEAL

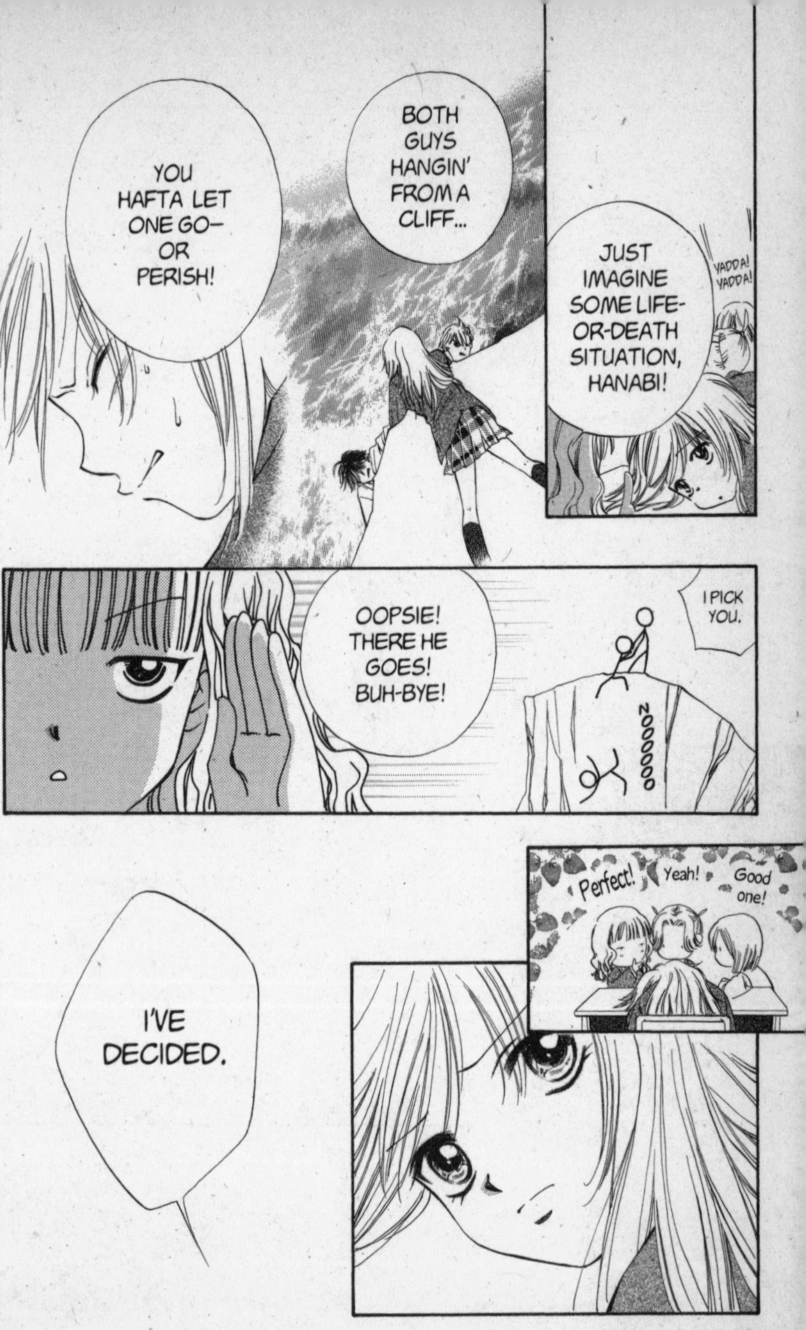
YADDA! YADDA!
JUST IMAGINE SOME LIFE-OR-DEATH SITUATION, HANABI!
BOTH GUYS HANGIN' FROM A CLIFF...
YOU HAFTA LET ONE GO— OR PERISH!
I PICK YOU.
NOOOOOO
OOPSIE! THERE HE GOES! BUH-BYE!
Good one!
Yeah!
Perfect!
I'VE DECIDED.

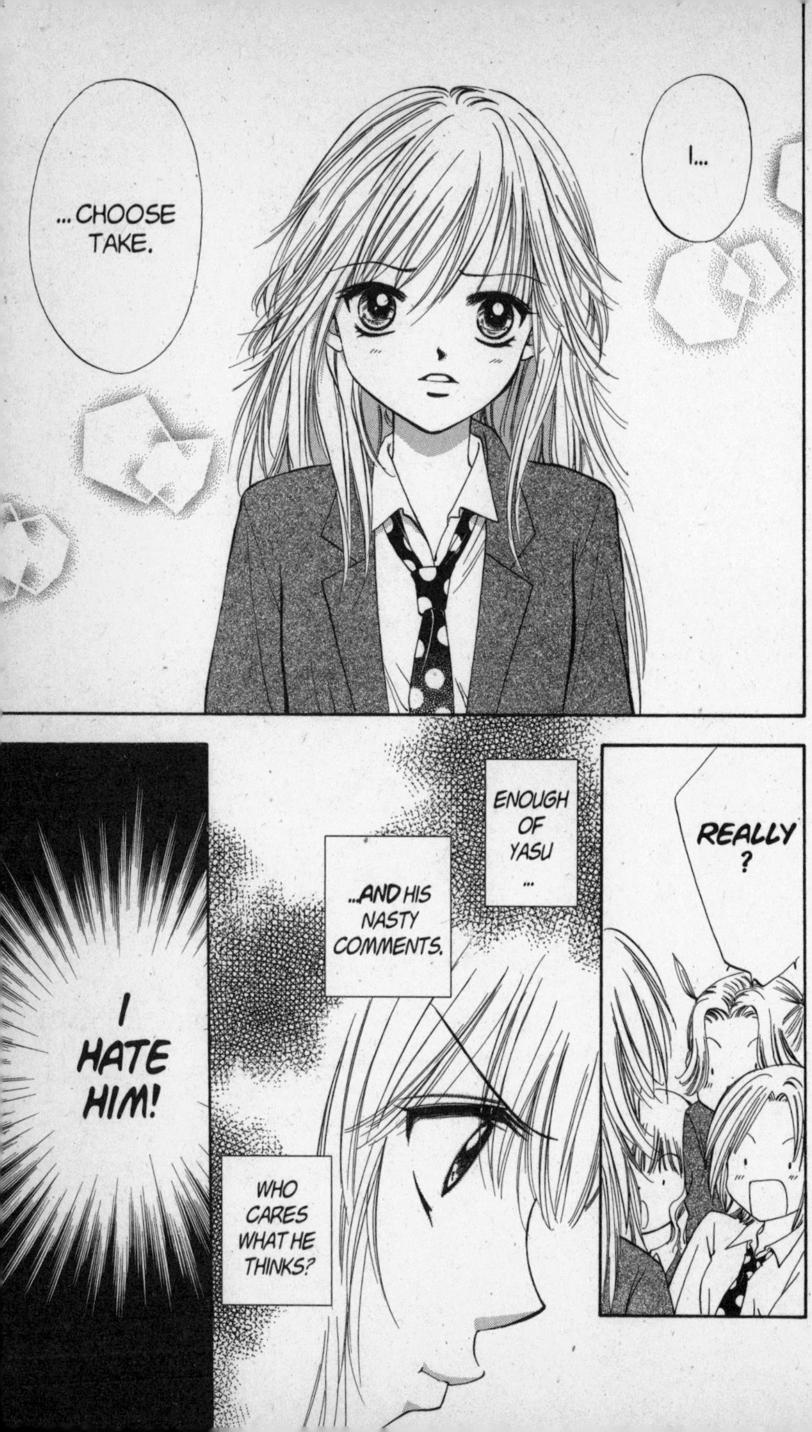
I...
...CHOOSE TAKE.
REALLY ?
ENOUGH OF YASU ...
...AND HIS NASTY COMMENTS.
WHO CARES WHAT HE THINKS?
I HATE HIM!

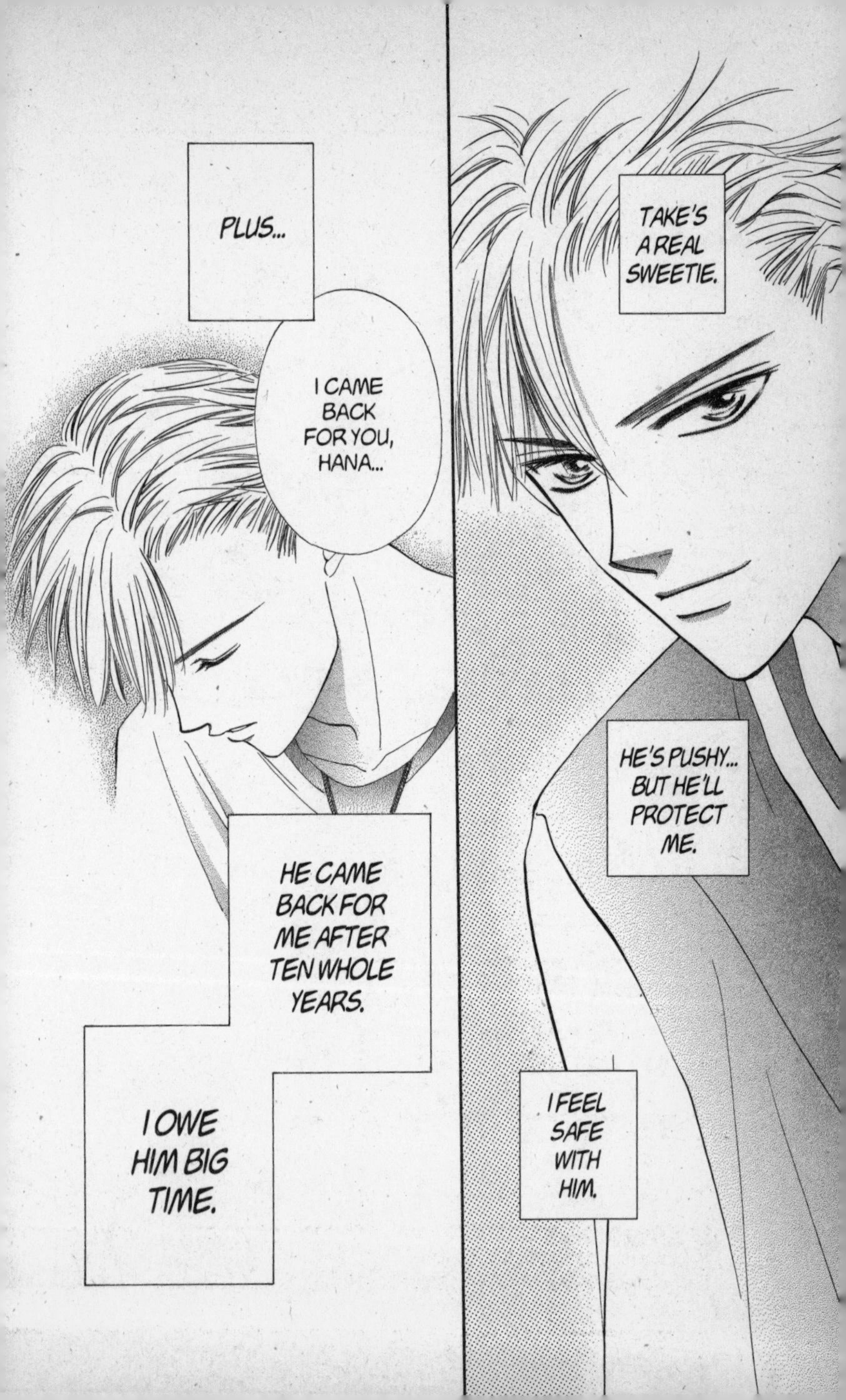
TAKE'S A REAL SWEETIE.
HE'S PUSHY... BUT HE'LL PROTECT ME.
I FEEL SAFE WITH HIM.
PLUS...
I CAME BACK FOR YOU, HANA...
HE CAME BACK FOR ME AFTER TEN WHOLE YEARS.
I OWE HIM BIG TIME.

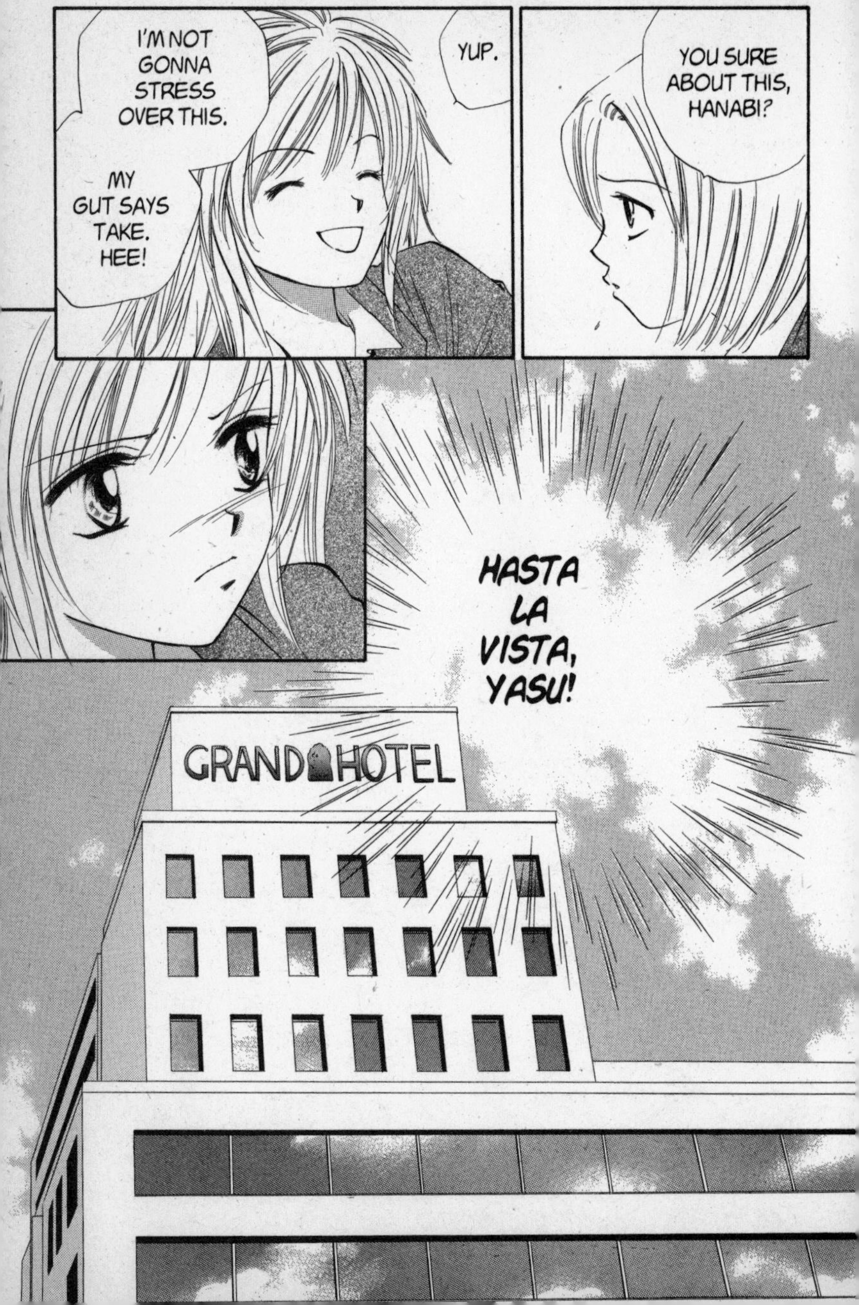
YOU SURE ABOUT THIS, HANABI?
YUP.
I'M NOT GONNA STRESS OVER THIS.
MY GUT SAYS TAKE. HEE!
HASTA LA VISTA, YASU!
GRAND HOTEL

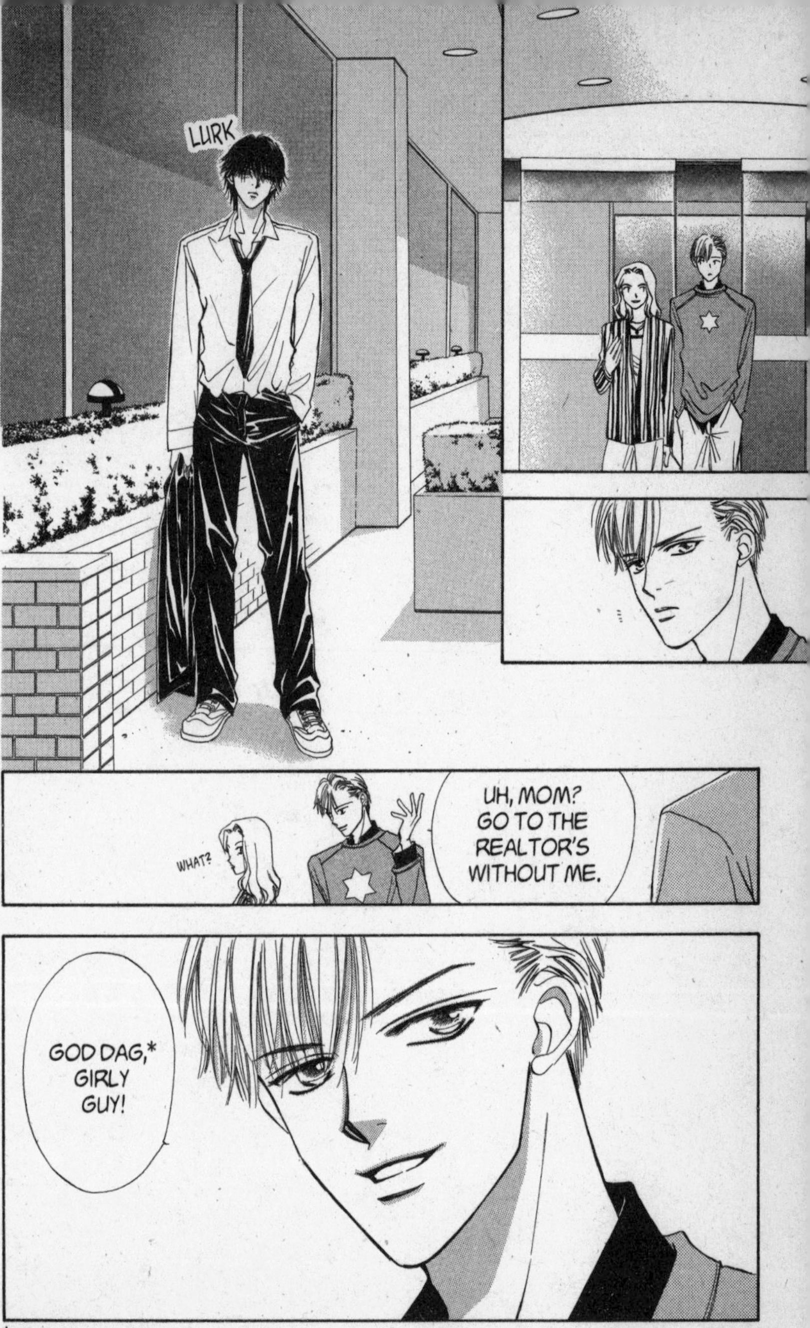
LURK
UH, MOM? GO TO THE REALTOR'S WITHOUT ME.
WHAT?
GOD DAG,* GIRLY GUY!

*HELLO IN DANISH

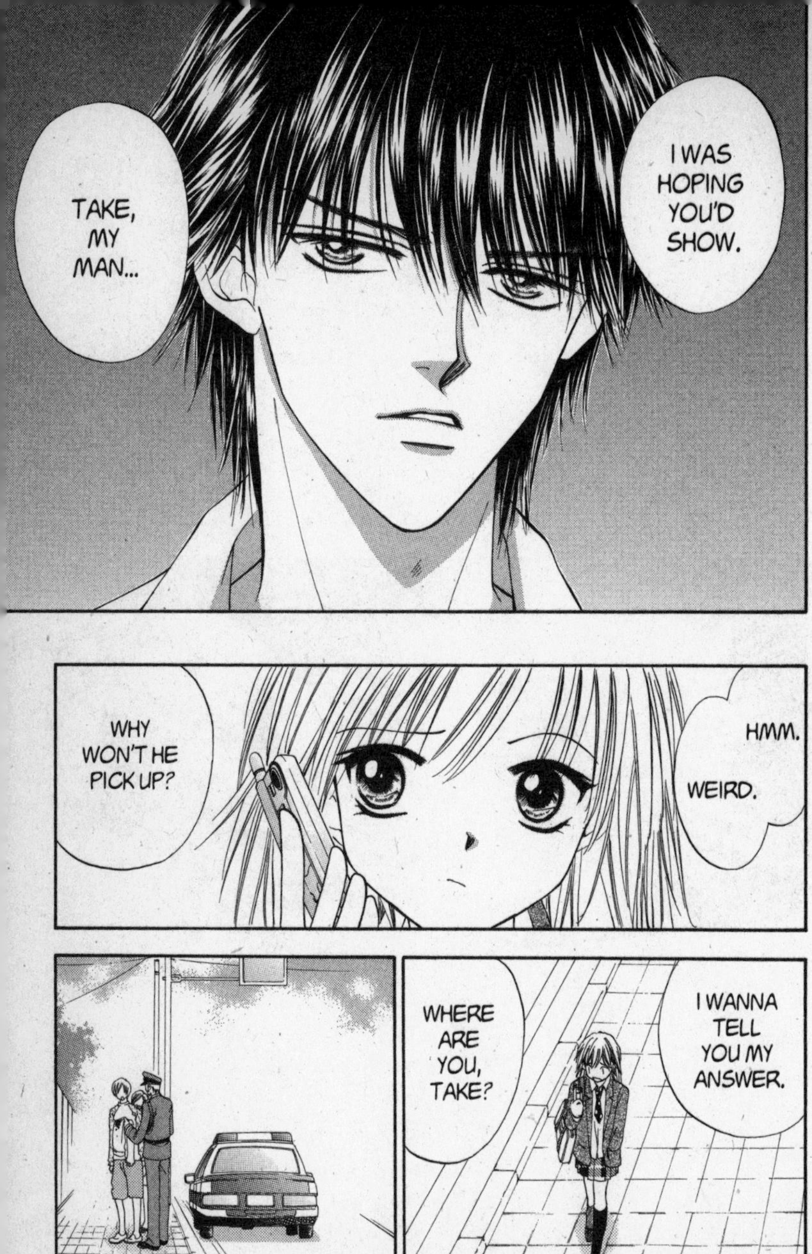
I WAS HOPING YOU'D SHOW.
TAKE, MY MAN...
HMM.
WEIRD.
WHY WON'T HE PICK UP?
I WANNA TELL YOU MY ANSWER.
WHERE ARE YOU, TAKE?

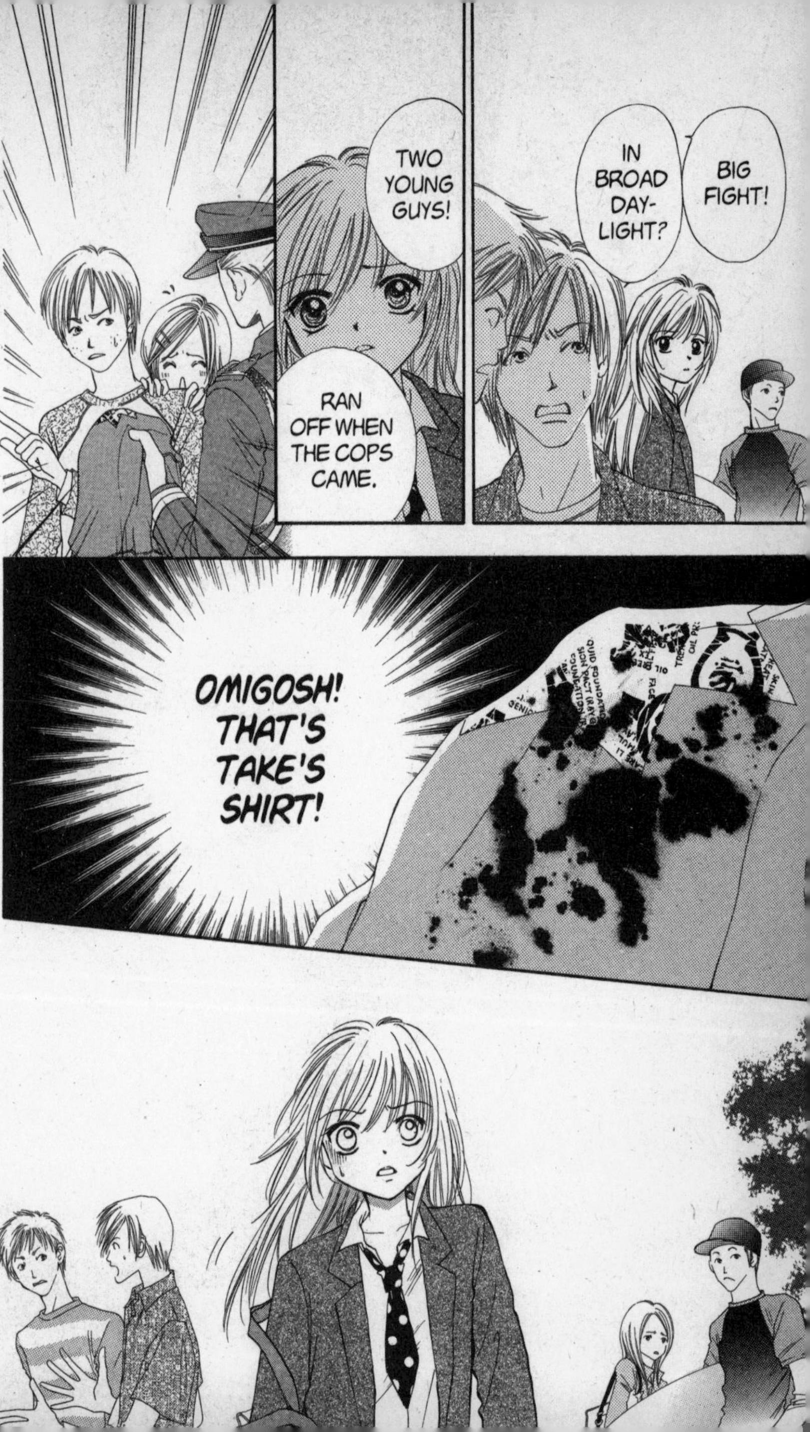
BIG FIGHT!
IN BROAD DAY-LIGHT?
TWO YOUNG GUYS!
RAN OFF WHEN THE COPS CAME.
OMIGOSH! THAT'S TAKE'S SHIRT!

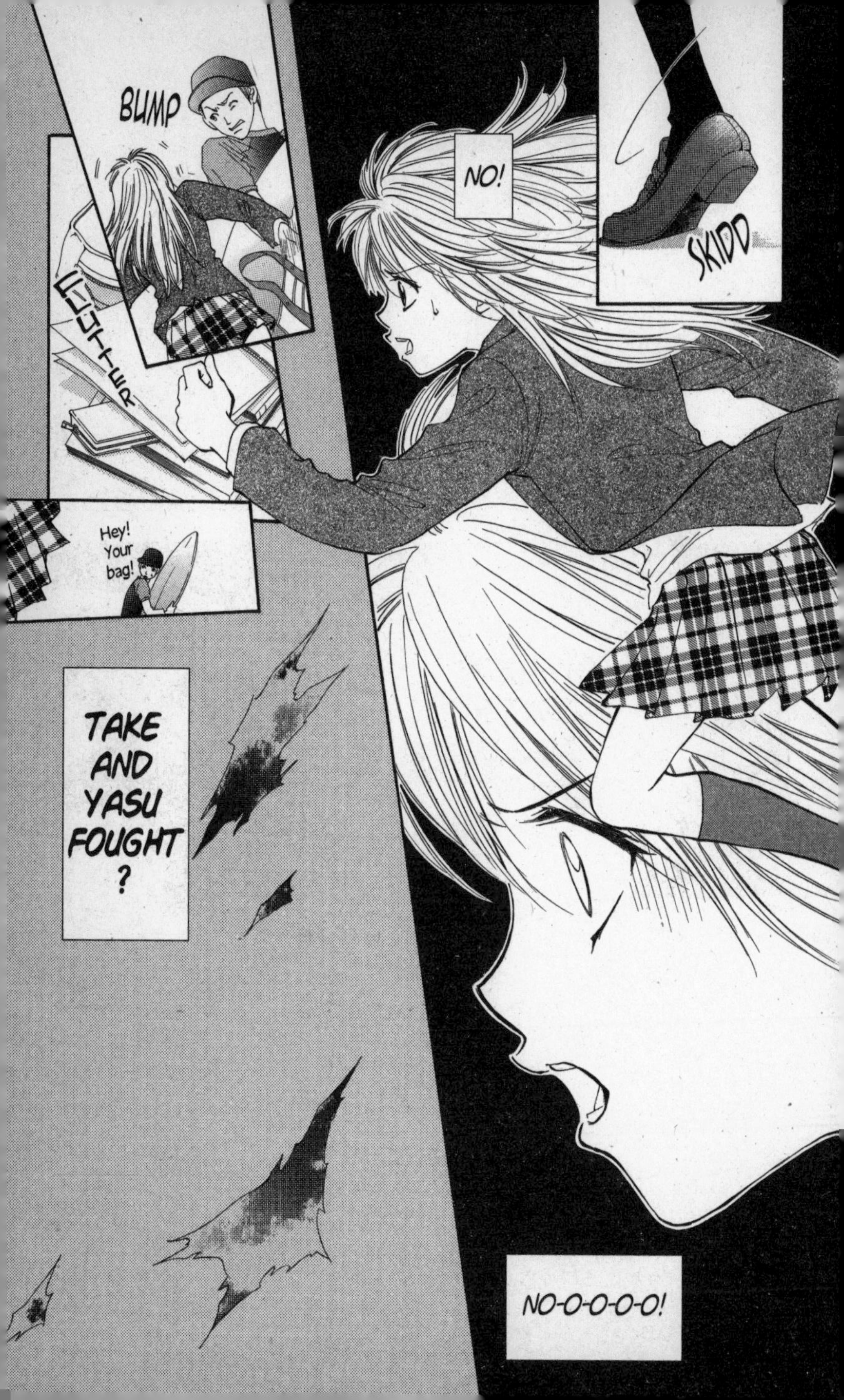
SKIDD
NO!
BUMP
CLUTTER
Hey! Your bag!
TAKE AND YASU FOUGHT?
NO-O-O-O-O!

HAPPY HUSTLE HIGH

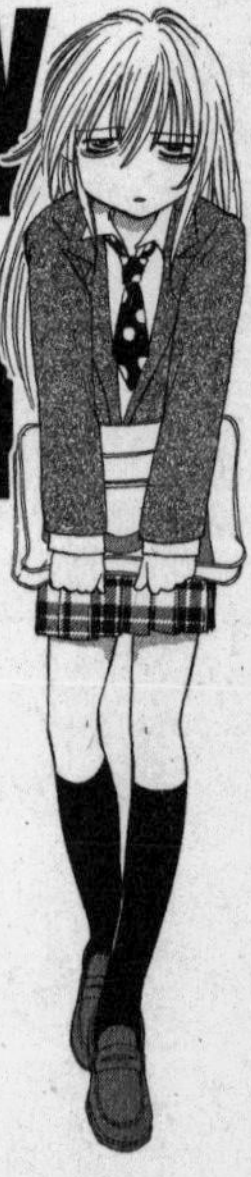

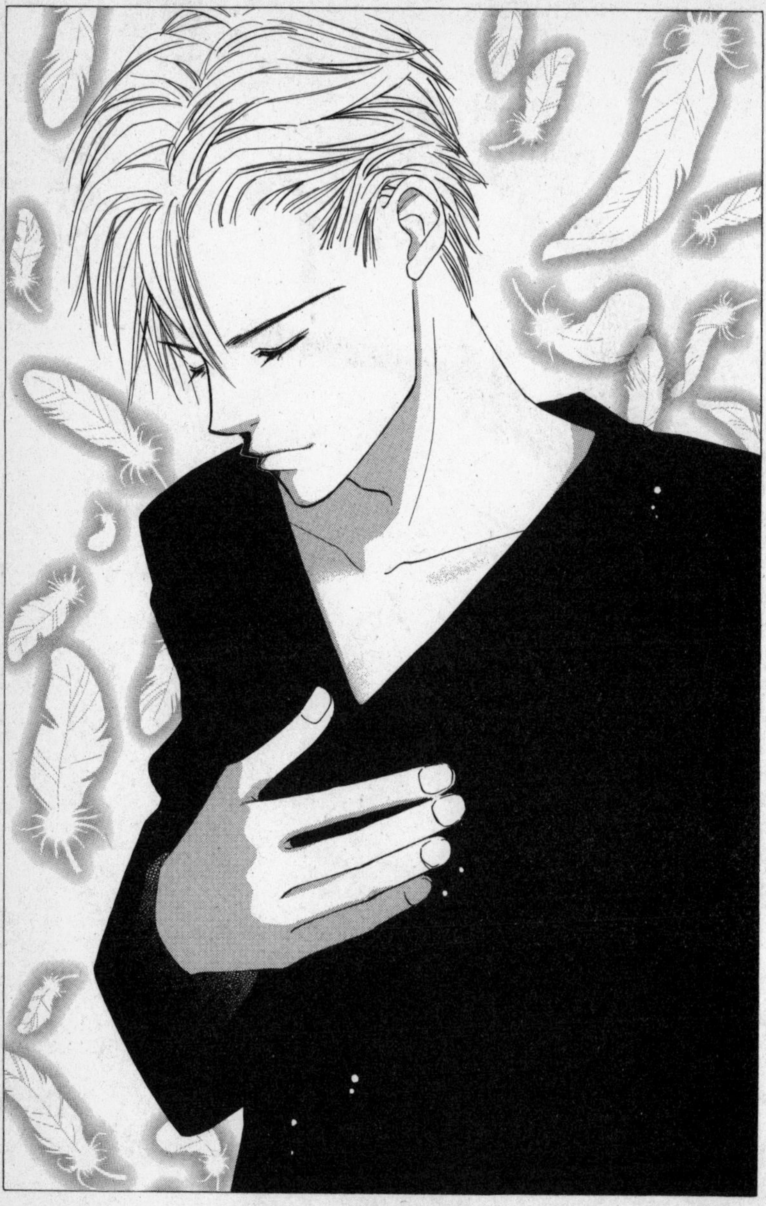

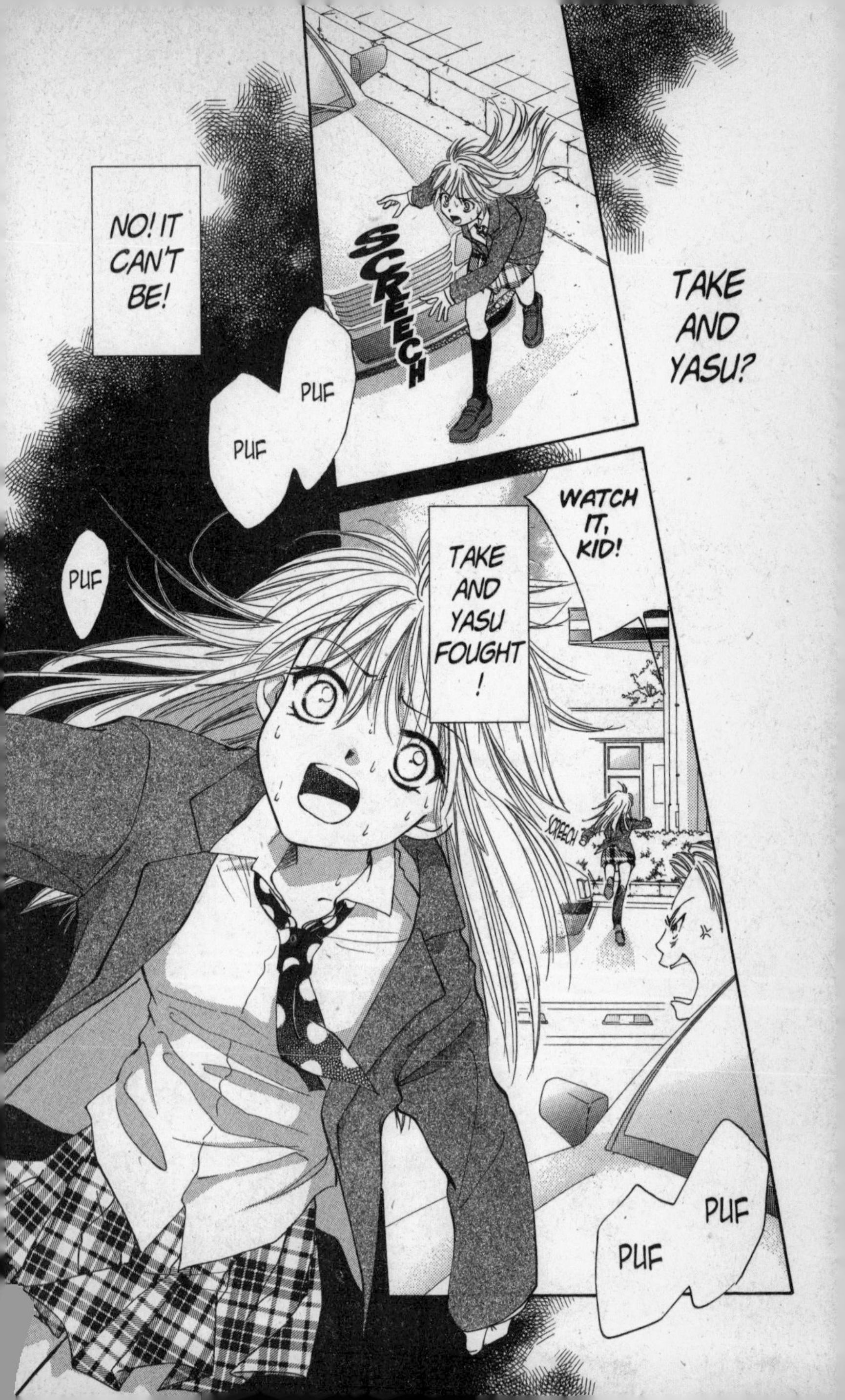
TAKE AND YASU?
SCREECH
PUF
PUF
NO! IT CAN'T BE!
WATCH IT, KID!
TAKE AND YASU FOUGHT!
SCREECH
PUF
PUF
PUF

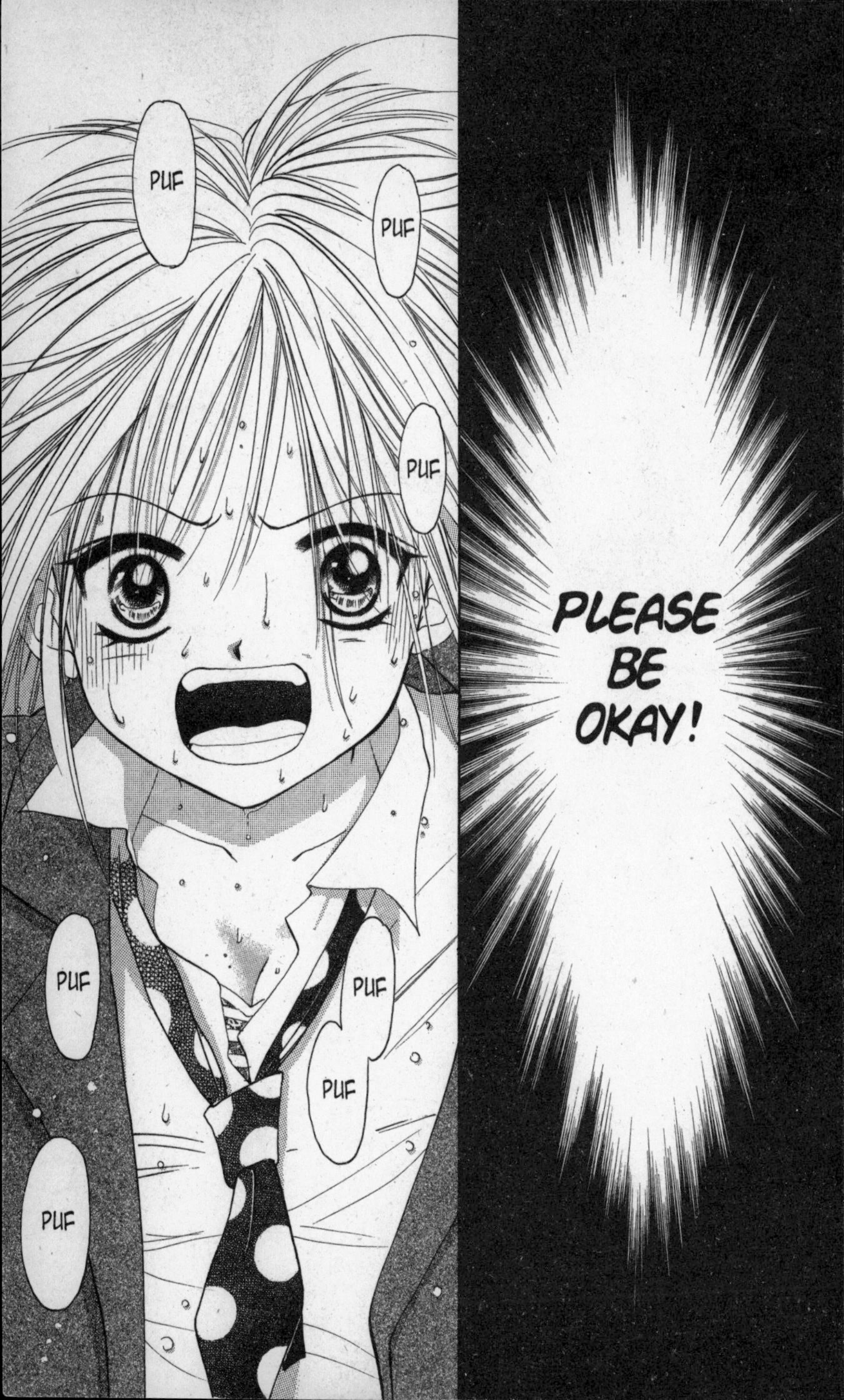
PLEASE BE OKAY!
PUF
PUF
PUF
PUF
PUF
PUF
PUF

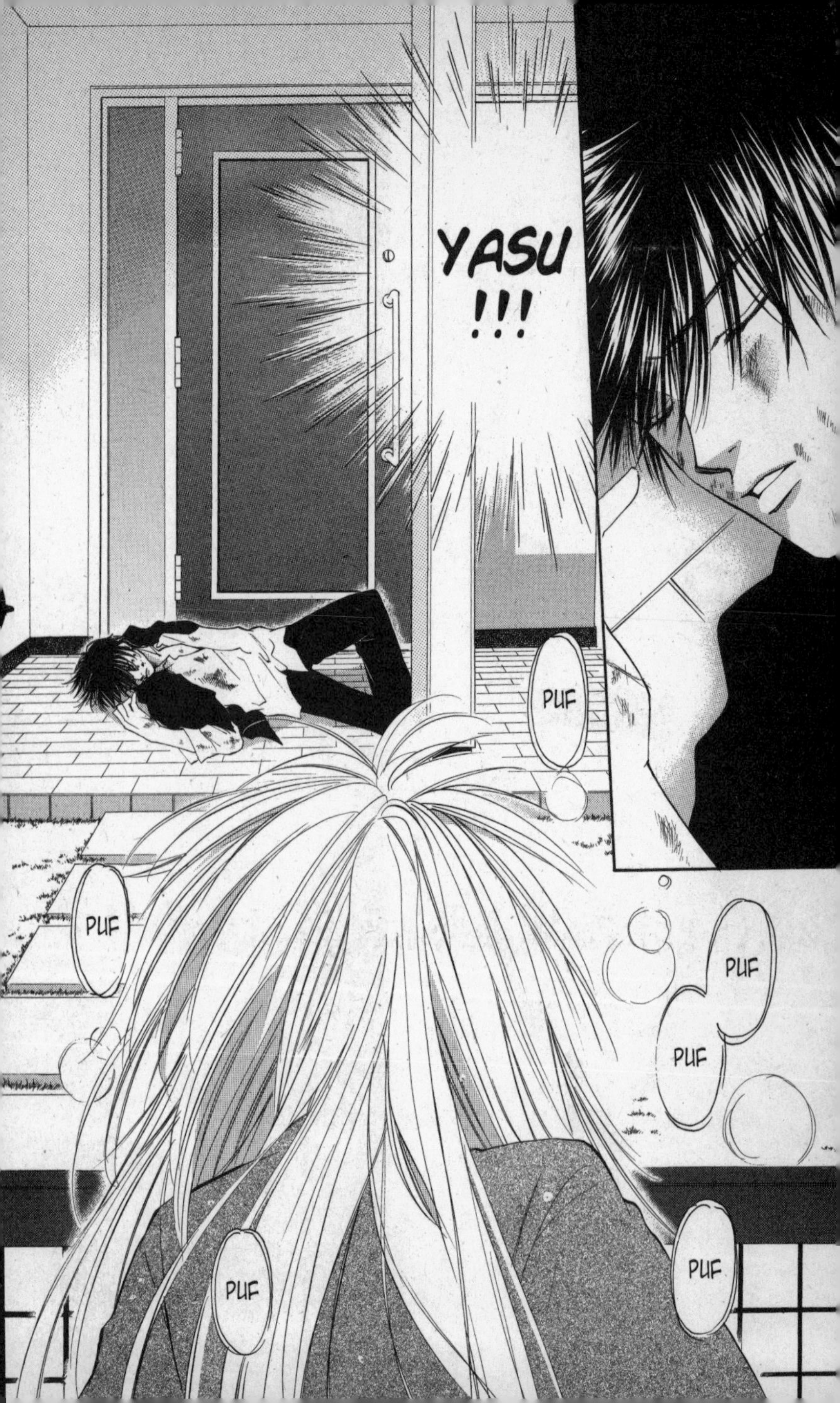
YASU !!!
PUF
PUF
PUF
PUF
PUF
PUF

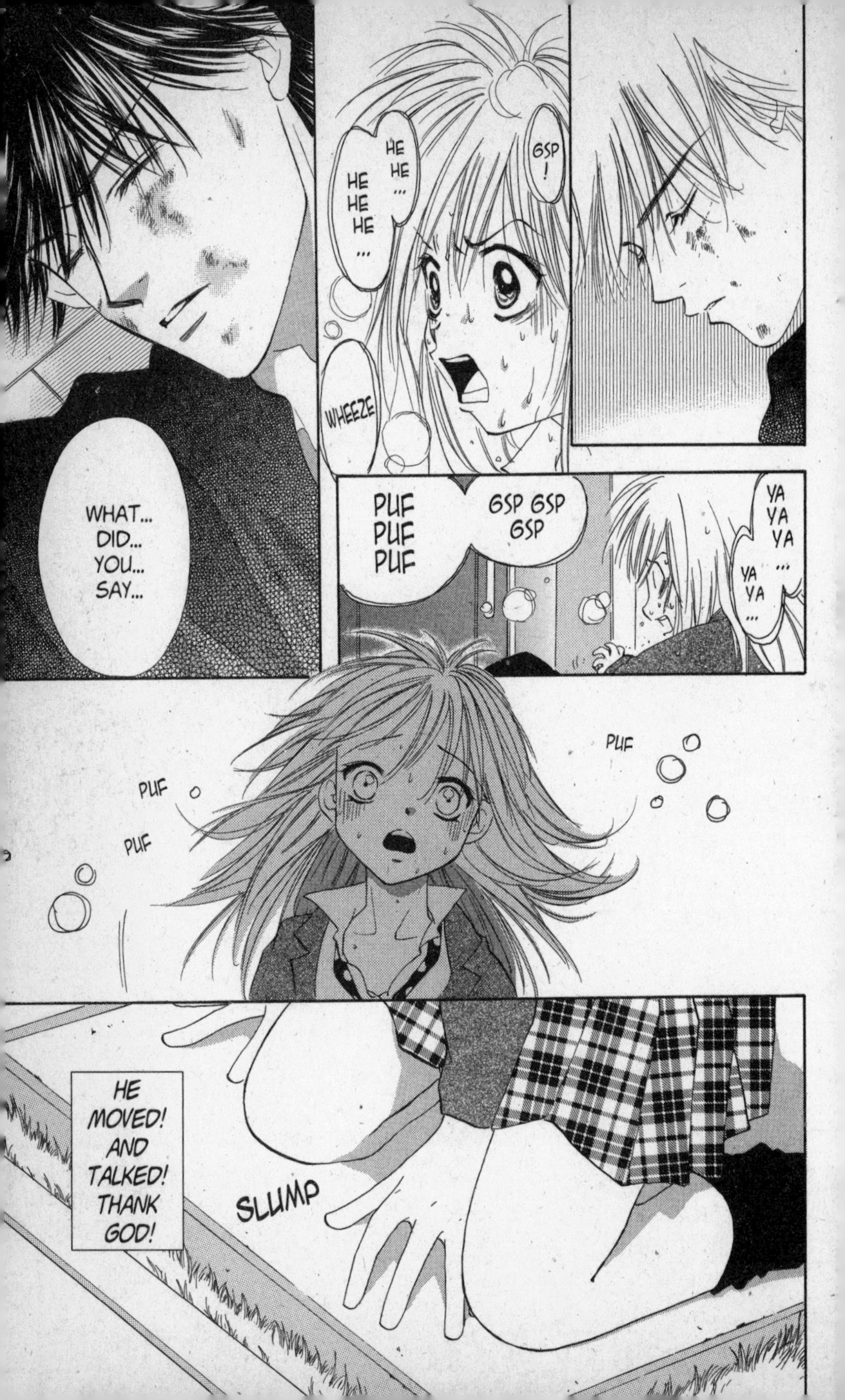
GSP!
HE HE ... HE HE HE ...
WHEEZE
YA YA YA ...
YA YA ...
GSP GSP GSP
PUF PUF PUF
WHAT... DID... YOU... SAY...
PUF
PUF
PUF
HE MOVED! AND TALKED! THANK GOD!
SLUMP

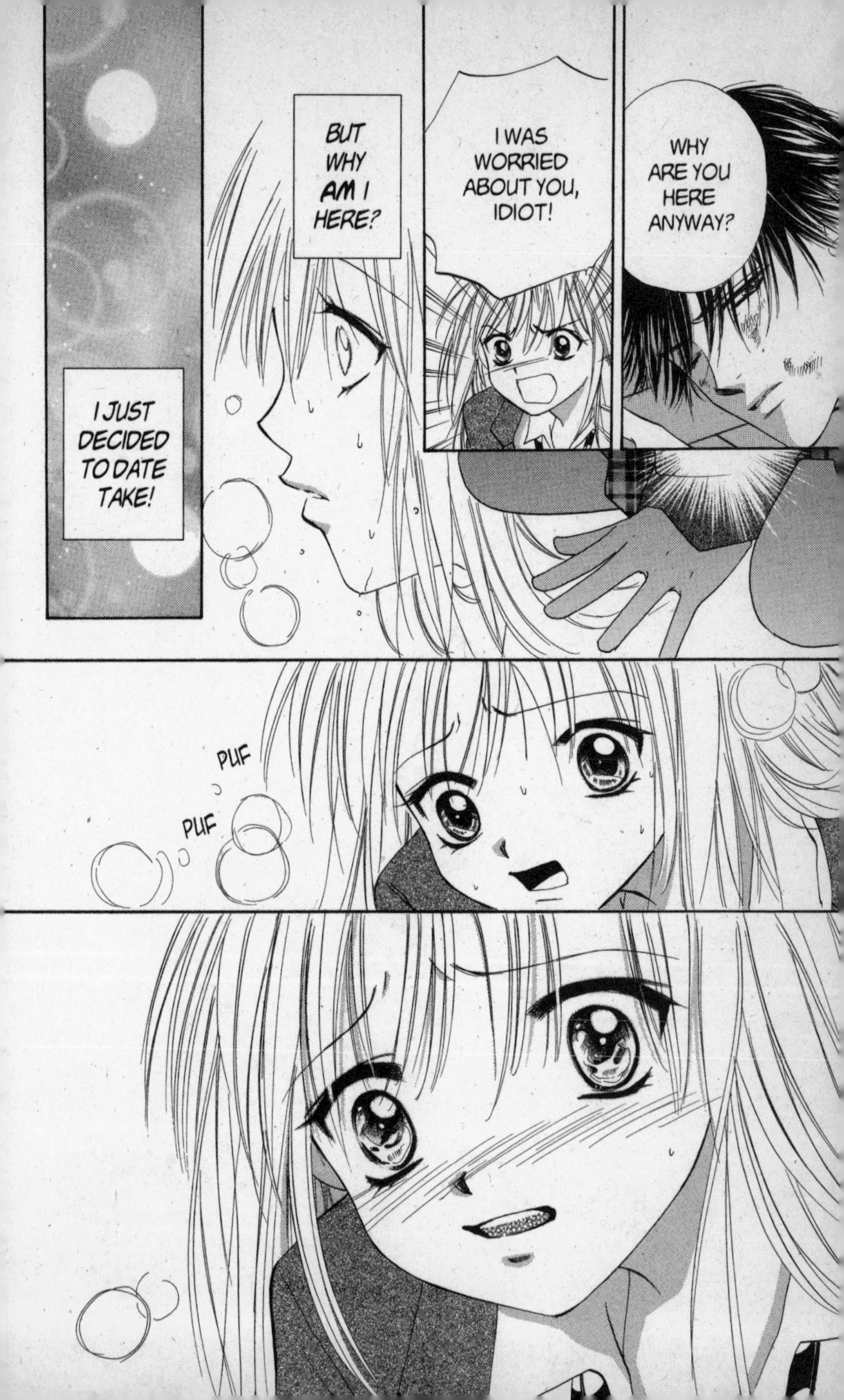
WHY ARE YOU HERE ANYWAY?
I WAS WORRIED ABOUT YOU, IDIOT!
BUT WHY **AM** I HERE?
I JUST DECIDED TO DATE TAKE!
PUF
PUF

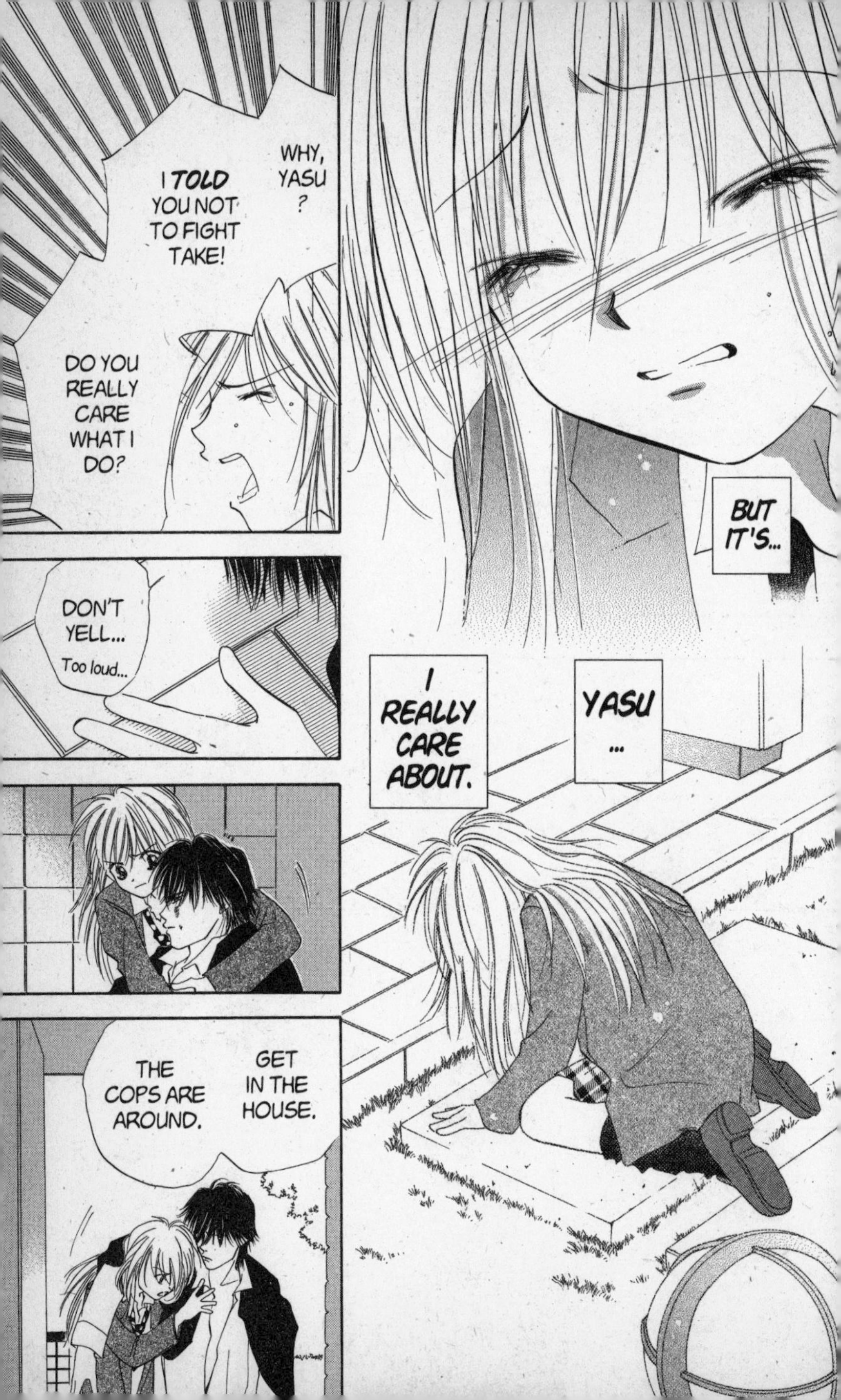
BUT IT'S...
YASU...
I REALLY CARE ABOUT.
WHY, YASU?
I TOLD YOU NOT TO FIGHT TAKE!
DO YOU REALLY CARE WHAT I DO?
DON'T YELL...
Too loud...
GET IN THE HOUSE.
THE COPS ARE AROUND.

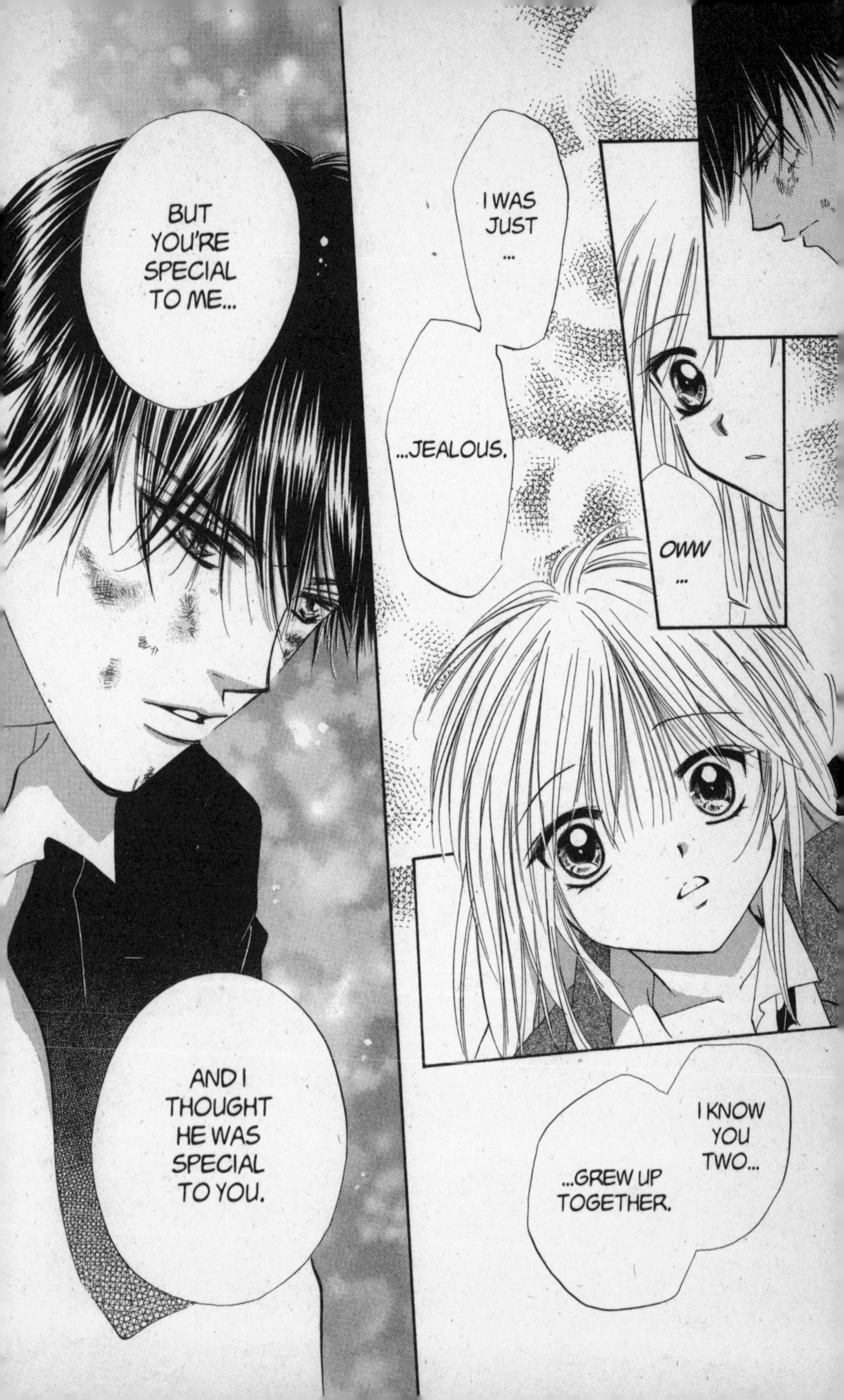
I WAS JUST ...
...JEALOUS.
OWW ...
I KNOW YOU TWO...
...GREW UP TOGETHER.
BUT YOU'RE SPECIAL TO ME...
AND I THOUGHT HE WAS SPECIAL TO YOU.

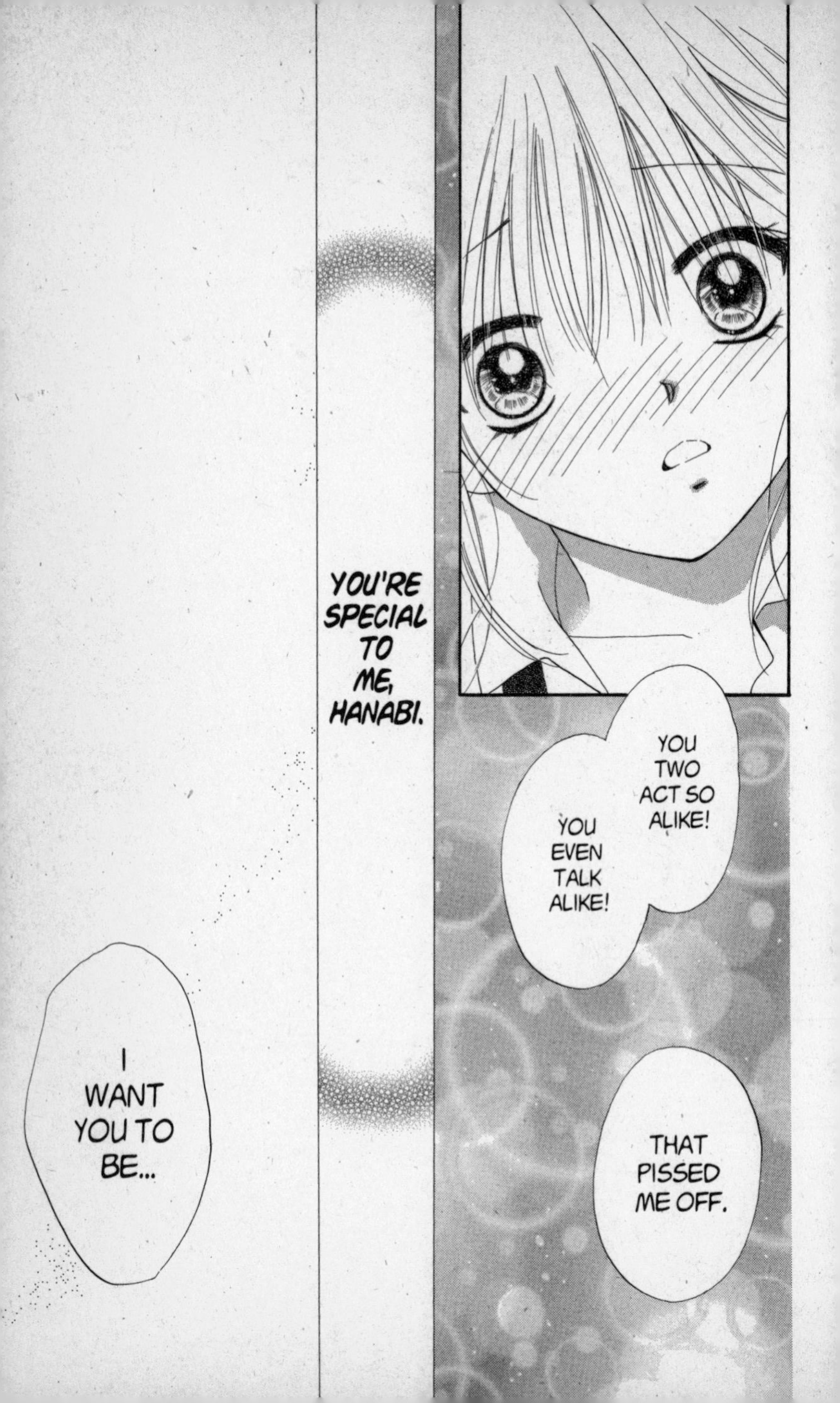
YOU TWO ACT SO ALIKE!
YOU EVEN TALK ALIKE!
THAT PISSED ME OFF.
YOU'RE SPECIAL TO ME, HANABI.
I WANT YOU TO BE...

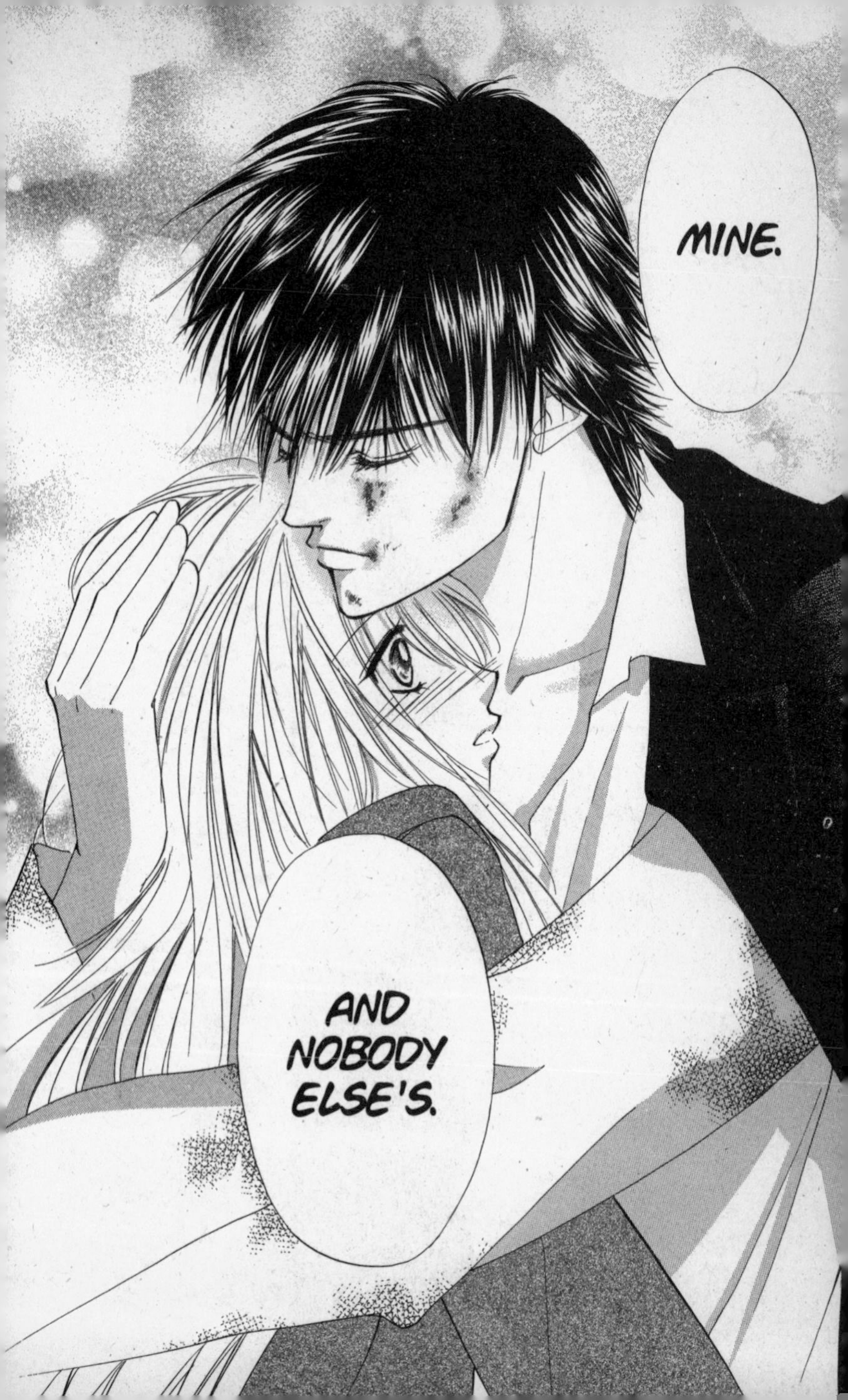
MINE.
AND NOBODY ELSE'S.

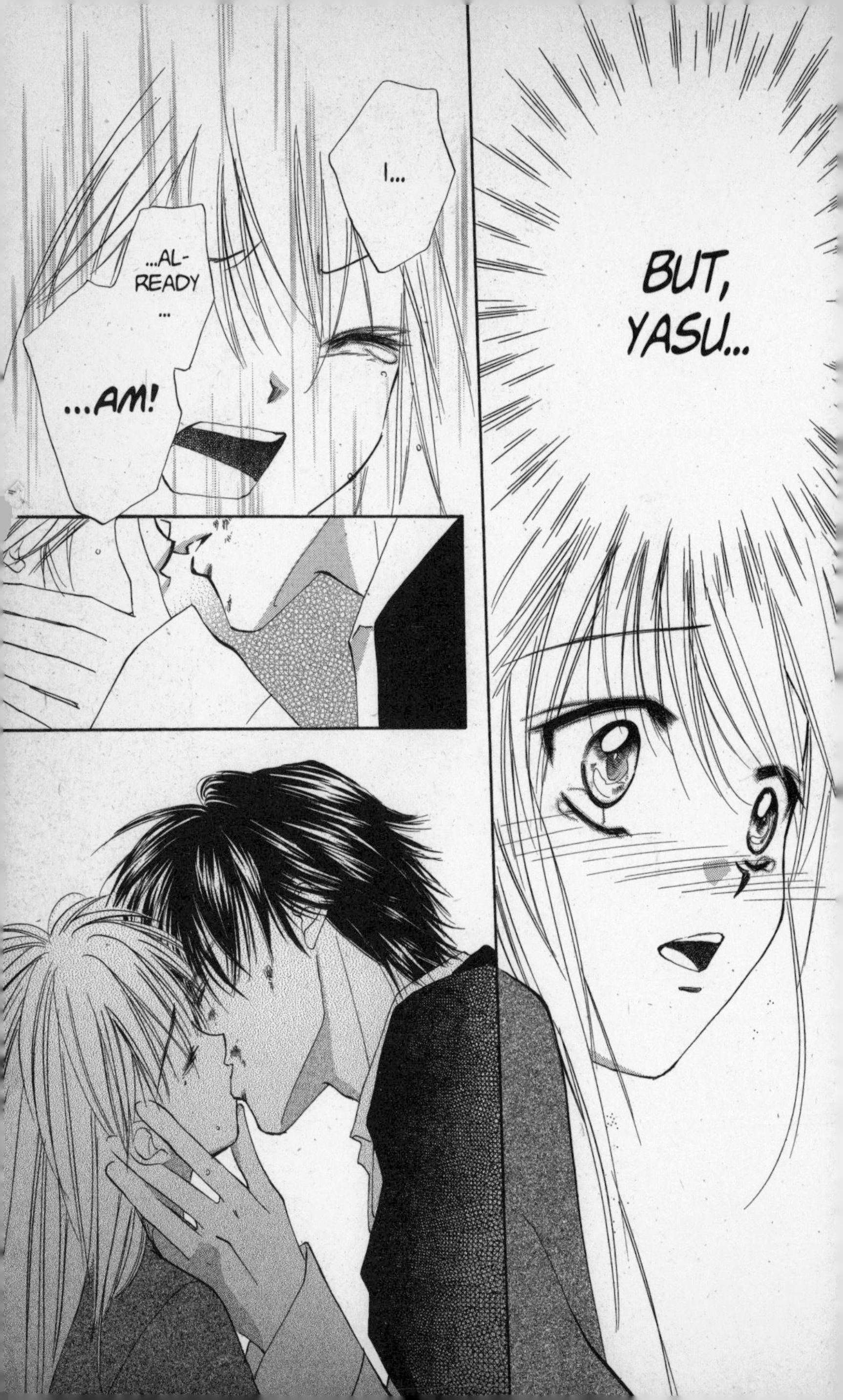
BUT, YASU...
I...
...AL-
READY
...
...AM!

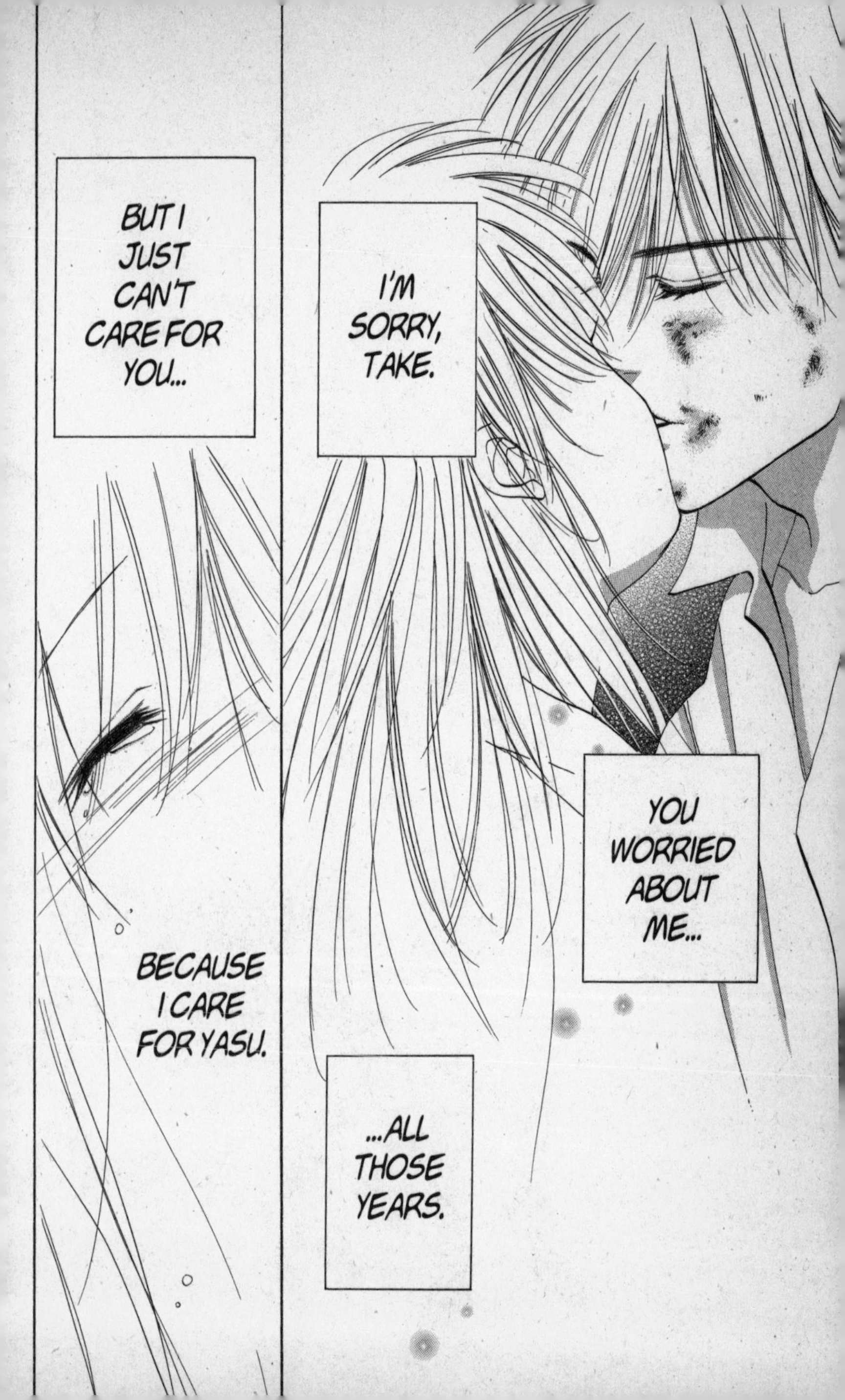
I'M SORRY, TAKE.
YOU WORRIED ABOUT ME...
...ALL THOSE YEARS.
BUT I JUST CAN'T CARE FOR YOU...
BECAUSE I CARE FOR YASU.

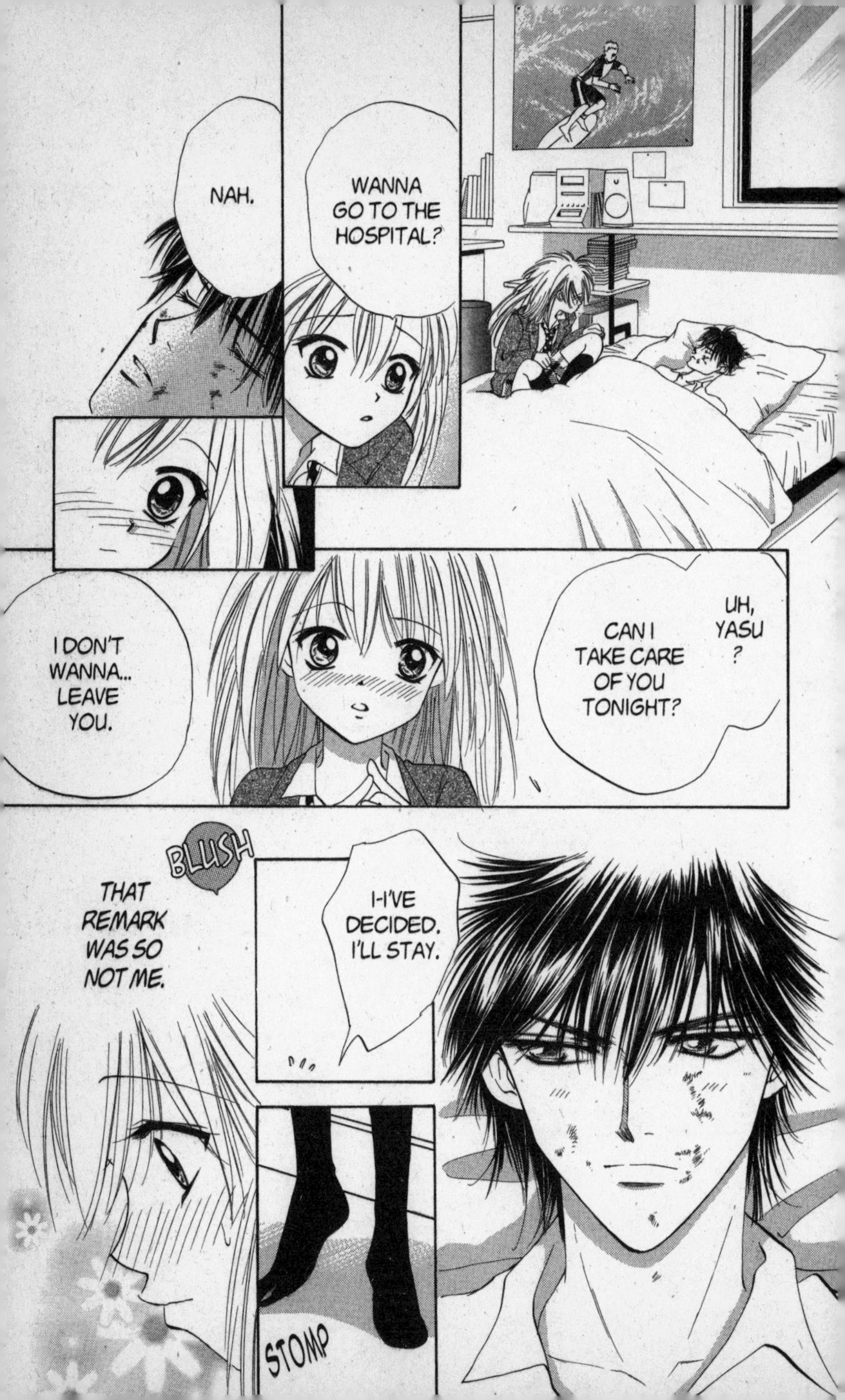
WANNA GO TO THE HOSPITAL?
NAH.
UH, YASU?
CAN I TAKE CARE OF YOU TONIGHT?
I DON'T WANNA... LEAVE YOU.
I-I'VE DECIDED. I'LL STAY.
STOMP
BLUSH
THAT REMARK WAS SO NOT ME.

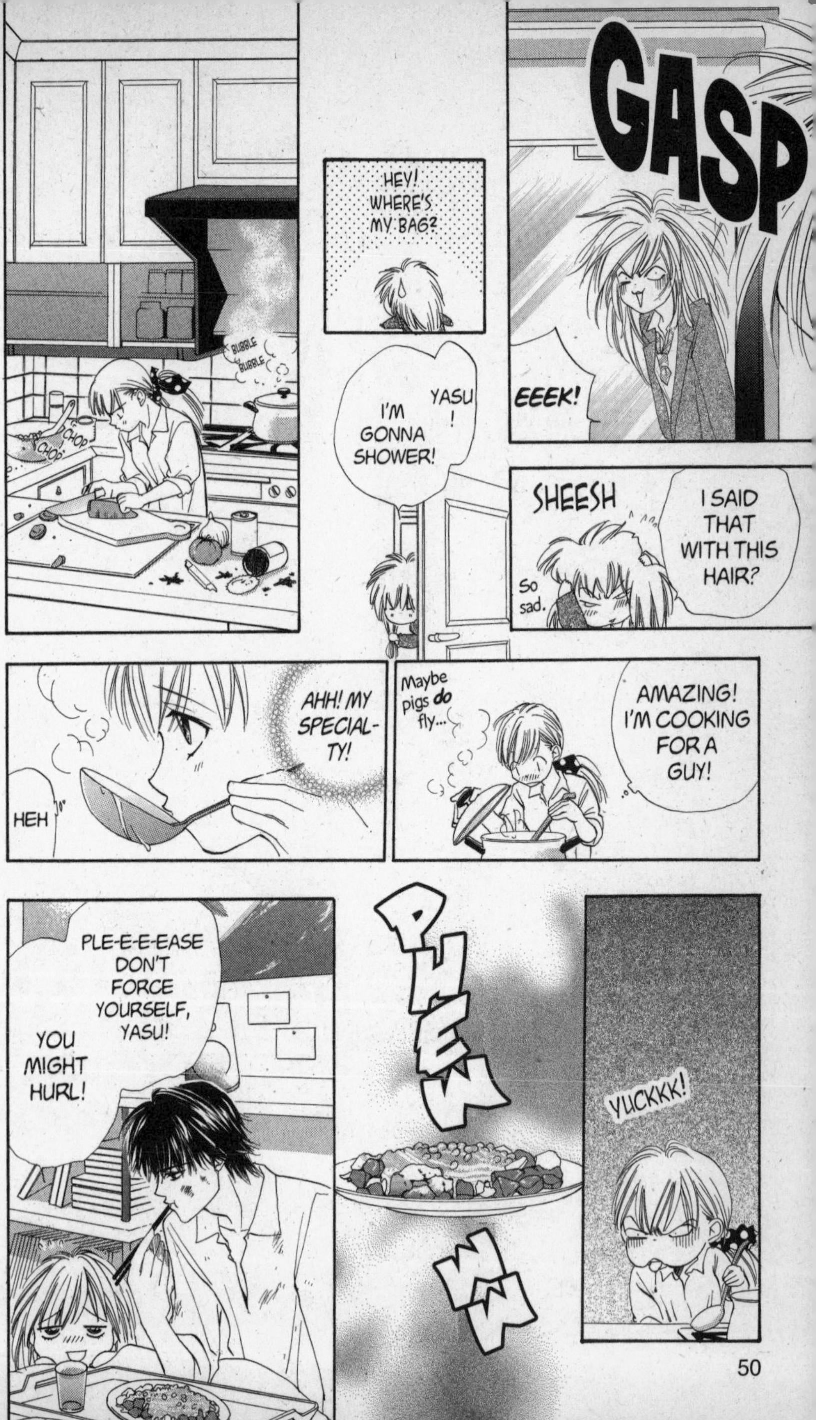
GASP
EEEK!
SHEESH
I SAID THAT WITH THIS HAIR?
So sad.
HEY! WHERE'S MY BAG?
YASU! I'M GONNA SHOWER!
BUBBLE BUBBLE
CHOP CHOP
AMAZING! I'M COOKING FOR A GUY!
Maybe pigs do fly...
AHH! MY SPECIAL-TY!
HEH
YUCKKK!
PHEW
PLE-E-E-EASE DON'T FORCE YOURSELF, YASU!
YOU MIGHT HURL!

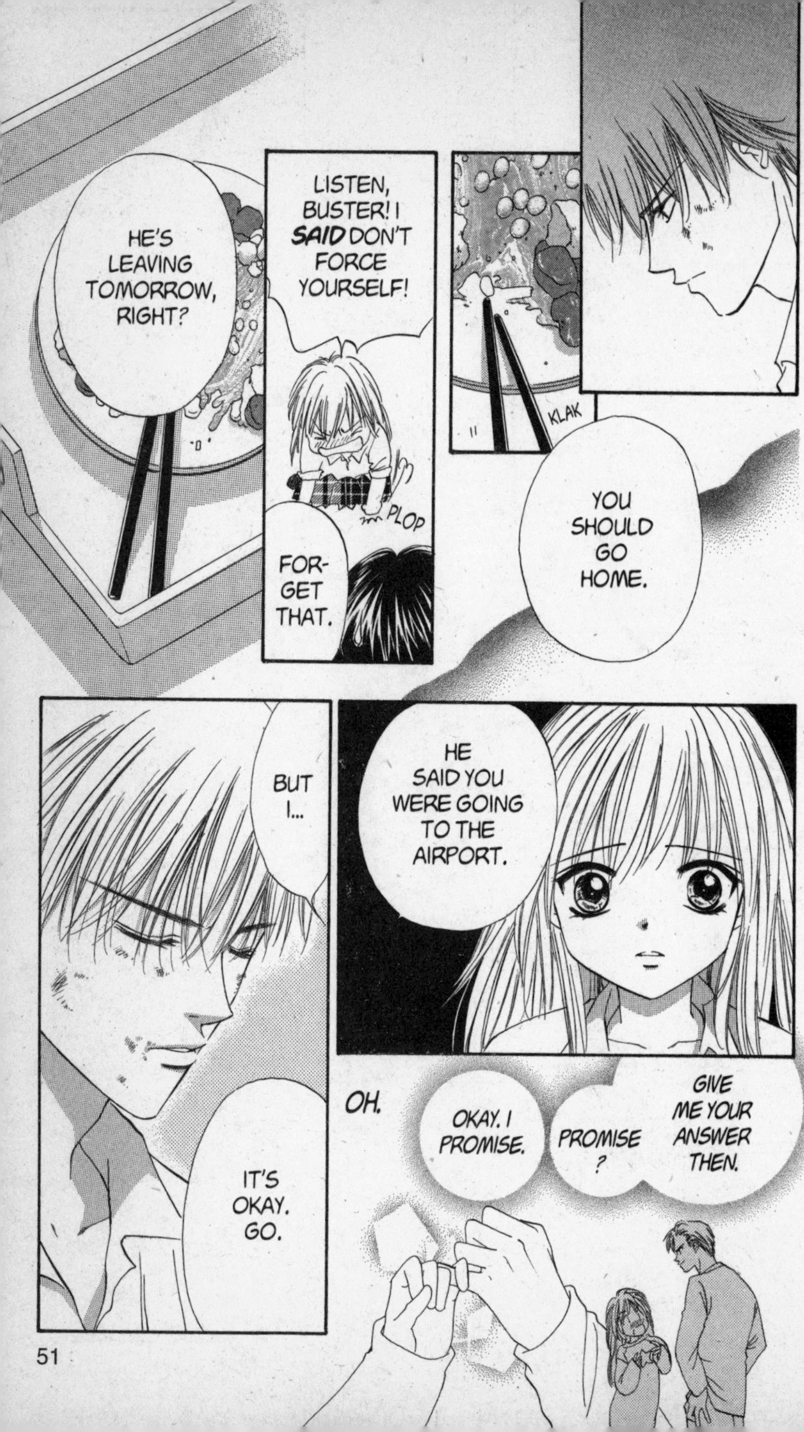
KLAK
YOU SHOULD GO HOME.
LISTEN, BUSTER! I **SAID** DON'T FORCE YOURSELF!
PLOP
FOR-GET THAT.
HE'S LEAVING TOMORROW, RIGHT?
HE SAID YOU WERE GOING TO THE AIRPORT.
BUT I...
IT'S OKAY. GO.
GIVE ME YOUR ANSWER THEN.
PROMISE?
OKAY. I PROMISE.
OH.

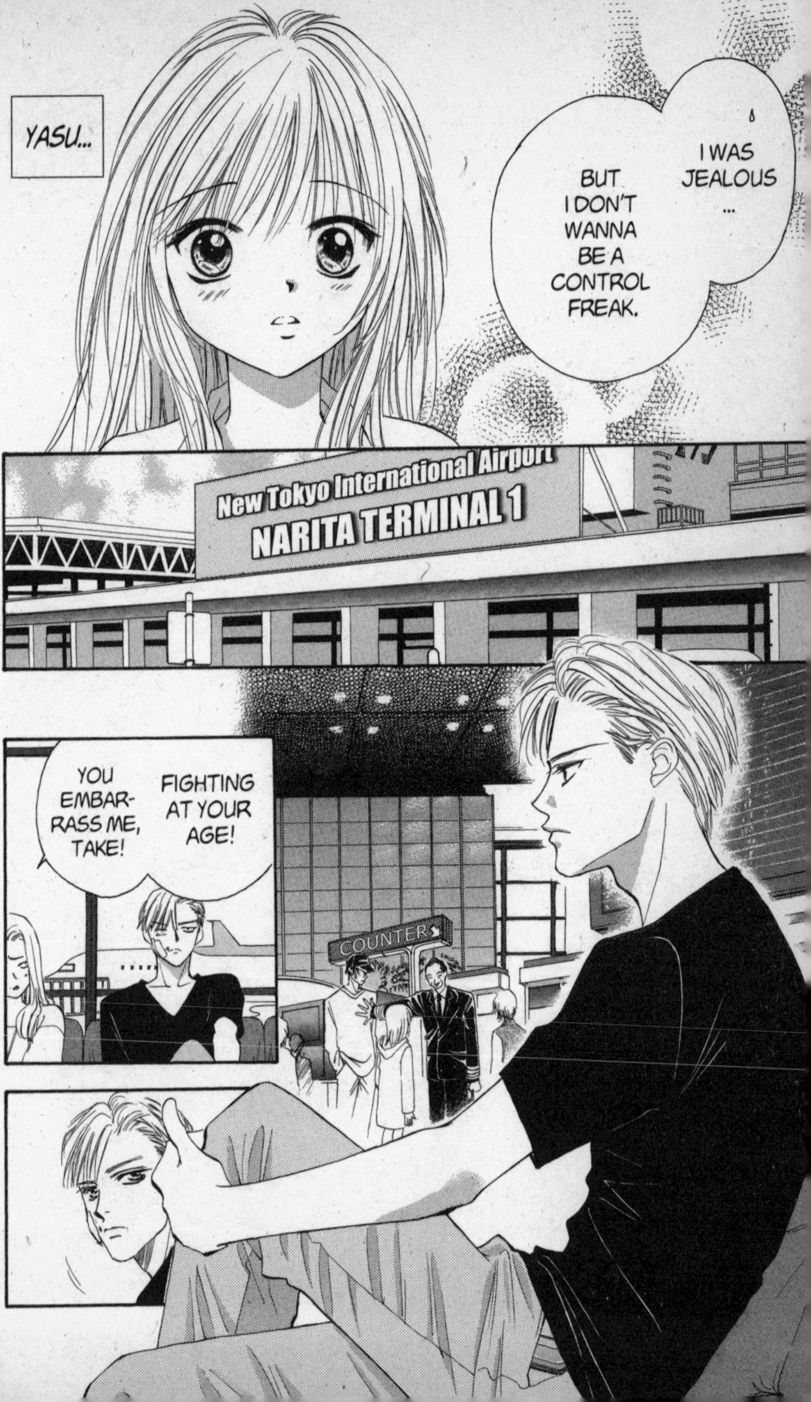
I WAS JEALOUS...
BUT I DON'T WANNA BE A CONTROL FREAK.
YASU...
New Tokyo International Airport
NARITA TERMINAL 1
COUNTER
YOU EMBARRASS ME, TAKE! FIGHTING AT YOUR AGE!

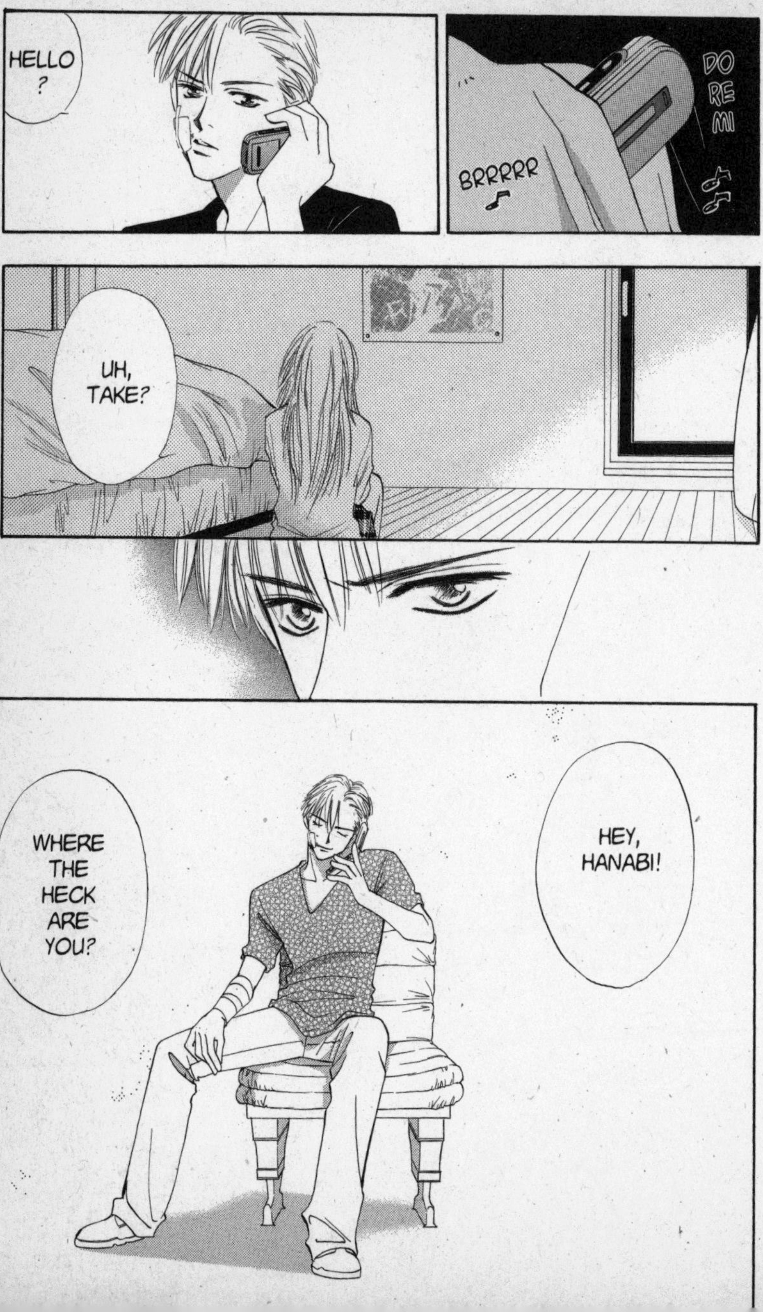
DO RE MI
BRRRRR
HELLO ?
UH, TAKE?
HEY, HANABI!
WHERE THE HECK ARE YOU?

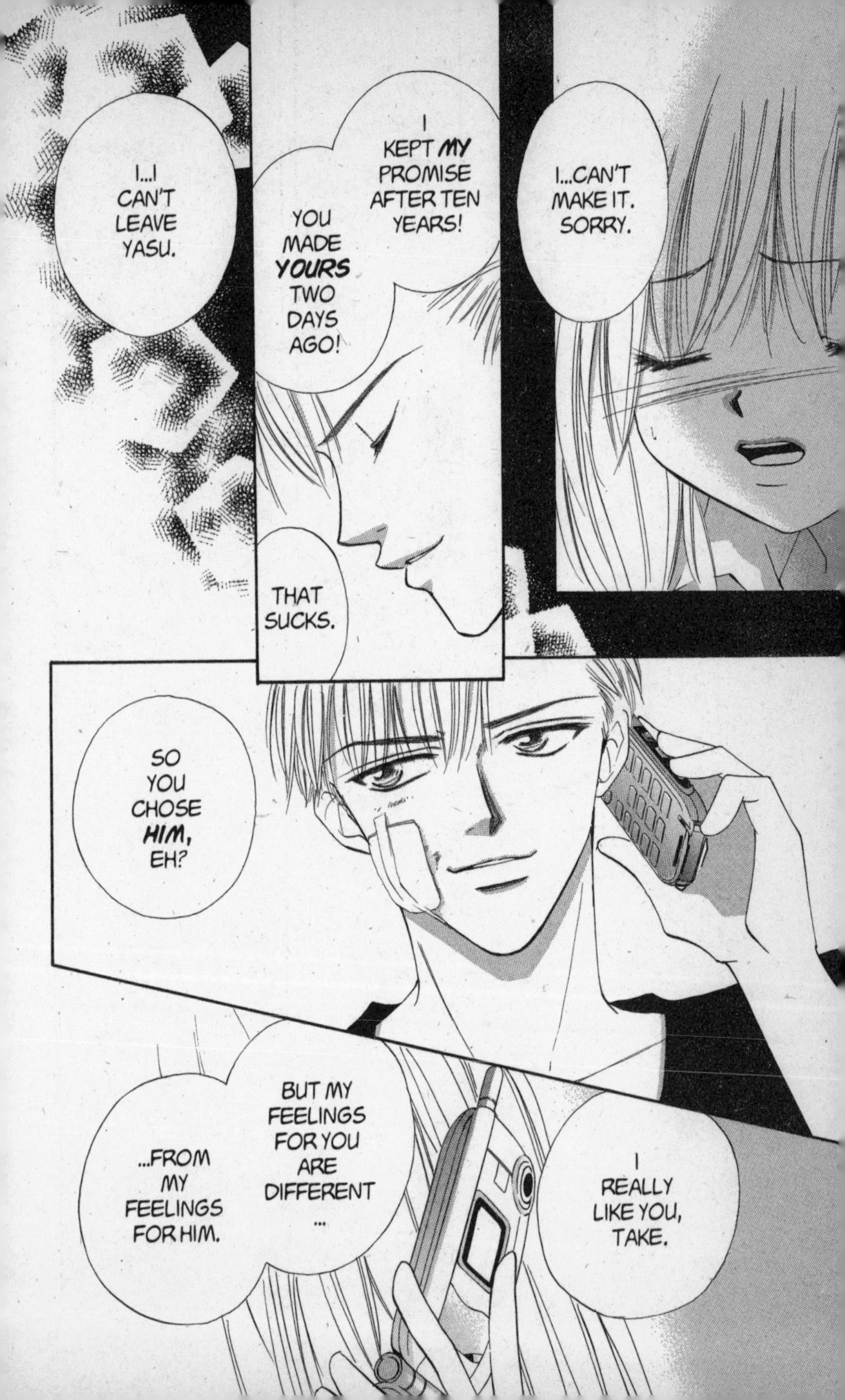
I...CAN'T MAKE IT. SORRY.
I KEPT MY PROMISE AFTER TEN YEARS!
YOU MADE YOURS TWO DAYS AGO!
THAT SUCKS.
I...I CAN'T LEAVE YASU.
SO YOU CHOSE HIM, EH?
I REALLY LIKE YOU, TAKE.
BUT MY FEELINGS FOR YOU ARE DIFFERENT...
...FROM MY FEELINGS FOR HIM.

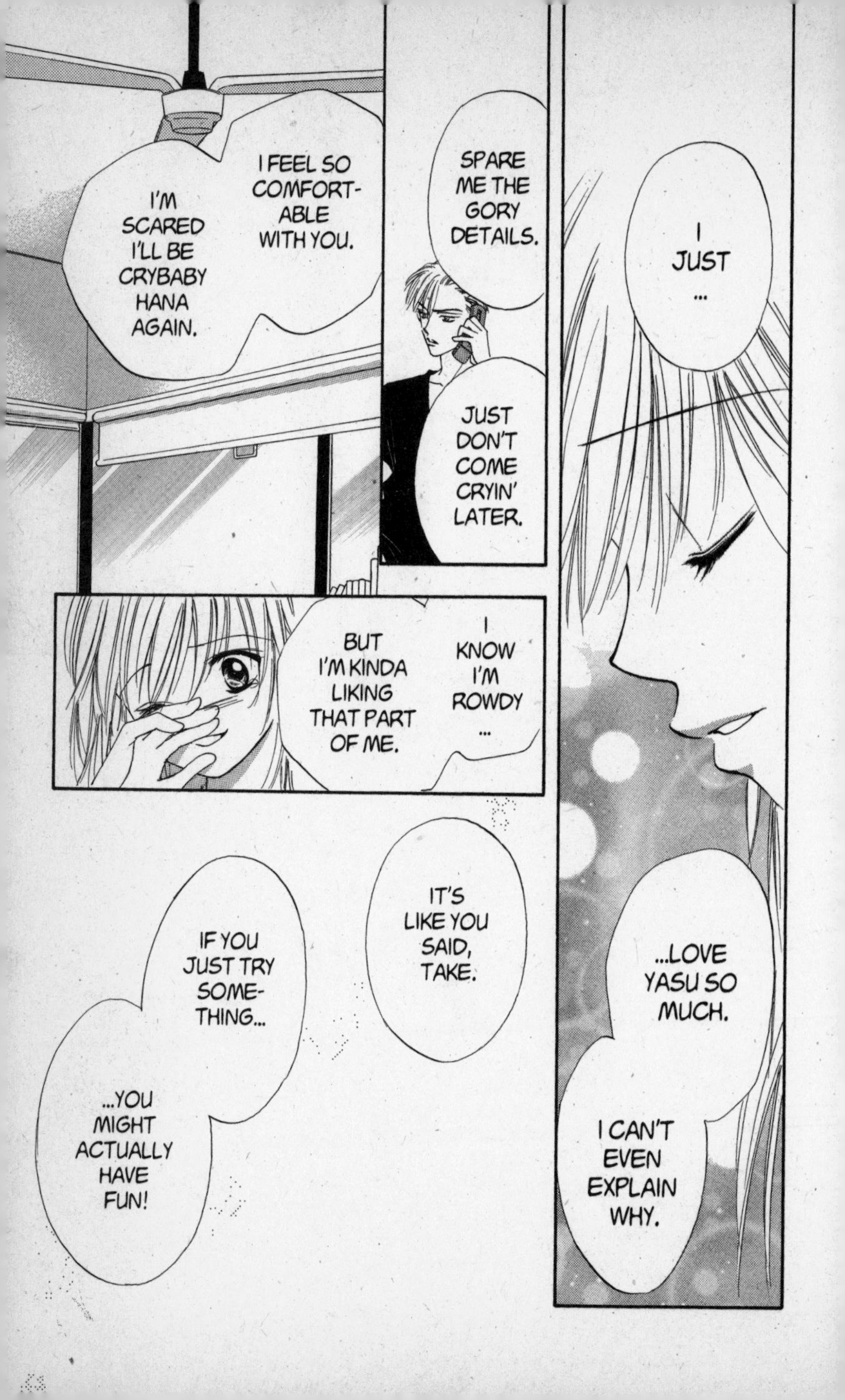
I JUST ...
...LOVE YASU SO MUCH.
I CAN'T EVEN EXPLAIN WHY.
SPARE ME THE GORY DETAILS.
JUST DON'T COME CRYIN' LATER.
I FEEL SO COMFORT-ABLE WITH YOU.
I'M SCARED I'LL BE CRYBABY HANA AGAIN.
I KNOW I'M ROWDY ...
BUT I'M KINDA LIKING THAT PART OF ME.
IT'S LIKE YOU SAID, TAKE.
IF YOU JUST TRY SOME-THING...
...YOU MIGHT ACTUALLY HAVE FUN!

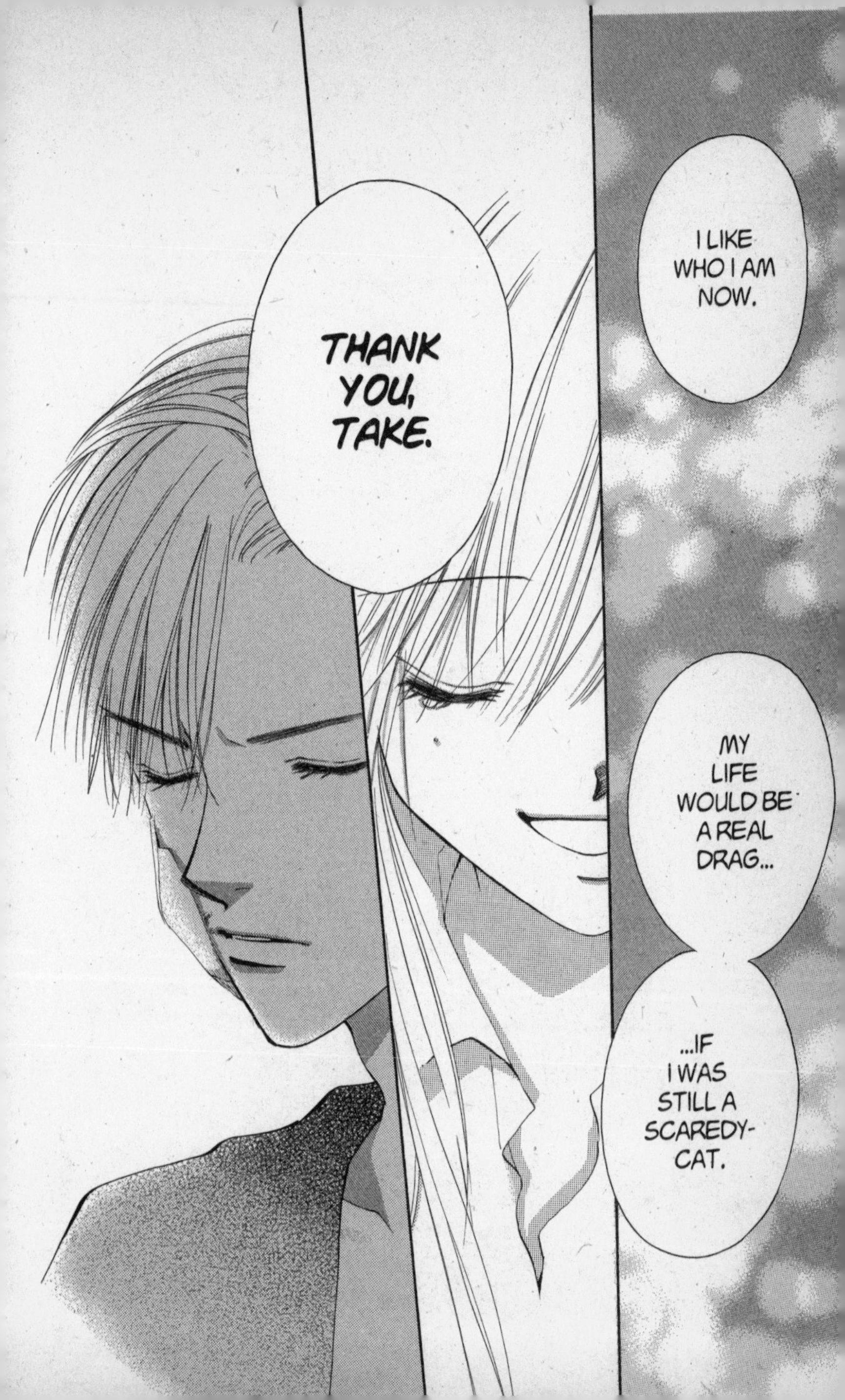
I LIKE WHO I AM NOW.
MY LIFE WOULD BE A REAL DRAG...
...IF I WAS STILL A SCAREDY-CAT.
THANK YOU, TAKE.

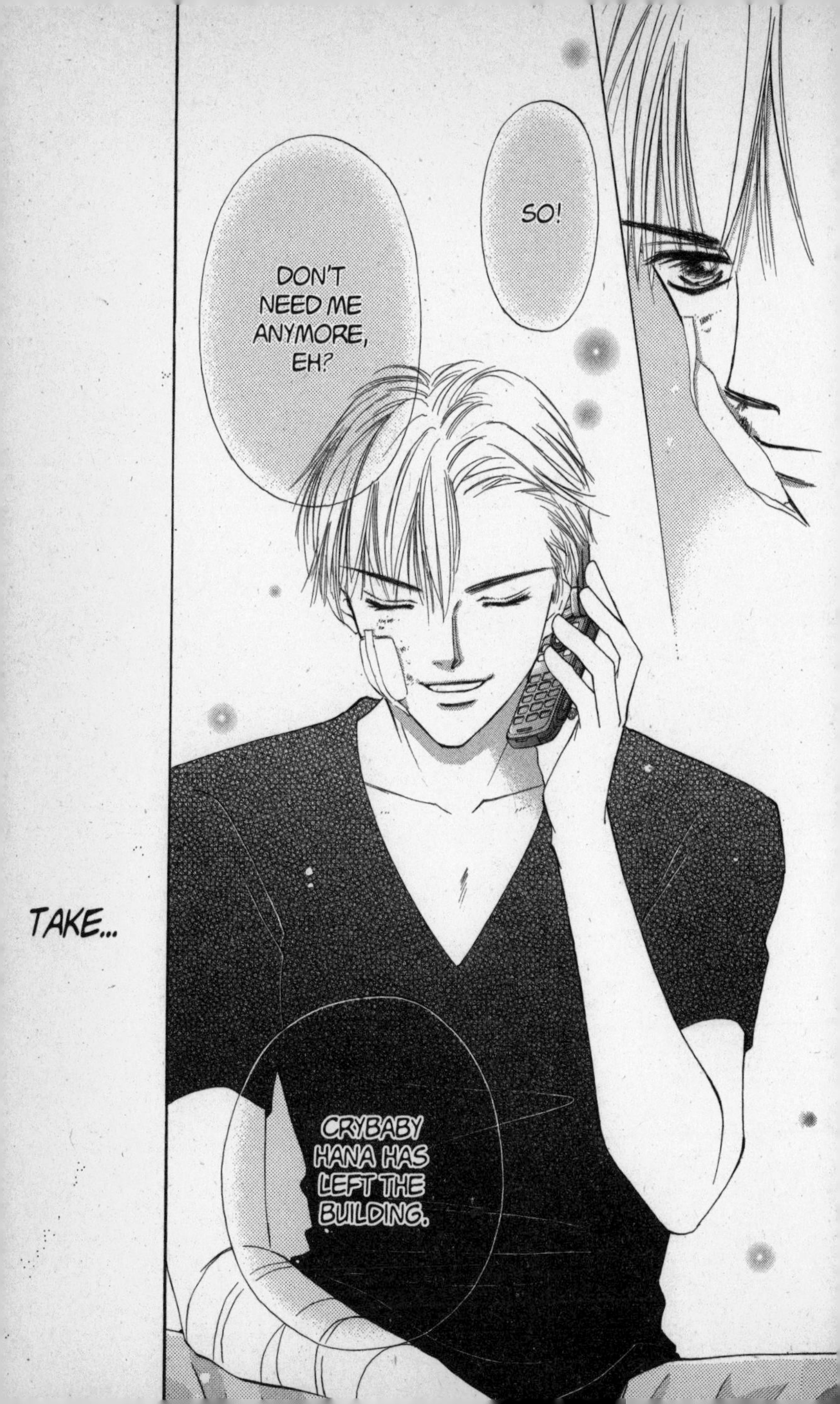
SO!
DON'T NEED ME ANYMORE, EH?
CRYBABY HANA HAS LEFT THE BUILDING.
TAKE...

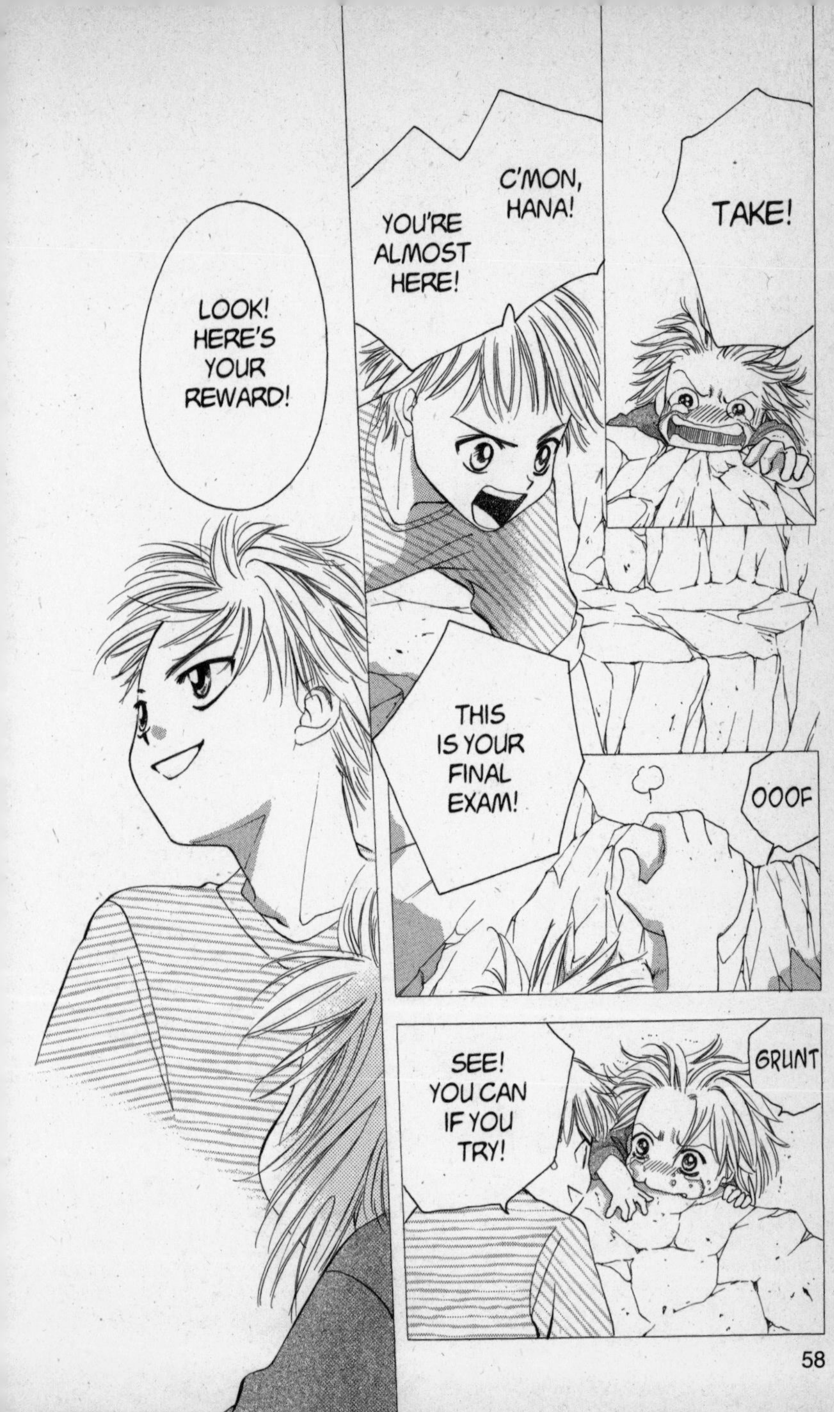
TAKE!
C'MON, HANA!
YOU'RE ALMOST HERE!
THIS IS YOUR FINAL EXAM!
OOOF
GRUNT
SEE! YOU CAN IF YOU TRY!
LOOK! HERE'S YOUR REWARD!

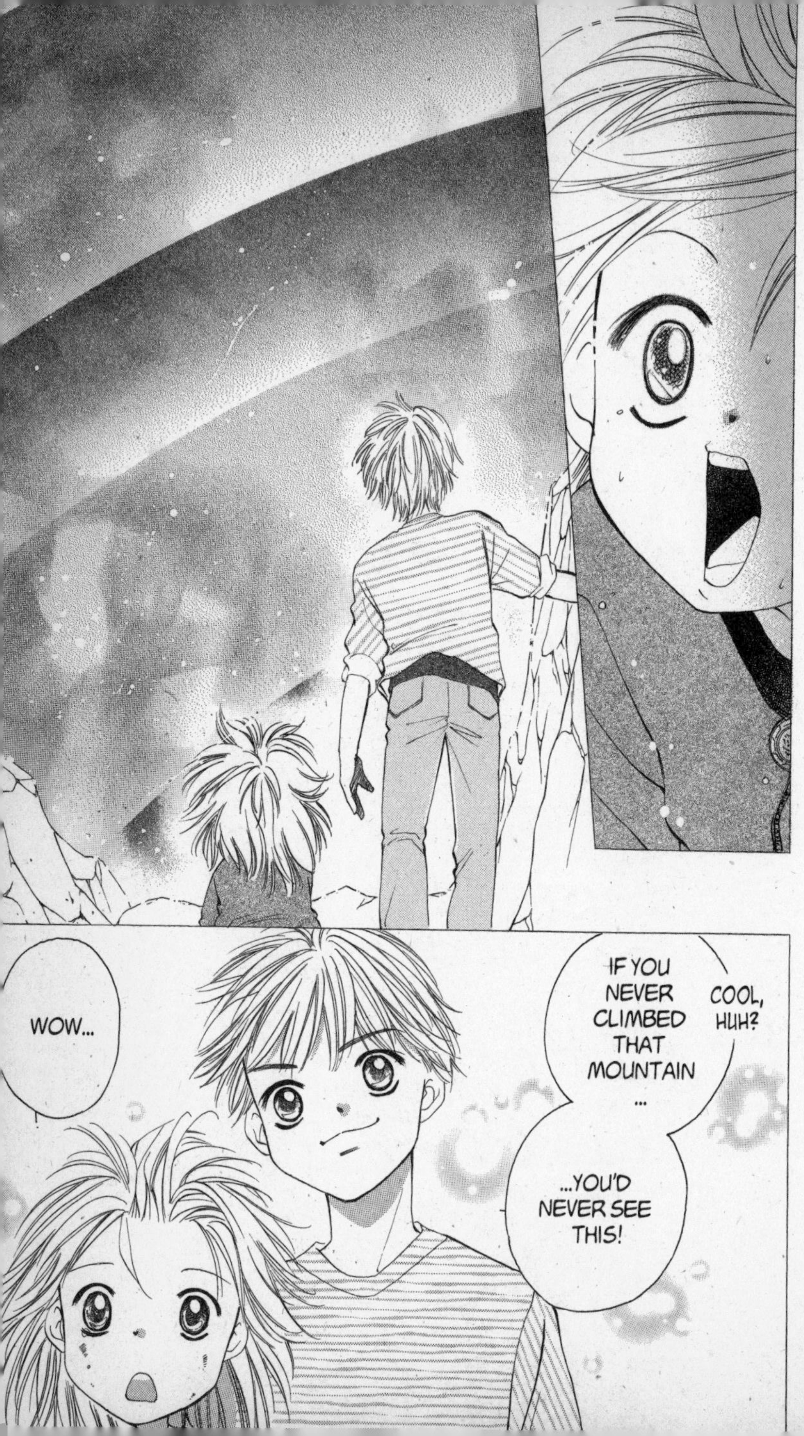
COOL, HUH?
IF YOU NEVER CLIMBED THAT MOUNTAIN ...
...YOU'D NEVER SEE THIS!
WOW...

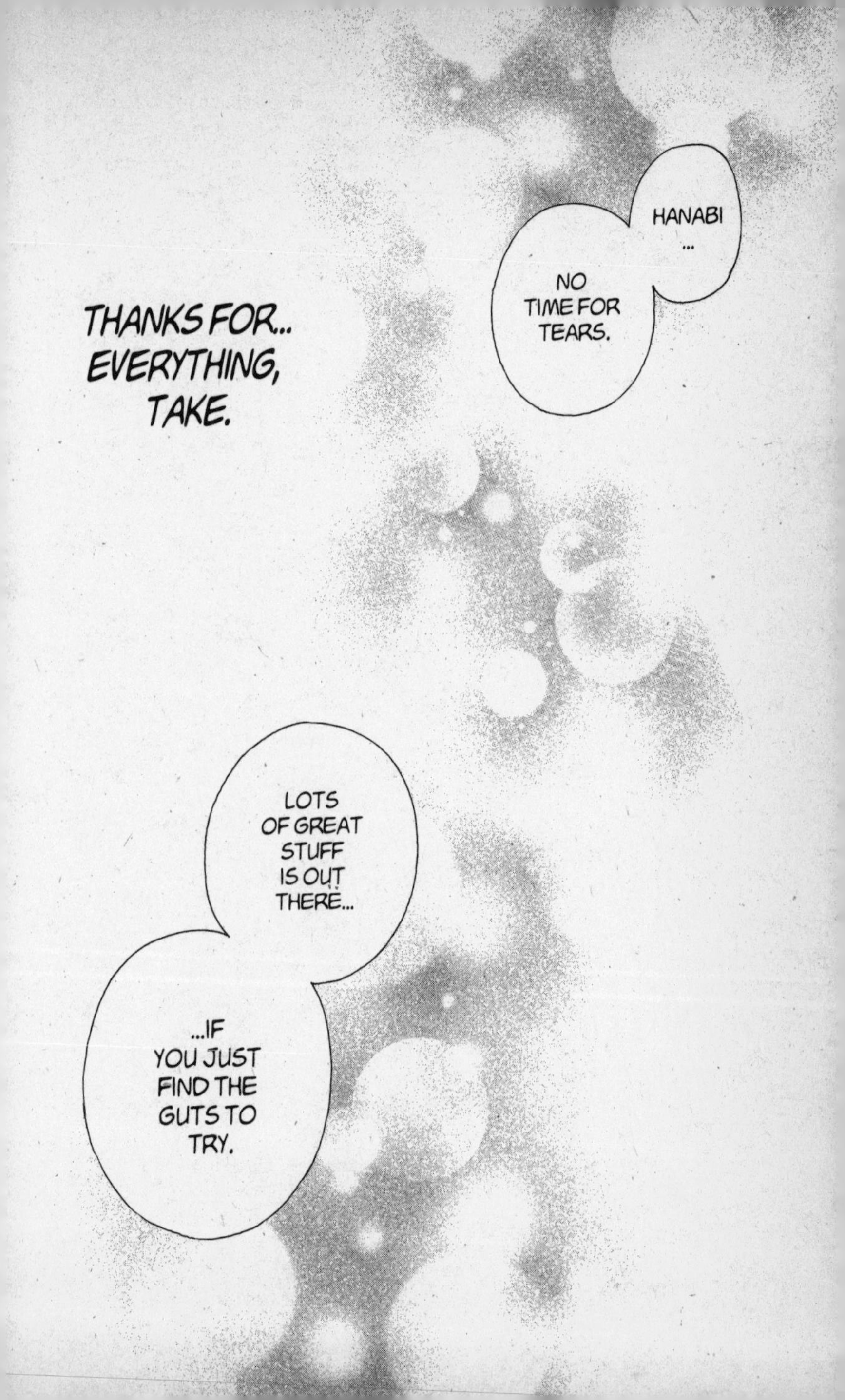
HANABI ...
NO TIME FOR TEARS.
THANKS FOR... EVERYTHING, TAKE.
LOTS OF GREAT STUFF IS OUT THERE...
...IF YOU JUST FIND THE GUTS TO TRY.

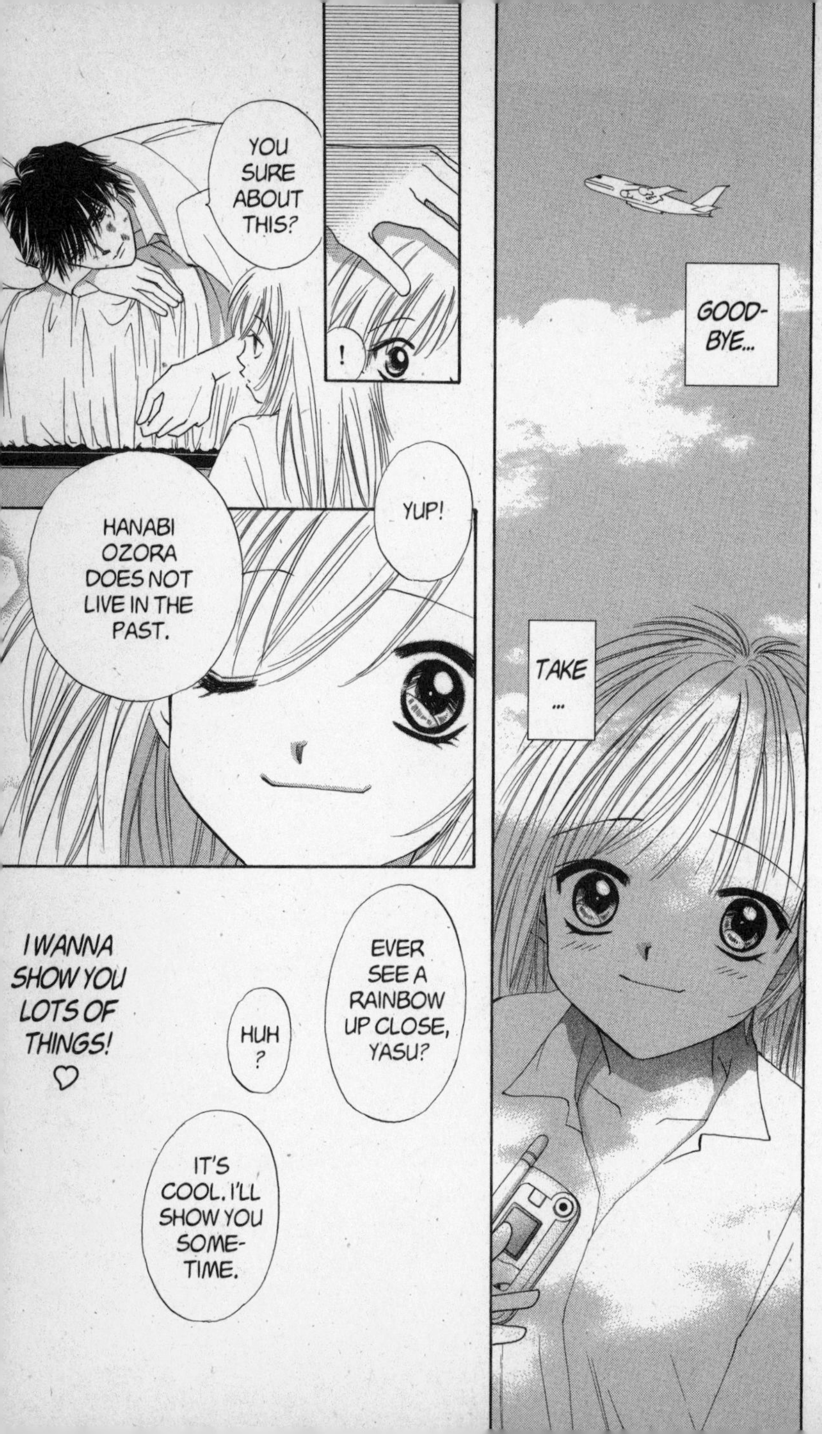
GOOD-BYE...
TAKE ...
!
YOU SURE ABOUT THIS?
YUP!
HANABI OZORA DOES NOT LIVE IN THE PAST.
EVER SEE A RAINBOW UP CLOSE, YASU?
HUH?
IT'S COOL. I'LL SHOW YOU SOME-TIME.
I WANNA SHOW YOU LOTS OF THINGS! ♡

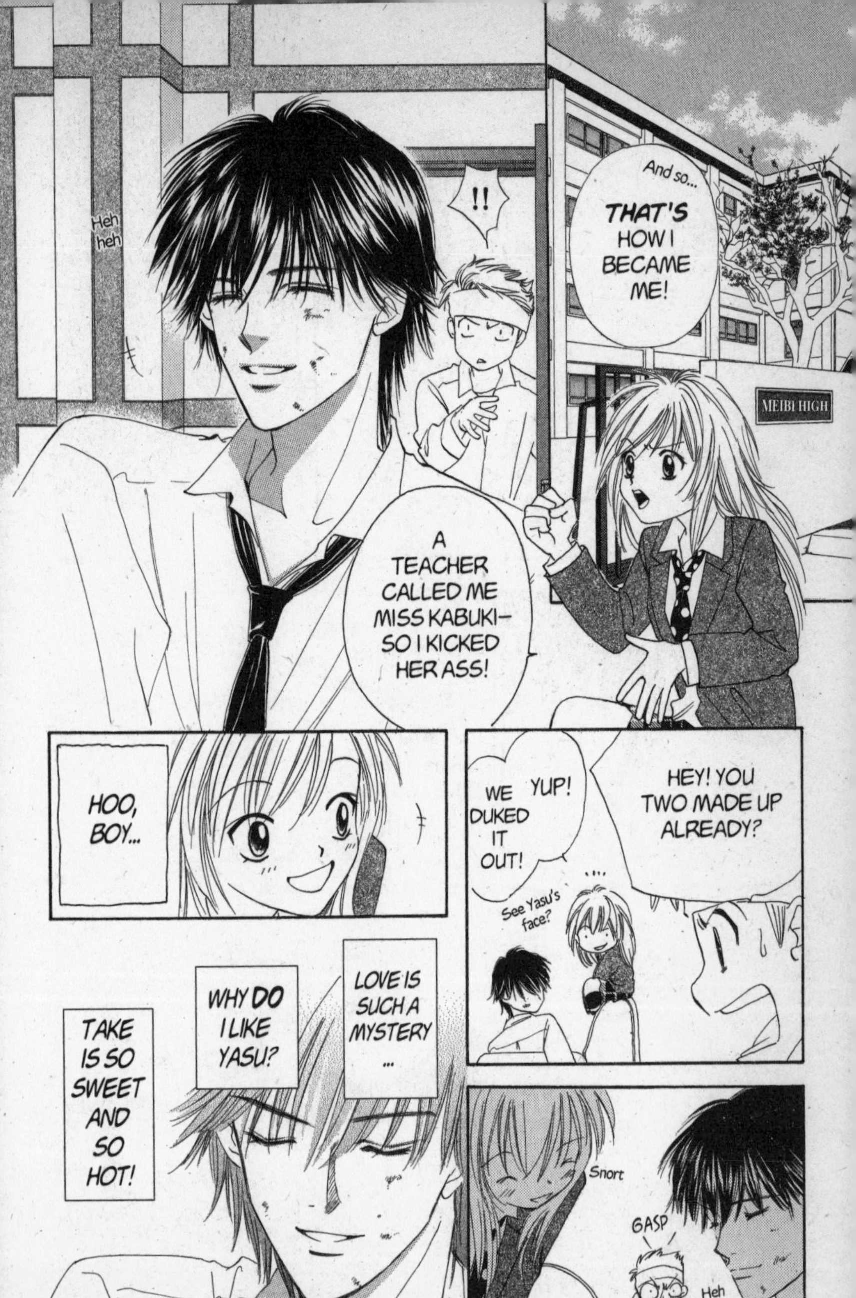
And so... THAT'S HOW I BECAME ME!
MEIBI HIGH
!!
Heh heh
A TEACHER CALLED ME MISS KABUKI— SO I KICKED HER ASS!
HEY! YOU TWO MADE UP ALREADY?
YUP! WE DUKED IT OUT!
...
See Yasu's face?
HOO, BOY...
Snort
GASP
Heh
LOVE IS SUCH A MYSTERY ...
WHY DO I LIKE YASU?
TAKE IS SO SWEET AND SO HOT!

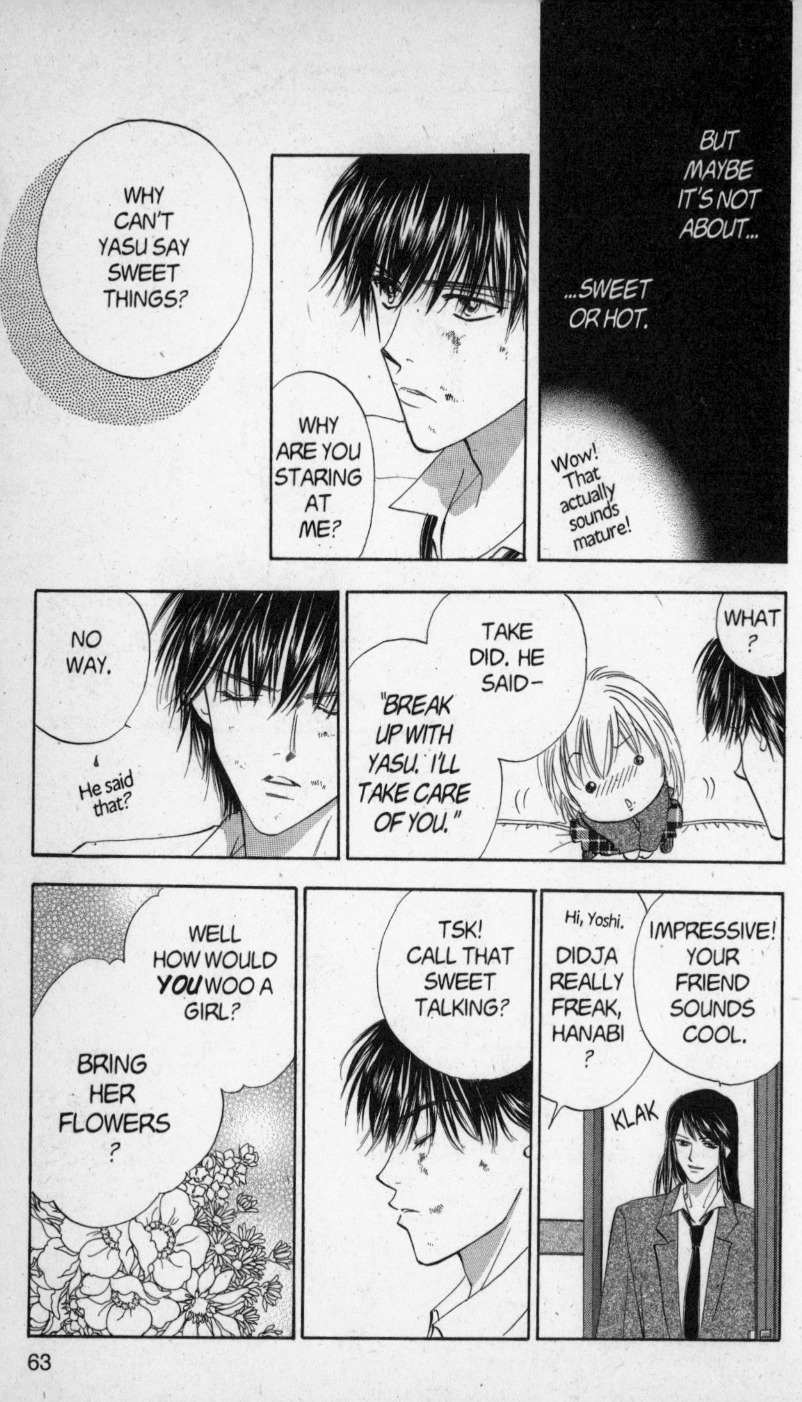
BUT MAYBE IT'S NOT ABOUT...
...SWEET OR HOT.
Wow! That actually sounds mature!
WHY ARE YOU STARING AT ME?
WHY CAN'T YASU SAY SWEET THINGS?
WHAT?
TAKE DID. HE SAID—
"BREAK UP WITH YASU. I'LL TAKE CARE OF YOU."
NO WAY.
He said that?
IMPRESSIVE! YOUR FRIEND SOUNDS COOL.
Hi, Yoshi.
DIDJA REALLY FREAK, HANABI?
KLAK
TSK! CALL THAT SWEET TALKING?
WELL HOW WOULD YOU WOO A GIRL?
BRING HER FLOWERS?

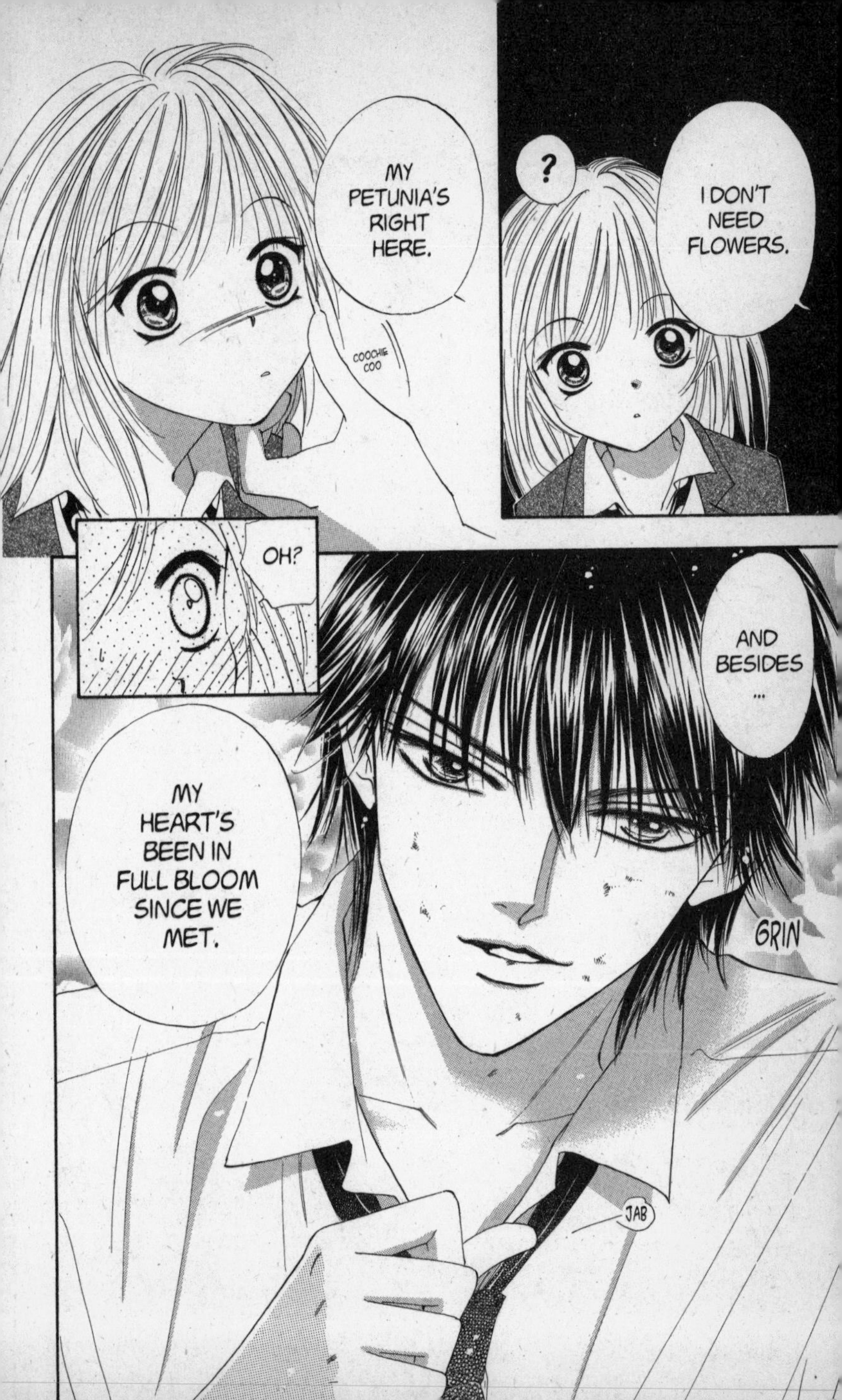

?
I DON'T NEED FLOWERS.
MY PETUNIA'S RIGHT HERE.
COOCHIE COO
AND BESIDES ...
OH?
MY HEART'S BEEN IN FULL BLOOM SINCE WE MET.
GRIN
JAB

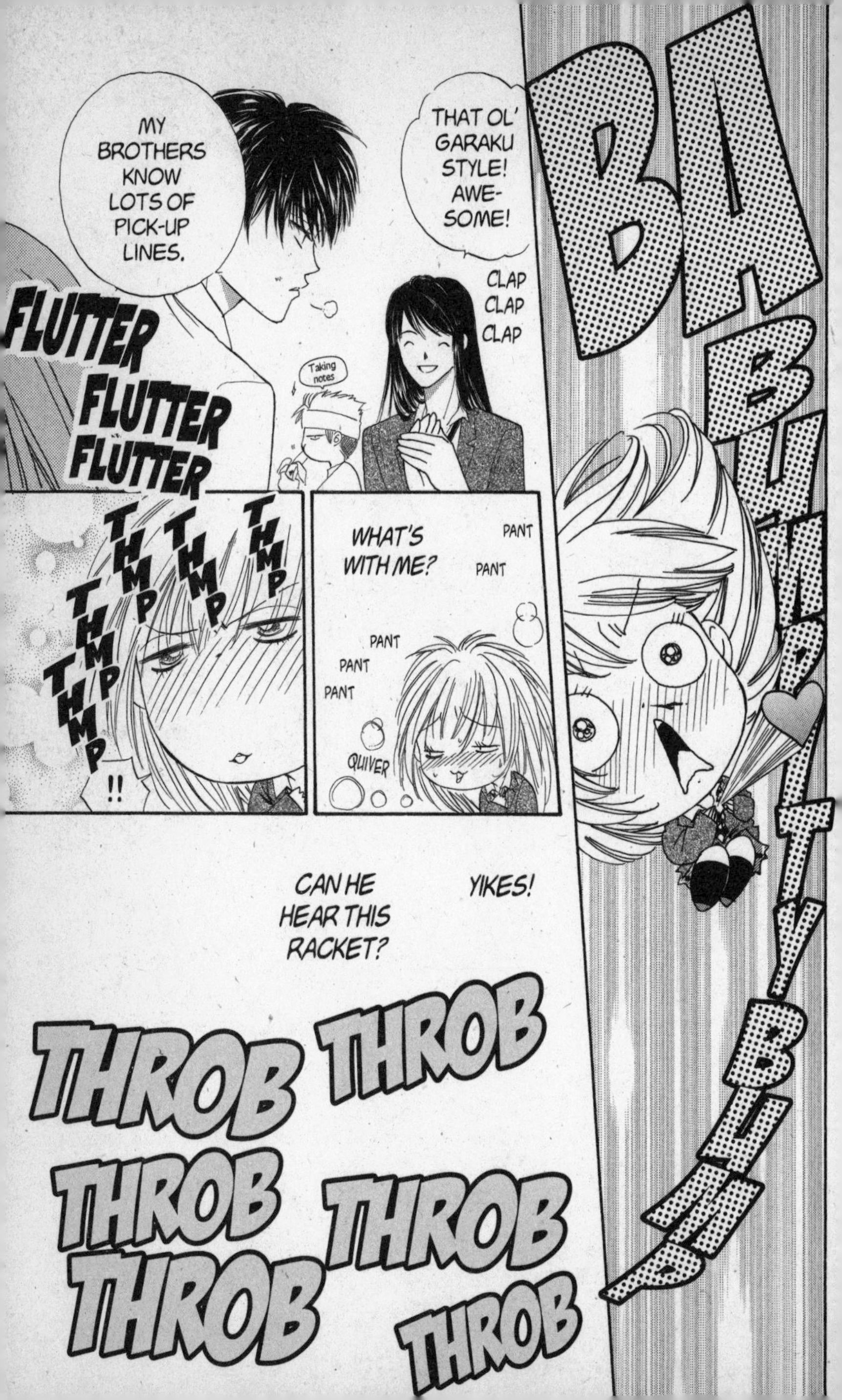
BA-BUMPITY-BUMP
THAT OL' GARAKU STYLE! AWE-SOME!
CLAP CLAP CLAP
MY BROTHERS KNOW LOTS OF PICK-UP LINES.
Taking notes
FLUTTER FLUTTER FLUTTER
WHAT'S WITH ME?
PANT PANT
PANT PANT PANT
QUIVER
THMP THMP THMP THMP THMP
!!
YIKES!
CAN HE HEAR THIS RACKET?
THROB THROB THROB THROB THROB THROB

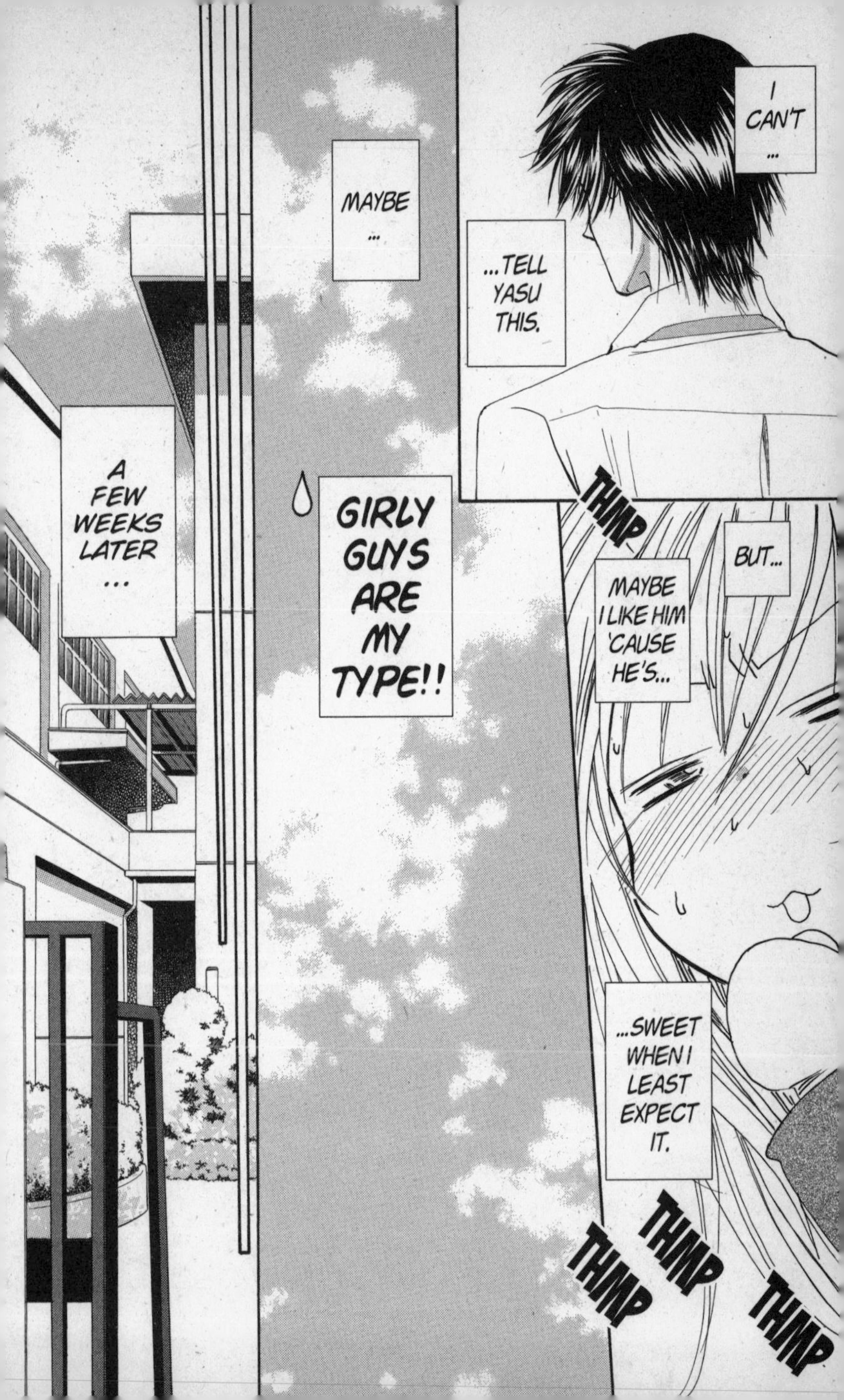
I CAN'T ...
...TELL YASU THIS.
THMP
BUT...
MAYBE I LIKE HIM 'CAUSE HE'S...
...SWEET WHEN I LEAST EXPECT IT.
THMP
THMP
THMP
MAYBE ...
GIRLY GUYS ARE MY TYPE!!
A FEW WEEKS LATER ...

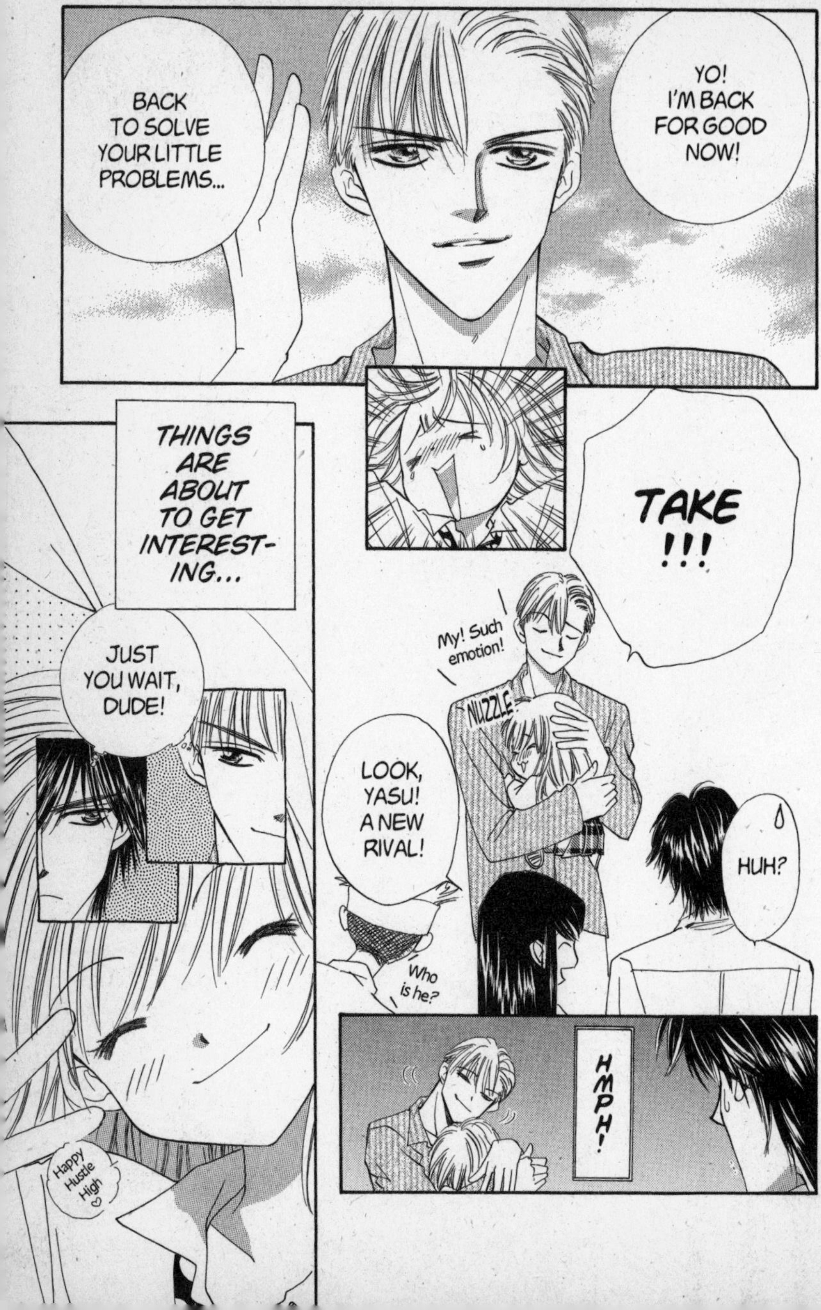

YO! I'M BACK FOR GOOD NOW!
BACK TO SOLVE YOUR LITTLE PROBLEMS...
TAKE !!!
My! Such emotion!
NUZZLE
HUH?
LOOK, YASU! A NEW RIVAL!
Who is he?
HMPH!
THINGS ARE ABOUT TO GET INTEREST-ING...
JUST YOU WAIT, DUDE!
Happy Hustle High ♡

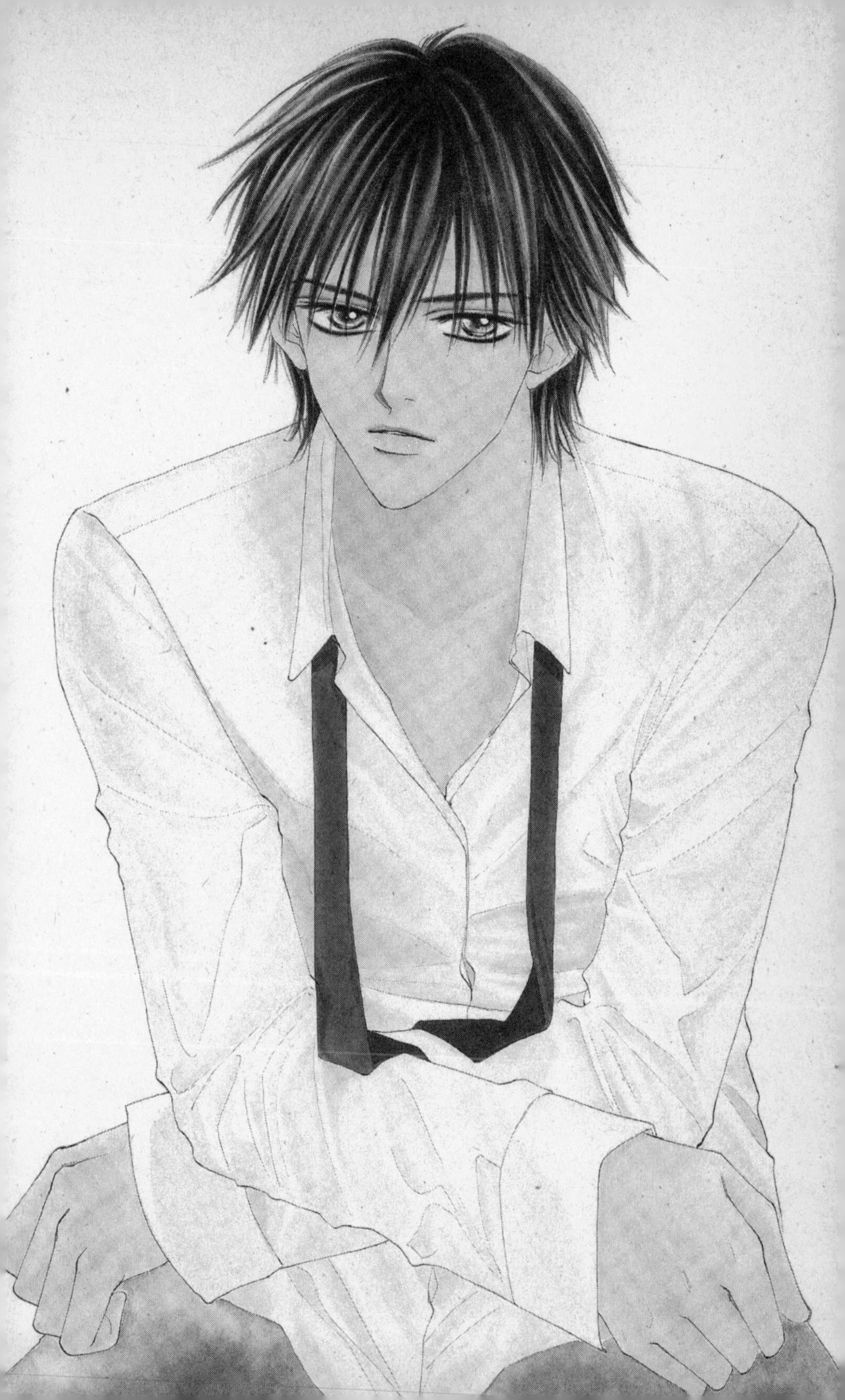

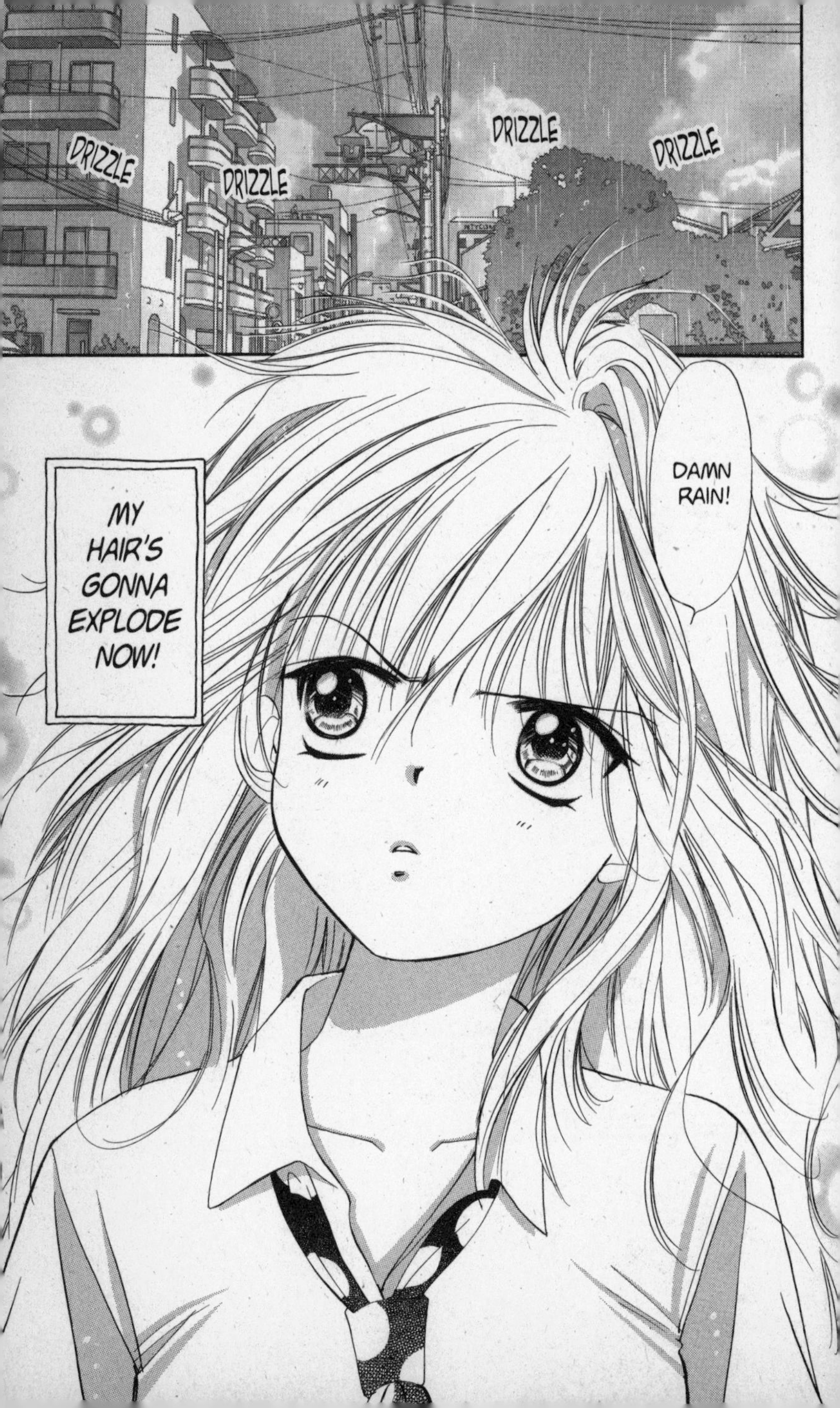
DRIZZLE
DRIZZLE
DRIZZLE
DRIZZLE
DAMN RAIN!
MY HAIR'S GONNA EXPLODE NOW!

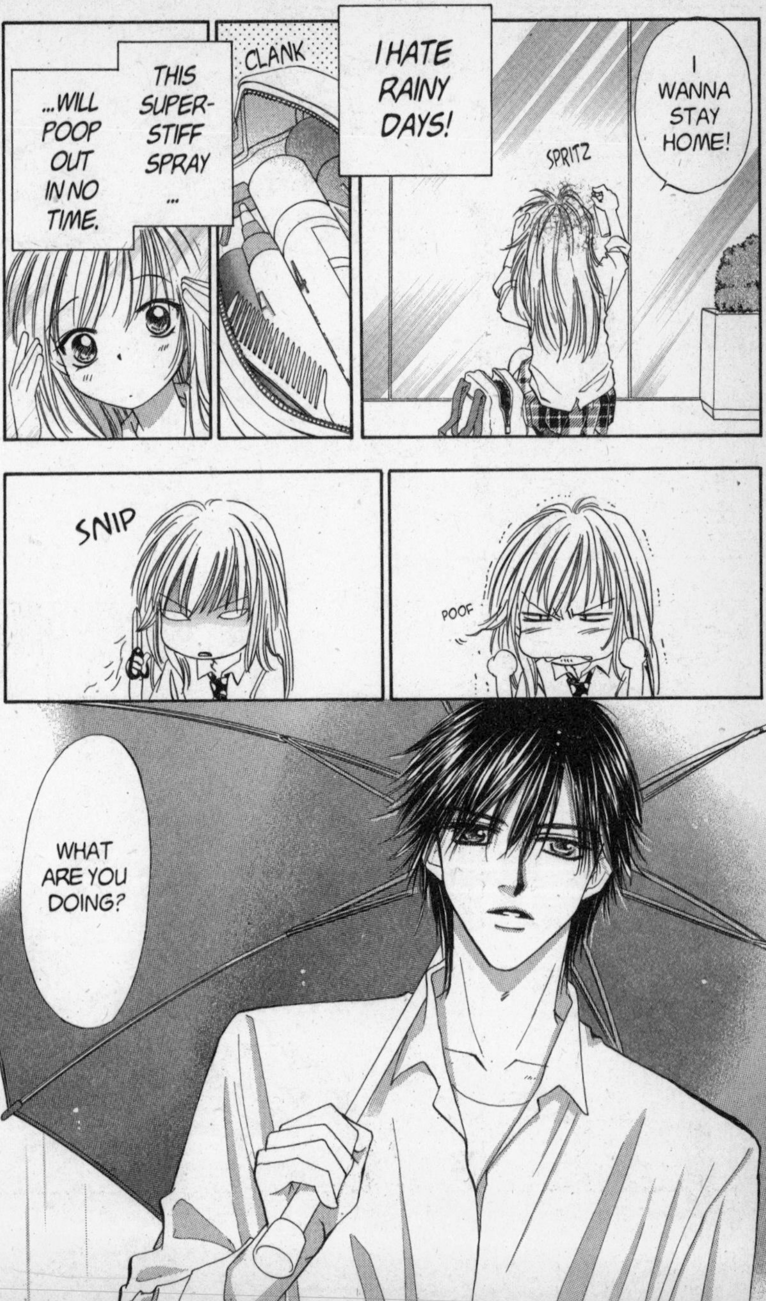

I WANNA STAY HOME!
SPRITZ
I HATE RAINY DAYS!
CLANK
THIS SUPER-STIFF SPRAY ...
...WILL POOP OUT IN NO TIME.
POOF
SNIP
WHAT ARE YOU DOING?

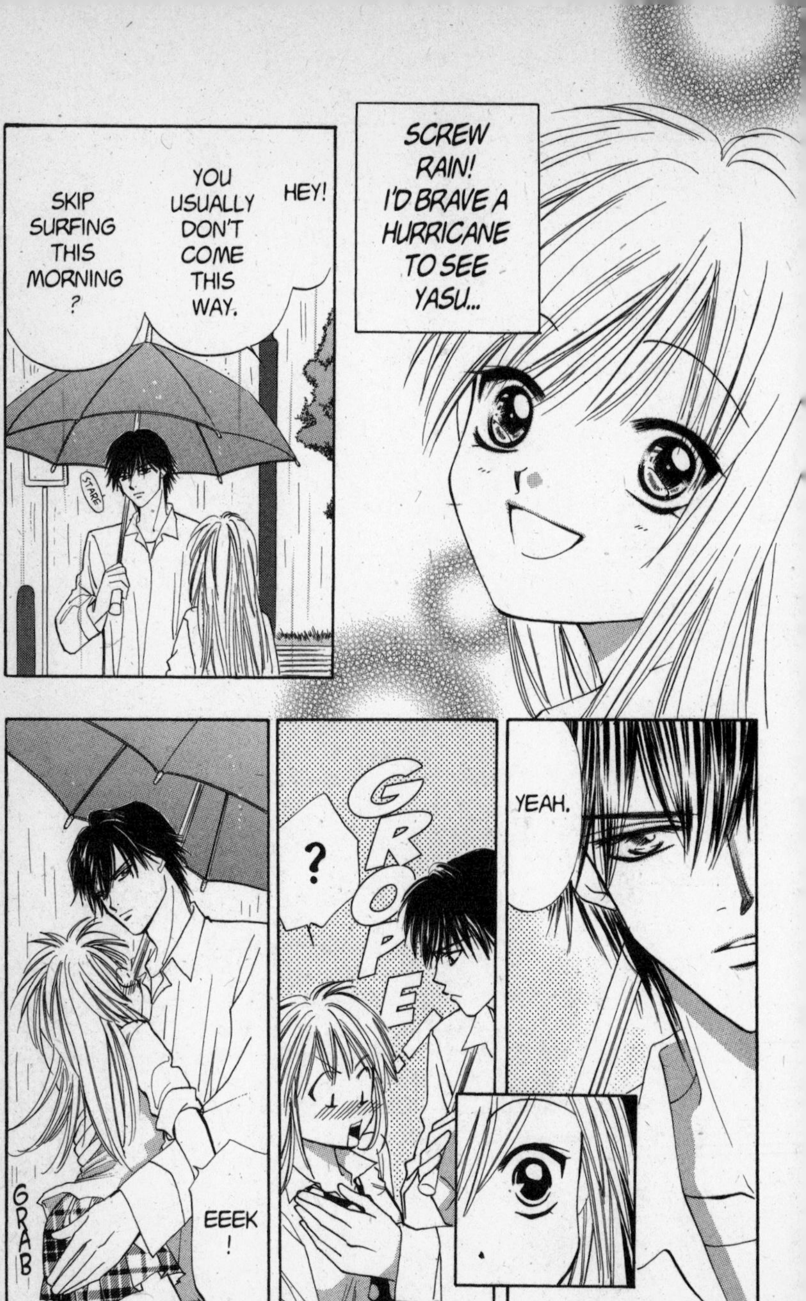
SCREW RAIN! I'D BRAVE A HURRICANE TO SEE YASU...
HEY!
YOU USUALLY DON'T COME THIS WAY.
SKIP SURFING THIS MORNING?
STARE
YEAH.
?
GROPE
GRAB
EEEK!

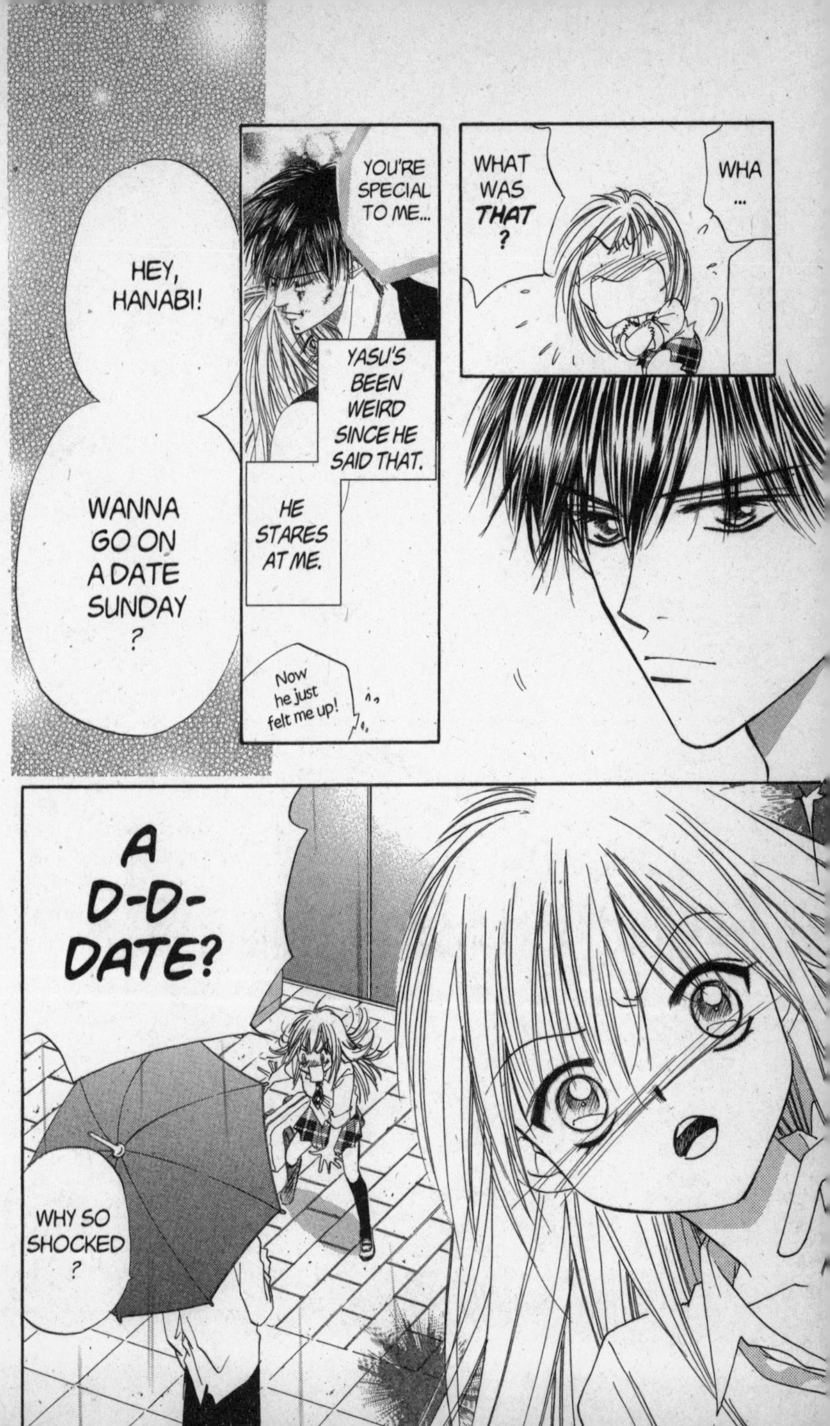
WHA ...
WHAT WAS THAT ?
YOU'RE SPECIAL TO ME...
YASU'S BEEN WEIRD SINCE HE SAID THAT.
HE STARES AT ME.
Now he just felt me up!
HEY, HANABI!
WANNA GO ON A DATE SUNDAY ?
A D-D-DATE?
WHY SO SHOCKED ?

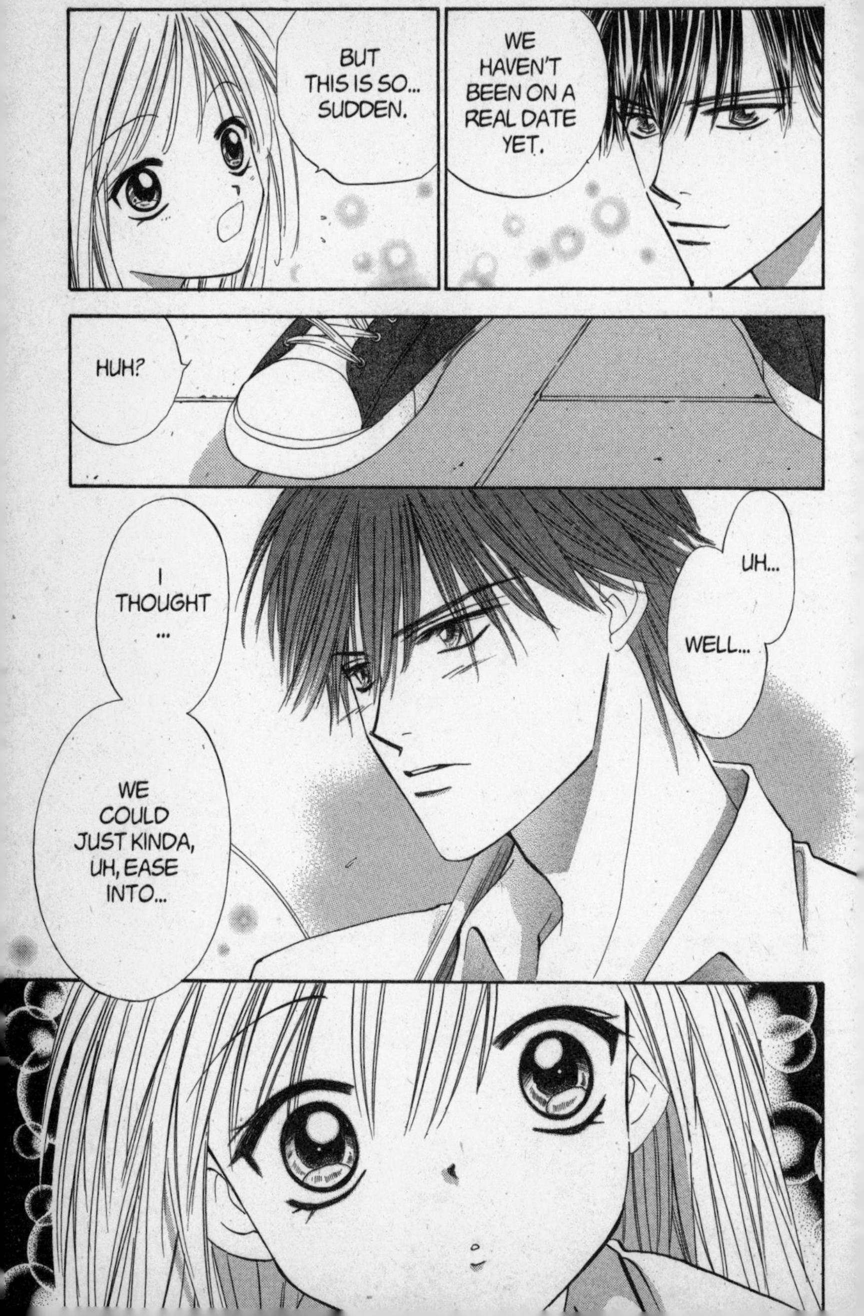
WE HAVEN'T BEEN ON A REAL DATE YET.
BUT THIS IS SO... SUDDEN.
HUH?
UH...
WELL...
I THOUGHT ...
WE COULD JUST KINDA, UH, EASE INTO...

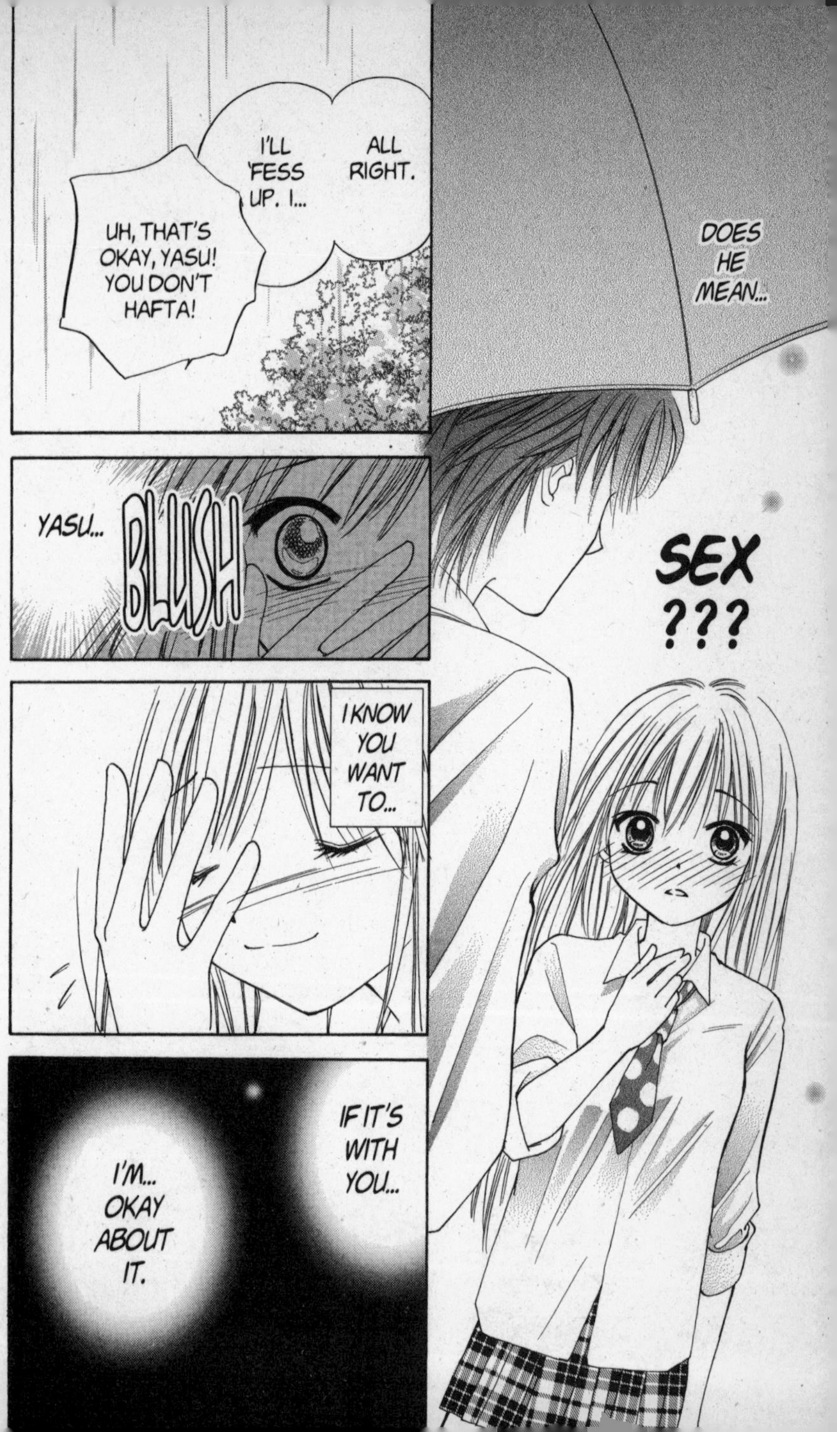
DOES HE MEAN...
SEX???
ALL RIGHT.
I'LL 'FESS UP. I...
UH, THAT'S OKAY, YASU! YOU DON'T HAFTA!
BLUSH
YASU...
I KNOW YOU WANT TO...
IF IT'S WITH YOU...
I'M... OKAY ABOUT IT.

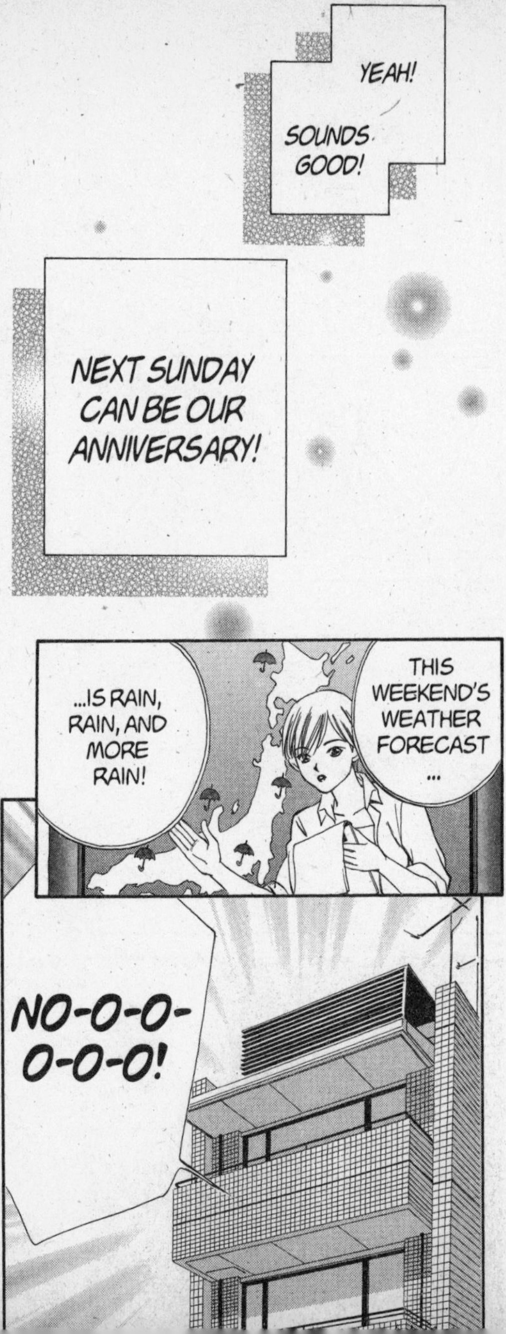
YEAH!
SOUNDS GOOD!
NEXT SUNDAY CAN BE OUR ANNIVERSARY!
THIS WEEKEND'S WEATHER FORECAST ...
...IS RAIN, RAIN, AND MORE RAIN!
NO-O-O-O-O-O!

SOUTH KOREA AND MY MOM

WHEN I WENT TO MY MOM'S RECENTLY, I WAS SURPRISED HOW MUCH HAS CHANGED. SHE HAS TONS OF SOUTH KOREAN STUFF NOW: POSTERS, DVDS, AND CDS OF POPULAR MALE STARS. "WHAT'S UP, MOM?" I ASKED. SHE REPLIED, "OH, RIE, AHN-NYUNG HA-SEH-YO!" MOM JUST ADORES RYU SIWON! ♡ ♥ ♥ ♥ SHE PLAYS HIS CDS AND POINTS OUT HIS PICTURE IN MAGAZINES. "ISN'T HE HANDSOME?" SHE'LL SAY. SHE'S JUST LIKE A TEENAGER! SEEING HER FACE LIGHT UP MADE ME THINK ABOUT MY SHOJO MANGA. THE POWER OF LOVE TRULY *IS* AMAZING...

BY THE WAY, THE FIRST KOREAN WORD I EVER LEARNED WAS "OPPA" ("DAD").

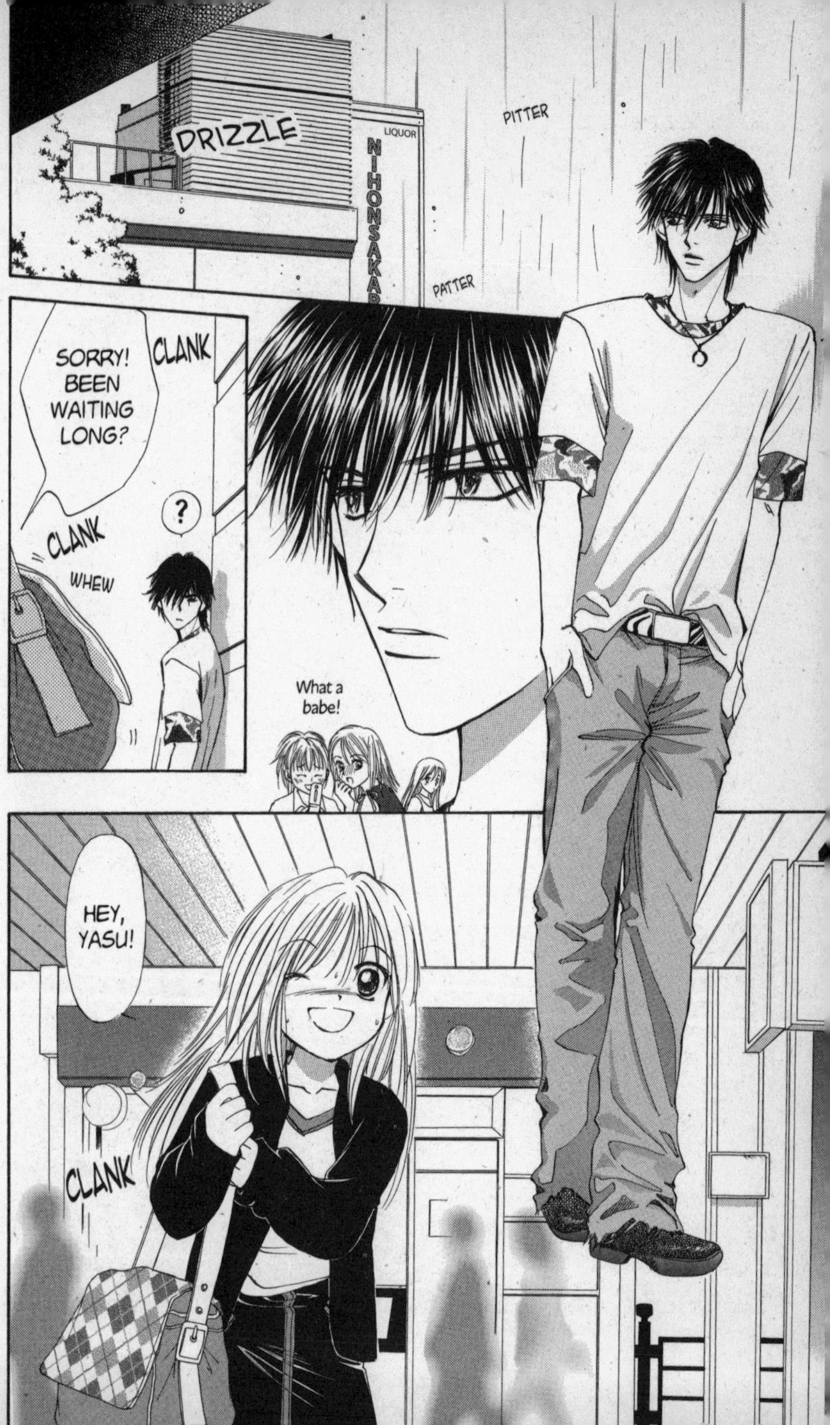
PITTER
PATTER
LIQUOR
DRIZZLE
What a babe!
SORRY! BEEN WAITING LONG?
CLANK
?
CLANK
WHEW
HEY, YASU!
CLANK

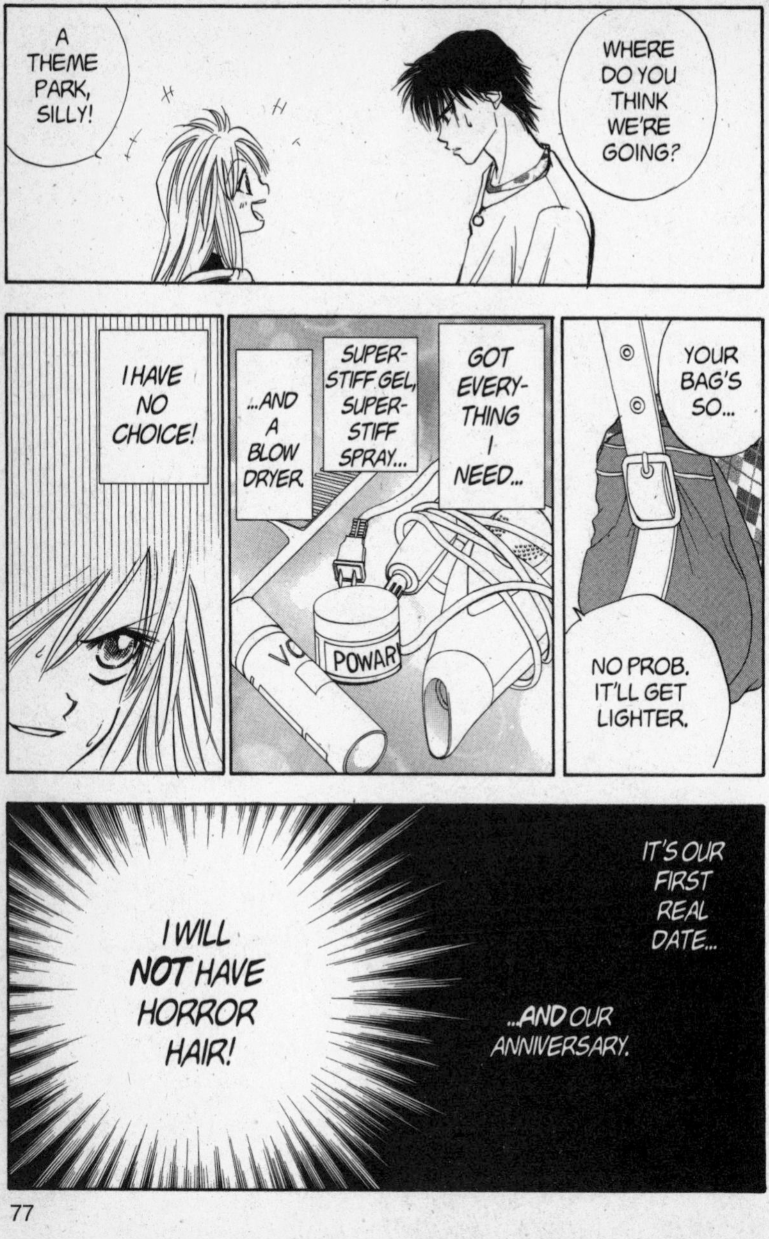
WHERE DO YOU THINK WE'RE GOING?
A THEME PARK, SILLY!
YOUR BAG'S SO...
NO PROB. IT'LL GET LIGHTER.
GOT EVERY-THING I NEED...
SUPER-STIFF GEL, SUPER-STIFF SPRAY...
...AND A BLOW DRYER.
POWAR
I HAVE NO CHOICE!
IT'S OUR FIRST REAL DATE...
...AND OUR ANNIVERSARY.
I WILL **NOT** HAVE HORROR HAIR!

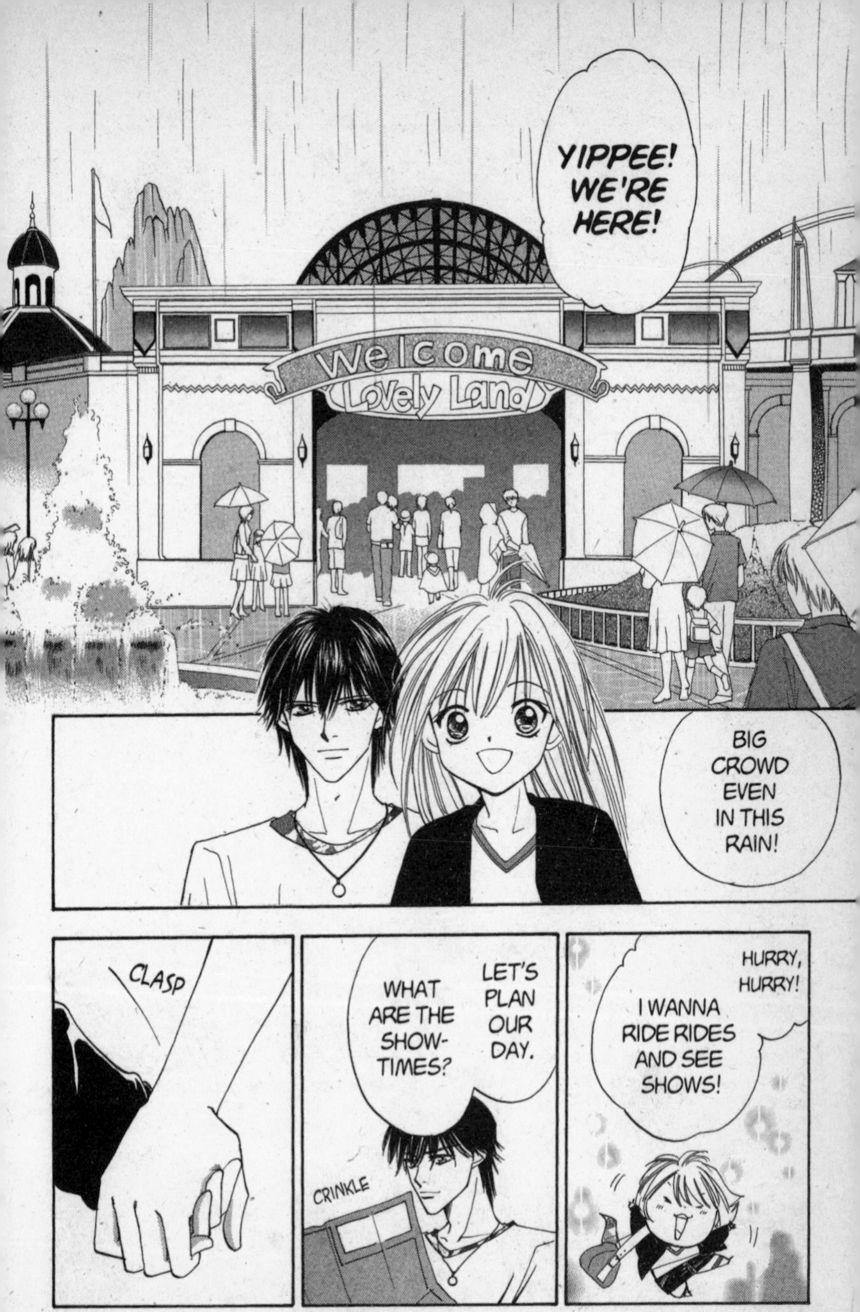
YIPPEE! WE'RE HERE!
Welcome
Lovely Land
BIG CROWD EVEN IN THIS RAIN!
HURRY, HURRY!
I WANNA RIDE RIDES AND SEE SHOWS!
LET'S PLAN OUR DAY.
WHAT ARE THE SHOW-TIMES?
CRINKLE
CLASP

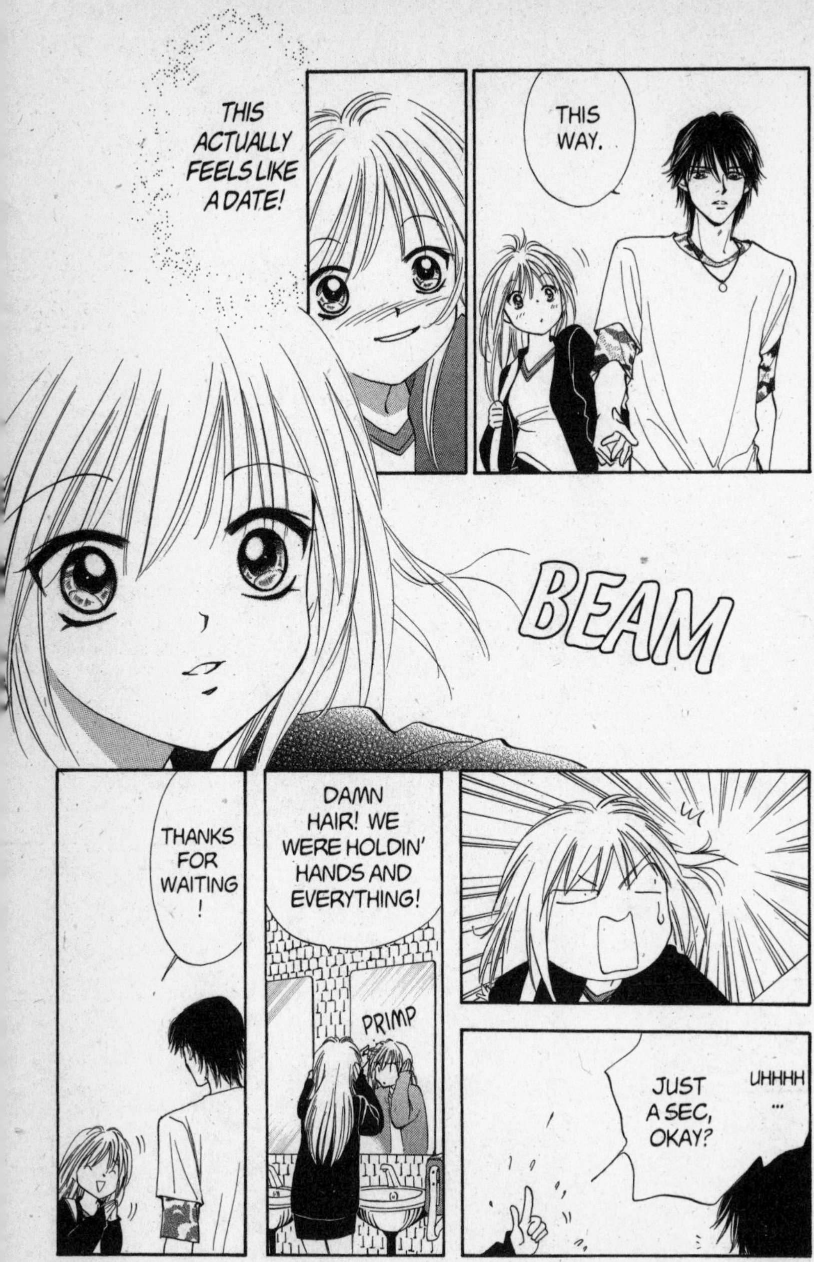
THIS WAY.
THIS ACTUALLY FEELS LIKE A DATE!
BEAM
UHHHH ...
JUST A SEC, OKAY?
DAMN HAIR! WE WERE HOLDIN' HANDS AND EVERYTHING!
PRIMP
THANKS FOR WAITING!

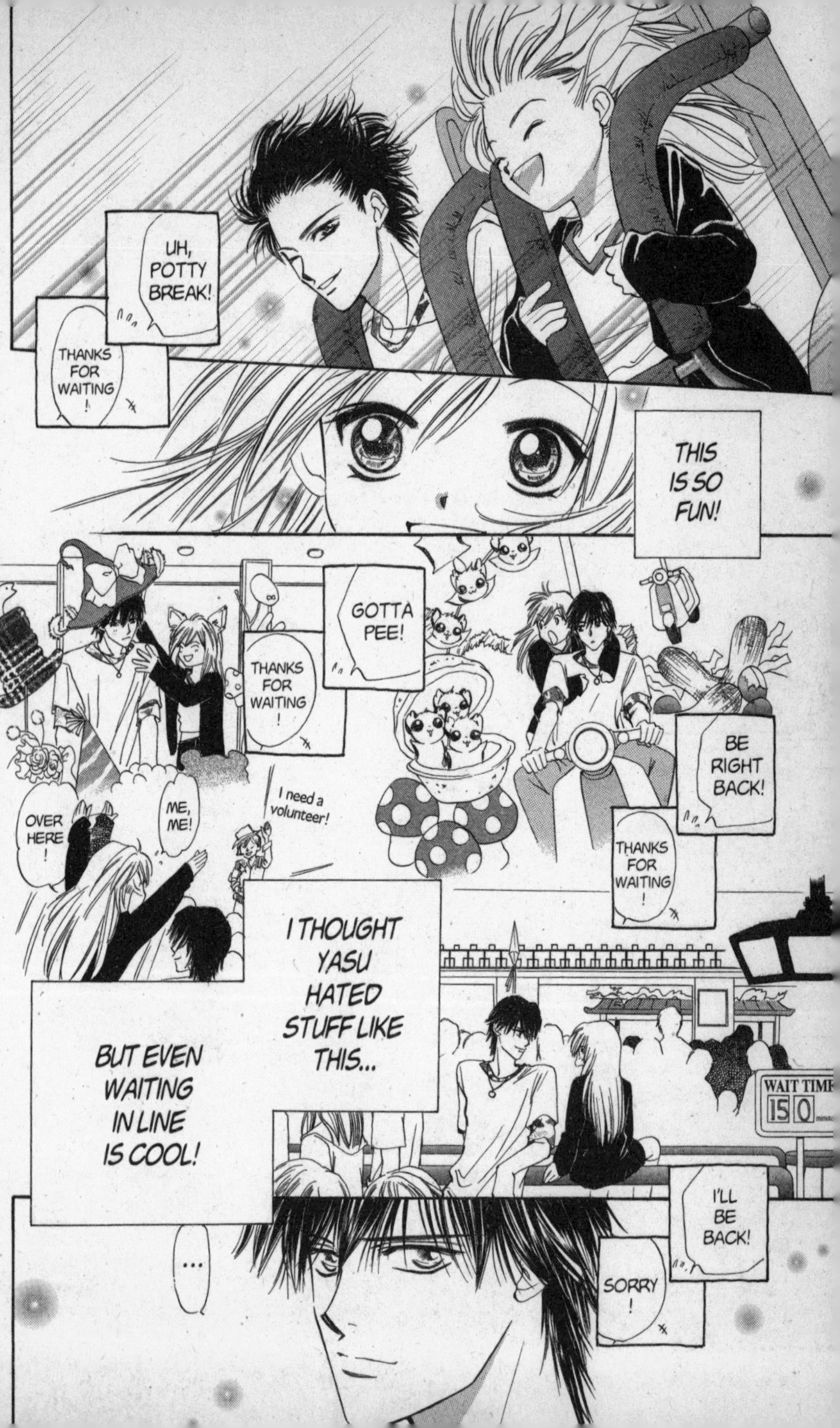
UH, POTTY BREAK!
THANKS FOR WAITING!
THIS IS SO FUN!
BE RIGHT BACK!
THANKS FOR WAITING!
GOTTA PEE!
THANKS FOR WAITING!
I need a volunteer!
ME, ME!
OVER HERE!
I THOUGHT YASU HATED STUFF LIKE THIS...
BUT EVEN WAITING IN LINE IS COOL!
WAIT TIM
150
I'LL BE BACK!
SORRY!
...

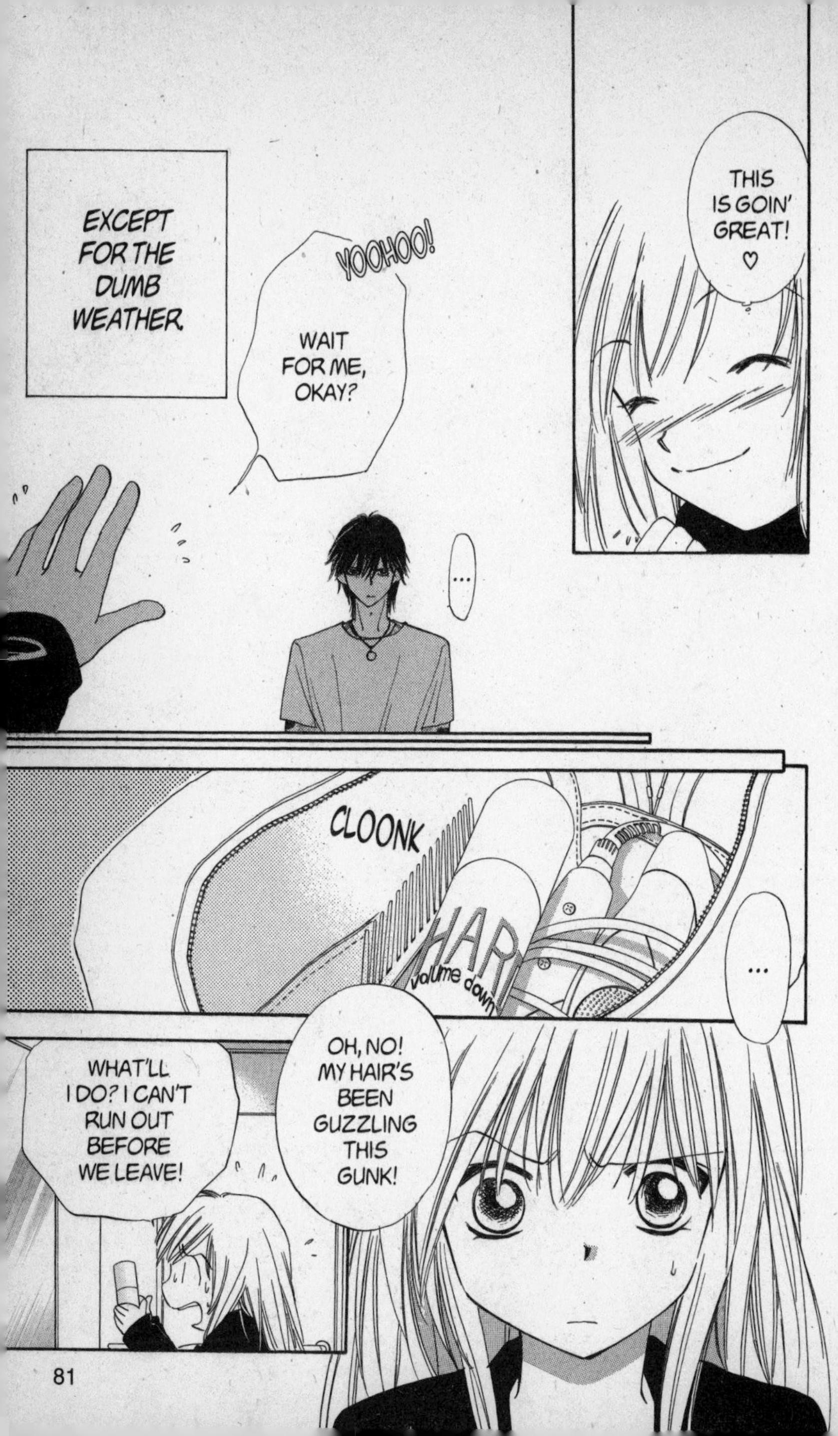
THIS IS GOIN' GREAT! ♡
YOOHOO!
WAIT FOR ME, OKAY?
EXCEPT FOR THE DUMB WEATHER.
...
CLOONK
HAIR volume down
...
OH, NO! MY HAIR'S BEEN GUZZLING THIS GUNK!
WHAT'LL I DO? I CAN'T RUN OUT BEFORE WE LEAVE!

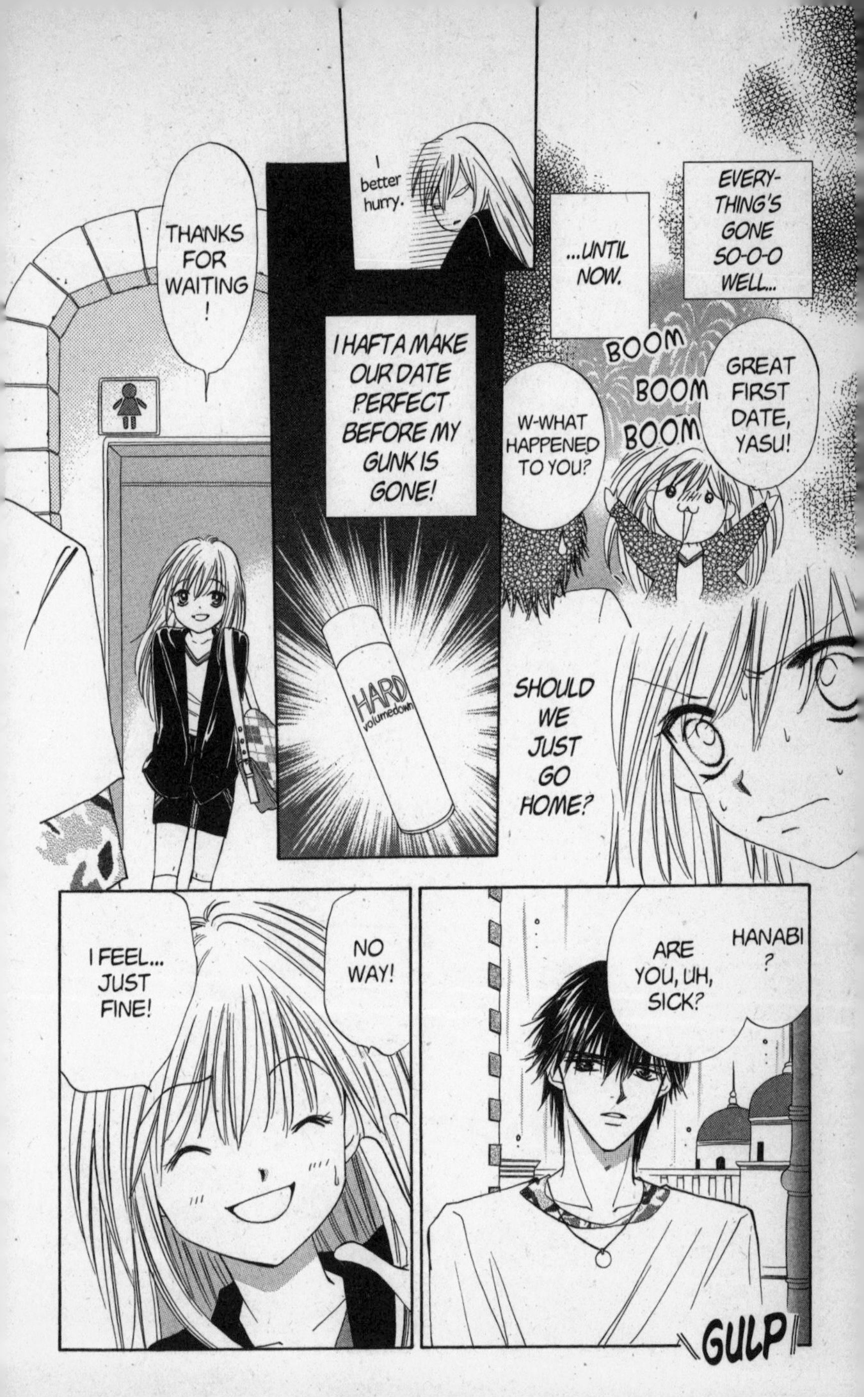
EVERY-THING'S GONE SO-O-O WELL...
...UNTIL NOW.
GREAT FIRST DATE, YASU!
BOOM BOOM BOOM
W-WHAT HAPPENED TO YOU?
SHOULD WE JUST GO HOME?
I better hurry.
I HAFTA MAKE OUR DATE PERFECT BEFORE MY GUNK IS GONE!
HARD volumedown
THANKS FOR WAITING!
HANABI?
ARE YOU, UH, SICK?
GULP
NO WAY!
I FEEL... JUST FINE!

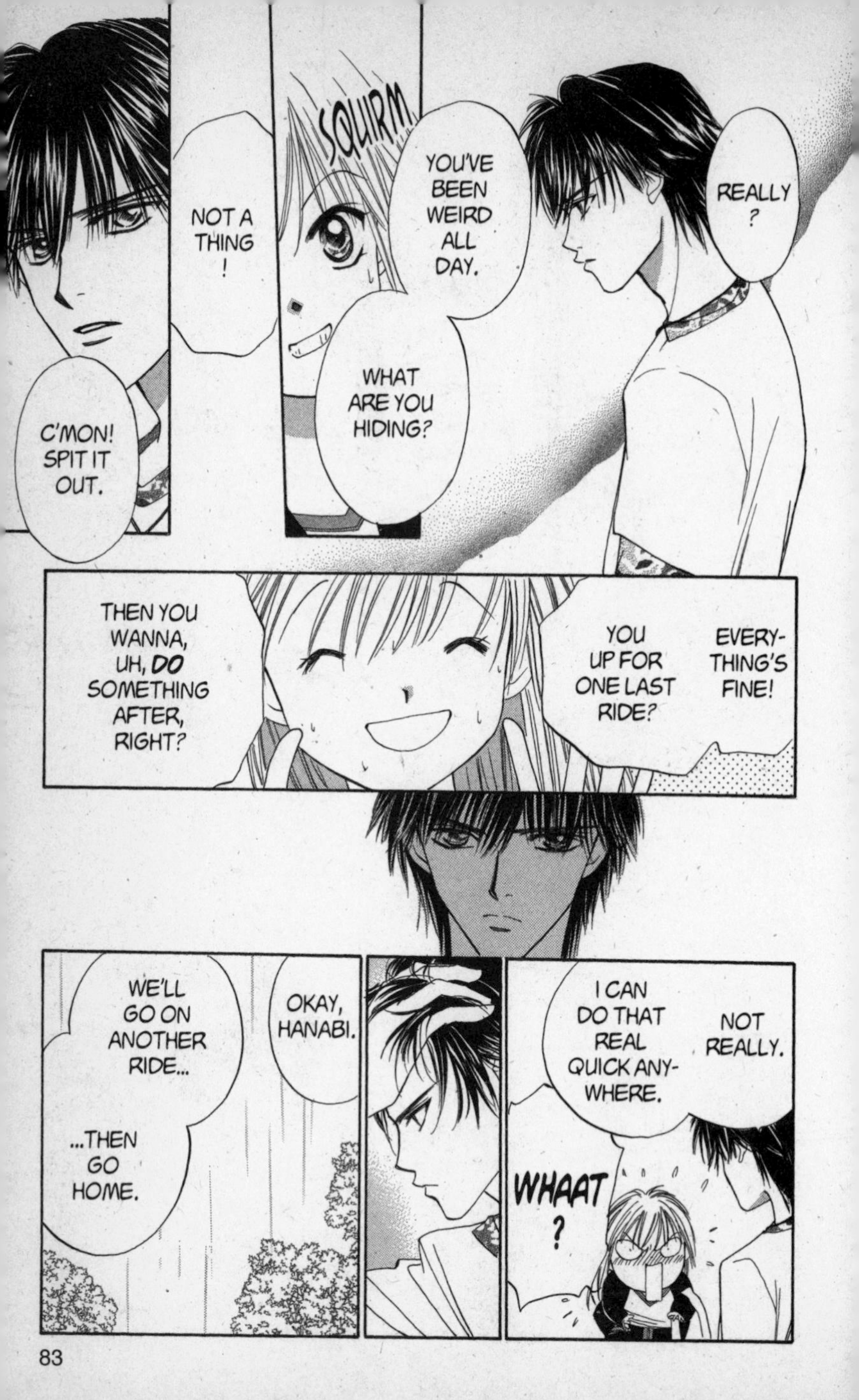
REALLY?
SQUIRM
YOU'VE BEEN WEIRD ALL DAY.
WHAT ARE YOU HIDING?
NOT A THING!
C'MON! SPIT IT OUT.
EVERY-THING'S FINE!
YOU UP FOR ONE LAST RIDE?
THEN YOU WANNA, UH, **DO** SOMETHING AFTER, RIGHT?
NOT REALLY.
I CAN DO THAT REAL QUICK ANY-WHERE.
WHAAT?
OKAY, HANABI.
WE'LL GO ON ANOTHER RIDE...
...THEN GO HOME.

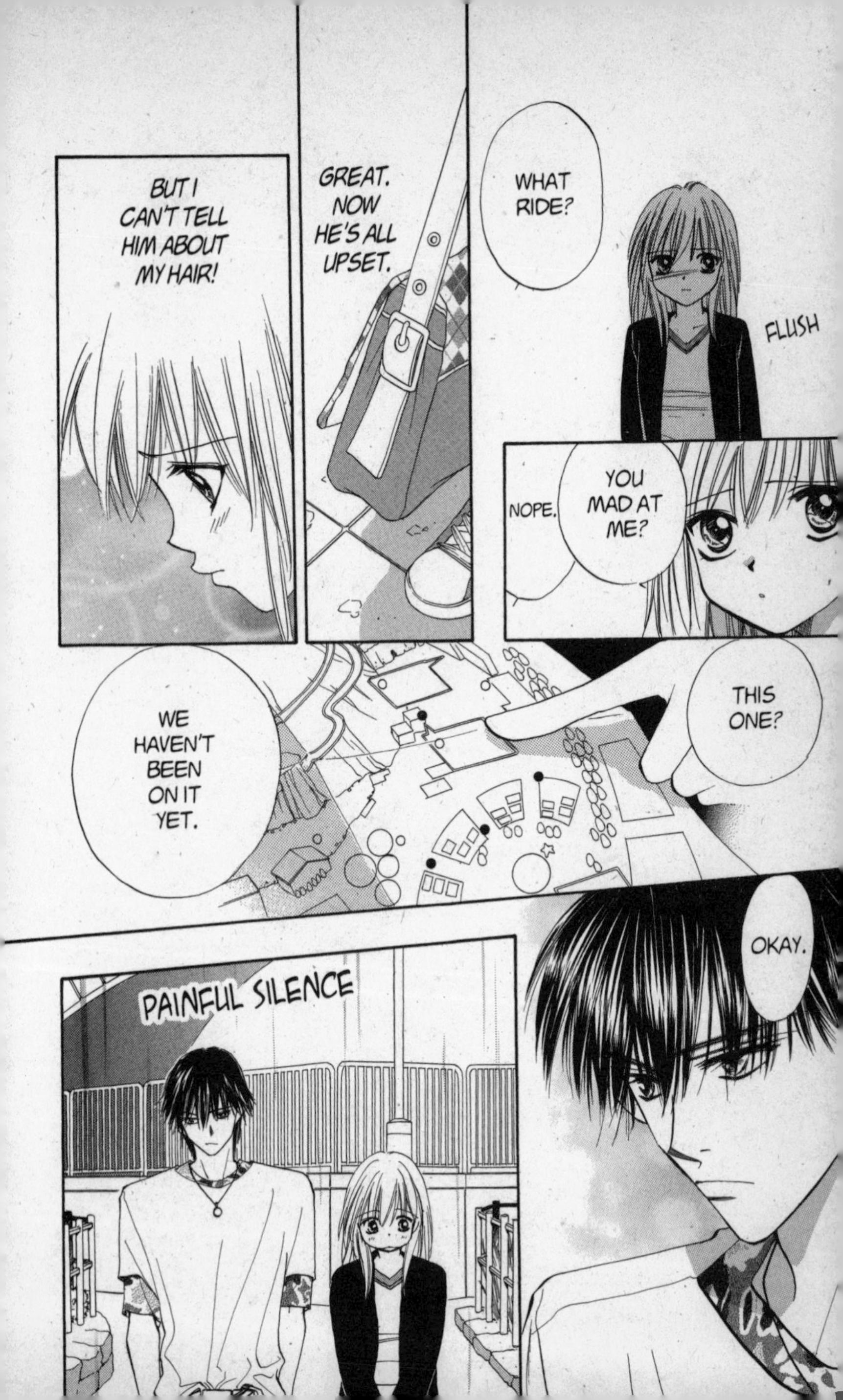
WHAT RIDE?
FLUSH
YOU MAD AT ME?
NOPE.
GREAT. NOW HE'S ALL UPSET.
BUT I CAN'T TELL HIM ABOUT MY HAIR!
THIS ONE?
WE HAVEN'T BEEN ON IT YET.
OKAY.
PAINFUL SILENCE

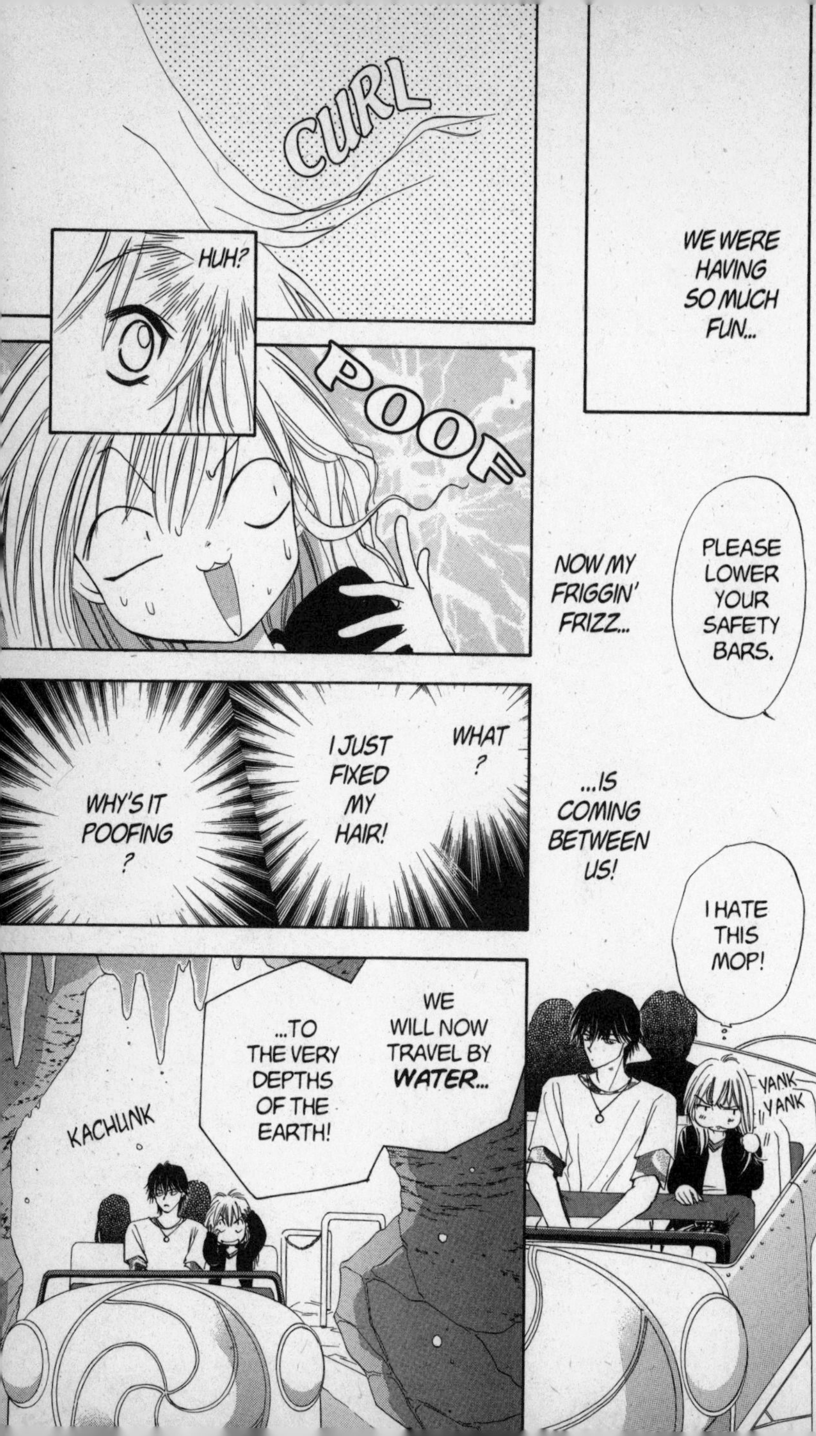
WE WERE HAVING SO MUCH FUN...
CURL
HUH?
POOF
PLEASE LOWER YOUR SAFETY BARS.
NOW MY FRIGGIN' FRIZZ...
WHAT?
I JUST FIXED MY HAIR!
WHY'S IT POOFING?
...IS COMING BETWEEN US!
I HATE THIS MOP!
YANK YANK
WE WILL NOW TRAVEL BY **WATER**...
...TO THE VERY DEPTHS OF THE EARTH!
KACHUNK

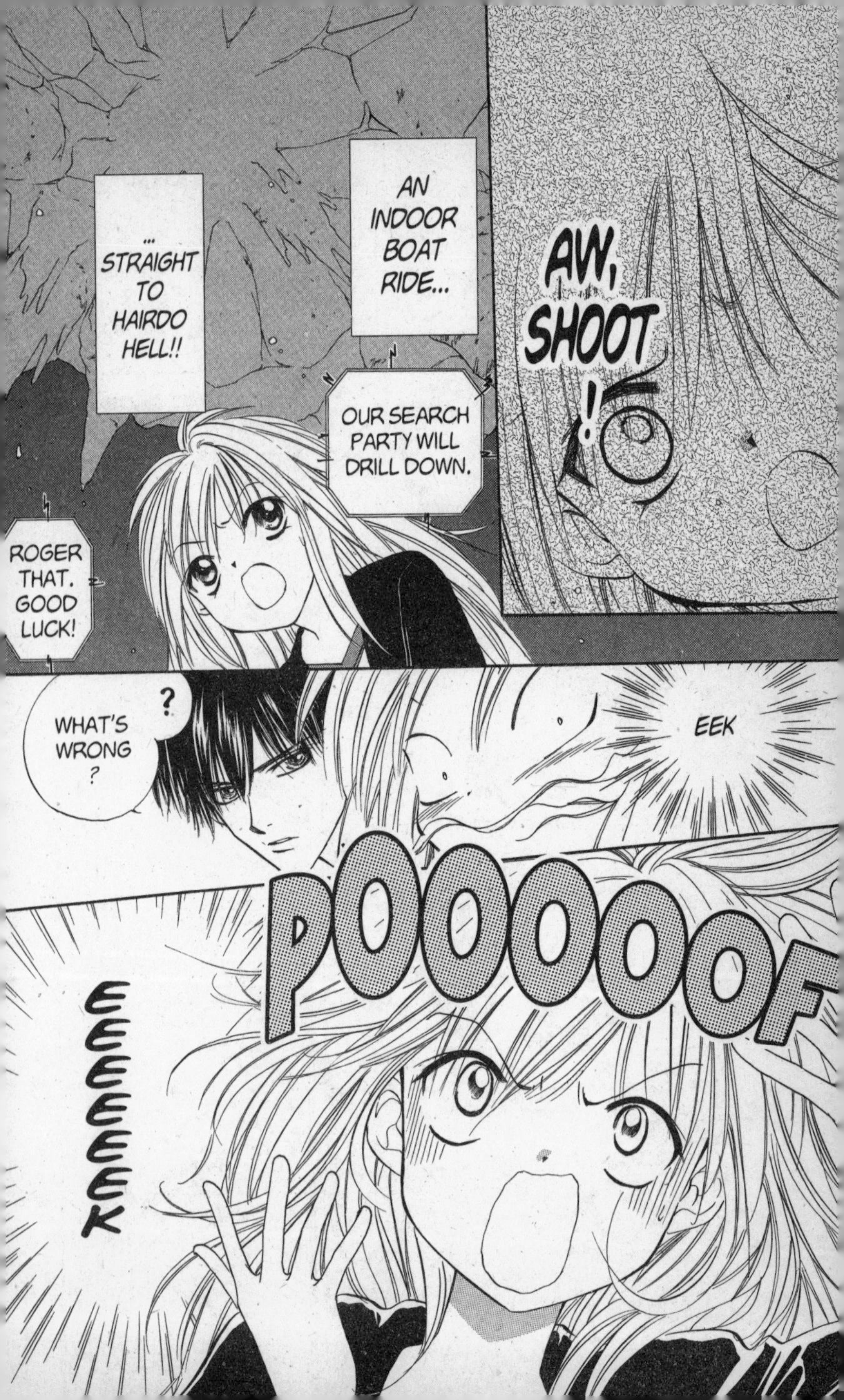
AW, SHOOT!
AN INDOOR BOAT RIDE...
...STRAIGHT TO HAIRDO HELL!!
OUR SEARCH PARTY WILL DRILL DOWN.
ROGER THAT. GOOD LUCK!
EEK
?
WHAT'S WRONG?
POOOOOF
EEEEEEEK

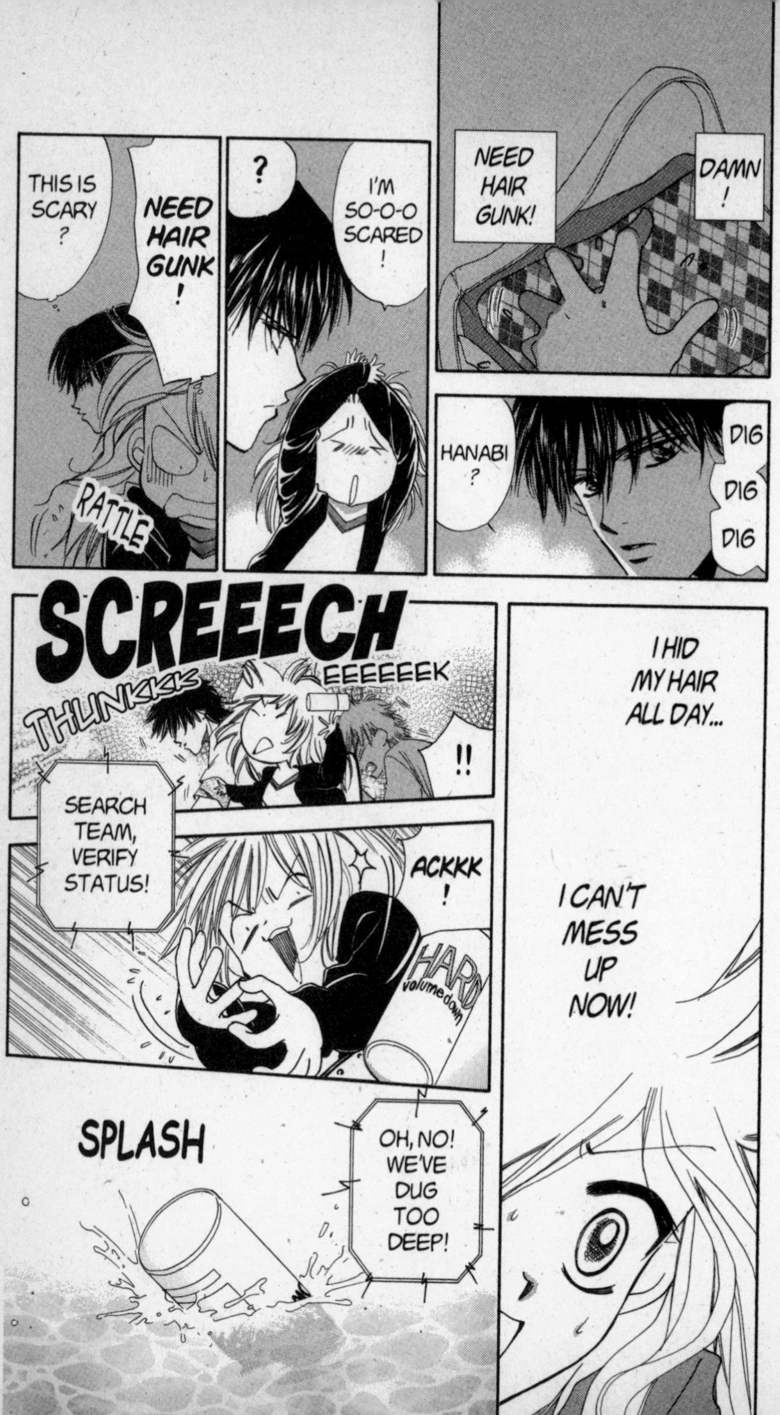
DAMN!
NEED HAIR GUNK!
DIG
DIG
DIG
HANABI?
I'M SO-O-O SCARED!
?
NEED HAIR GUNK!
THIS IS SCARY?
RATTLE
I HID MY HAIR ALL DAY...
I CAN'T MESS UP NOW!
SCREEECH
EEEEEEK
!!
THUNKKK
SEARCH TEAM, VERIFY STATUS!
ACKKK!
HARD
volume down
OH, NO! WE'VE DUG TOO DEEP!
SPLASH

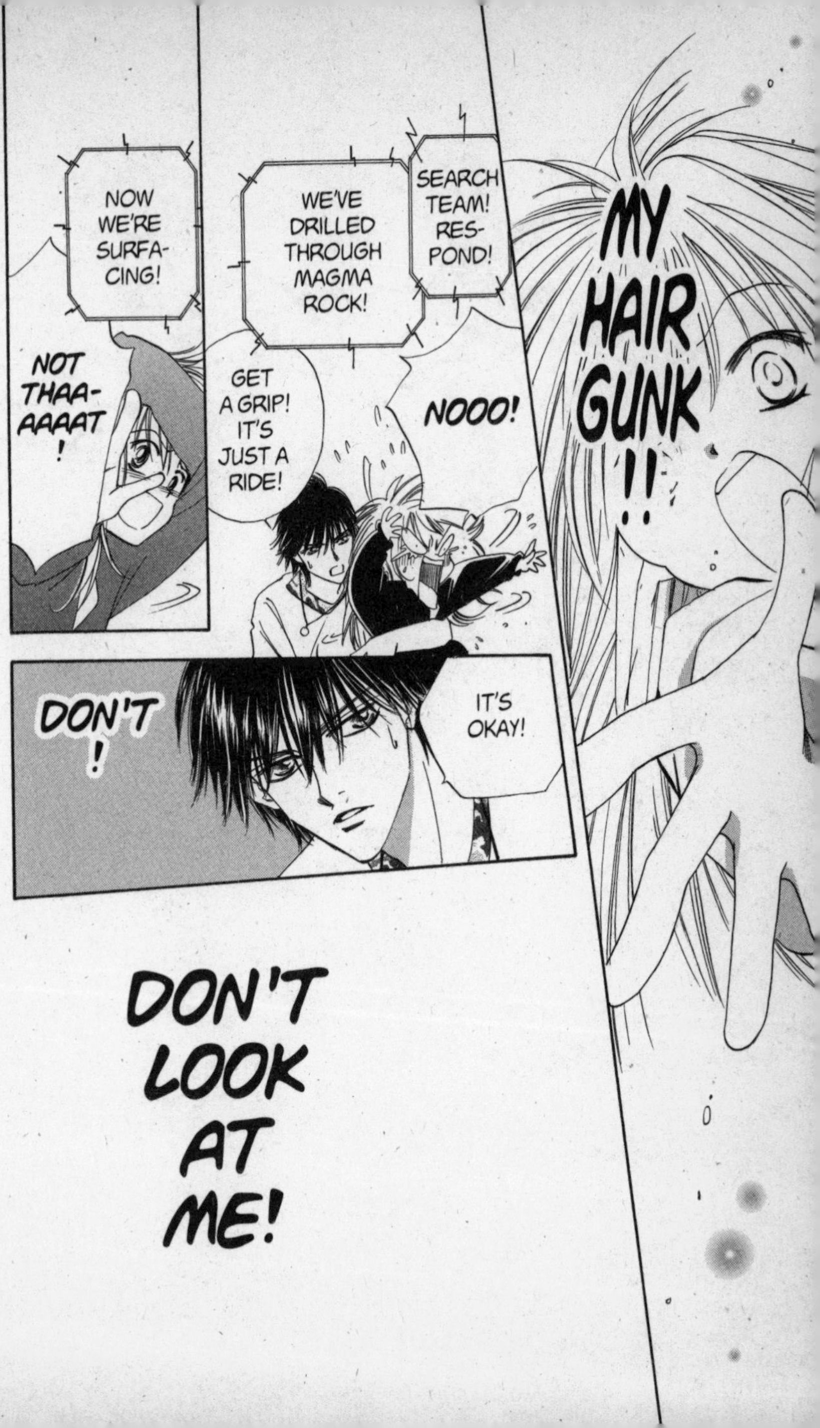
MY HAIR GUNK!!
DON'T LOOK AT ME!
SEARCH TEAM! RES-POND!
WE'VE DRILLED THROUGH MAGMA ROCK!
NOOO!
GET A GRIP! IT'S JUST A RIDE!
NOW WE'RE SURFA-CING!
NOT THAA-AAAAT!
IT'S OKAY!
DON'T!

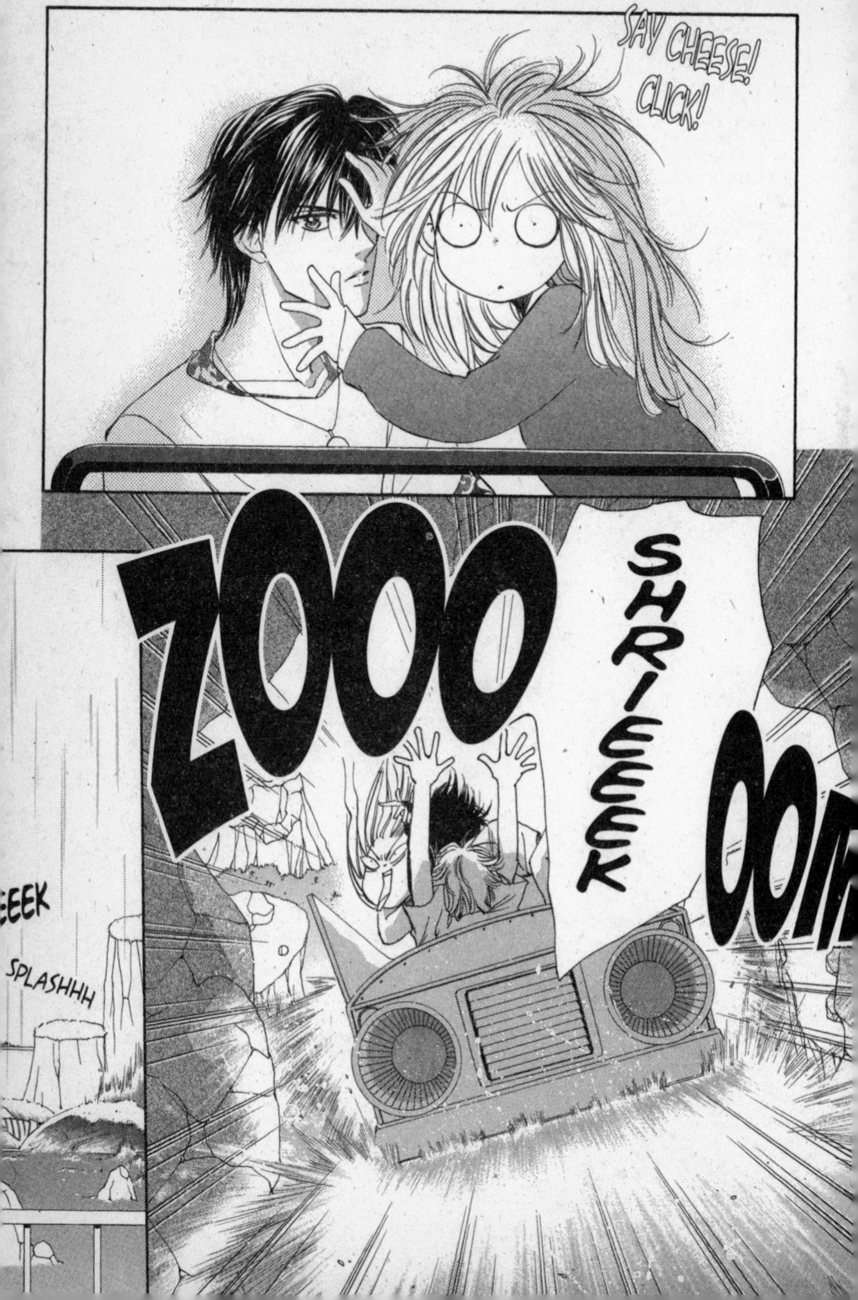
SAY CHEESE!
CLICK!
ZOOO
SHRIEEEK
OOM
EEEK
SPLASHHH

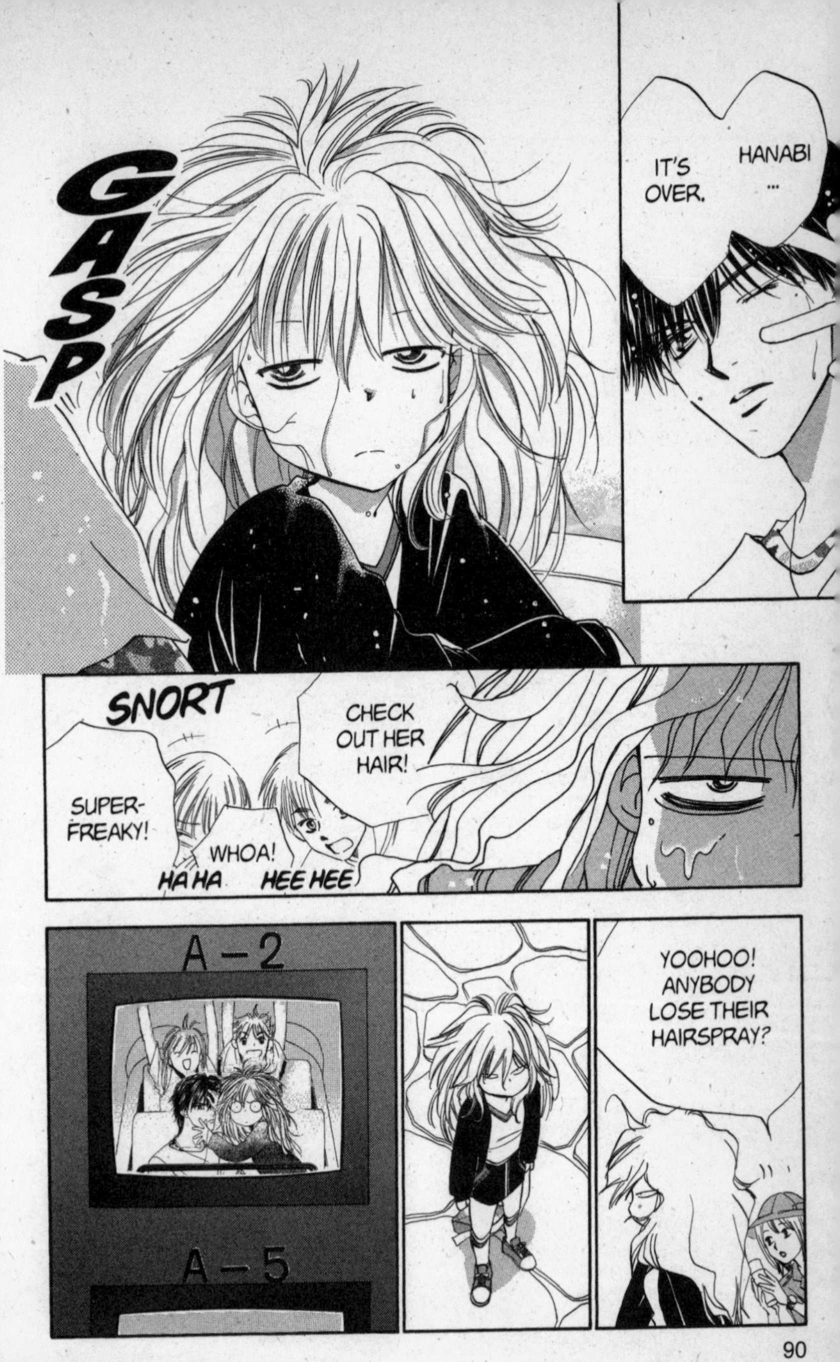
HANABI ...
IT'S OVER.
GASP
CHECK OUT HER HAIR!
SNORT
SUPER-FREAKY!
WHOA!
HEE HEE
HA HA
YOOHOO! ANYBODY LOSE THEIR HAIRSPRAY?
A-2
A-5

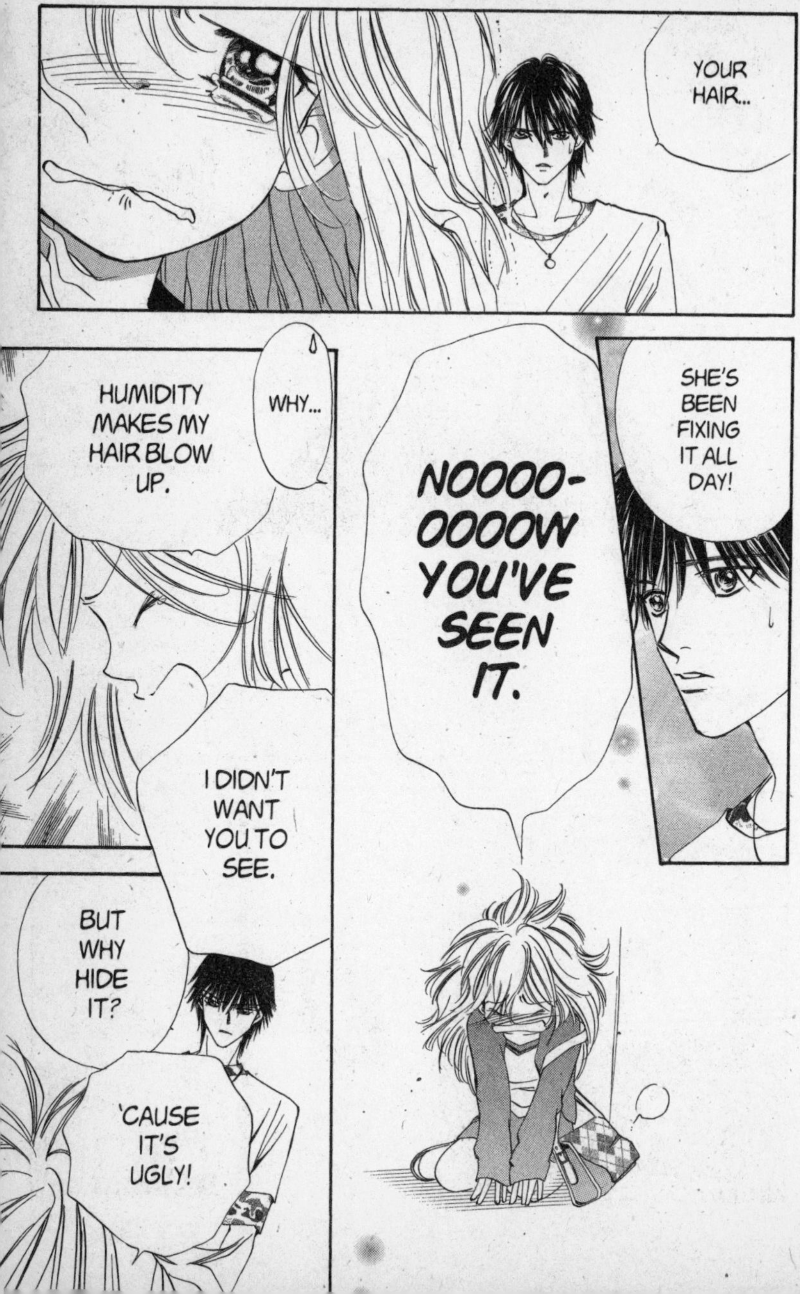
YOUR HAIR...
SHE'S BEEN FIXING IT ALL DAY!
NOOOO-OOOOW YOU'VE SEEN IT.
WHY...
HUMIDITY MAKES MY HAIR BLOW UP.
I DIDN'T WANT YOU TO SEE.
BUT WHY HIDE IT?
'CAUSE IT'S UGLY!

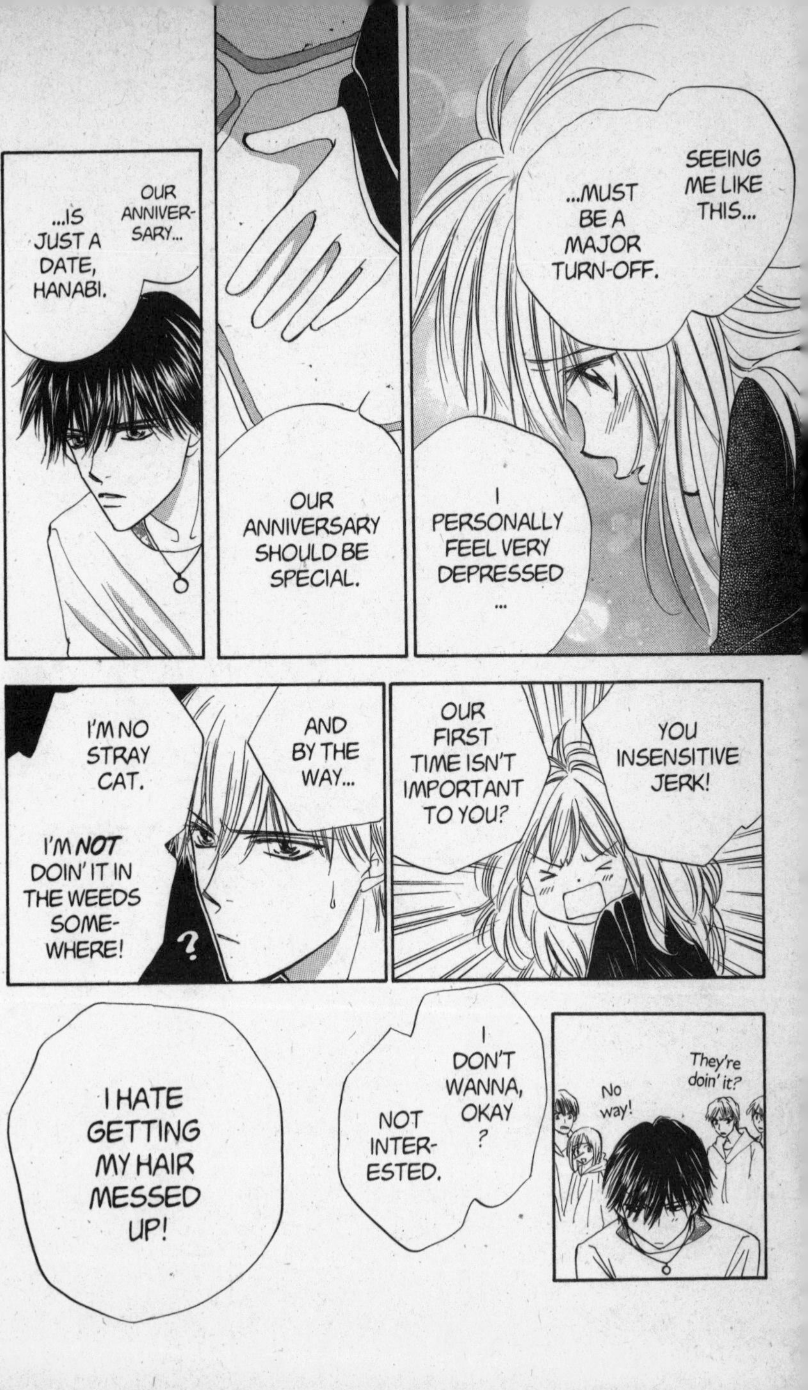
SEEING ME LIKE THIS...
...MUST BE A MAJOR TURN-OFF.
I PERSONALLY FEEL VERY DEPRESSED ...
OUR ANNIVERSARY SHOULD BE SPECIAL.
OUR ANNIVERSARY...
...IS JUST A DATE, HANABI.
YOU INSENSITIVE JERK!
OUR FIRST TIME ISN'T IMPORTANT TO YOU?
AND BY THE WAY...
I'M NO STRAY CAT.
I'M **NOT** DOIN' IT IN THE WEEDS SOMEWHERE!
?
They're doin' it?
No way!
I DON'T WANNA, OKAY?
NOT INTERESTED.
I HATE GETTING MY HAIR MESSED UP!

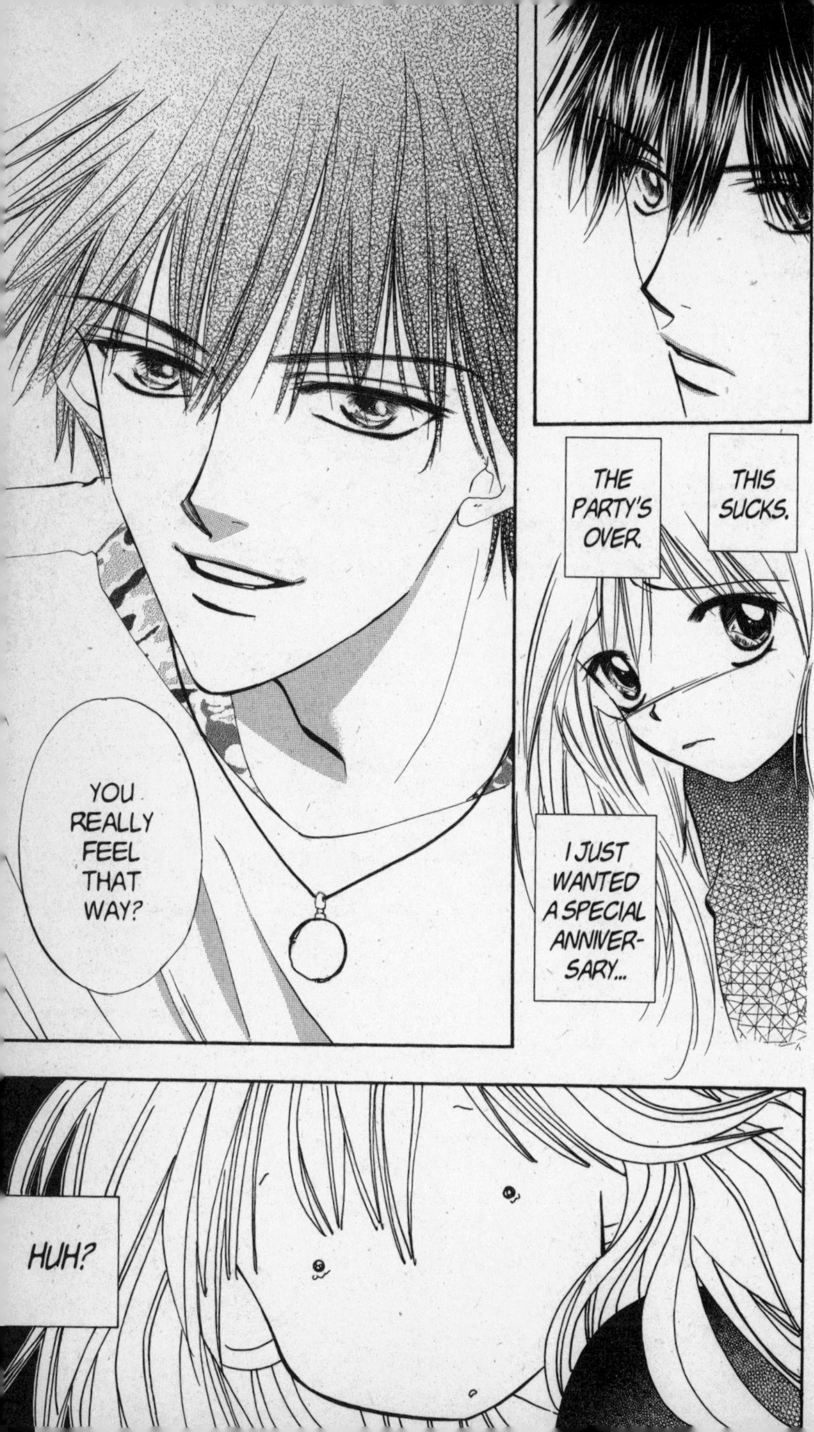
THIS SUCKS.
THE PARTY'S OVER.
I JUST WANTED A SPECIAL ANNIVER-SARY...
YOU REALLY FEEL THAT WAY?
HUH?

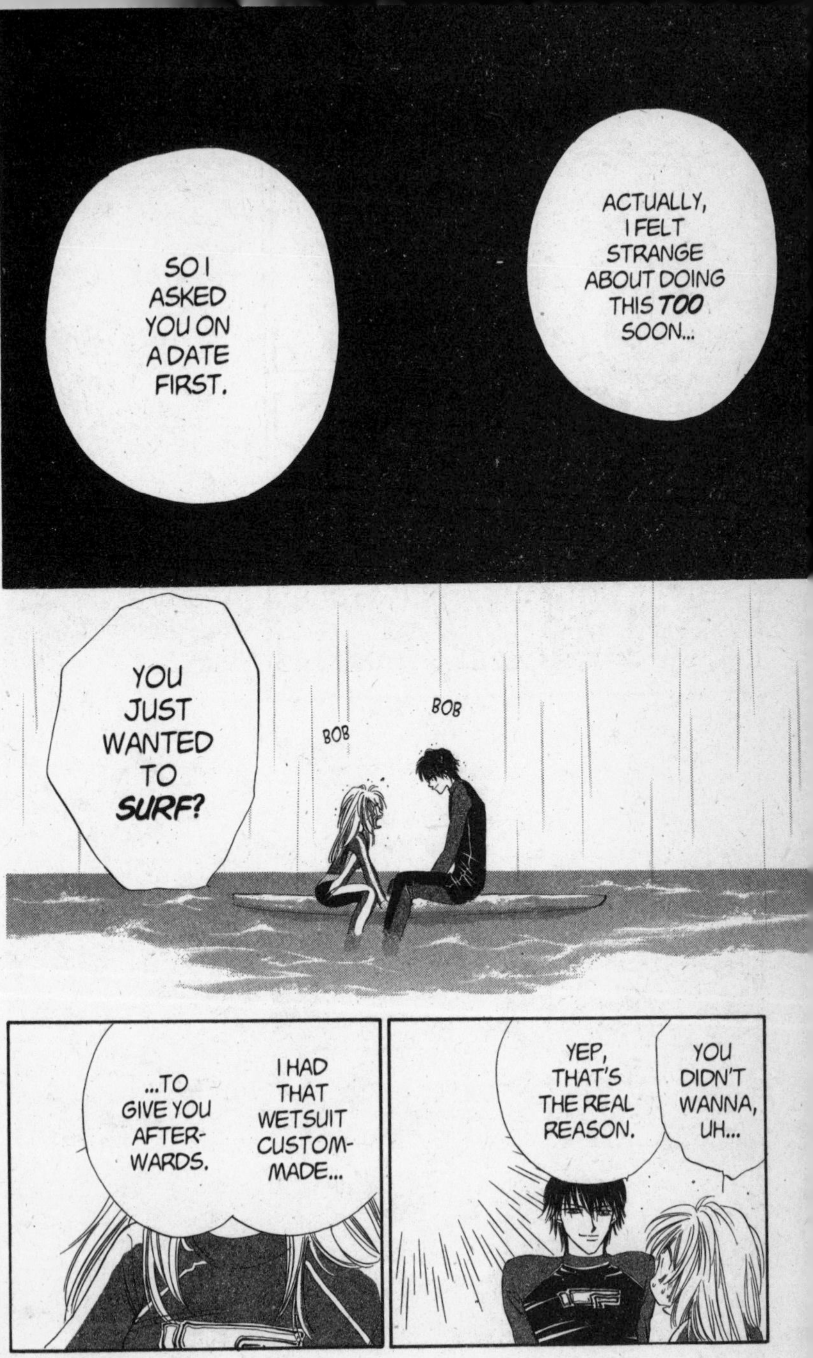
ACTUALLY, I FELT STRANGE ABOUT DOING THIS **TOO** SOON...
SO I ASKED YOU ON A DATE FIRST.
YOU JUST WANTED TO **SURF?**
BOB
BOB
YOU DIDN'T WANNA, UH...
YEP, THAT'S THE REAL REASON.
I HAD THAT WETSUIT CUSTOM-MADE...
...TO GIVE YOU AFTER-WARDS.

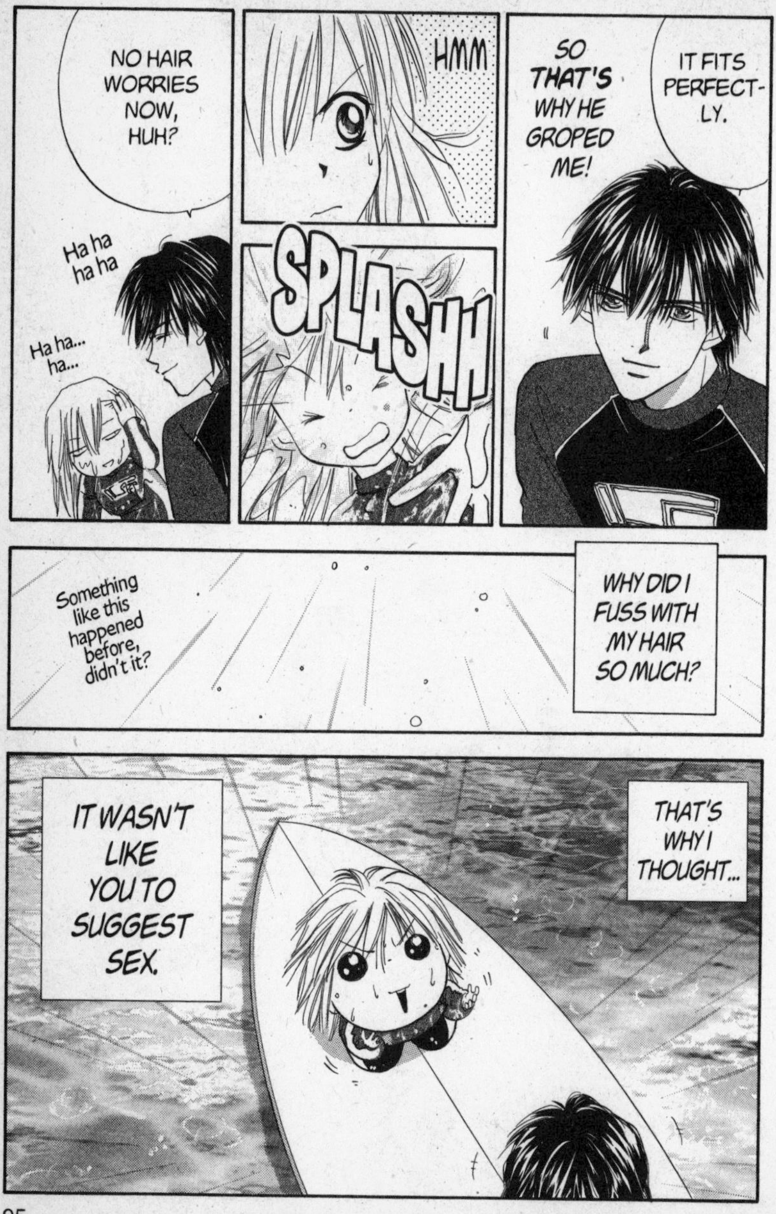
IT FITS PERFECT-LY.
SO THAT'S WHY HE GROPED ME!
HMM
SPLASHH
NO HAIR WORRIES NOW, HUH?
Ha ha ha ha
Ha ha... ha...
WHY DID I FUSS WITH MY HAIR SO MUCH?
Something like this happened before, didn't it?
THAT'S WHY I THOUGHT...
IT WASN'T LIKE YOU TO SUGGEST SEX.

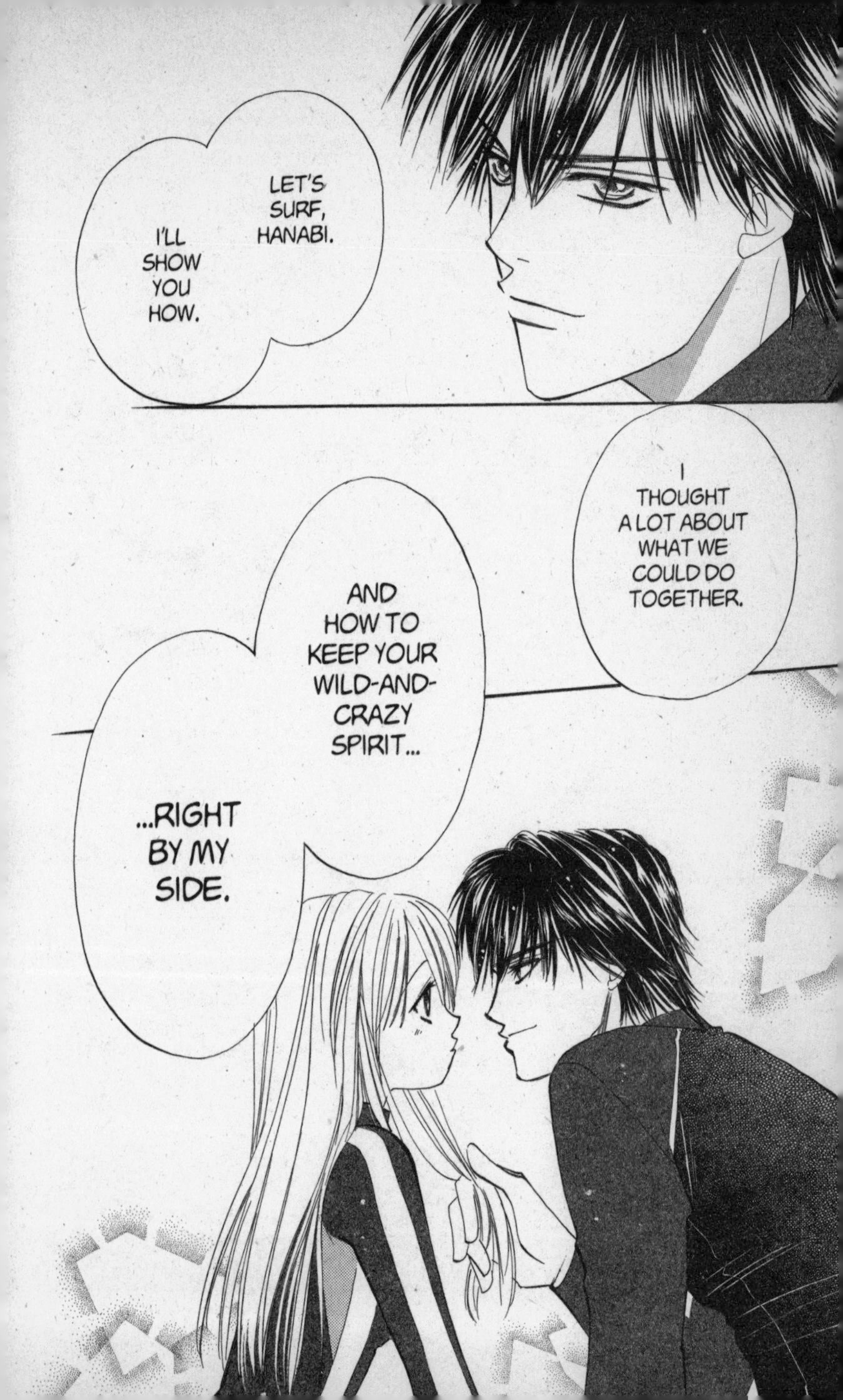
LET'S SURF, HANABI.
I'LL SHOW YOU HOW.
I THOUGHT A LOT ABOUT WHAT WE COULD DO TOGETHER.
AND HOW TO KEEP YOUR WILD-AND-CRAZY SPIRIT...
...RIGHT BY MY SIDE.

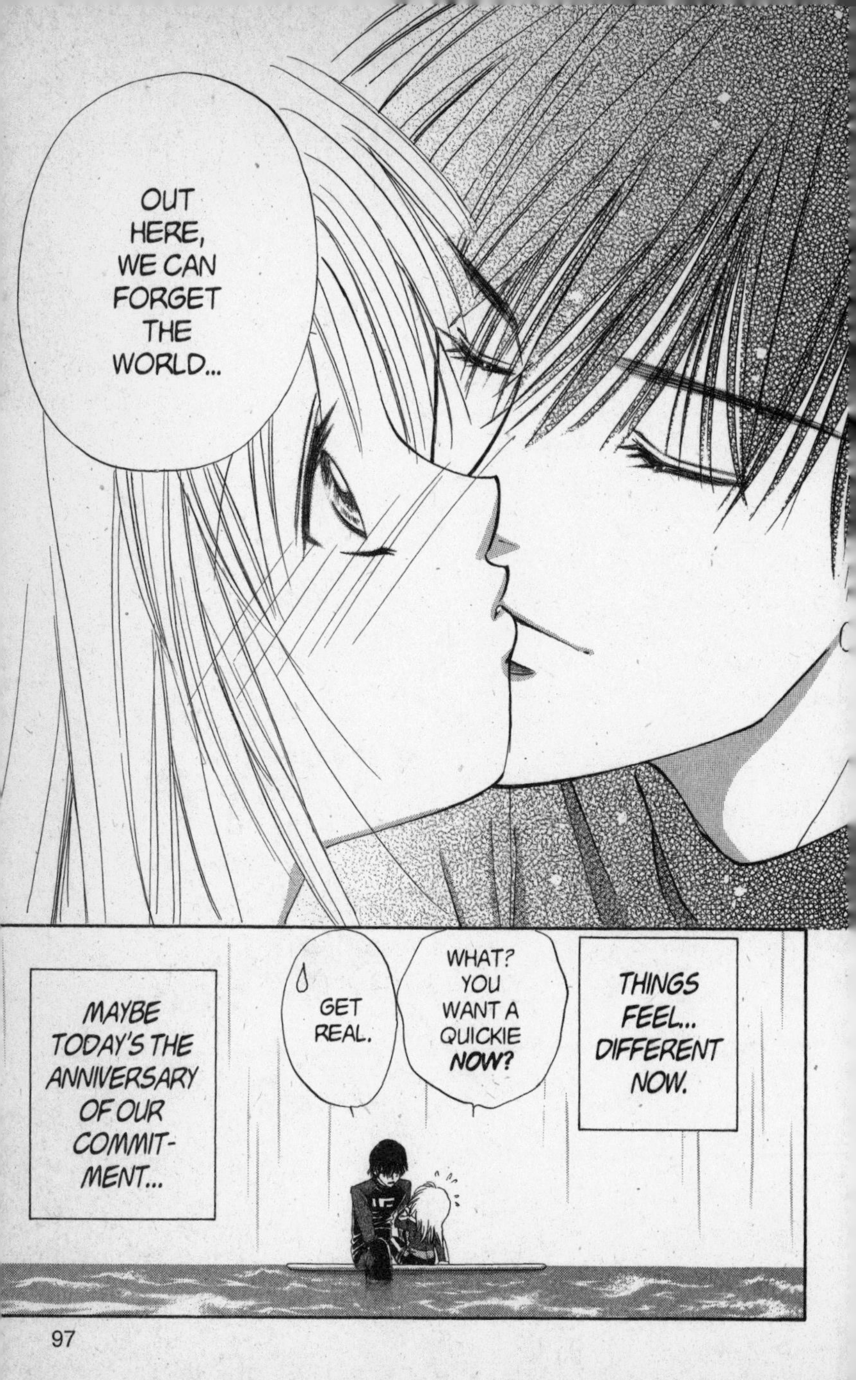
OUT HERE, WE CAN FORGET THE WORLD...
THINGS FEEL... DIFFERENT NOW.
WHAT? YOU WANT A QUICKIE NOW?
GET REAL.
MAYBE TODAY'S THE ANNIVERSARY OF OUR COMMIT-MENT...

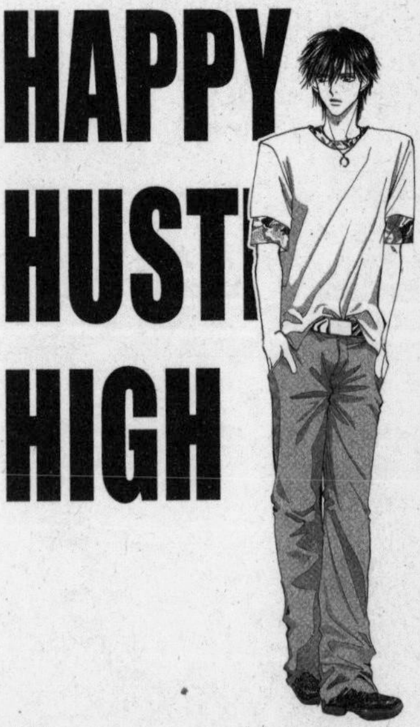
HAPPY
HUST
HIGH

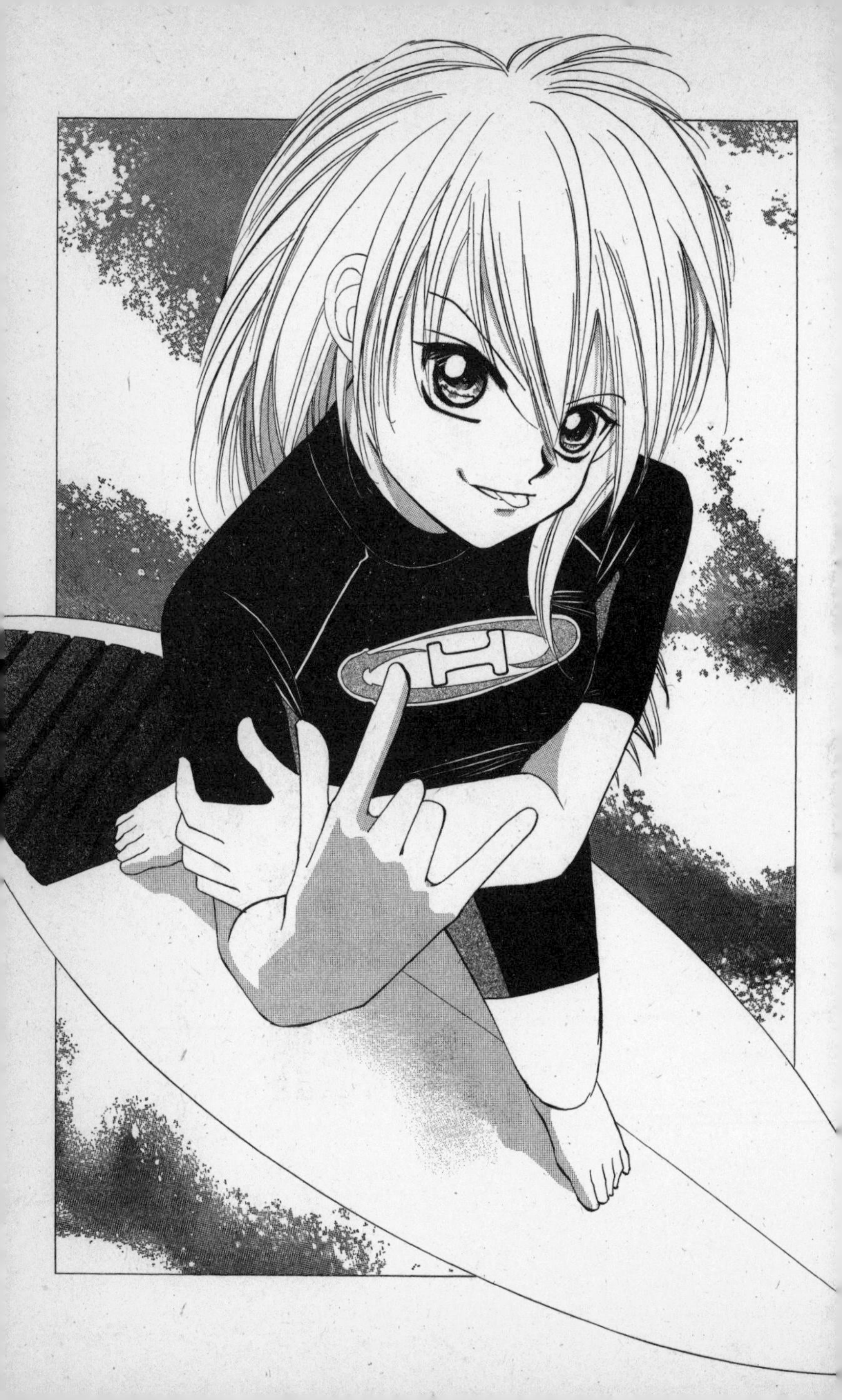

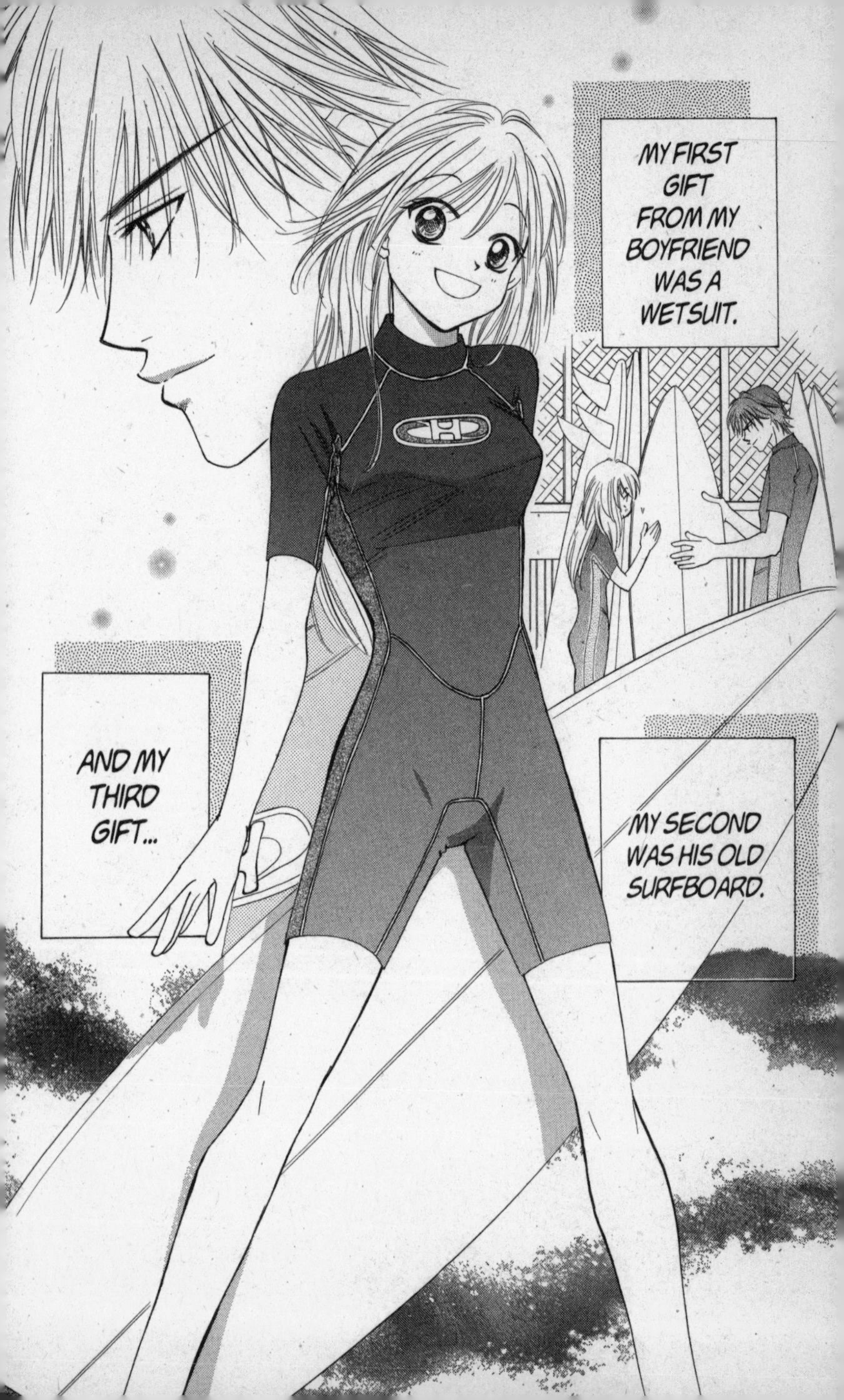
MY FIRST GIFT FROM MY BOYFRIEND WAS A WETSUIT.
MY SECOND WAS HIS OLD SURFBOARD.
AND MY THIRD GIFT...

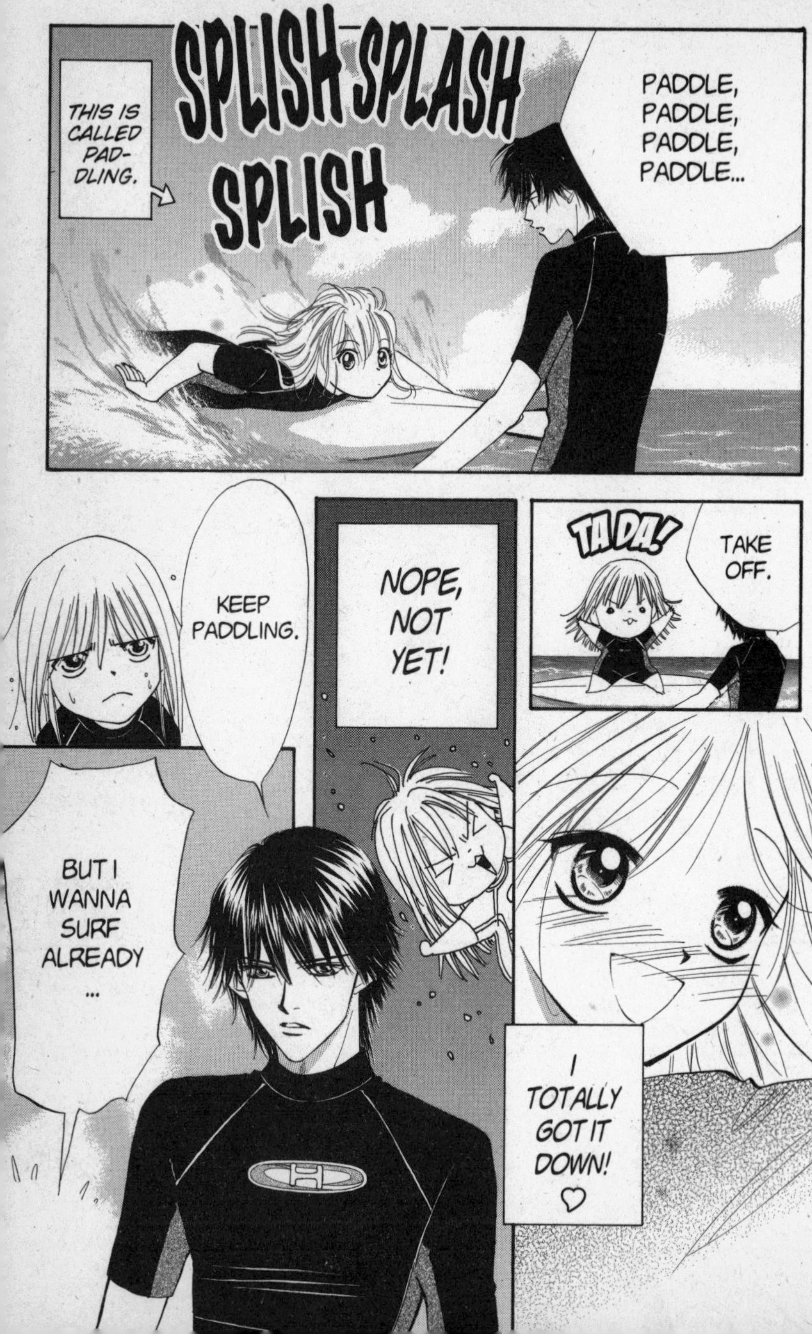
PADDLE, PADDLE, PADDLE, PADDLE...
SPLISH SPLASH SPLISH
THIS IS CALLED PAD-DLING.
TA DA!
TAKE OFF.
I TOTALLY GOT IT DOWN! ♡
NOPE, NOT YET!
KEEP PADDLING.
BUT I WANNA SURF ALREADY ...

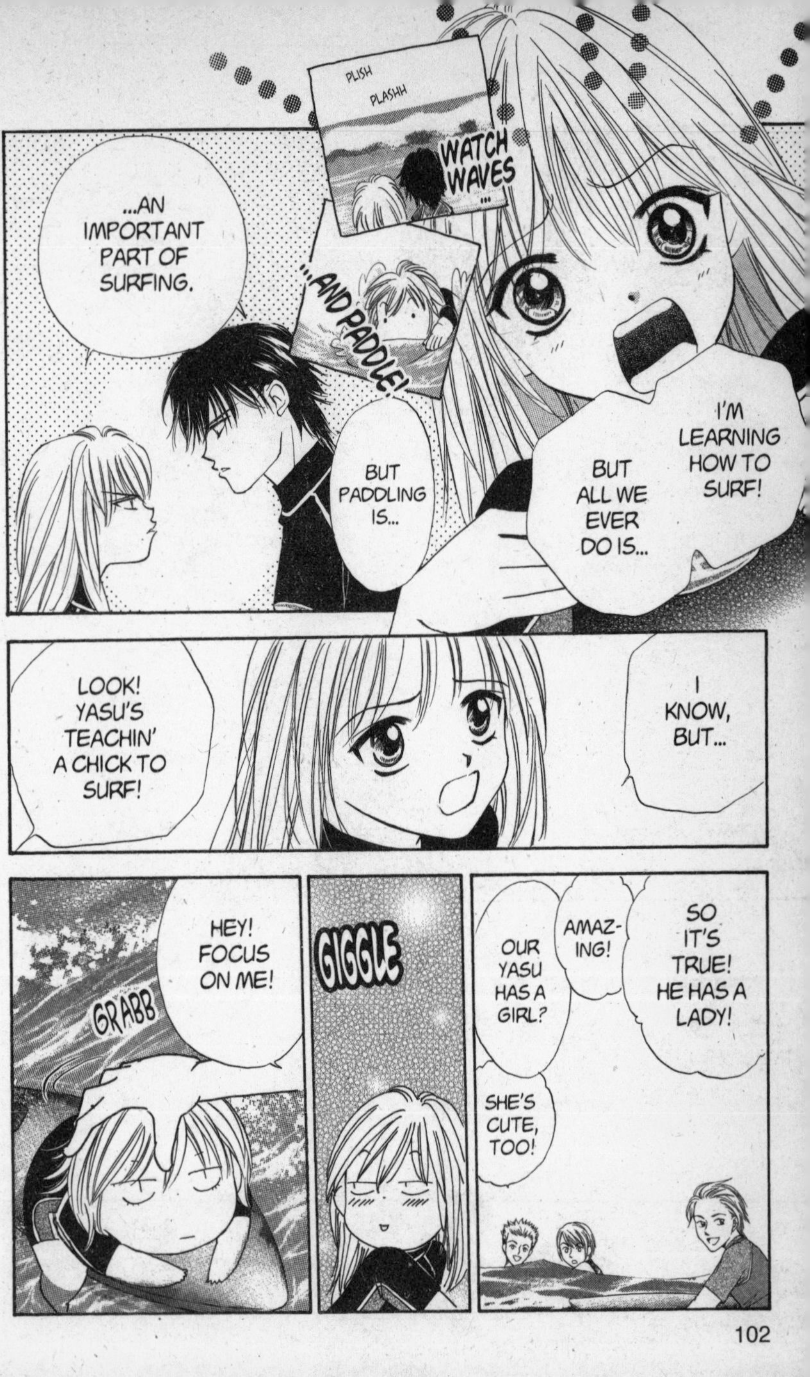
I'M LEARNING HOW TO SURF!
BUT ALL WE EVER DO IS...
PLISH
PLASHH
WATCH WAVES...
...AND PADDLE!
BUT PADDLING IS...
...AN IMPORTANT PART OF SURFING.
I KNOW, BUT...
LOOK! YASU'S TEACHIN' A CHICK TO SURF!
SO IT'S TRUE! HE HAS A LADY!
AMAZ-ING!
OUR YASU HAS A GIRL?
SHE'S CUTE, TOO!
GIGGLE
HEY! FOCUS ON ME!
GRABB

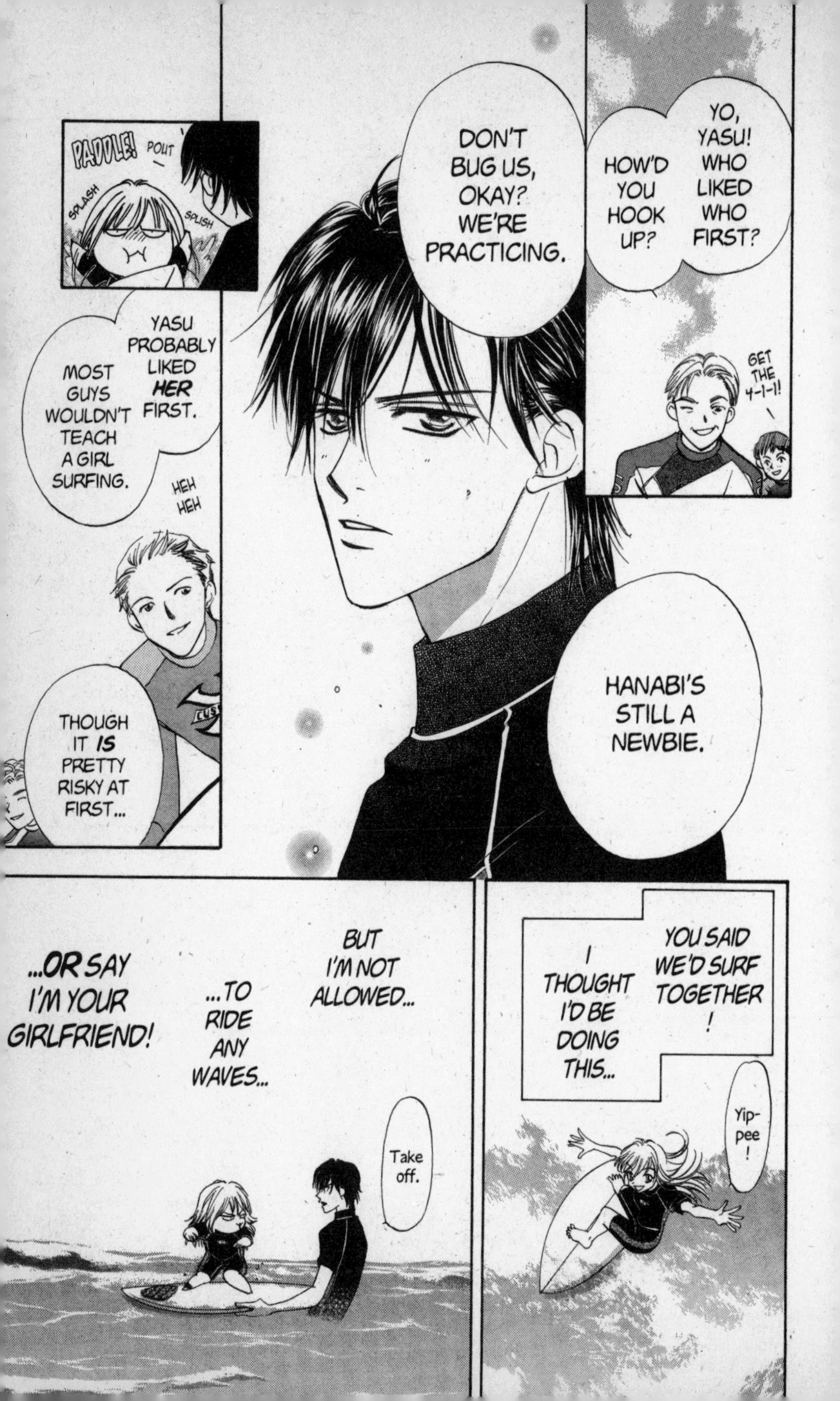
YO, YASU! WHO LIKED WHO FIRST?
HOW'D YOU HOOK UP?
GET THE 4-1-1!
DON'T BUG US, OKAY? WE'RE PRACTICING.
HANABI'S STILL A NEWBIE.
PADDLE!
POUT
SPLASH
SPLISH
YASU PROBABLY LIKED **HER** FIRST.
MOST GUYS WOULDN'T TEACH A GIRL SURFING.
HEH HEH
THOUGH IT ***IS*** PRETTY RISKY AT FIRST...
YOU SAID WE'D SURF TOGETHER!
I THOUGHT I'D BE DOING THIS...
Yip-pee!
BUT I'M NOT ALLOWED...
...TO RIDE ANY WAVES...
...**OR** SAY I'M YOUR GIRLFRIEND!
Take off.

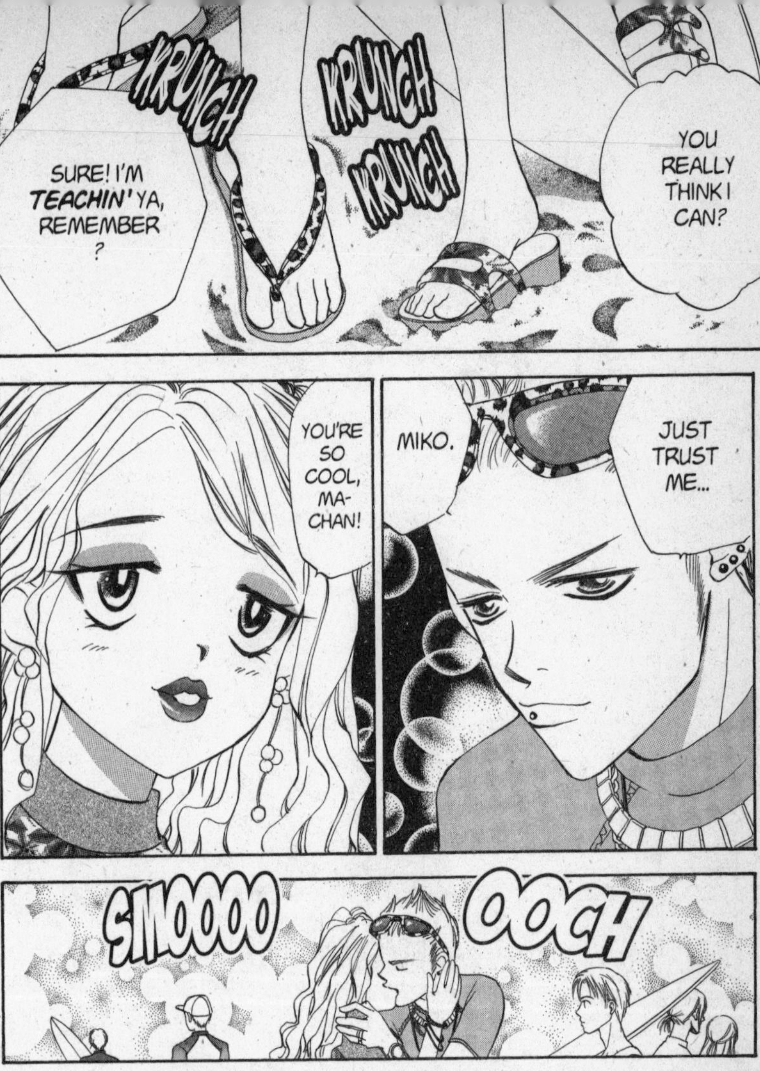

YOU REALLY THINK I CAN?
KRUNCH
KRUNCH
KRUNCH
SURE! I'M **TEACHIN'** YA, REMEMBER?
JUST TRUST ME...
MIKO.
YOU'RE SO COOL, MA-CHAN!
SMOOOOOOCH
I ♡ YOU!
I ♡ YOU, TOO!

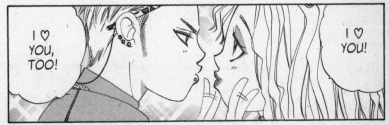

THEY ARE SO INTO EACH OTHER!
I'M JEALOUS!
OH! SOME-BODY'S WATCHING, MA-CHAN!
WHO CARES? LET 'EM LOOK, BABE.
!?
THEY SURE LOOK CUTE TOGETHER!
DAMN! I WANTED TO GO WITH YASU...
Bend your elbows.

VIDEO GAMES

A FEW YEARS AGO, MY HEALTH WAS POOR AND MY ADORABLE DOG MOMON WAS GETTING OLDER. SO I STOPPED TRAVELING SO MUCH, STARTED PLAYING RPGS—AND GOT MYSELF HOOKED!

THESE DAYS I'VE BEEN PLAYING A GAME THAT'S BEEN OUT AWHILE. STRATEGY GUIDES ARE HARD TO FIND, SO I ASK FRIENDS AND SURF THE INTERNET FOR TIPS.

I'VE BUGGED SOME FRIENDS SO MUCH, I THINK SOMEONE WILL JUST SOCK ME SOMEDAY! LOL! ONCE I EVEN CALLED MY FRIEND ASHI-SAN AT 2 A.M., ALMOST IN TEARS! I HAD PLAYED THROUGH THE GAME FOUR TIMES—AND STILL DIDN'T SEE THE GOOD ENDING!

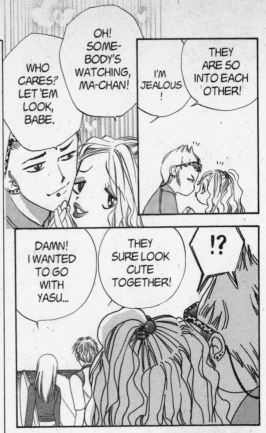

That was fun!
Phew! Finally!

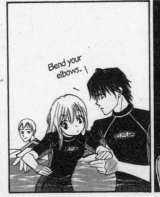

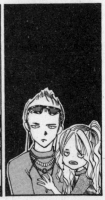

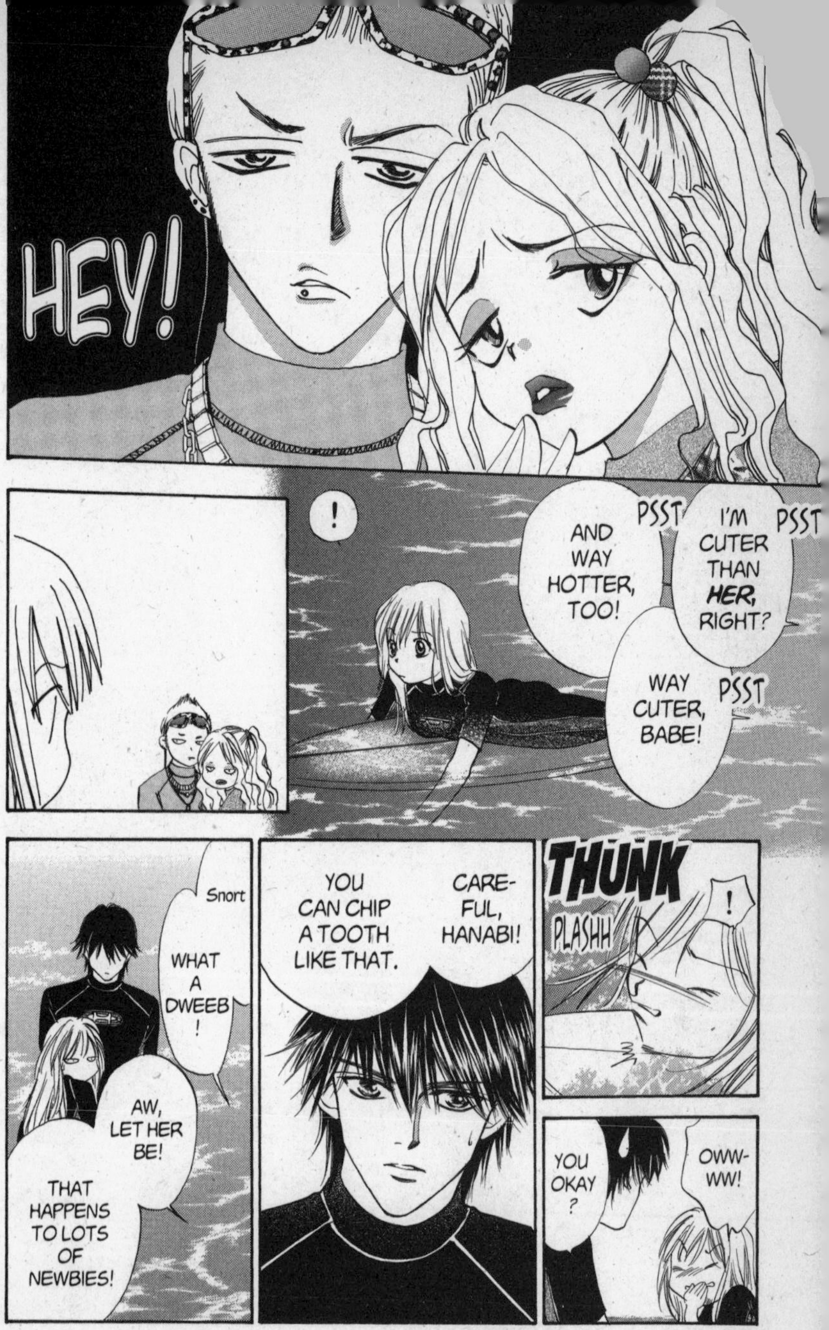
HEY!
PSST
I'M CUTER THAN HER, RIGHT?
PSST
AND WAY HOTTER, TOO!
PSST
WAY CUTER, BABE!
!
THUNK
PLASHH
!
OWW-WW!
YOU OKAY?
CARE-FUL, HANABI!
YOU CAN CHIP A TOOTH LIKE THAT.
Snort
WHAT A DWEEB!
AW, LET HER BE!
THAT HAPPENS TO LOTS OF NEWBIES!

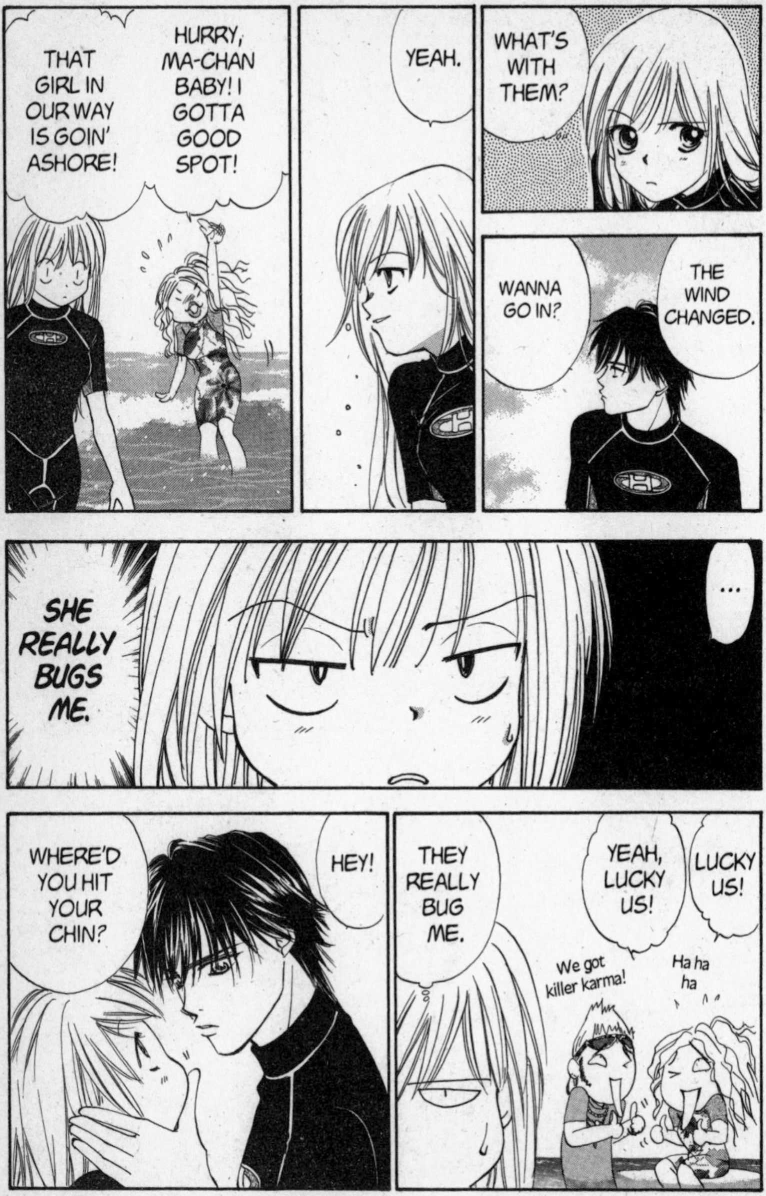
WHAT'S WITH THEM?
THE WIND CHANGED.
WANNA GO IN?
YEAH.
HURRY, MA-CHAN BABY! I GOTTA GOOD SPOT!
THAT GIRL IN OUR WAY IS GOIN' ASHORE!
...
SHE REALLY BUGS ME.
LUCKY US!
YEAH, LUCKY US!
Ha ha ha
We got killer karma!
THEY REALLY BUG ME.
HEY!
WHERE'D YOU HIT YOUR CHIN?

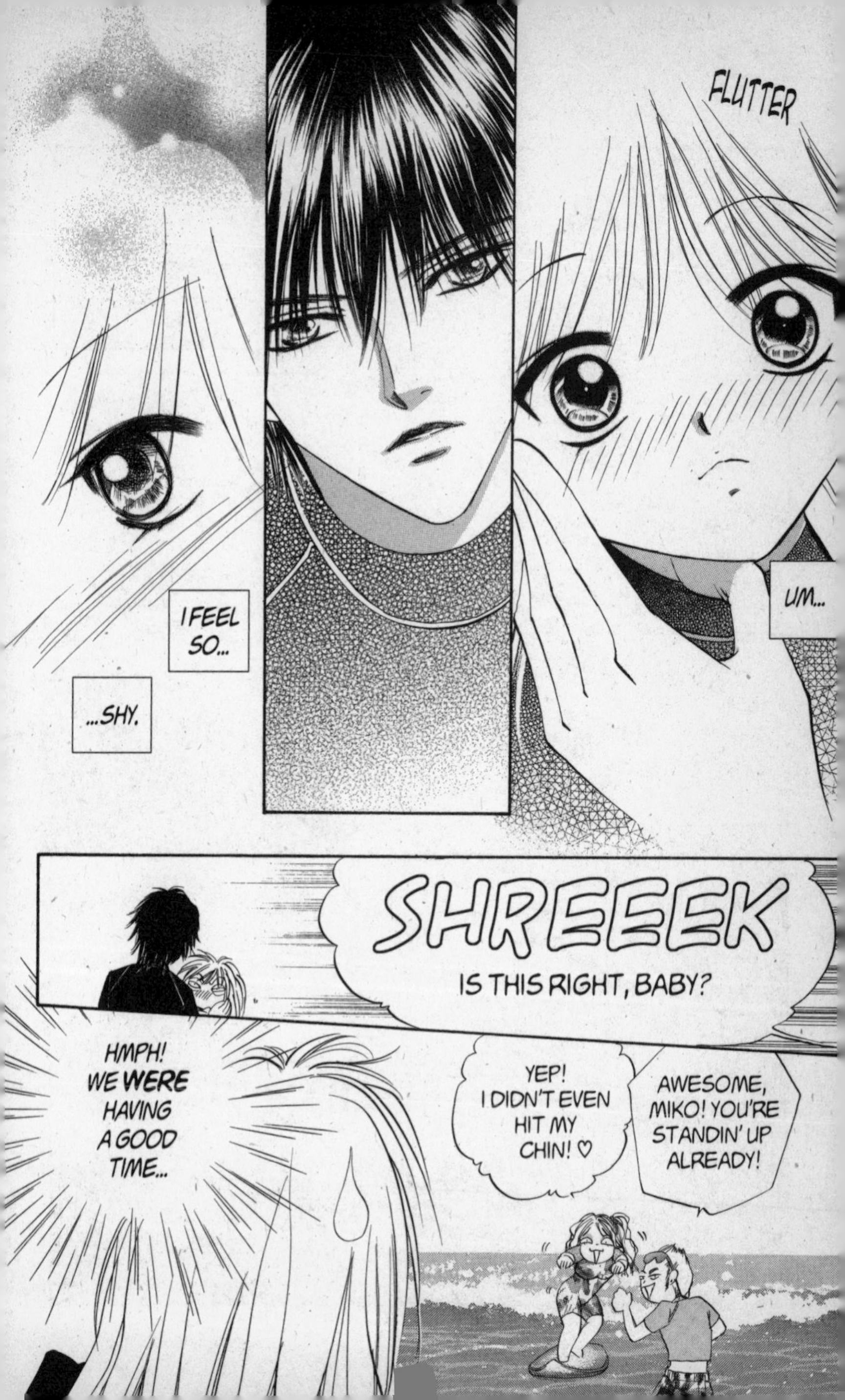
FLUTTER
UM...
I FEEL SO...
...SHY.
SHREEEK
IS THIS RIGHT, BABY?
AWESOME, MIKO! YOU'RE STANDIN' UP ALREADY!
YEP! I DIDN'T EVEN HIT MY CHIN! ♡
HMPH! WE WERE HAVING A GOOD TIME...

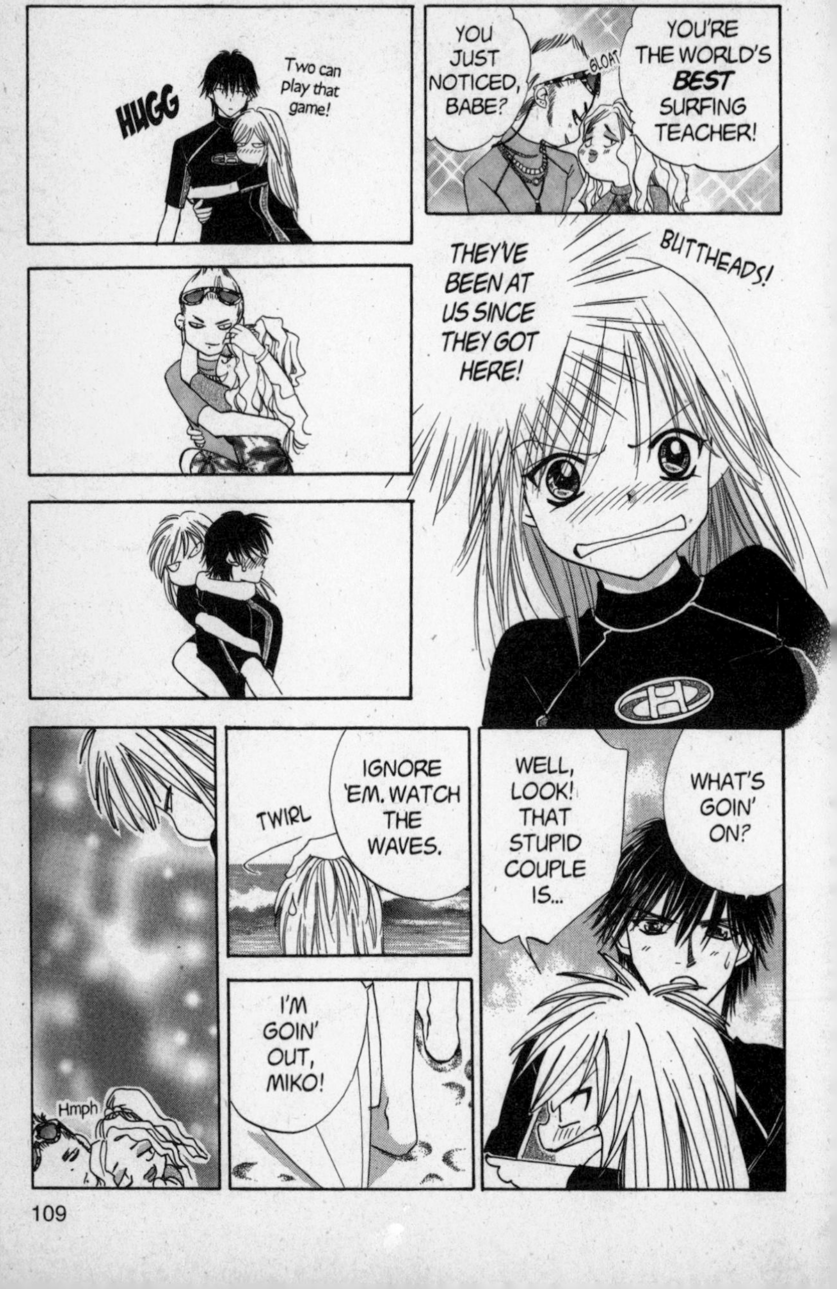
YOU'RE THE WORLD'S BEST SURFING TEACHER!
GLOAT
YOU JUST NOTICED, BABE?
HUGG
Two can play that game!
BUTTHEADS!
THEY'VE BEEN AT US SINCE THEY GOT HERE!
WHAT'S GOIN' ON?
WELL, LOOK! THAT STUPID COUPLE IS...
IGNORE 'EM. WATCH THE WAVES.
TWIRL
I'M GOIN' OUT, MIKO!
Hmph

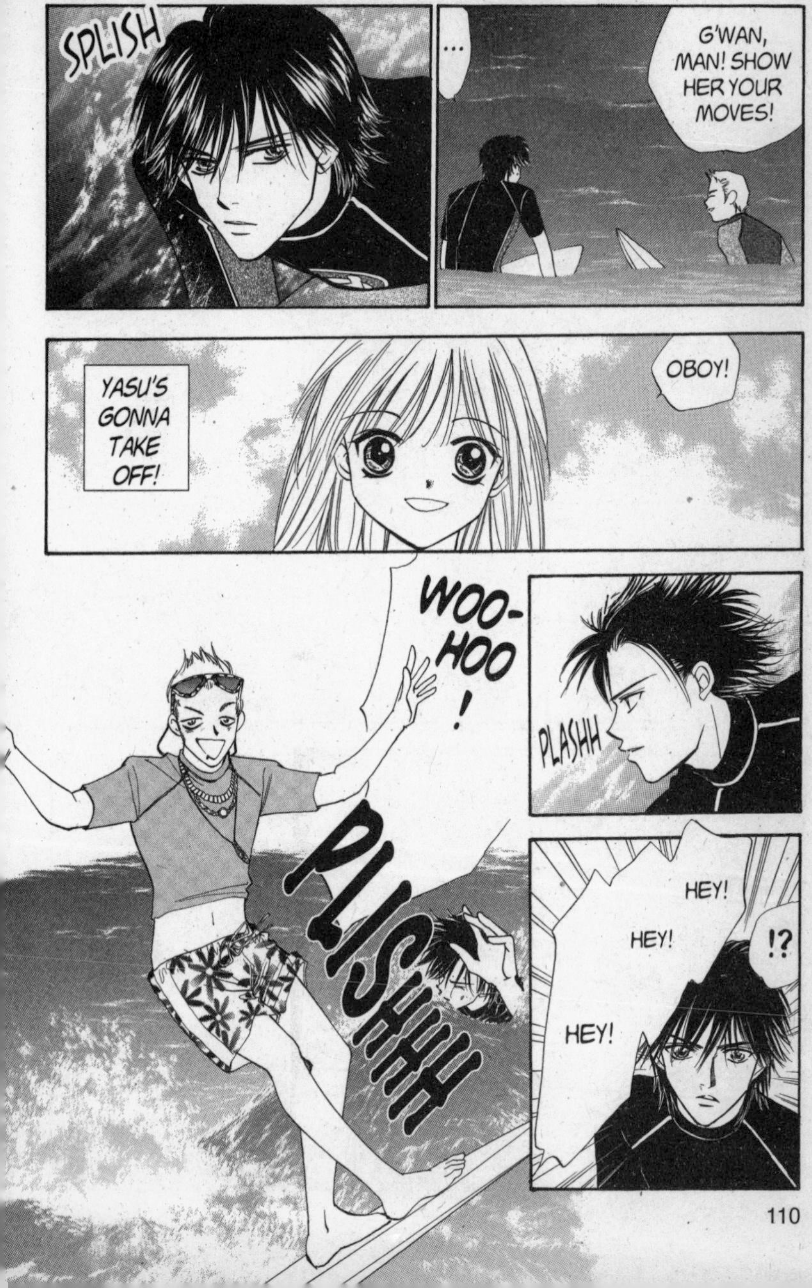
G'WAN, MAN! SHOW HER YOUR MOVES!
...
SPLISH
OBOY!
YASU'S GONNA TAKE OFF!
PLASHH
HEY!
!?
HEY!
HEY!
WOO-HOO!
PLISHH

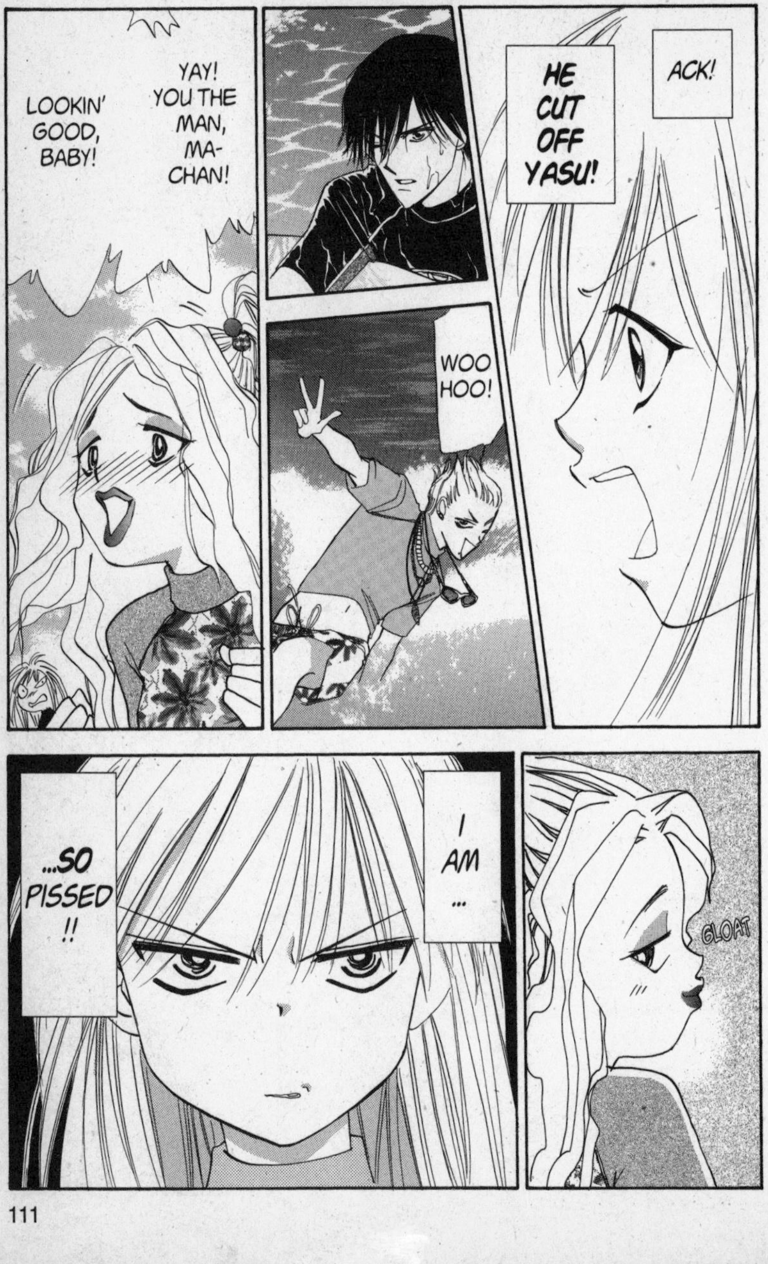
ACK!
HE CUT OFF YASU!
WOO HOO!
YAY! YOU THE MAN, MA-CHAN!
LOOKIN' GOOD, BABY!
GLOAT
I AM ...
...SO PISSED !!

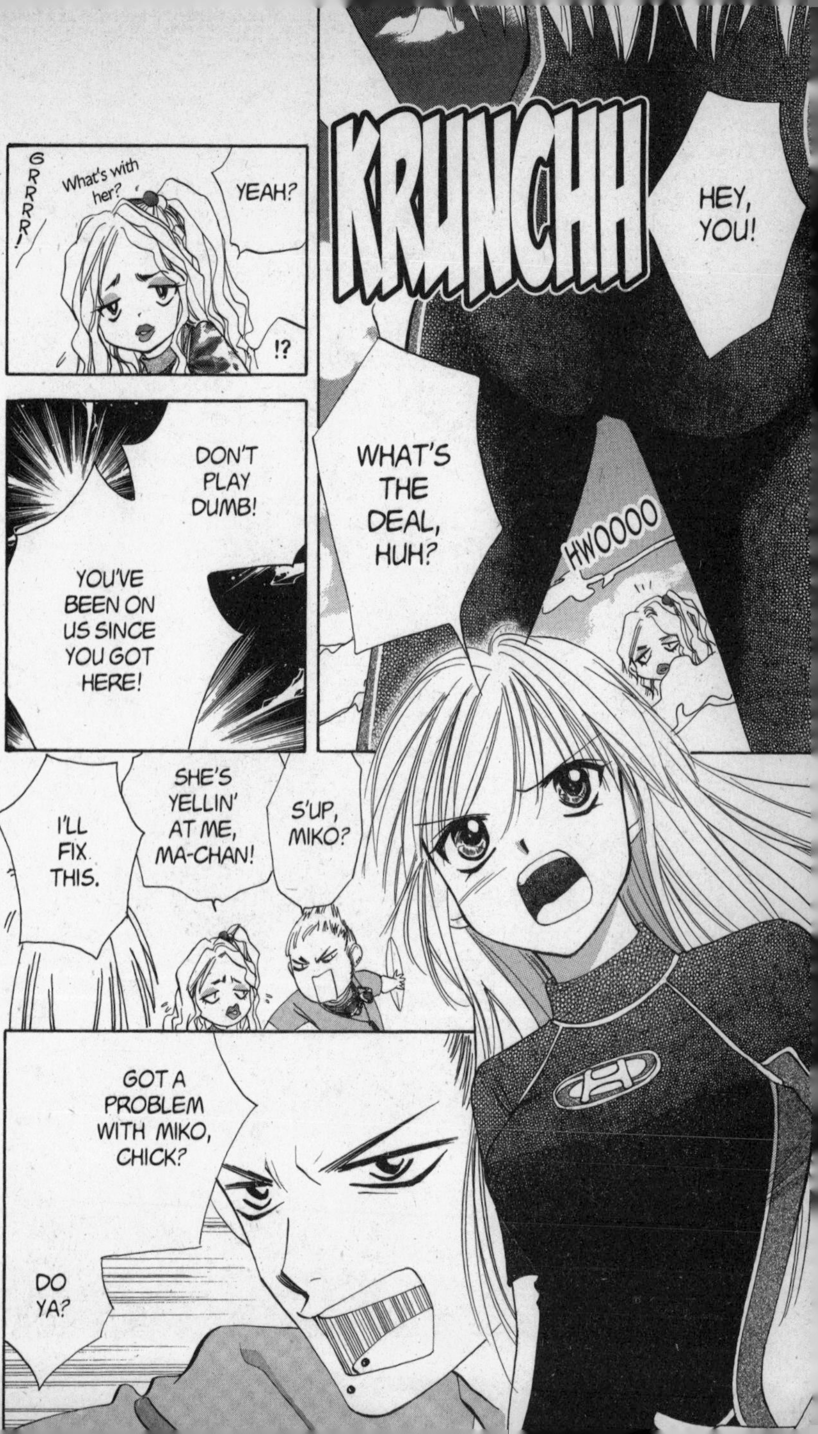
KRUNCHH
HEY, YOU!
WHAT'S THE DEAL, HUH?
HWOOOO
YEAH?
What's with her?
GRRRR!
!?
DON'T PLAY DUMB!
YOU'VE BEEN ON US SINCE YOU GOT HERE!
S'UP, MIKO?
SHE'S YELLIN' AT ME, MA-CHAN!
I'LL FIX THIS.
GOT A PROBLEM WITH MIKO, CHICK?
DO YA?

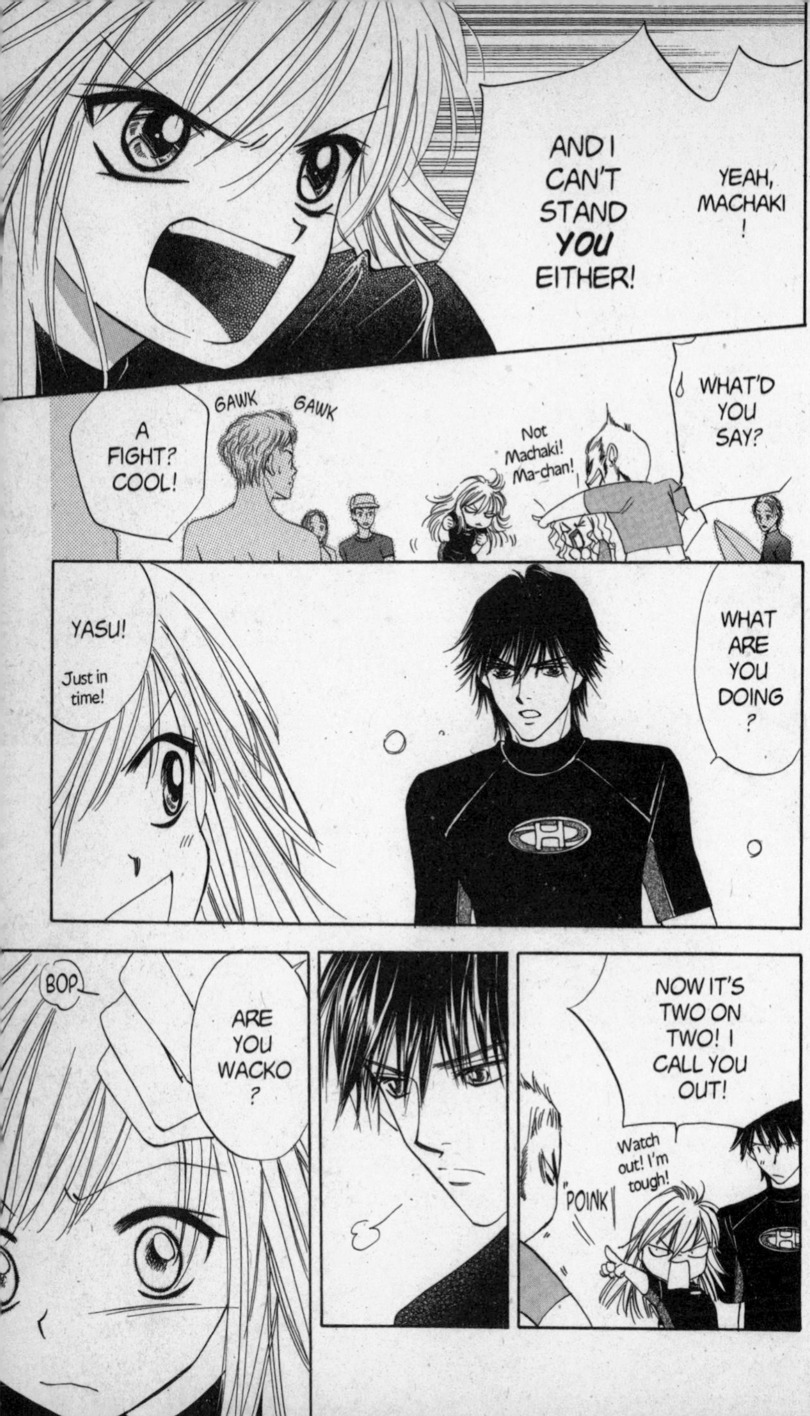
YEAH, MACHAKI!
AND I CAN'T STAND **YOU** EITHER!
WHAT'D YOU SAY?
Not Machaki! Ma-chan!
GAWK GAWK
A FIGHT? COOL!
WHAT ARE YOU DOING?
YASU!
Just in time!
NOW IT'S TWO ON TWO! I CALL YOU OUT!
Watch out! I'm tough!
POINK
ARE YOU WACKO?
BOP

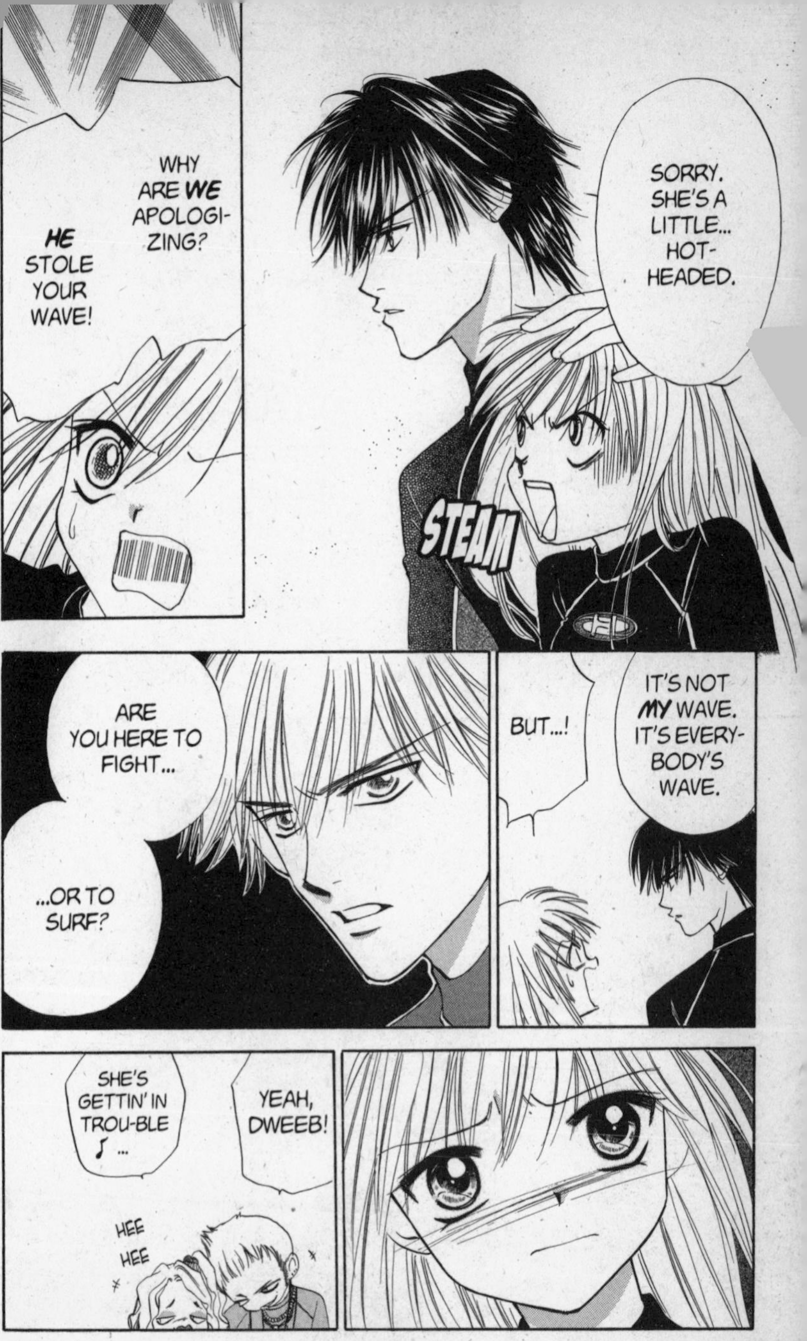
SORRY. SHE'S A LITTLE... HOT-HEADED.
STEAM
WHY ARE **WE** APOLOGI-ZING?
HE STOLE YOUR WAVE!
IT'S NOT **MY** WAVE. IT'S EVERY-BODY'S WAVE.
BUT...!
ARE YOU HERE TO FIGHT...
...OR TO SURF?
YEAH, DWEEB!
SHE'S GETTIN' IN TROU-BLE ♪ ...
HEE HEE

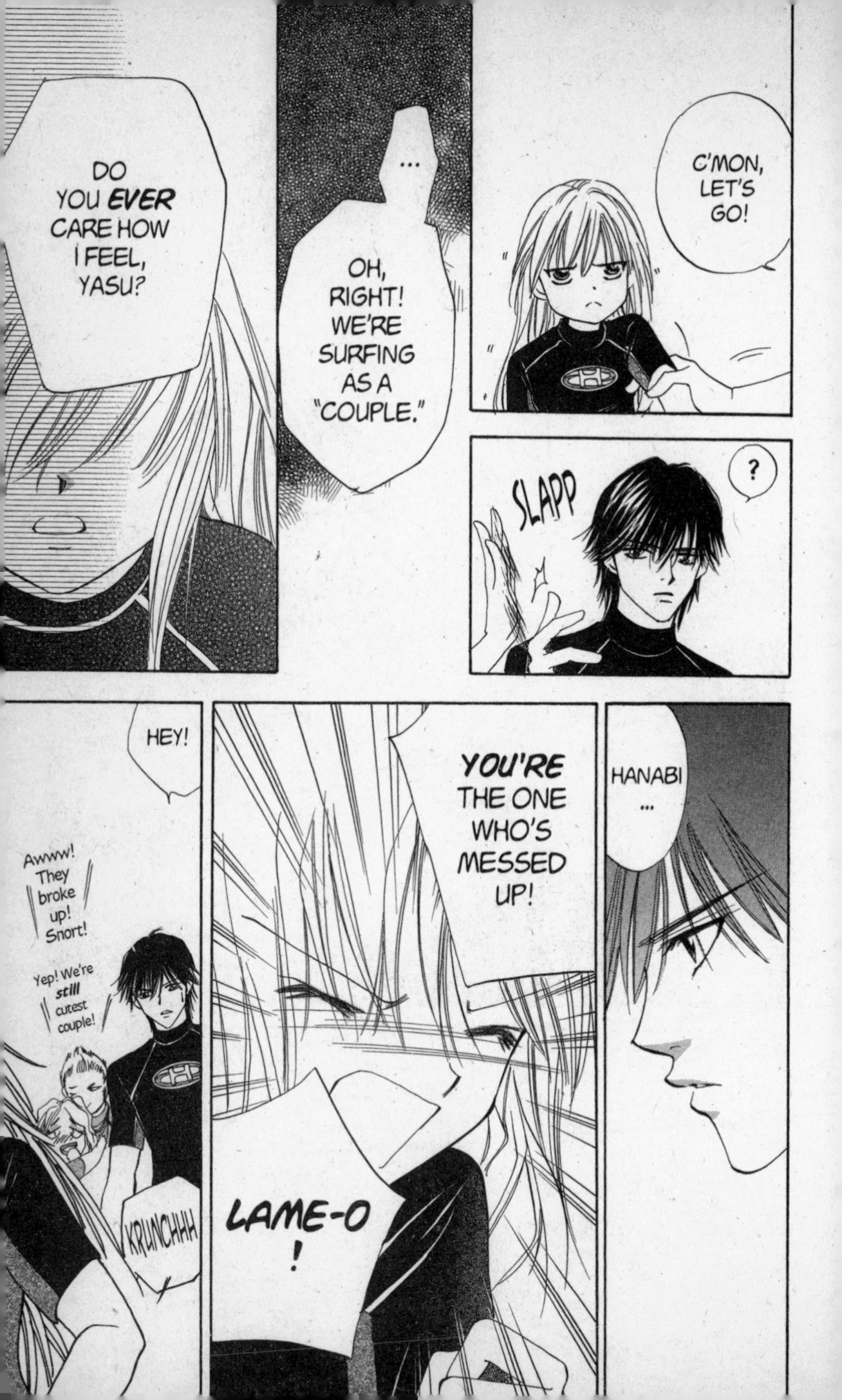
C'MON, LET'S GO!
?
SLAPP
...
OH, RIGHT! WE'RE SURFING AS A "COUPLE."
DO YOU EVER CARE HOW I FEEL, YASU?
HANABI ...
YOU'RE THE ONE WHO'S MESSED UP!
LAME-O !
HEY!
Awww! They broke up! Snort!
Yep! We're still cutest couple!
KRUNCHHH

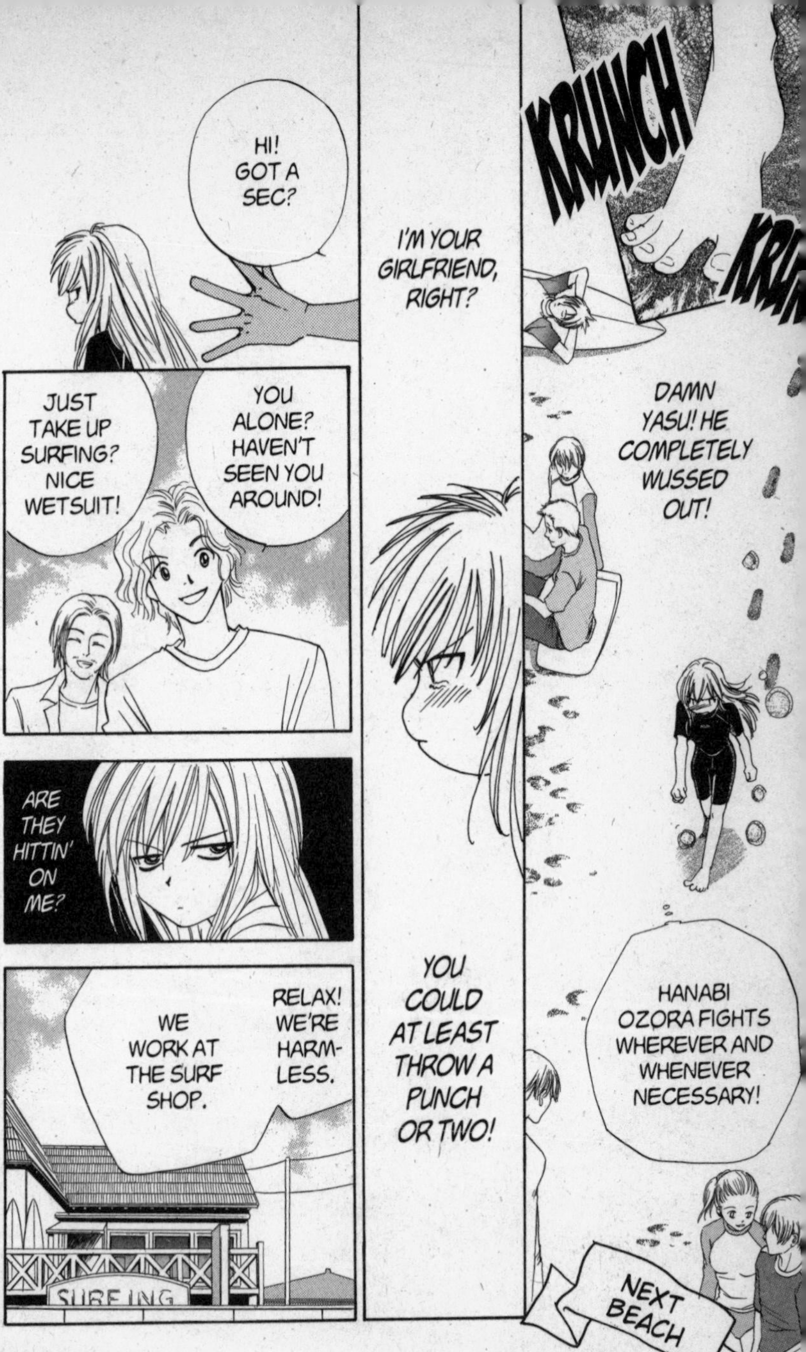
KRUNCH
DAMN YASU! HE COMPLETELY WUSSED OUT!
HANABI OZORA FIGHTS WHEREVER AND WHENEVER NECESSARY!
NEXT BEACH
I'M YOUR GIRLFRIEND, RIGHT?
YOU COULD AT LEAST THROW A PUNCH OR TWO!
HI! GOT A SEC?
YOU ALONE? HAVEN'T SEEN YOU AROUND!
JUST TAKE UP SURFING? NICE WETSUIT!
ARE THEY HITTIN' ON ME?
RELAX! WE'RE HARMLESS.
WE WORK AT THE SURF SHOP.
SURFING

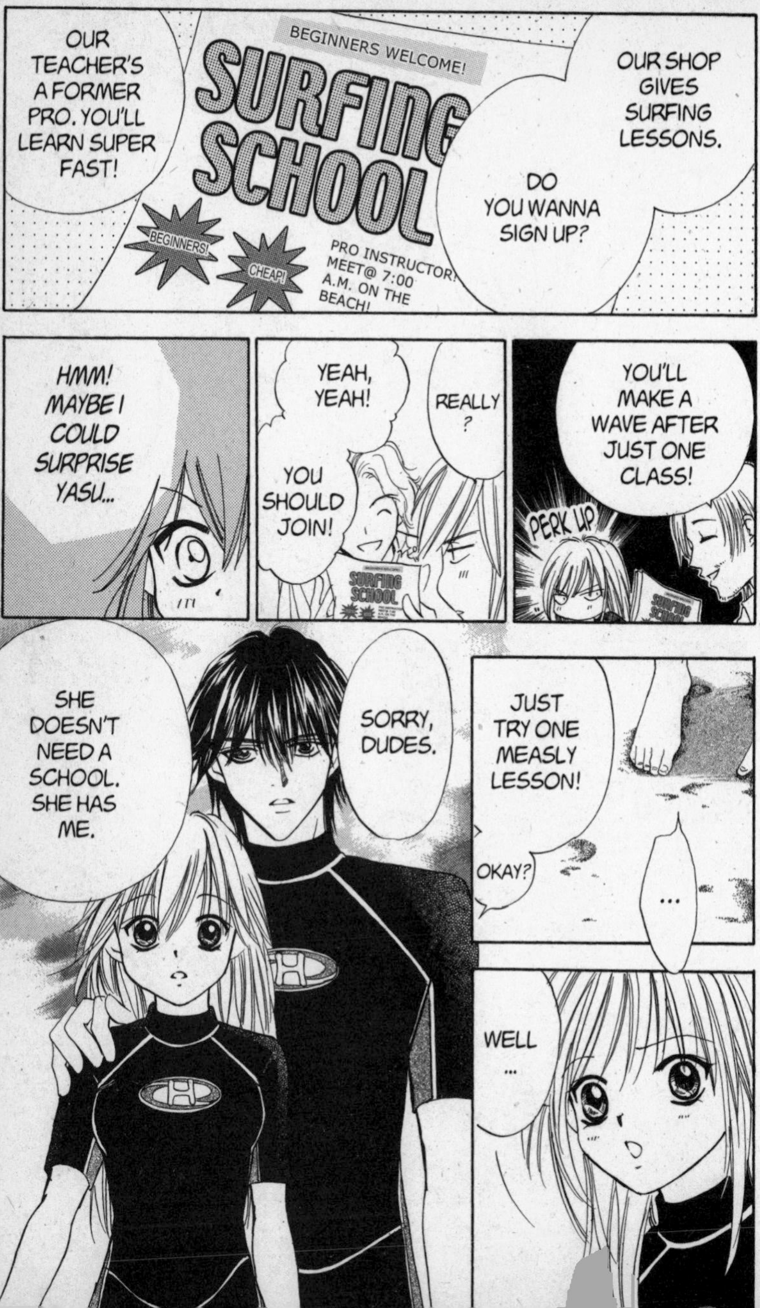
OUR SHOP GIVES SURFING LESSONS.
DO YOU WANNA SIGN UP?
BEGINNERS WELCOME!
SURFING SCHOOL
PRO INSTRUCTOR! MEET@ 7:00 A.M. ON THE BEACH!
CHEAP!
BEGINNERS!
OUR TEACHER'S A FORMER PRO. YOU'LL LEARN SUPER FAST!
YOU'LL MAKE A WAVE AFTER JUST ONE CLASS!
PERK UP
REALLY?
YEAH, YEAH!
YOU SHOULD JOIN!
HMM! MAYBE I COULD SURPRISE YASU...
JUST TRY ONE MEASLY LESSON!
OKAY?
...
WELL ...
SORRY, DUDES.
SHE DOESN'T NEED A SCHOOL. SHE HAS ME.

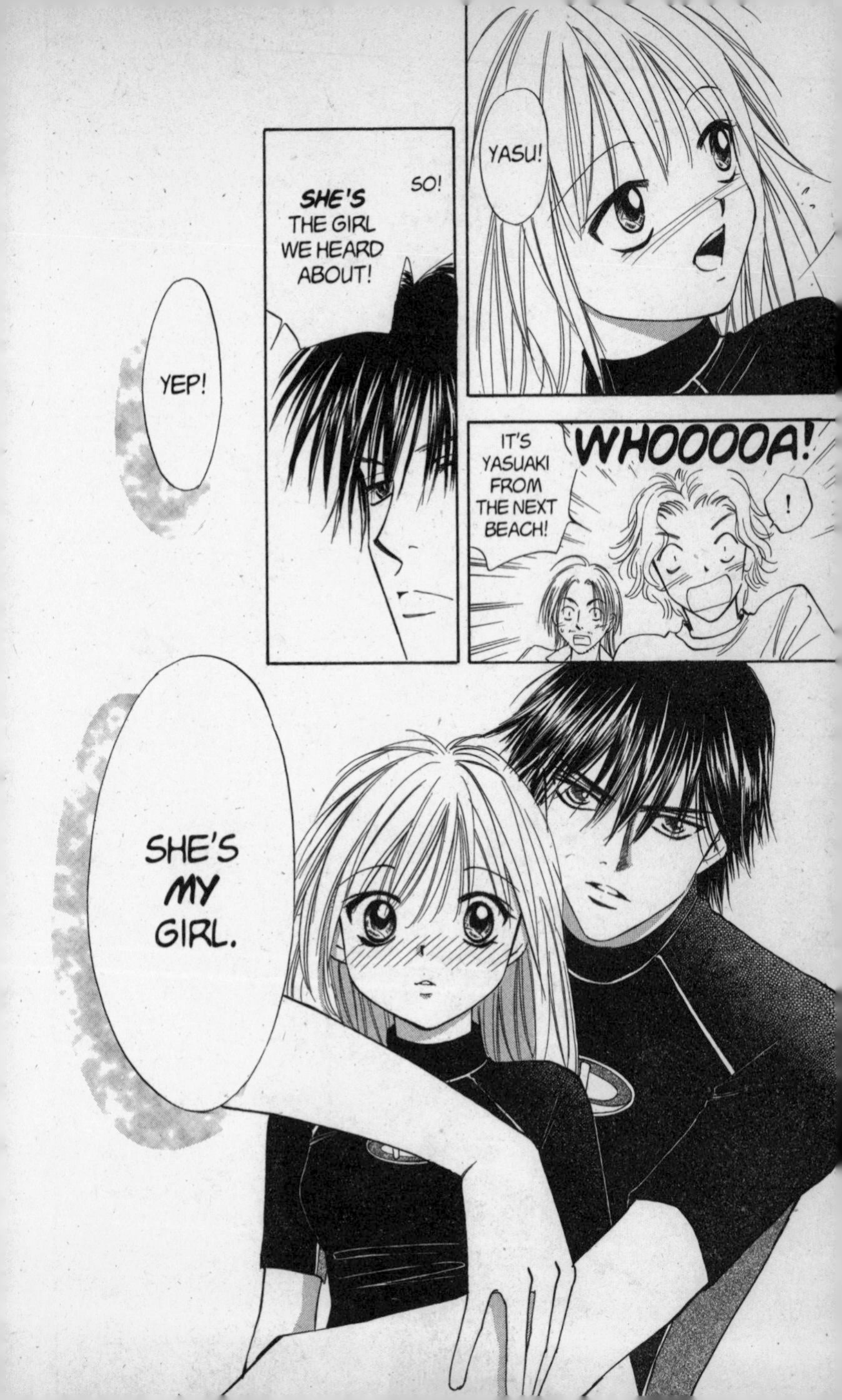
YASU!
WHOOOOA!
!
IT'S YASUAKI FROM THE NEXT BEACH!
SO!
SHE'S THE GIRL WE HEARD ABOUT!
YEP!
SHE'S MY GIRL.

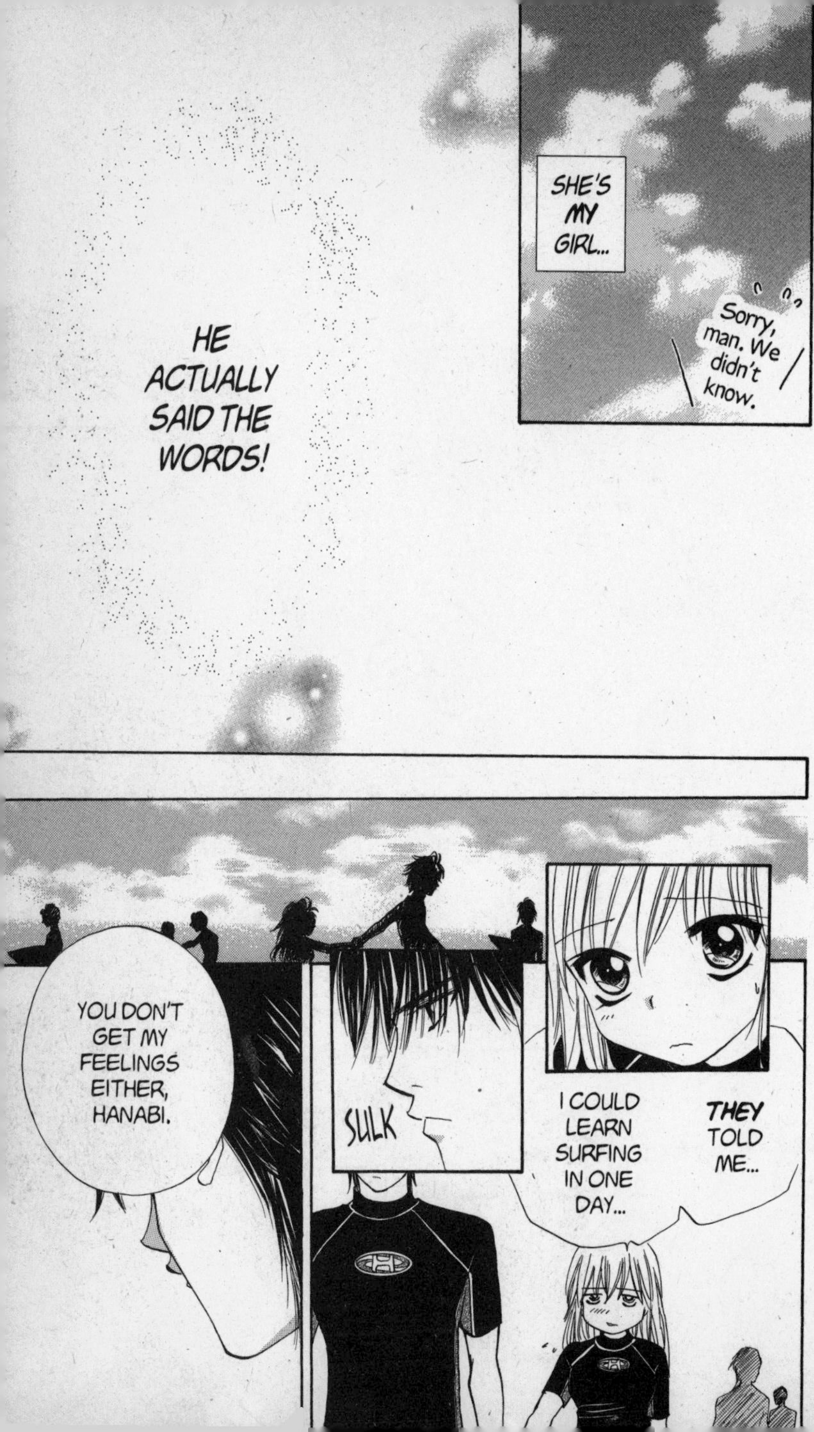
SHE'S MY GIRL...
Sorry, man. We didn't know.
HE ACTUALLY SAID THE WORDS!
THEY TOLD ME...
I COULD LEARN SURFING IN ONE DAY...
SULK
YOU DON'T GET MY FEELINGS EITHER, HANABI.

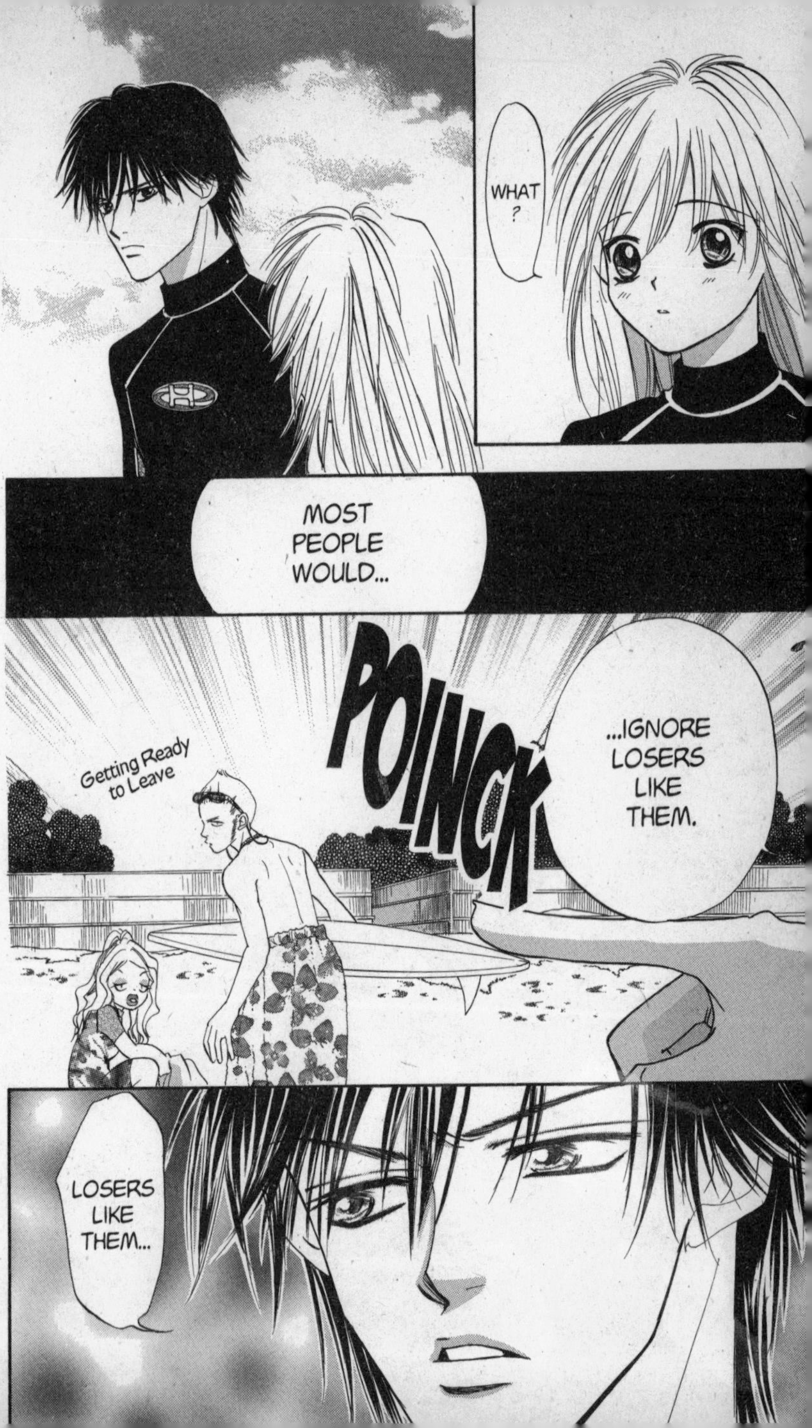
WHAT?
MOST PEOPLE WOULD...
...IGNORE LOSERS LIKE THEM.
POINCK
Getting Ready to Leave
LOSERS LIKE THEM...

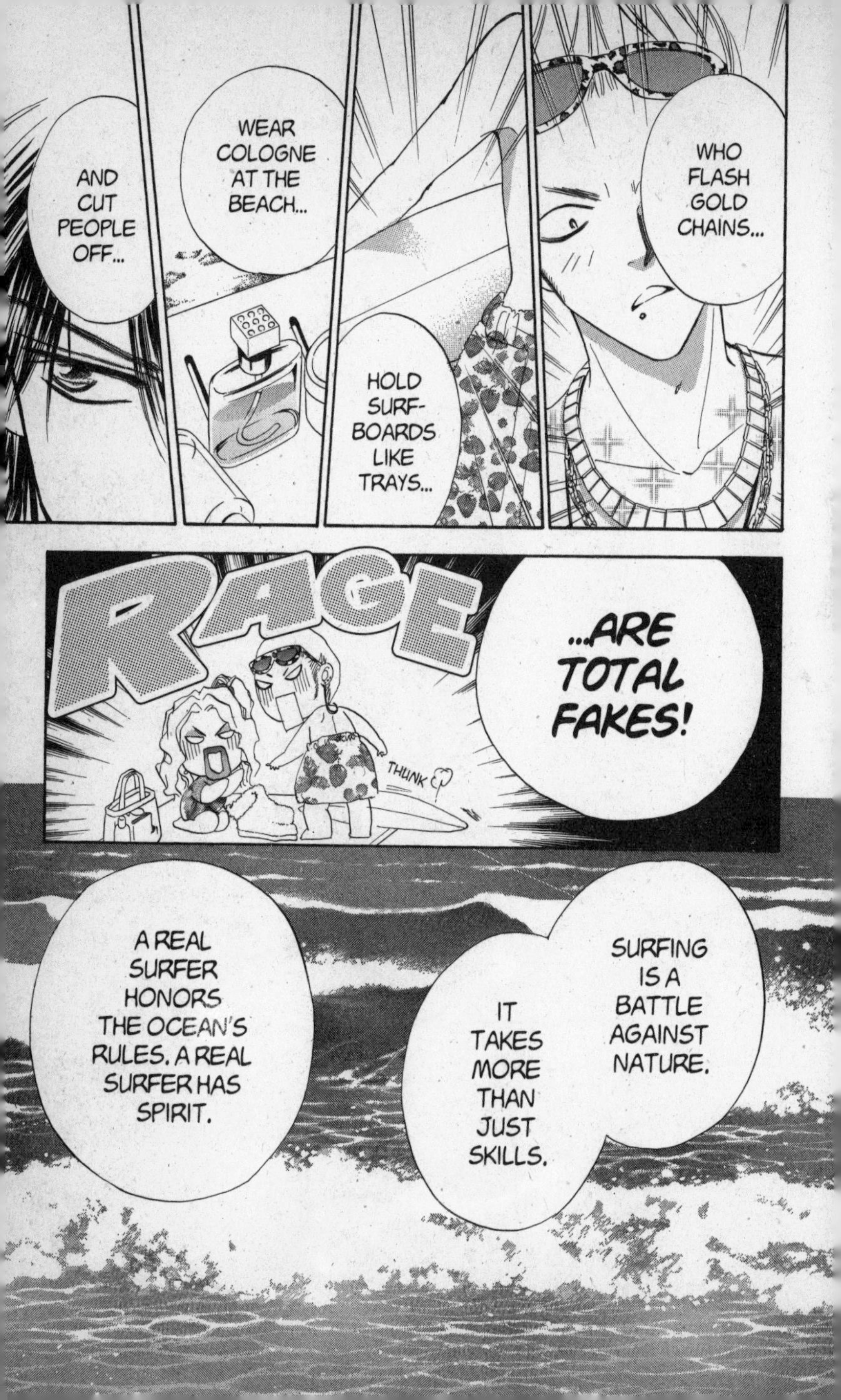
WHO FLASH GOLD CHAINS...
HOLD SURF-BOARDS LIKE TRAYS...
WEAR COLOGNE AT THE BEACH...
AND CUT PEOPLE OFF...
...ARE TOTAL FAKES!
RAGE
THUNK
SURFING IS A BATTLE AGAINST NATURE.
IT TAKES MORE THAN JUST SKILLS.
A REAL SURFER HONORS THE OCEAN'S RULES. A REAL SURFER HAS SPIRIT.

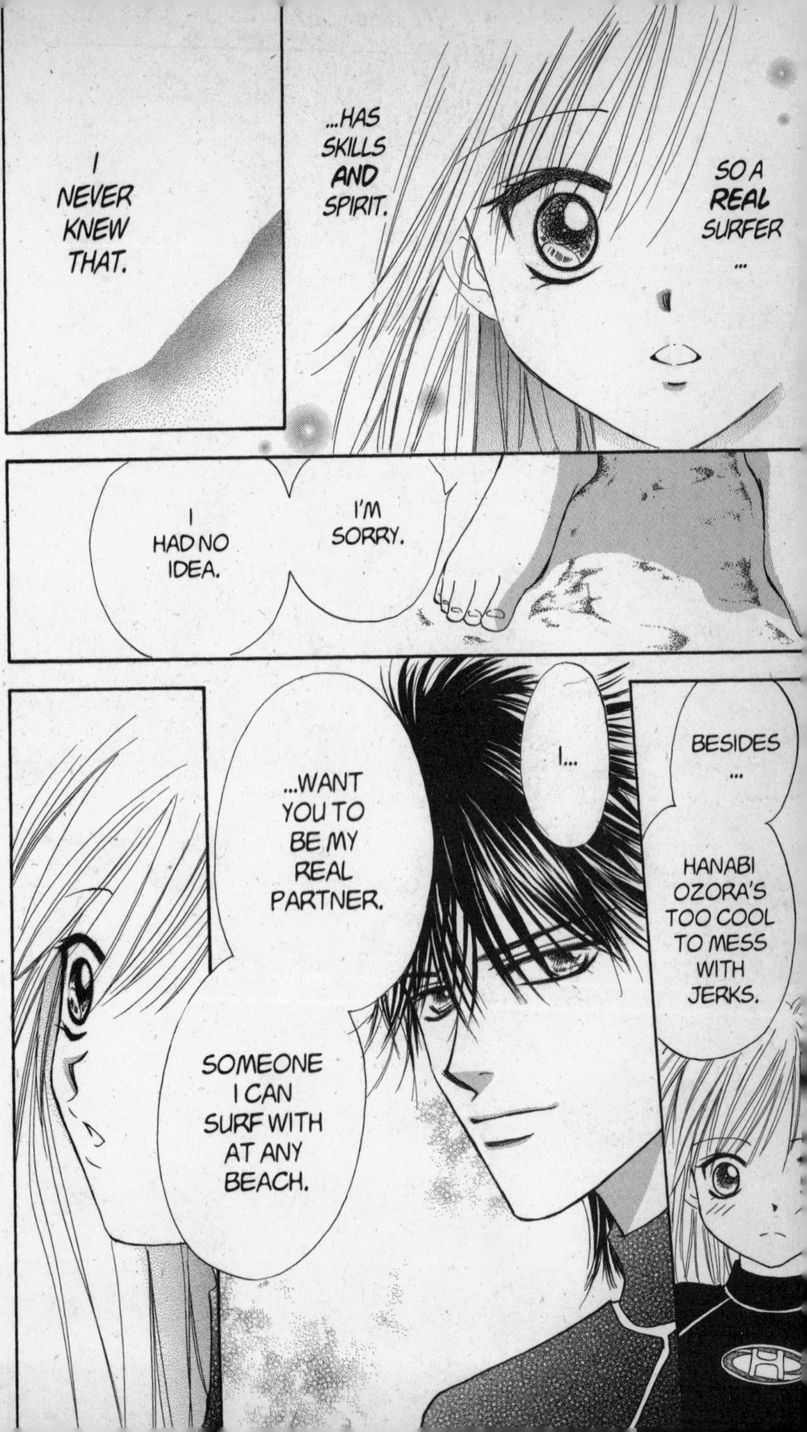
SO A REAL SURFER ...
...HAS SKILLS AND SPIRIT.
I NEVER KNEW THAT.
I'M SORRY.
I HAD NO IDEA.
BESIDES ...
HANABI OZORA'S TOO COOL TO MESS WITH JERKS.
I...
...WANT YOU TO BE MY REAL PARTNER.
SOMEONE I CAN SURF WITH AT ANY BEACH.

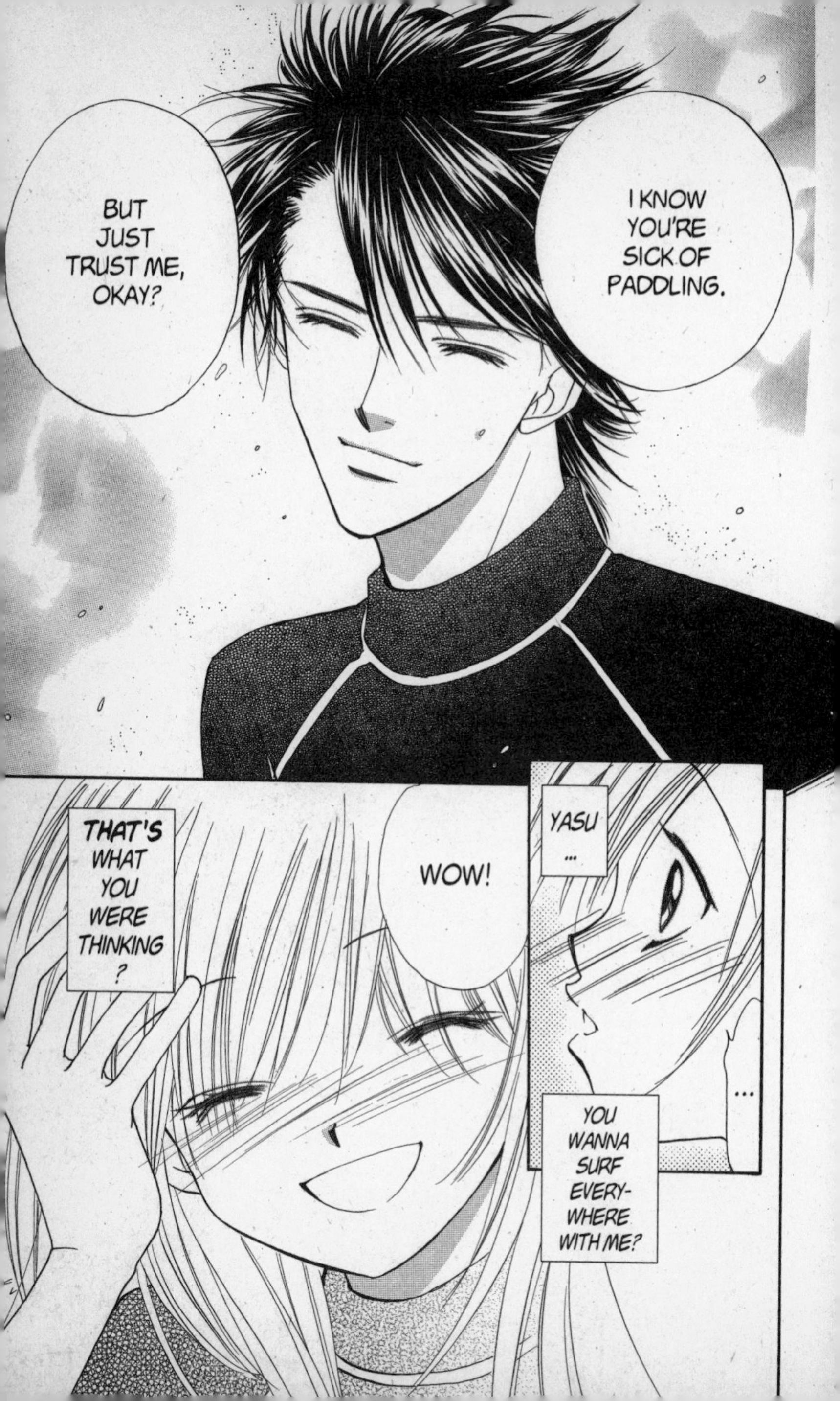
I KNOW YOU'RE SICK OF PADDLING.
BUT JUST TRUST ME, OKAY?
YASU ...
...
YOU WANNA SURF EVERY-WHERE WITH ME?
WOW!
THAT'S WHAT YOU WERE THINKING?

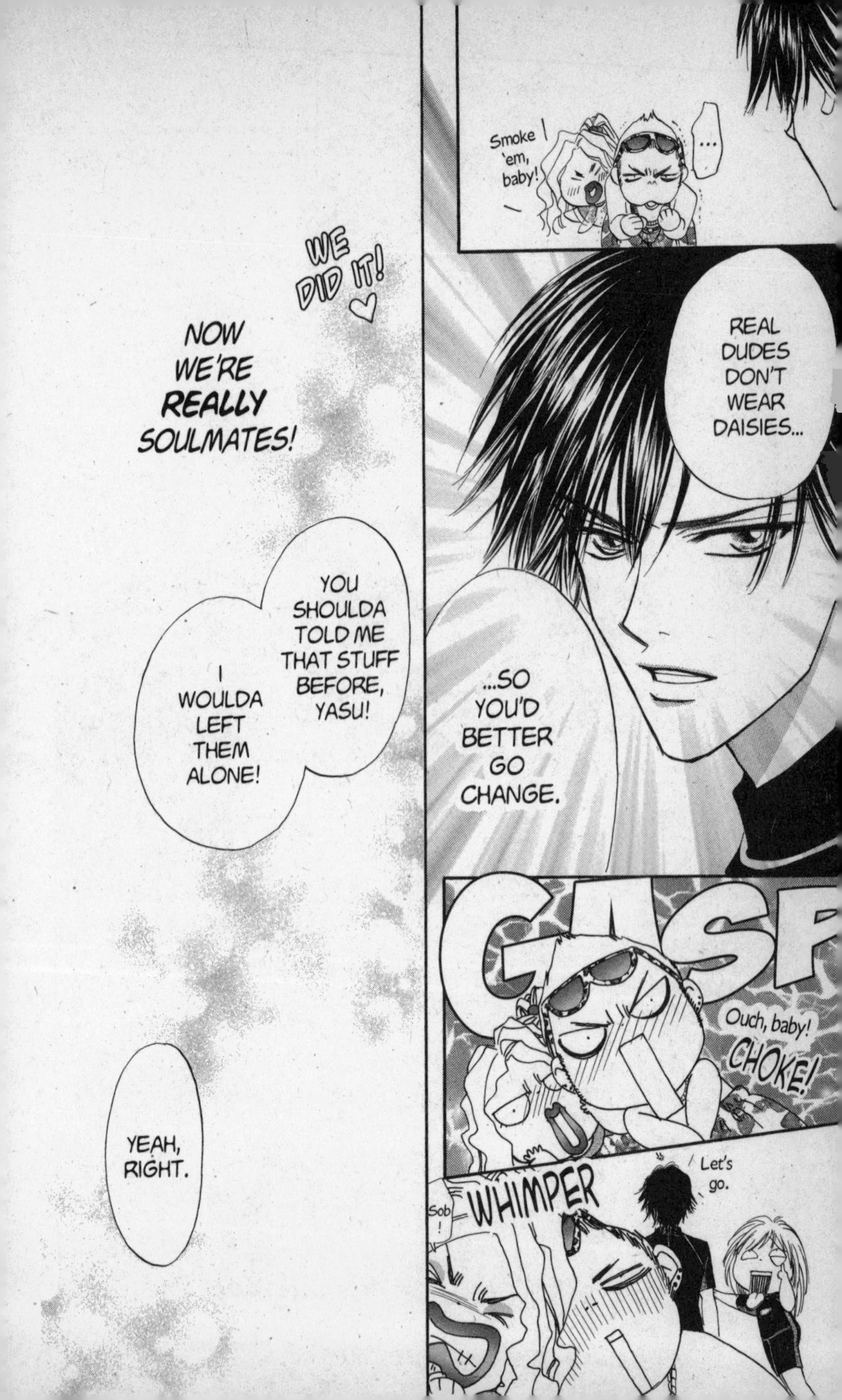
...
Smoke 'em, baby!
REAL DUDES DON'T WEAR DAISIES...
...SO YOU'D BETTER GO CHANGE.
GASP
Ouch, baby!
CHOKE!
Let's go.
WHIMPER
Sob!
WE DID IT! ♡
NOW WE'RE **REALLY** SOULMATES!
YOU SHOULDA TOLD ME THAT STUFF BEFORE, YASU!
I WOULDA LEFT THEM ALONE!
YEAH, RIGHT.

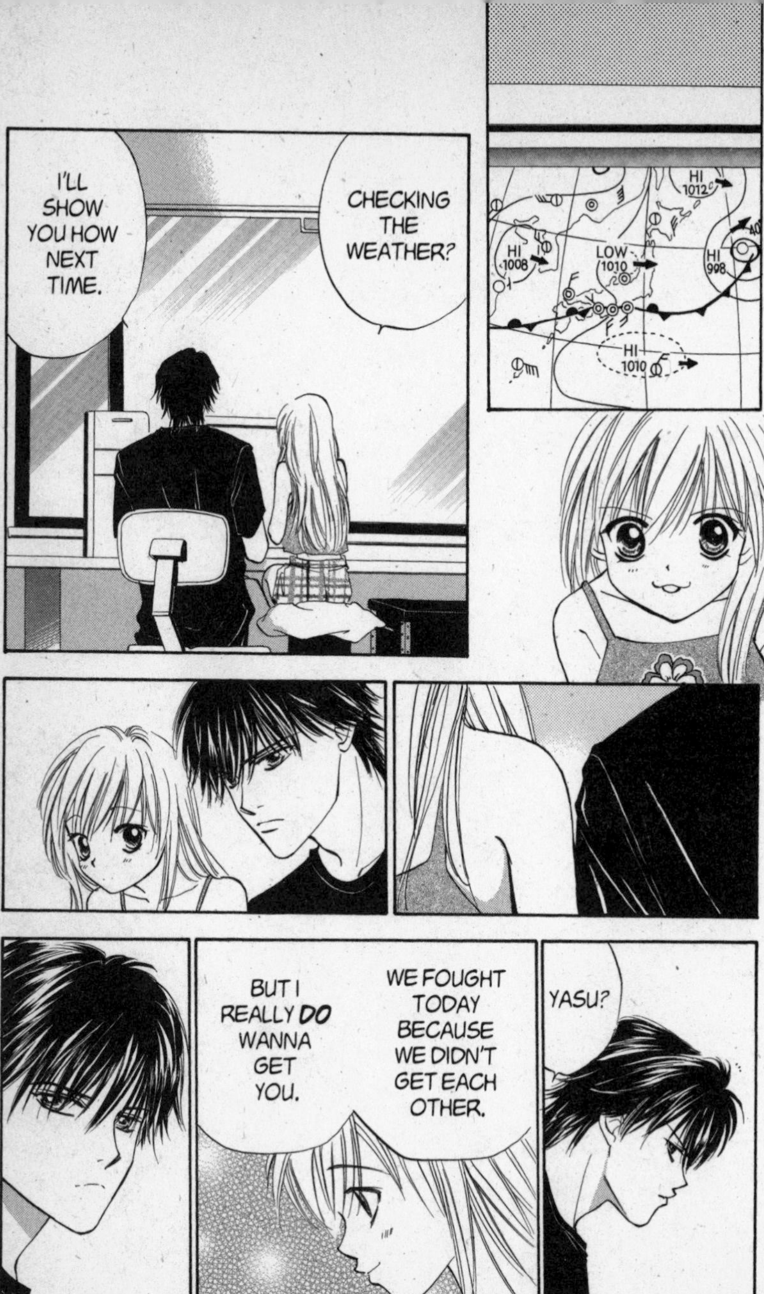
HI 1012
HI 1008
LOW 1010
HI 998
HI 1010
CHECKING THE WEATHER?
I'LL SHOW YOU HOW NEXT TIME.
YASU?
WE FOUGHT TODAY BECAUSE WE DIDN'T GET EACH OTHER.
BUT I REALLY **DO** WANNA GET YOU.

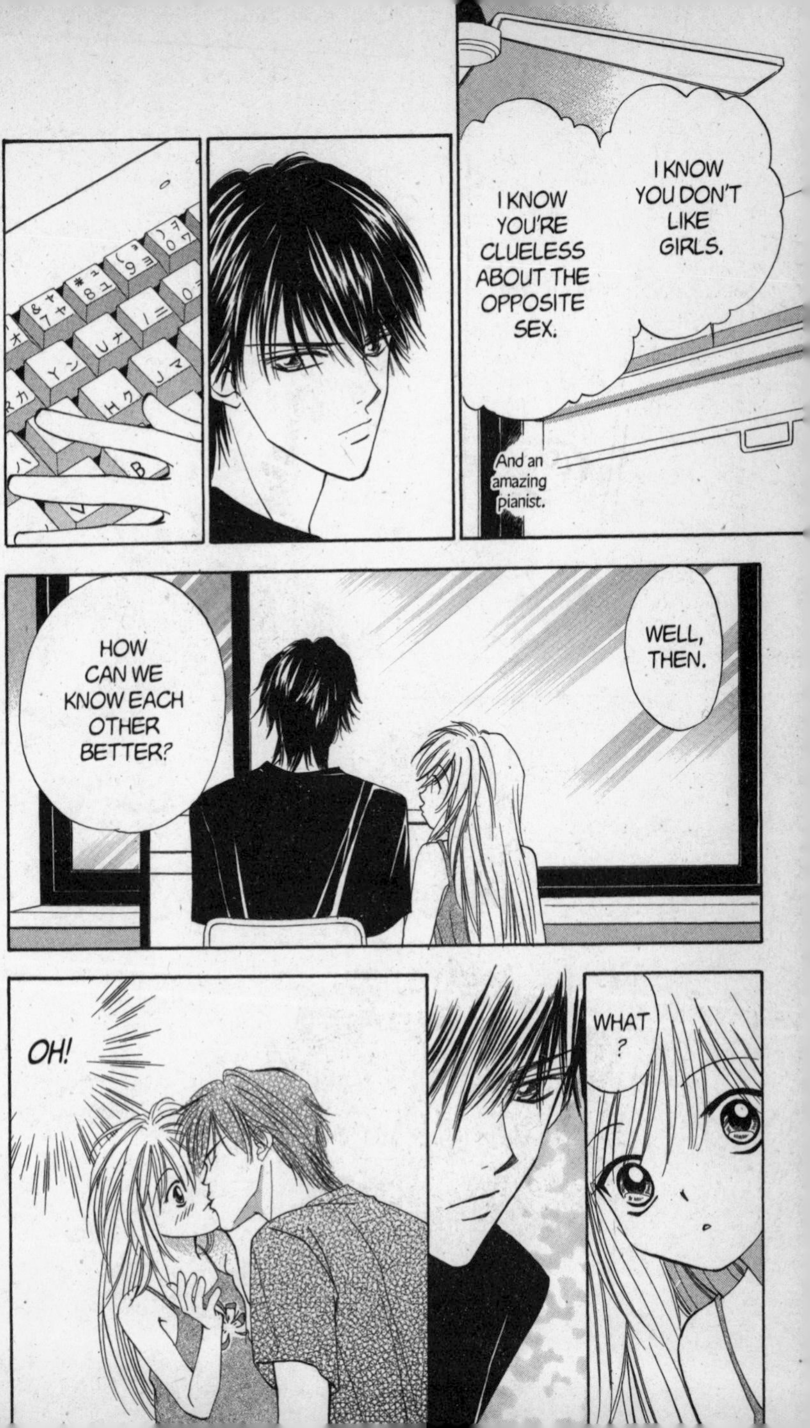
I KNOW YOU DON'T LIKE GIRLS.
I KNOW YOU'RE CLUELESS ABOUT THE OPPOSITE SEX.
And an amazing pianist.
WELL, THEN.
HOW CAN WE KNOW EACH OTHER BETTER?
WHAT ?
OH!

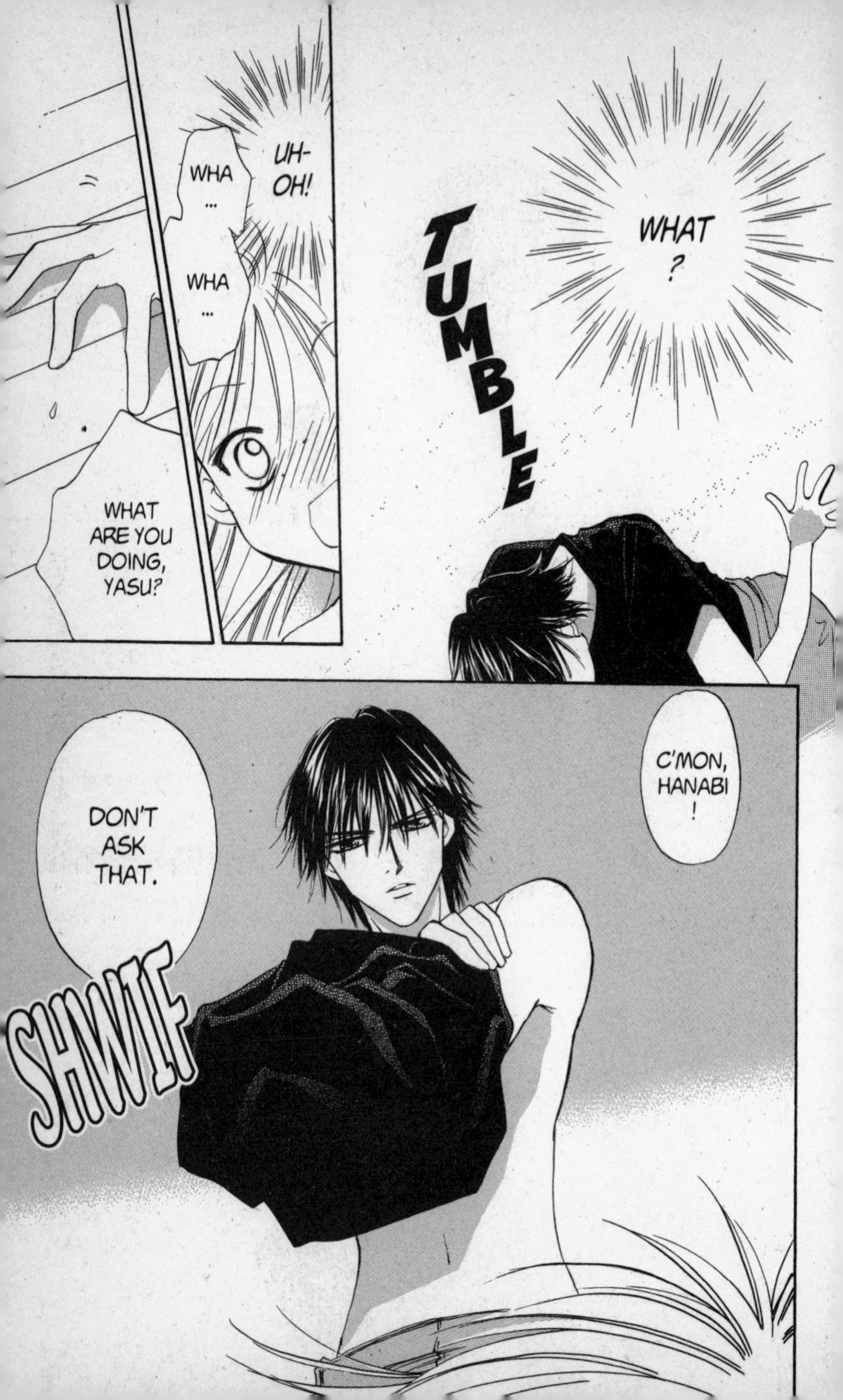
WHAT?
TUMBLE
UH-OH!
WHA...
WHA...
WHAT ARE YOU DOING, YASU?
C'MON, HANABI!
DON'T ASK THAT.
SHWIF

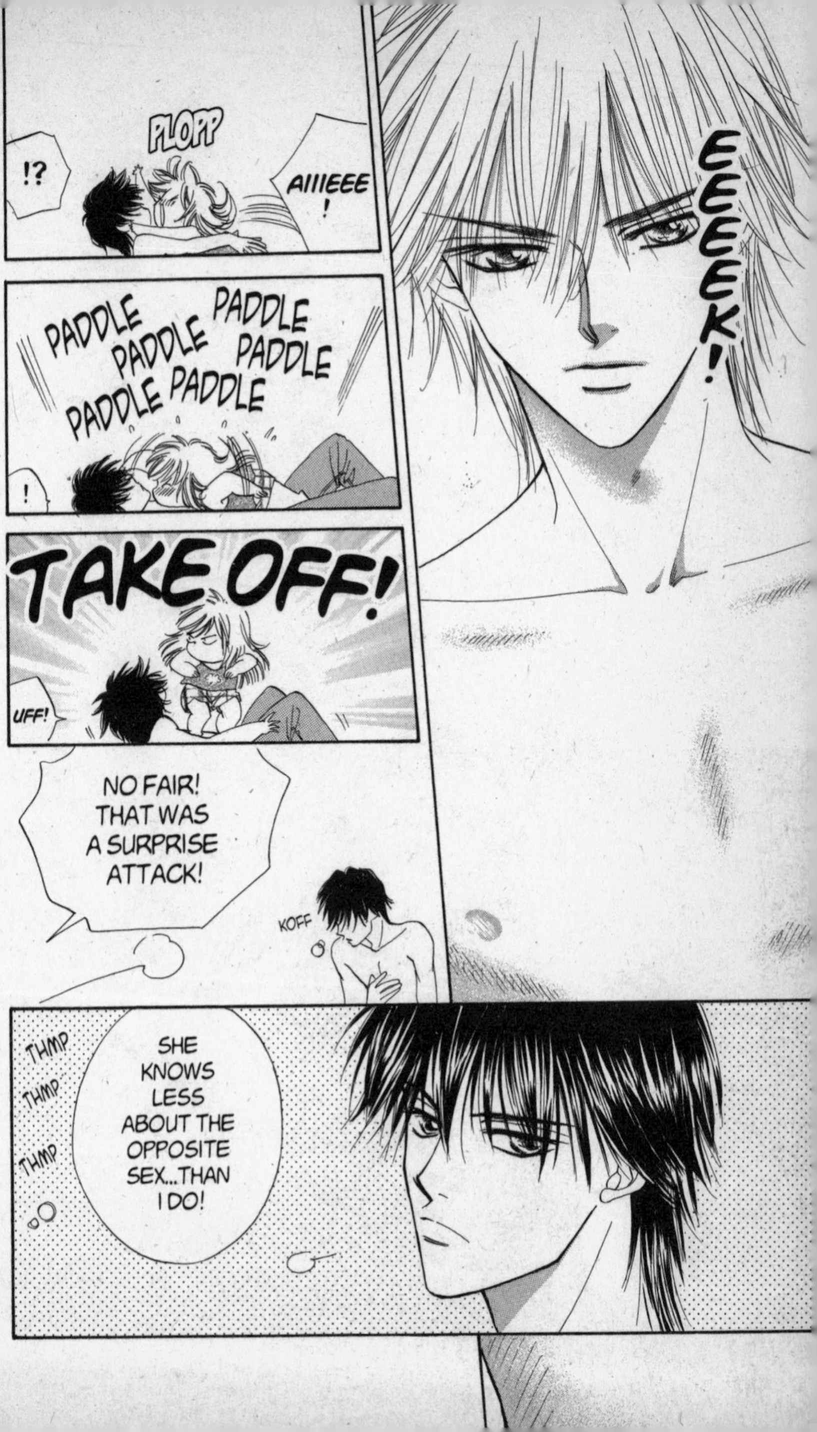
EEEEK!
AIIIEEE!
PLOPP
!?
PADDLE PADDLE PADDLE PADDLE PADDLE PADDLE
!
TAKE OFF!
UFF!
NO FAIR! THAT WAS A SURPRISE ATTACK!
KOFF
SHE KNOWS LESS ABOUT THE OPPOSITE SEX...THAN I DO!
THMP THMP THMP

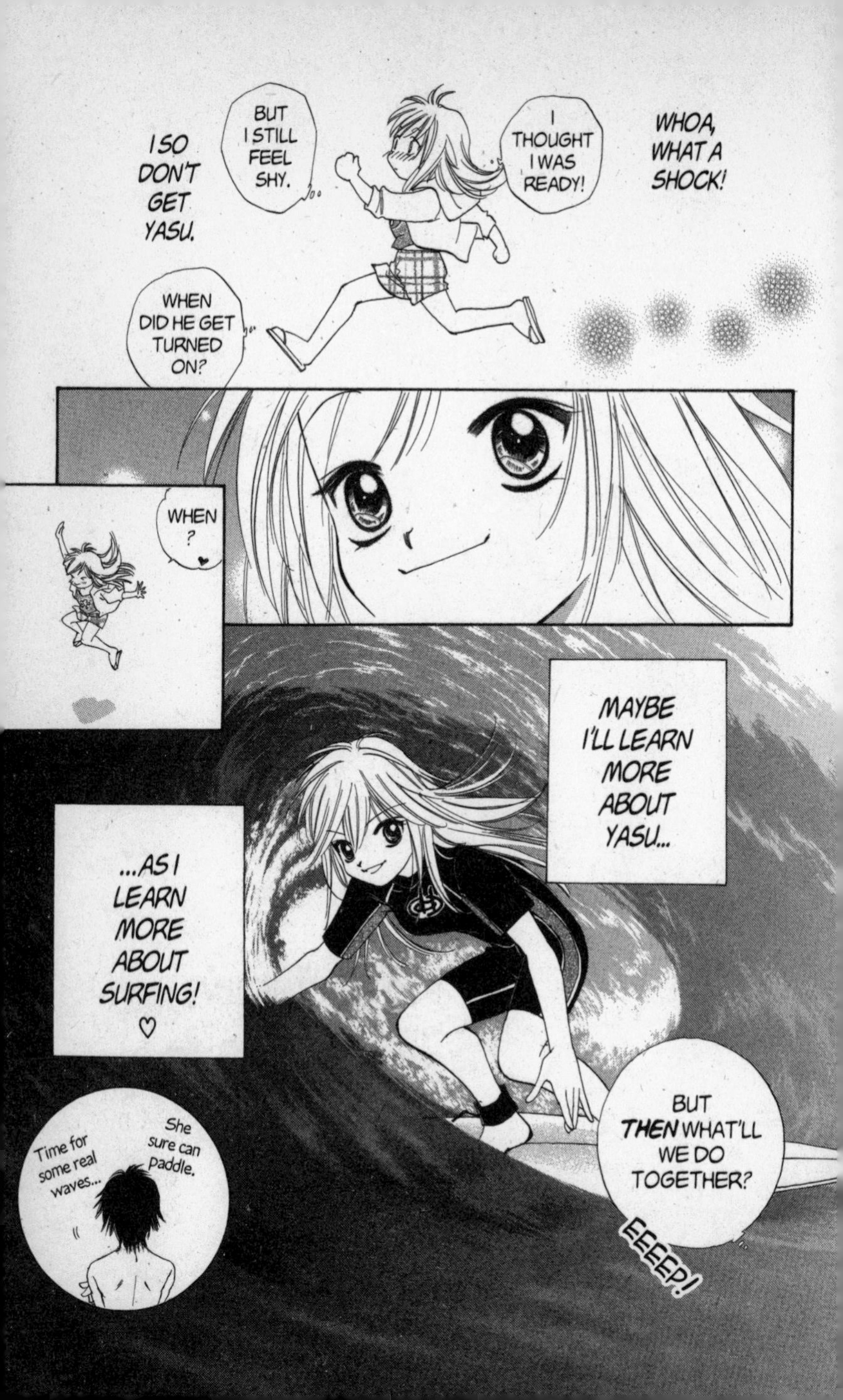
WHOA, WHAT A SHOCK!
I THOUGHT I WAS READY!
BUT I STILL FEEL SHY.
I SO DON'T GET YASU.
WHEN DID HE GET TURNED ON?
WHEN? ♥
MAYBE I'LL LEARN MORE ABOUT YASU...
...AS I LEARN MORE ABOUT SURFING! ♡
BUT **THEN** WHAT'LL WE DO TOGETHER?
EEEEP!
She sure can paddle.
Time for some real waves...

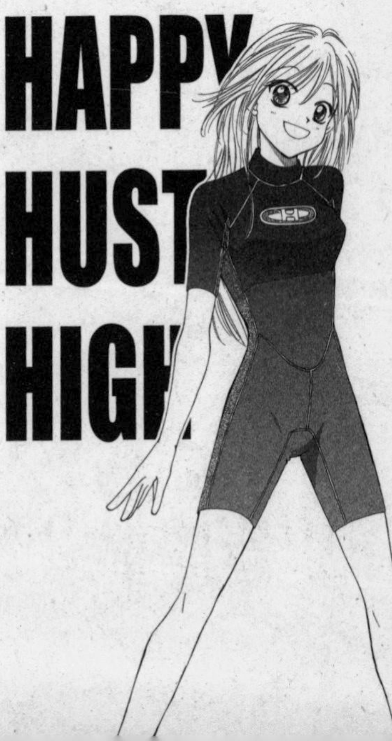
HAPPY
HUST
HIG

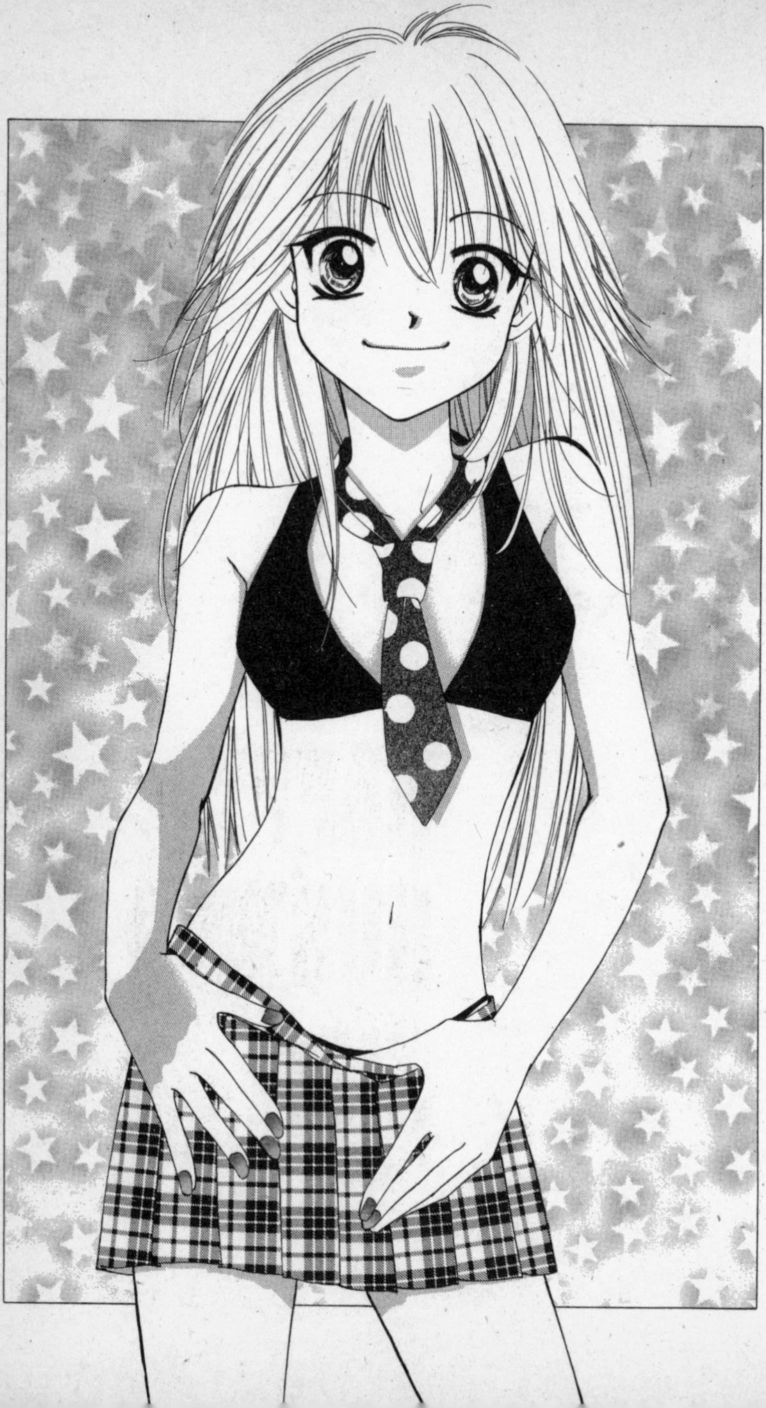

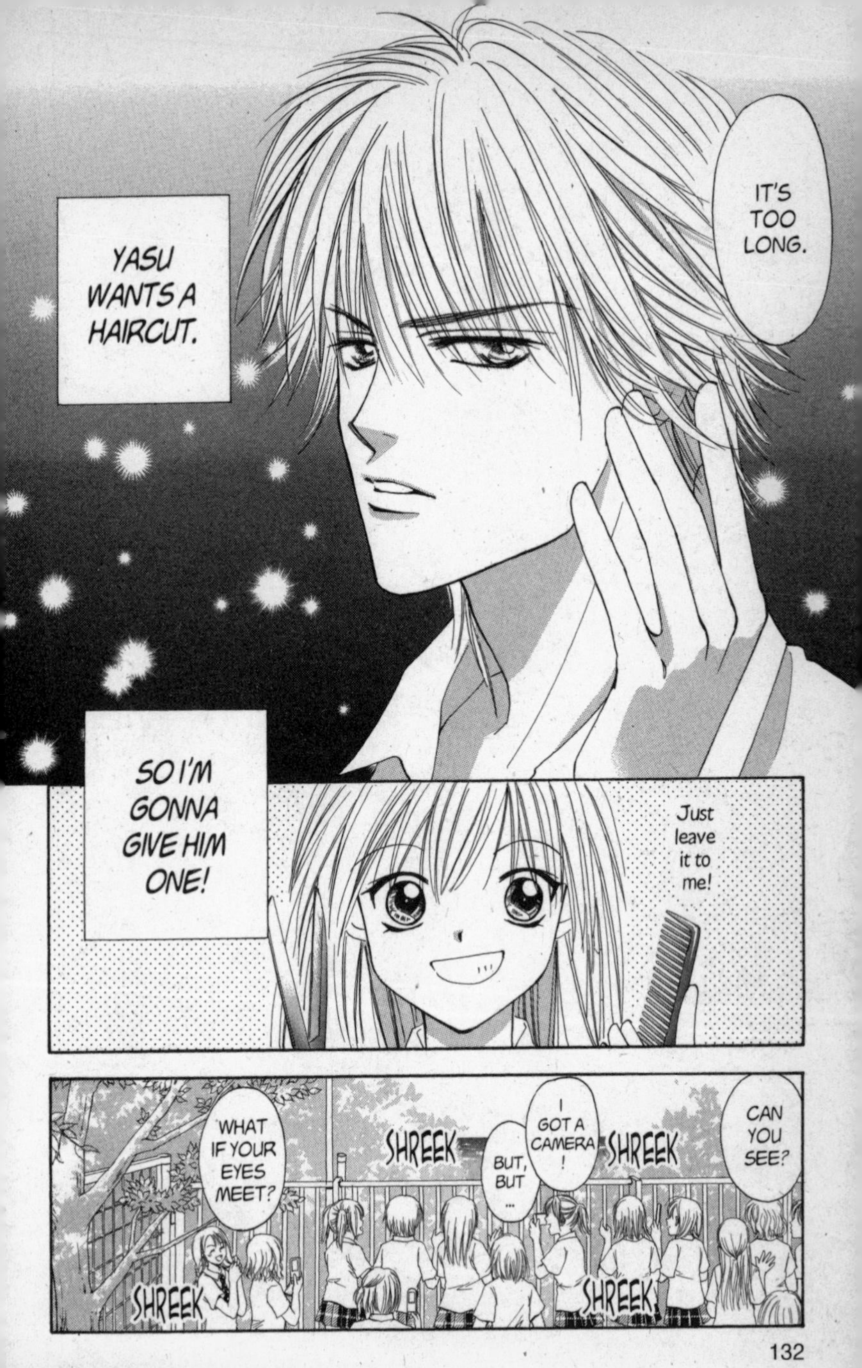
IT'S TOO LONG.
YASU WANTS A HAIRCUT.
SO I'M GONNA GIVE HIM ONE!
Just leave it to me!
CAN YOU SEE?
SHREEK
I GOT A CAMERA!
BUT, BUT...
SHREEK
WHAT IF YOUR EYES MEET?
SHREEK
SHREEK

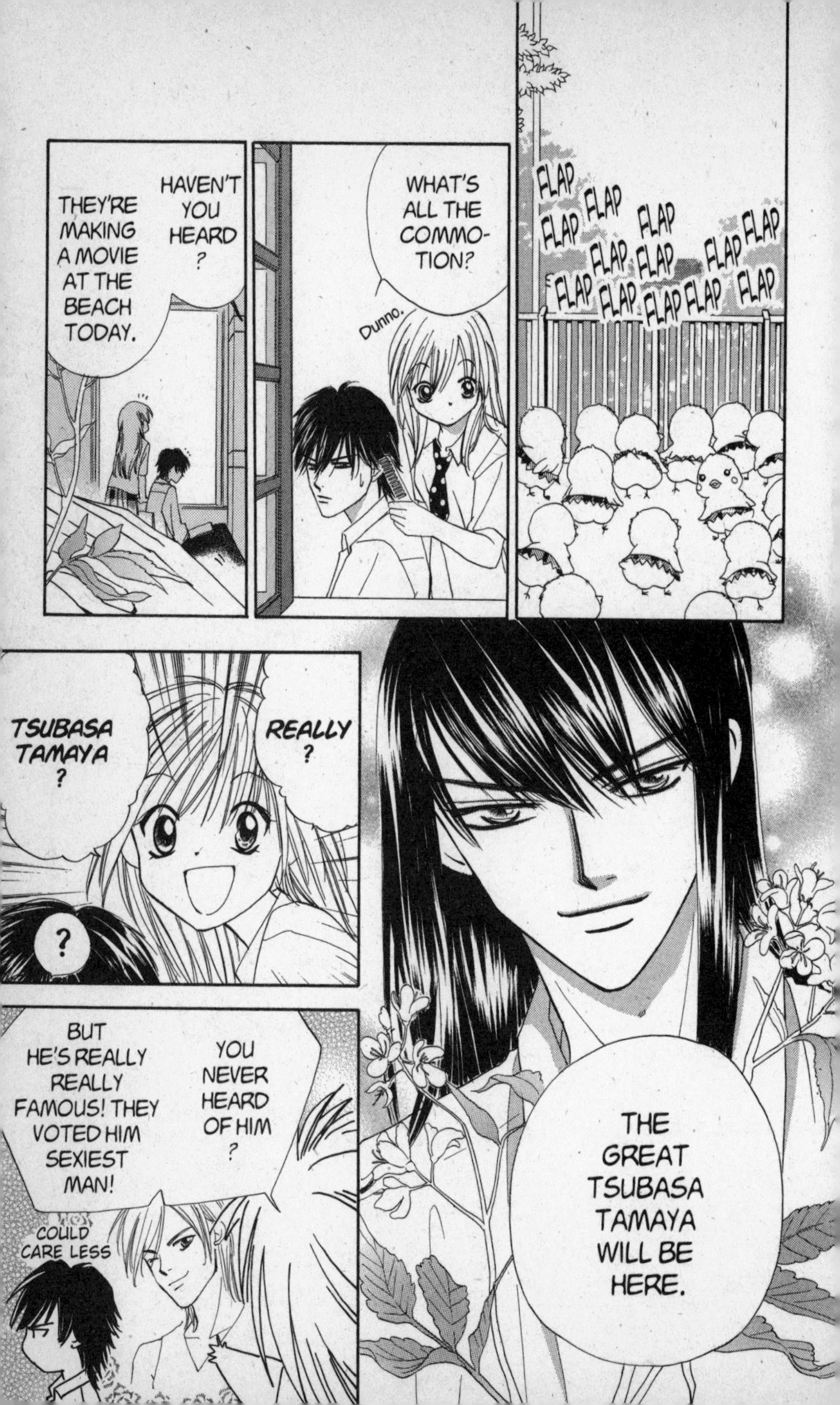
FLAP FLAP FLAP FLAP FLAP FLAP FLAP FLAP FLAP FLAP FLAP FLAP FLAP FLAP
WHAT'S ALL THE COMMOTION?
Dunno.
HAVEN'T YOU HEARD?
THEY'RE MAKING A MOVIE AT THE BEACH TODAY.
THE GREAT TSUBASA TAMAYA WILL BE HERE.
REALLY?
TSUBASA TAMAYA?
?
YOU NEVER HEARD OF HIM?
BUT HE'S REALLY REALLY FAMOUS! THEY VOTED HIM SEXIEST MAN!
COULD CARE LESS

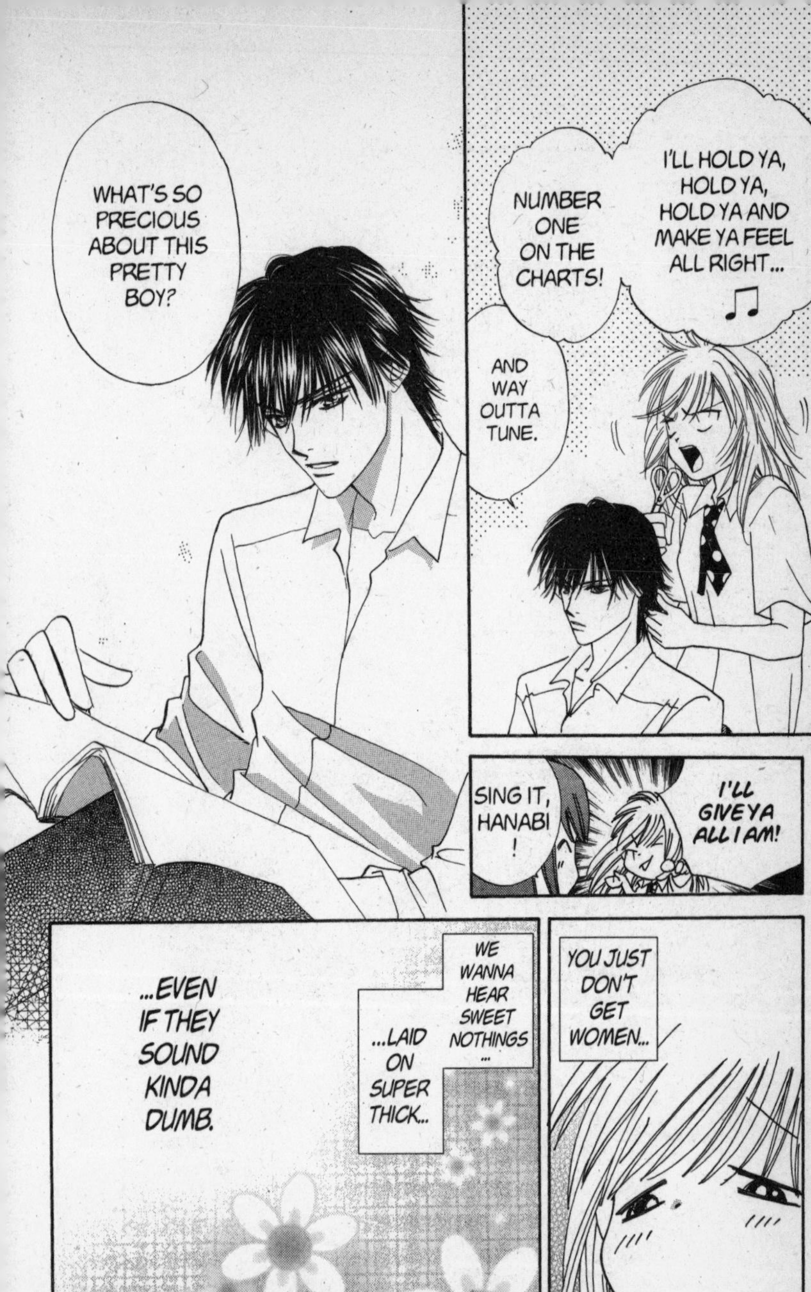
I'LL HOLD YA, HOLD YA, HOLD YA AND MAKE YA FEEL ALL RIGHT... ♫
NUMBER ONE ON THE CHARTS!
AND WAY OUTTA TUNE.
I'LL GIVE YA ALL I AM!
SING IT, HANABI!
WHAT'S SO PRECIOUS ABOUT THIS PRETTY BOY?
YOU JUST DON'T GET WOMEN...
WE WANNA HEAR SWEET NOTHINGS...
...LAID ON SUPER THICK...
...EVEN IF THEY SOUND KINDA DUMB.

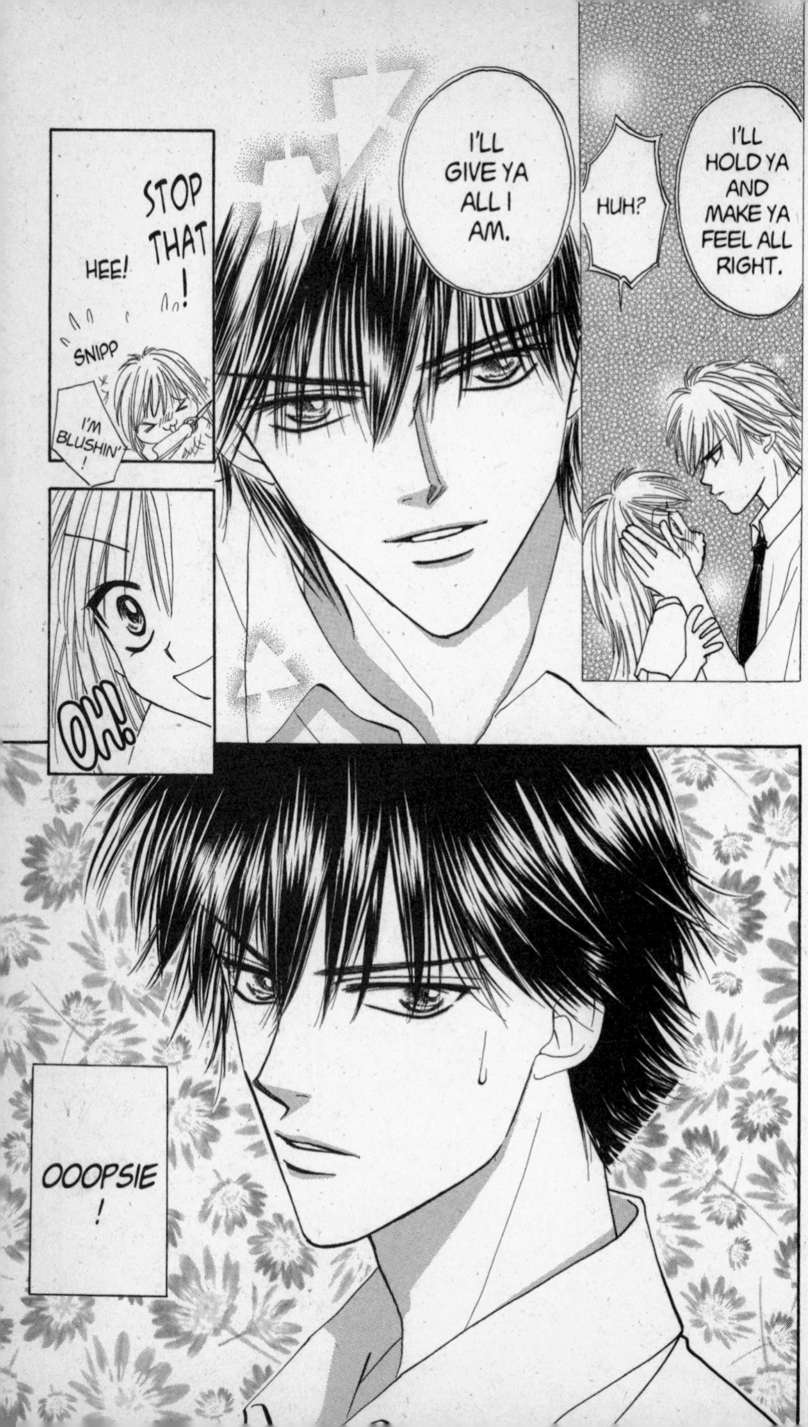
I'LL HOLD YA AND MAKE YA FEEL ALL RIGHT.
HUH?
I'LL GIVE YA ALL I AM.
STOP THAT!
HEE!
SNIPP
I'M BLUSHIN'!
OH!
OOOPSIE!

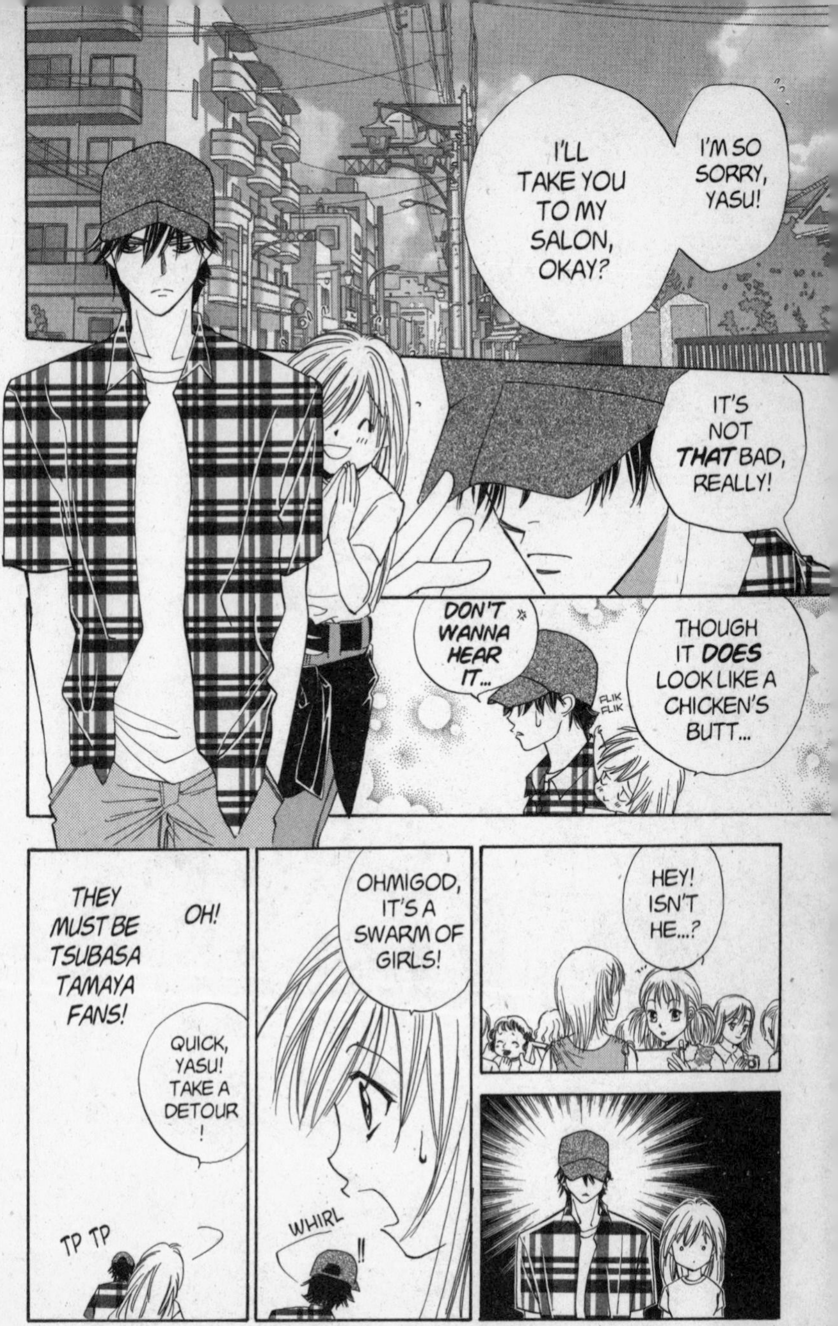
I'M SO SORRY, YASU!
I'LL TAKE YOU TO MY SALON, OKAY?
IT'S NOT **THAT** BAD, REALLY!
THOUGH IT **DOES** LOOK LIKE A CHICKEN'S BUTT...
FLIK FLIK
DON'T WANNA HEAR IT...
HEY! ISN'T HE...?
OHMIGOD, IT'S A SWARM OF GIRLS!
WHIRL
!!
OH!
THEY MUST BE TSUBASA TAMAYA FANS!
QUICK, YASU! TAKE A DETOUR!
TP TP

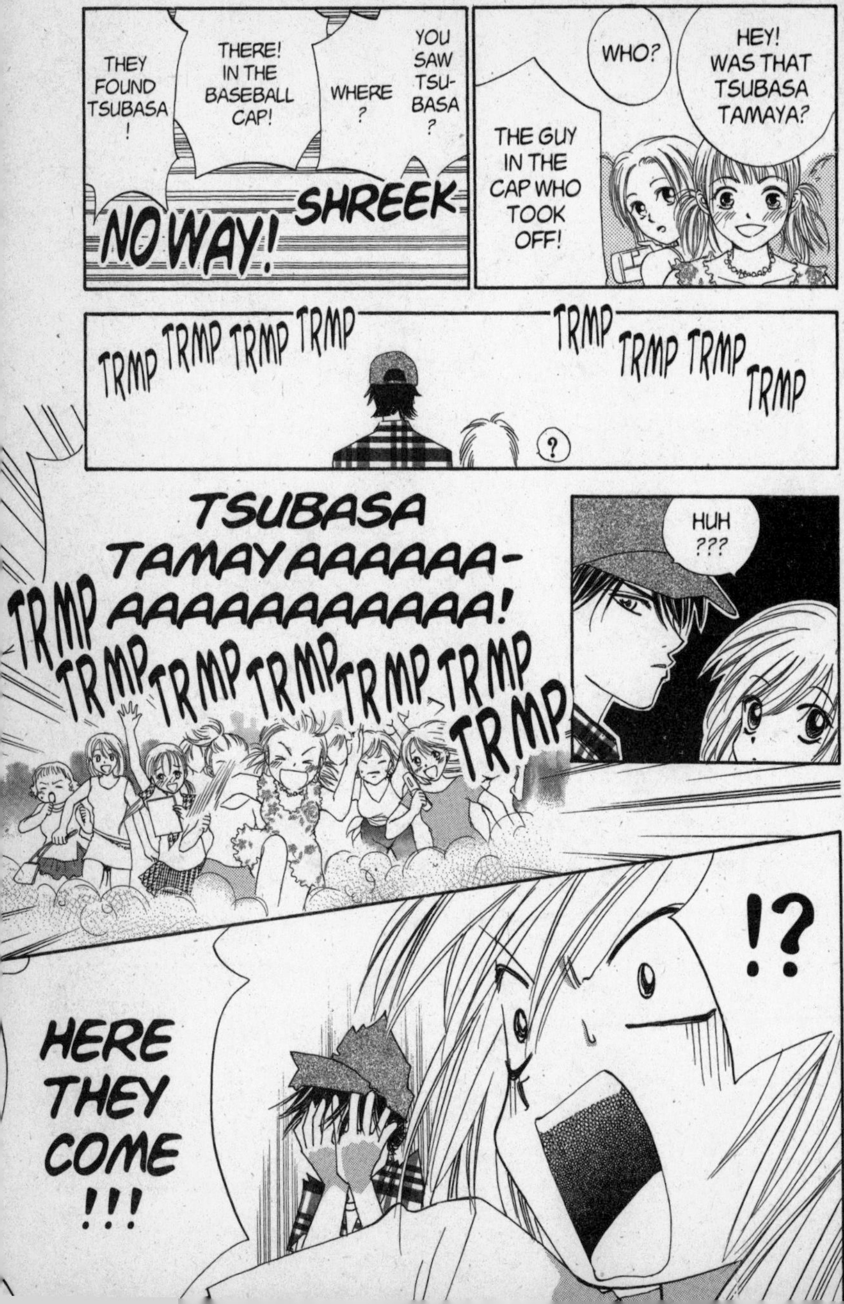

HEY! WAS THAT TSUBASA TAMAYA?
WHO?
THE GUY IN THE CAP WHO TOOK OFF!
YOU SAW TSU-BASA?
WHERE?
THERE! IN THE BASEBALL CAP!
THEY FOUND TSUBASA!
SHREEK
NO WAY!
TRMP TRMP TRMP TRMP
TRMP TRMP TRMP TRMP
?
HUH ???
TSUBASA TAMAYAAAAAA-AAAAAAAAAAAA!
TRMP TRMP TRMP TRMP TRMP TRMP TRMP
!?
HERE THEY COME!!!

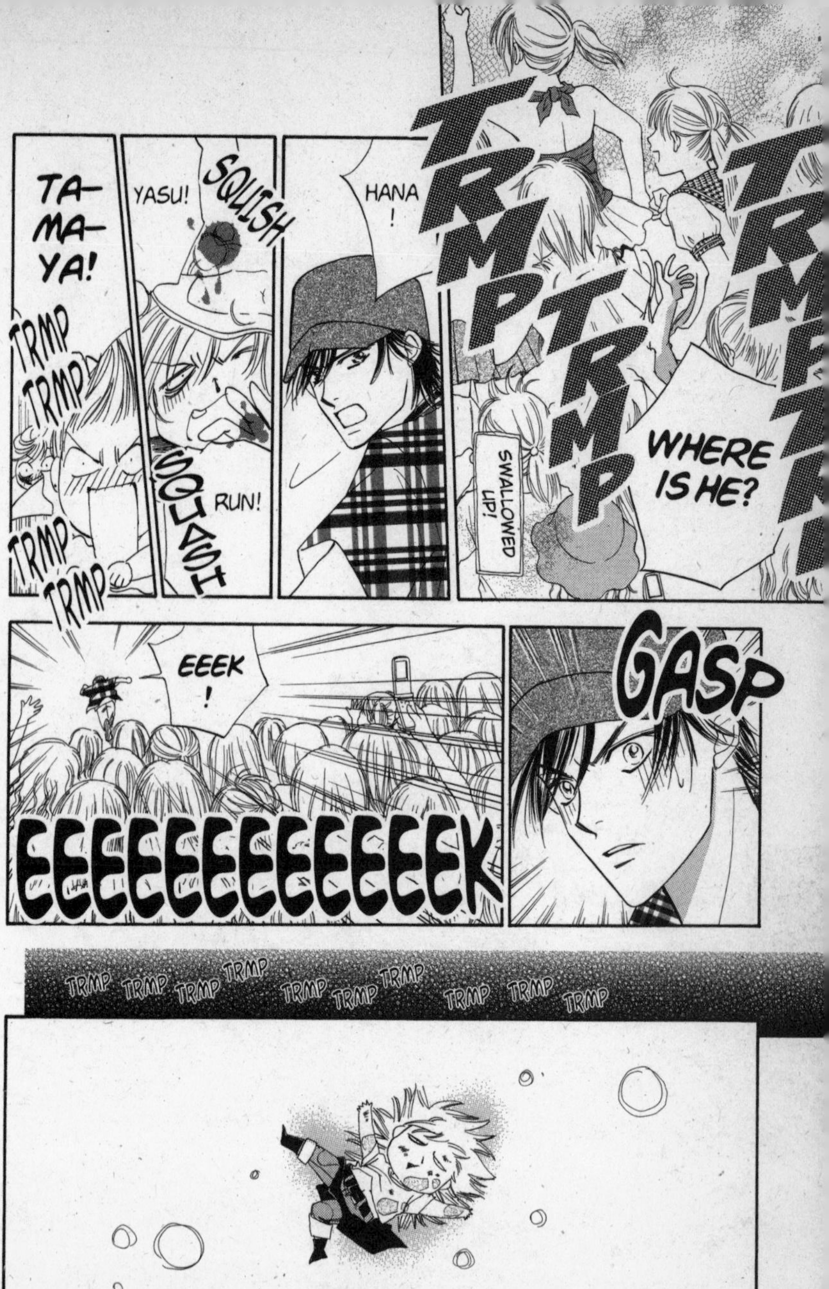
TRMP
TRMP
WHERE IS HE?
SWALLOWED UP!
TRMP
HANA!
YASU!
SQUISH
SQUASH
RUN!
TA-MA-YA!
TRMP TRMP
TRMP TRMP
GASP
EEEK!
EEEEEEEEEEEEEK
TRMP TRMP TRMP TRMP TRMP TRMP TRMP TRMP TRMP TRMP

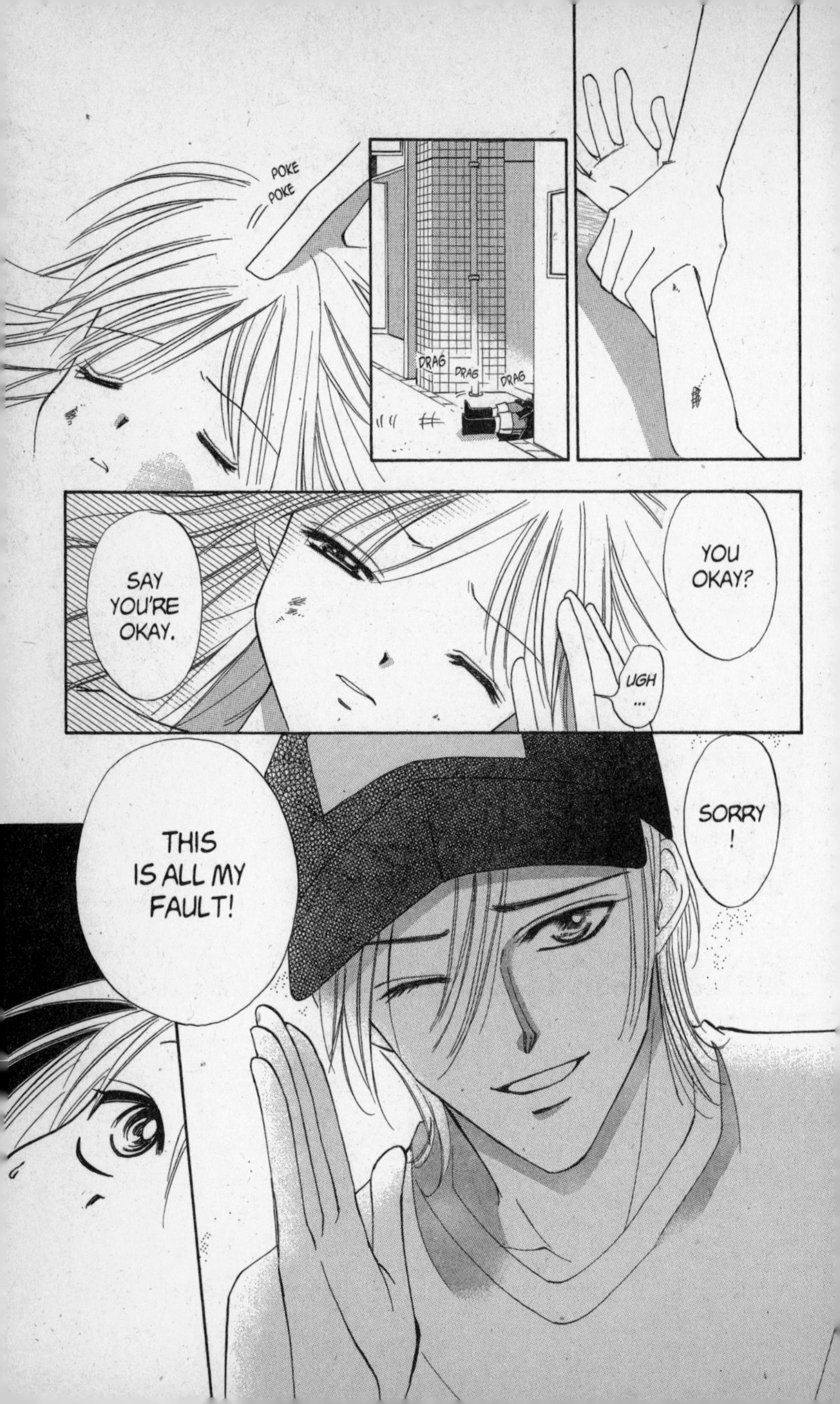
DRAG DRAG DRAG
POKE POKE
YOU OKAY?
UGH ...
SAY YOU'RE OKAY.
SORRY!
THIS IS ALL MY FAULT!

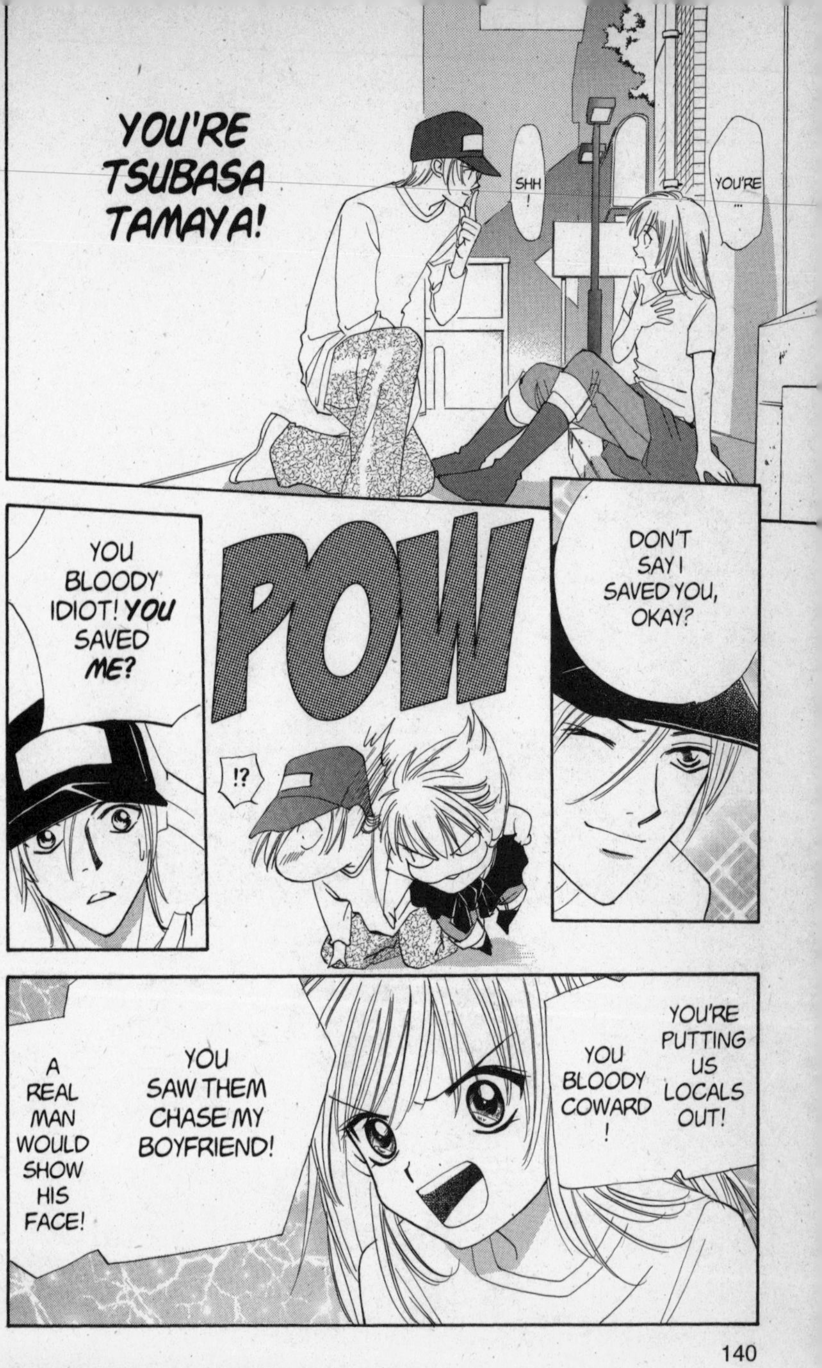
YOU'RE ...
SHH!
YOU'RE TSUBASA TAMAYA!
DON'T SAY I SAVED YOU, OKAY?
POW
!?
YOU BLOODY IDIOT! YOU SAVED ME?
YOU'RE PUTTING US LOCALS OUT!
YOU BLOODY COWARD!
YOU SAW THEM CHASE MY BOYFRIEND!
A REAL MAN WOULD SHOW HIS FACE!

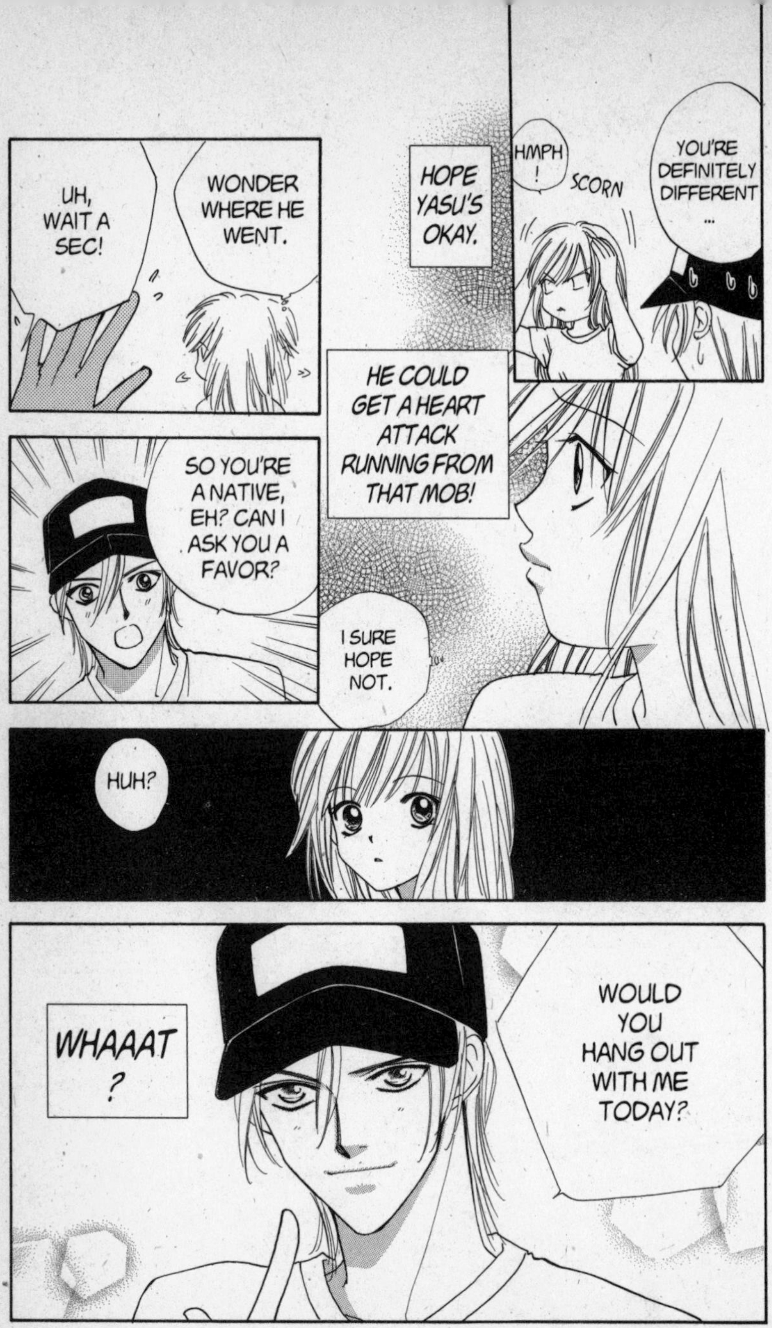
YOU'RE DEFINITELY DIFFERENT ...
HMPH !
SCORN
HOPE YASU'S OKAY.
WONDER WHERE HE WENT.
UH, WAIT A SEC!
HE COULD GET A HEART ATTACK RUNNING FROM THAT MOB!
I SURE HOPE NOT.
SO YOU'RE A NATIVE, EH? CAN I ASK YOU A FAVOR?
HUH?
WOULD YOU HANG OUT WITH ME TODAY?
WHAAAT ?

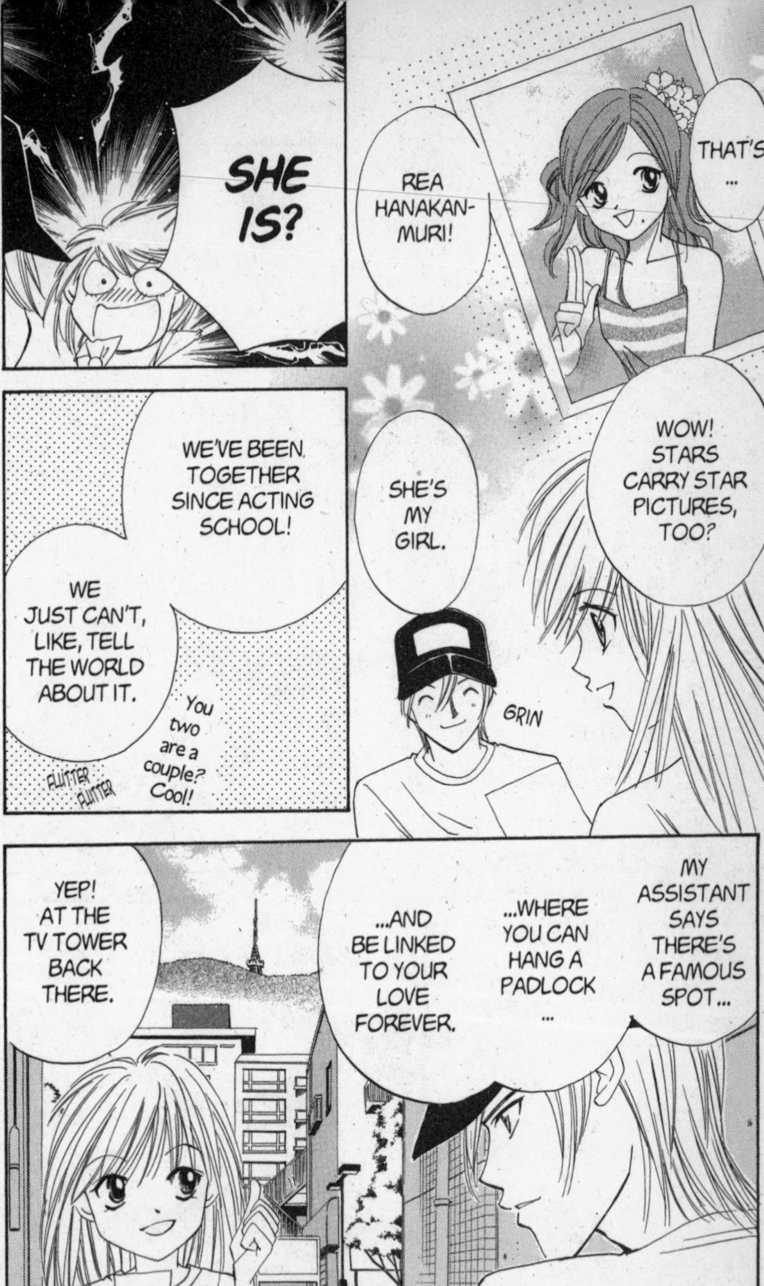
THAT'S ...
REA HANAKAN-MURI!
WOW! STARS CARRY STAR PICTURES, TOO?
SHE'S MY GIRL.
GRIN
SHE IS?
WE'VE BEEN TOGETHER SINCE ACTING SCHOOL!
WE JUST CAN'T, LIKE, TELL THE WORLD ABOUT IT.
You two are a couple? Cool!
FLUTTER FLUTTER
MY ASSISTANT SAYS THERE'S A FAMOUS SPOT...
...WHERE YOU CAN HANG A PADLOCK ...
...AND BE LINKED TO YOUR LOVE FOREVER.
YEP! AT THE TV TOWER BACK THERE.

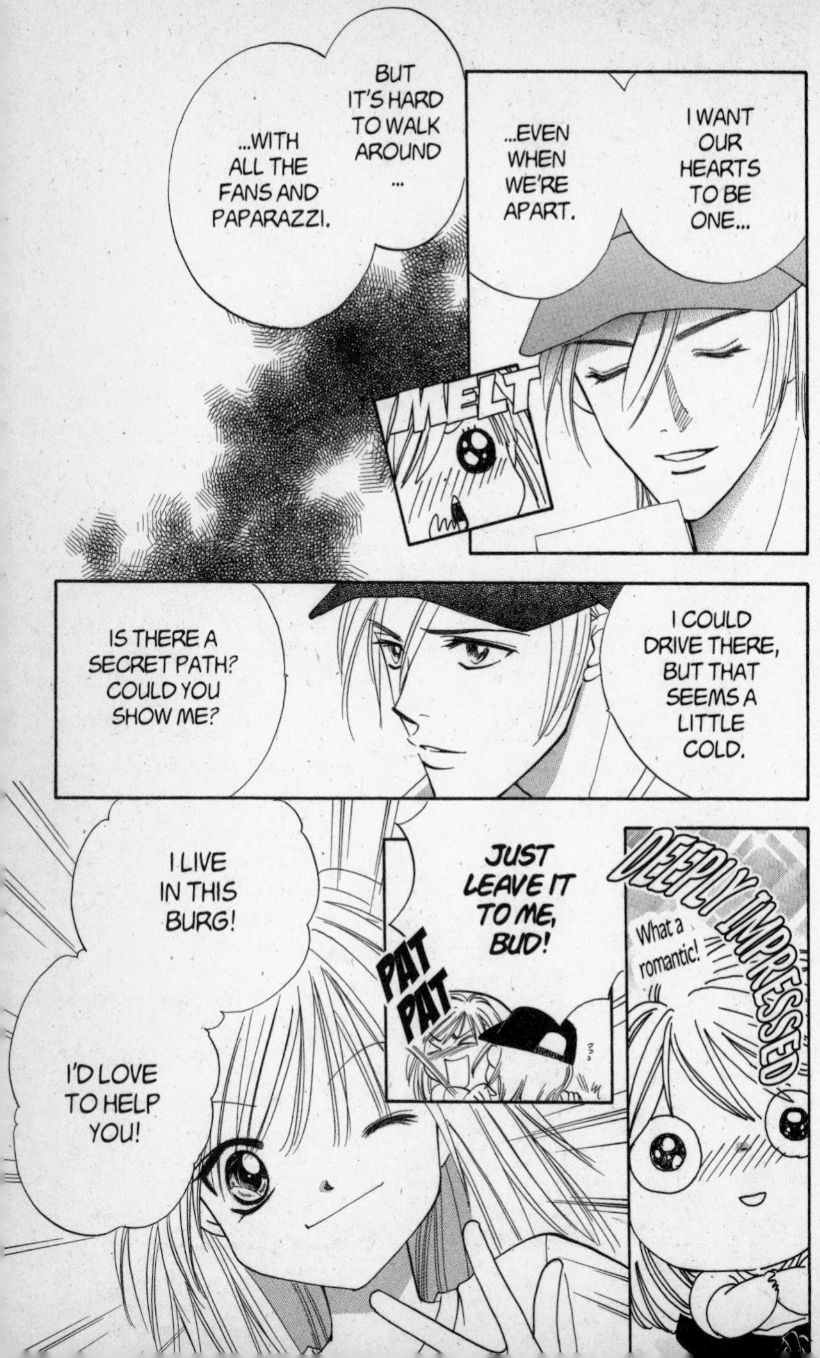
I WANT OUR HEARTS TO BE ONE...
...EVEN WHEN WE'RE APART.
MELT
BUT IT'S HARD TO WALK AROUND ...
...WITH ALL THE FANS AND PAPARAZZI.
I COULD DRIVE THERE, BUT THAT SEEMS A LITTLE COLD.
IS THERE A SECRET PATH? COULD YOU SHOW ME?
DEEPLY IMPRESSED
What a romantic!
JUST LEAVE IT TO ME, BUD!
PAT PAT
I LIVE IN THIS BURG!
I'D LOVE TO HELP YOU!

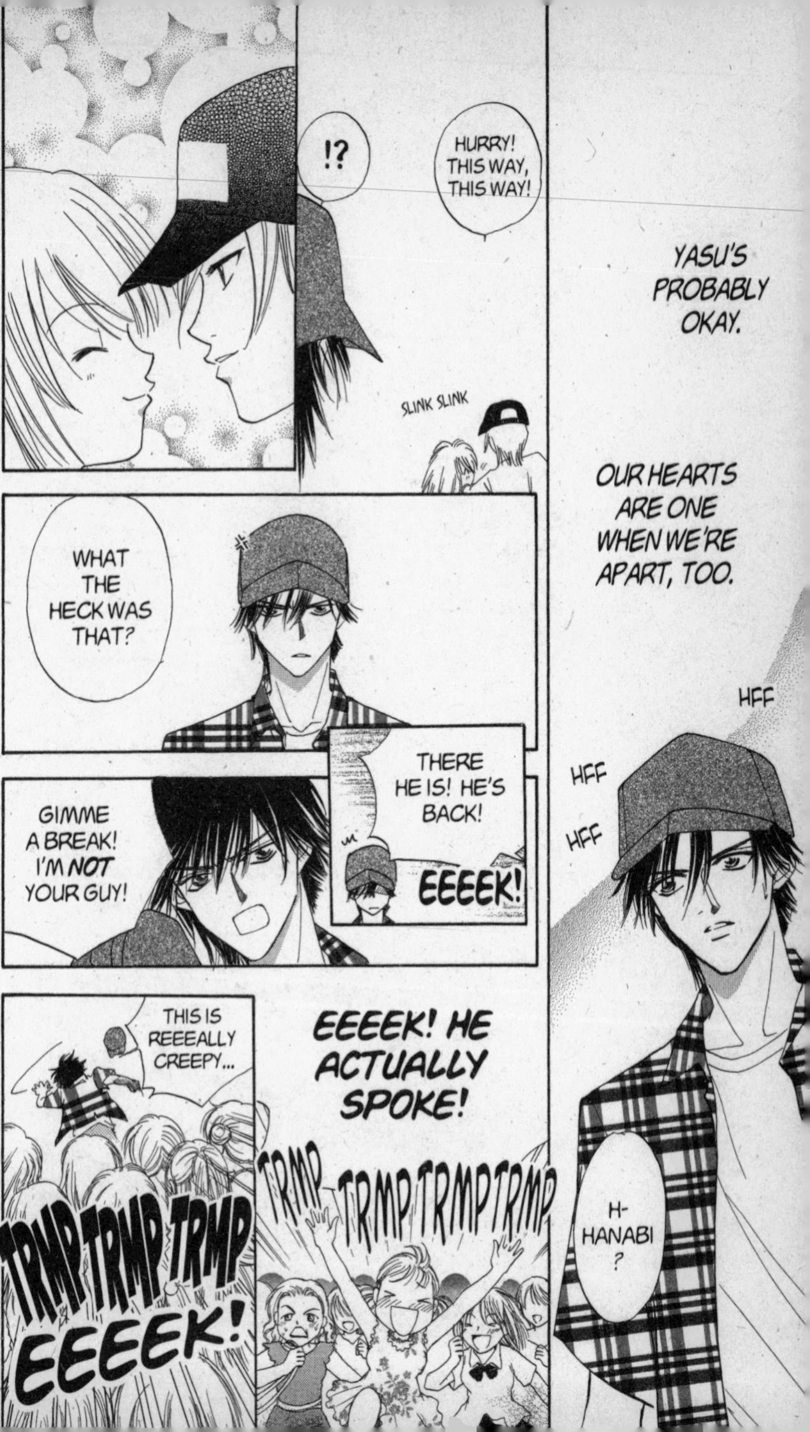
YASU'S PROBABLY OKAY.
OUR HEARTS ARE ONE WHEN WE'RE APART, TOO.
HFF
HFF
HFF
H- HANABI ?
HURRY! THIS WAY, THIS WAY!
!?
SLINK SLINK
WHAT THE HECK WAS THAT?
THERE HE IS! HE'S BACK!
EEEEK!
GIMME A BREAK! I'M *NOT* YOUR GUY!
EEEEK! HE ACTUALLY SPOKE!
TRMP TRMP TRMP TRMP
THIS IS REEEALLY CREEPY...
TRMP TRMP TRMP
EEEEK!

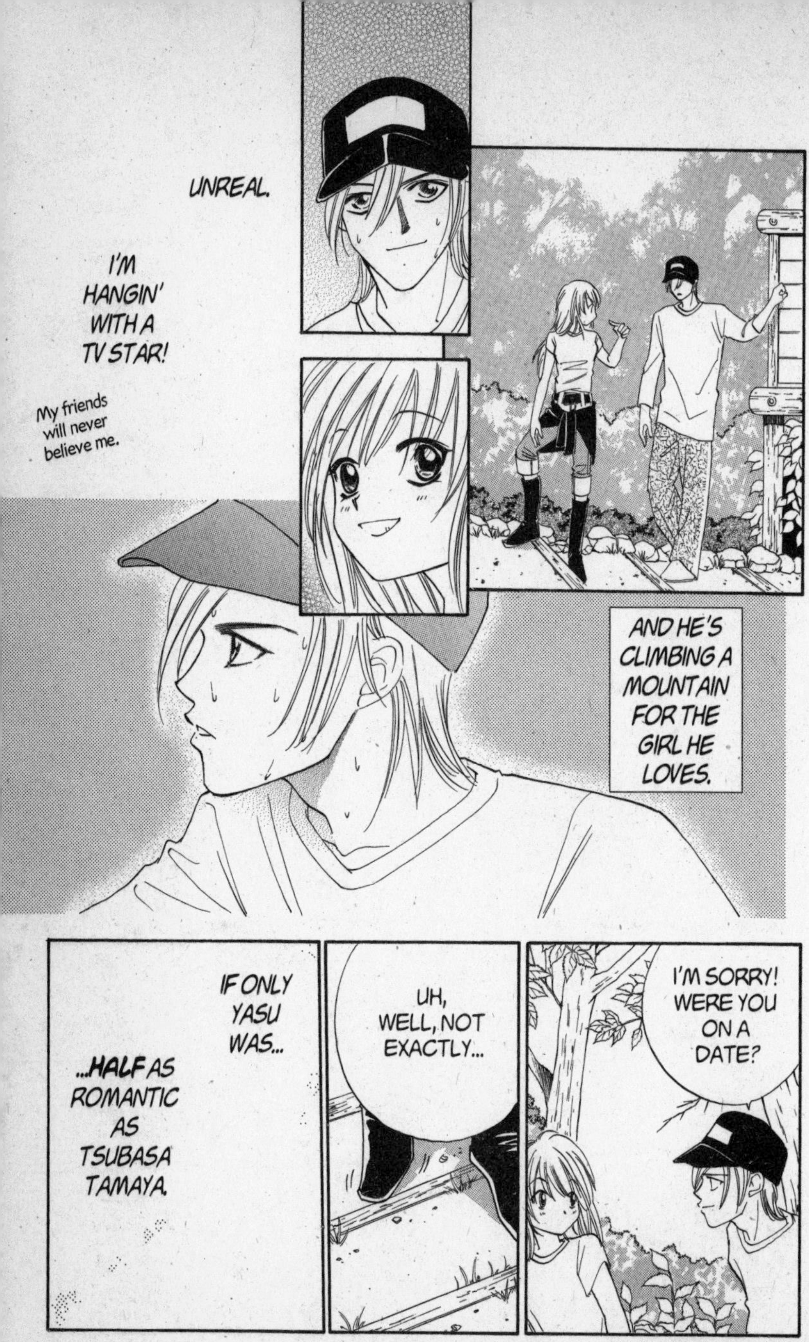
UNREAL.
I'M HANGIN' WITH A TV STAR!
My friends will never believe me.
AND HE'S CLIMBING A MOUNTAIN FOR THE GIRL HE LOVES.
I'M SORRY! WERE YOU ON A DATE?
UH, WELL, NOT EXACTLY...
IF ONLY YASU WAS...
...HALF AS ROMANTIC AS TSUBASA TAMAYA.

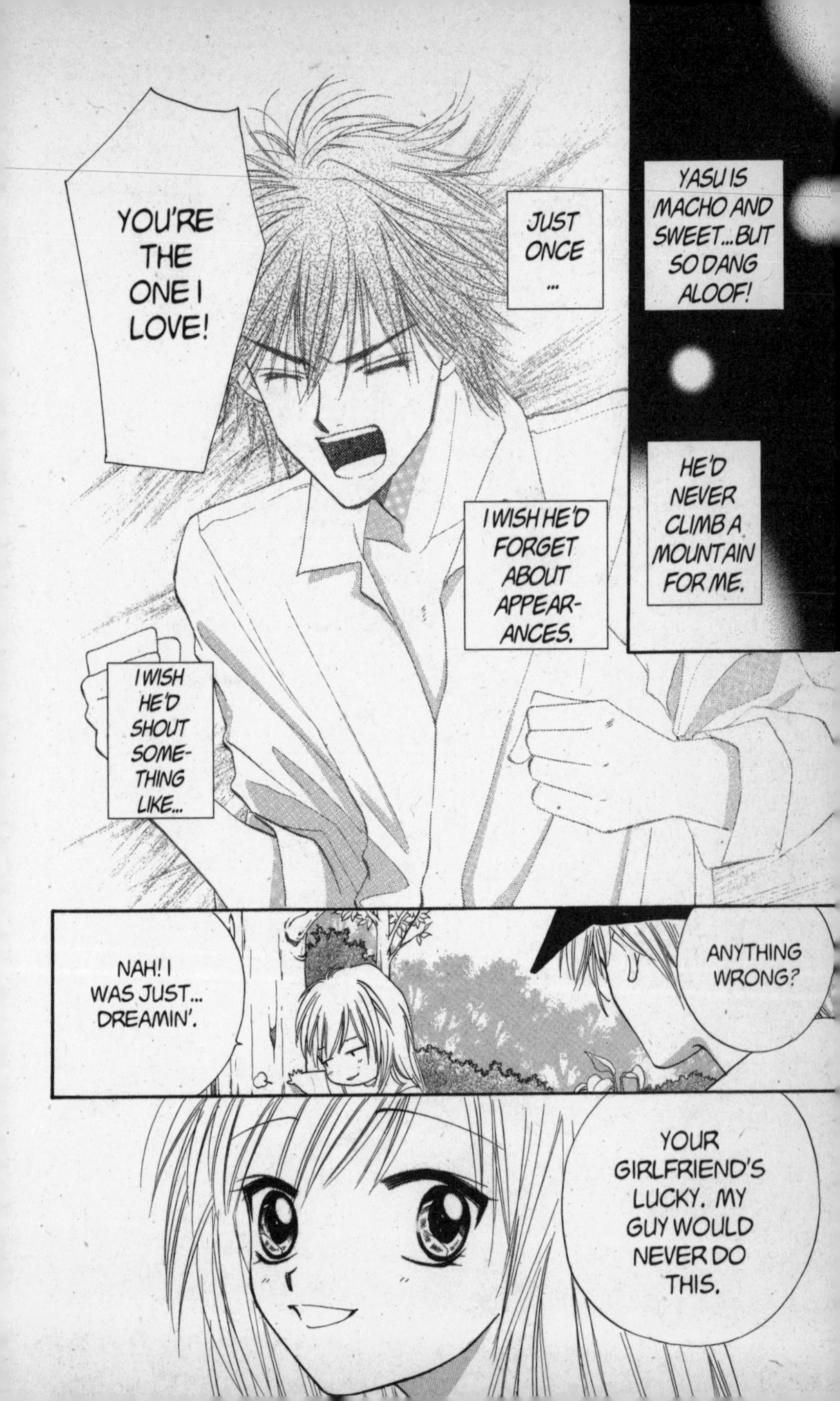
YASU IS MACHO AND SWEET...BUT SO DANG ALOOF!
HE'D NEVER CLIMB A MOUNTAIN FOR ME.
JUST ONCE ...
I WISH HE'D FORGET ABOUT APPEAR-ANCES.
I WISH HE'D SHOUT SOME-THING LIKE...
YOU'RE THE ONE I LOVE!
ANYTHING WRONG?
NAH! I WAS JUST... DREAMIN'.
YOUR GIRLFRIEND'S LUCKY. MY GUY WOULD NEVER DO THIS.

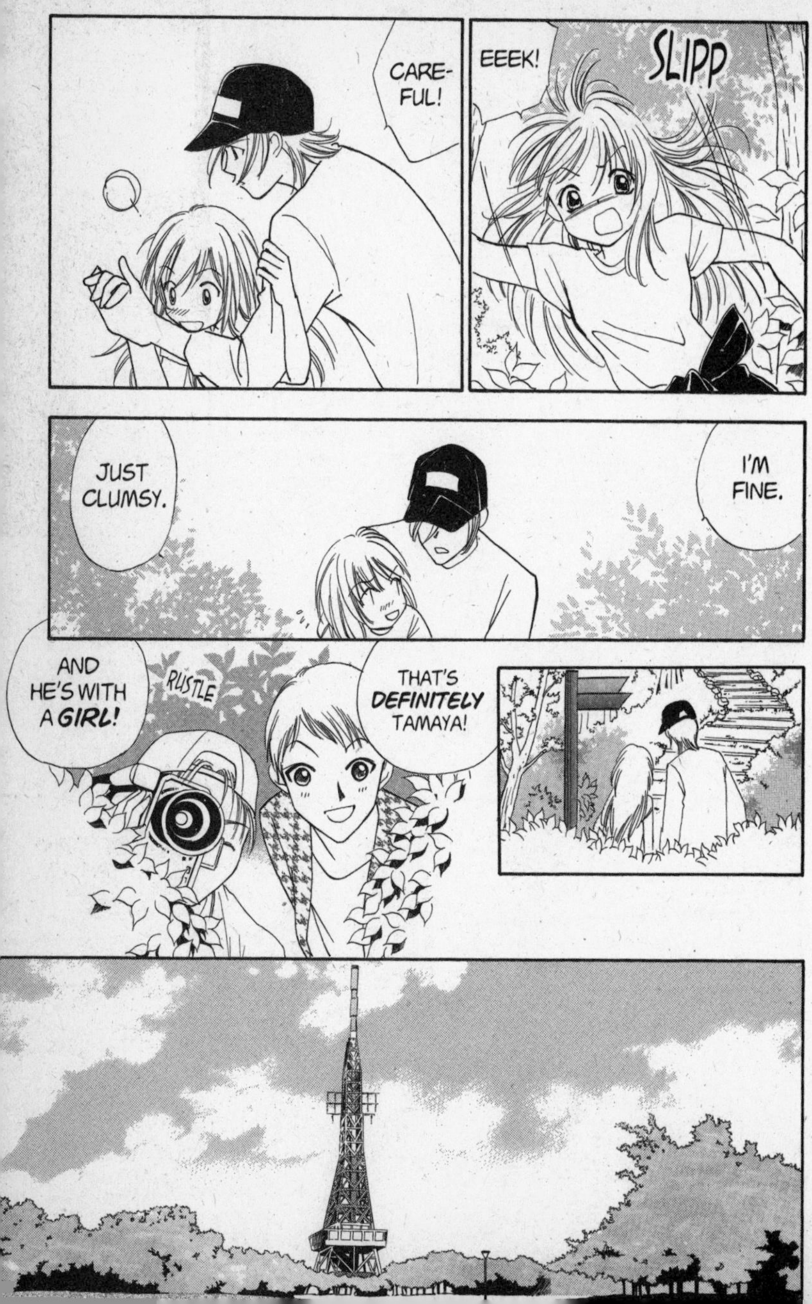
EEEK!
SLIPP
CARE-FUL!
I'M FINE.
JUST CLUMSY.
THAT'S DEFINITELY TAMAYA!
RUSTLE
AND HE'S WITH A GIRL!

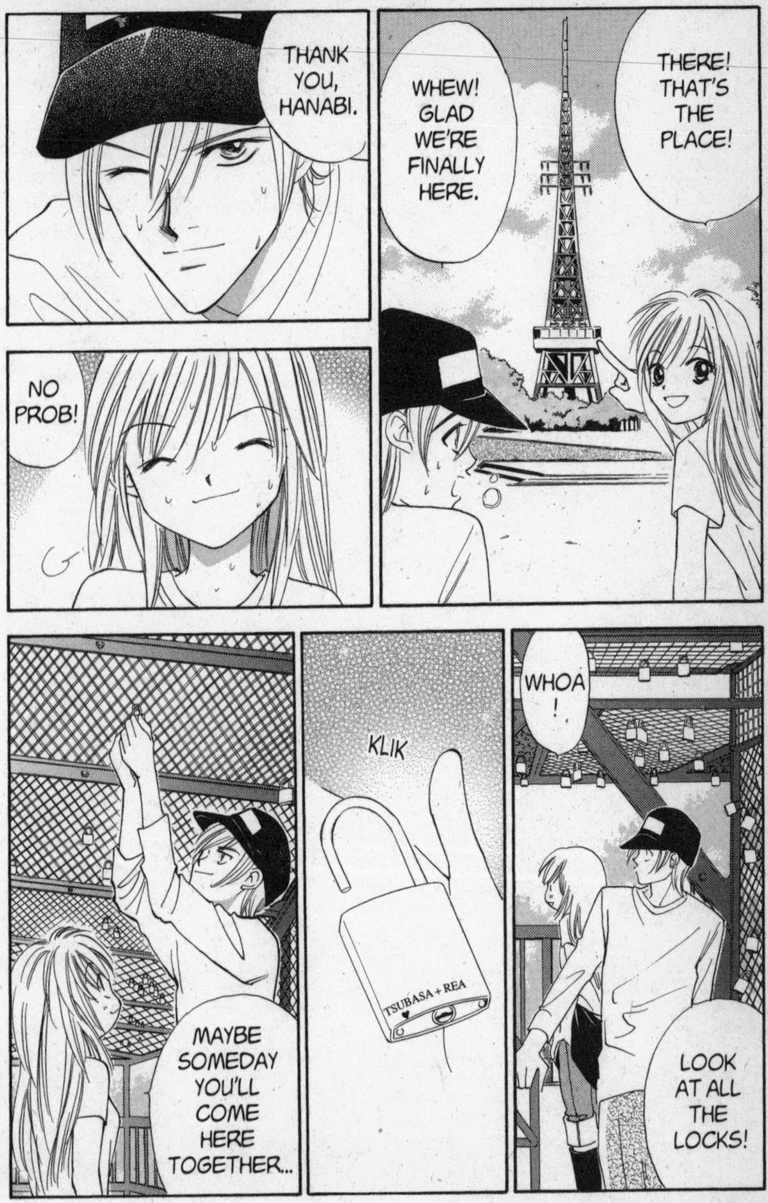
THERE! THAT'S THE PLACE!
WHEW! GLAD WE'RE FINALLY HERE.
THANK YOU, HANABI.
NO PROB!
WHOA!
LOOK AT ALL THE LOCKS!
KLIK
TSUBASA + REA
MAYBE SOMEDAY YOU'LL COME HERE TOGETHER...

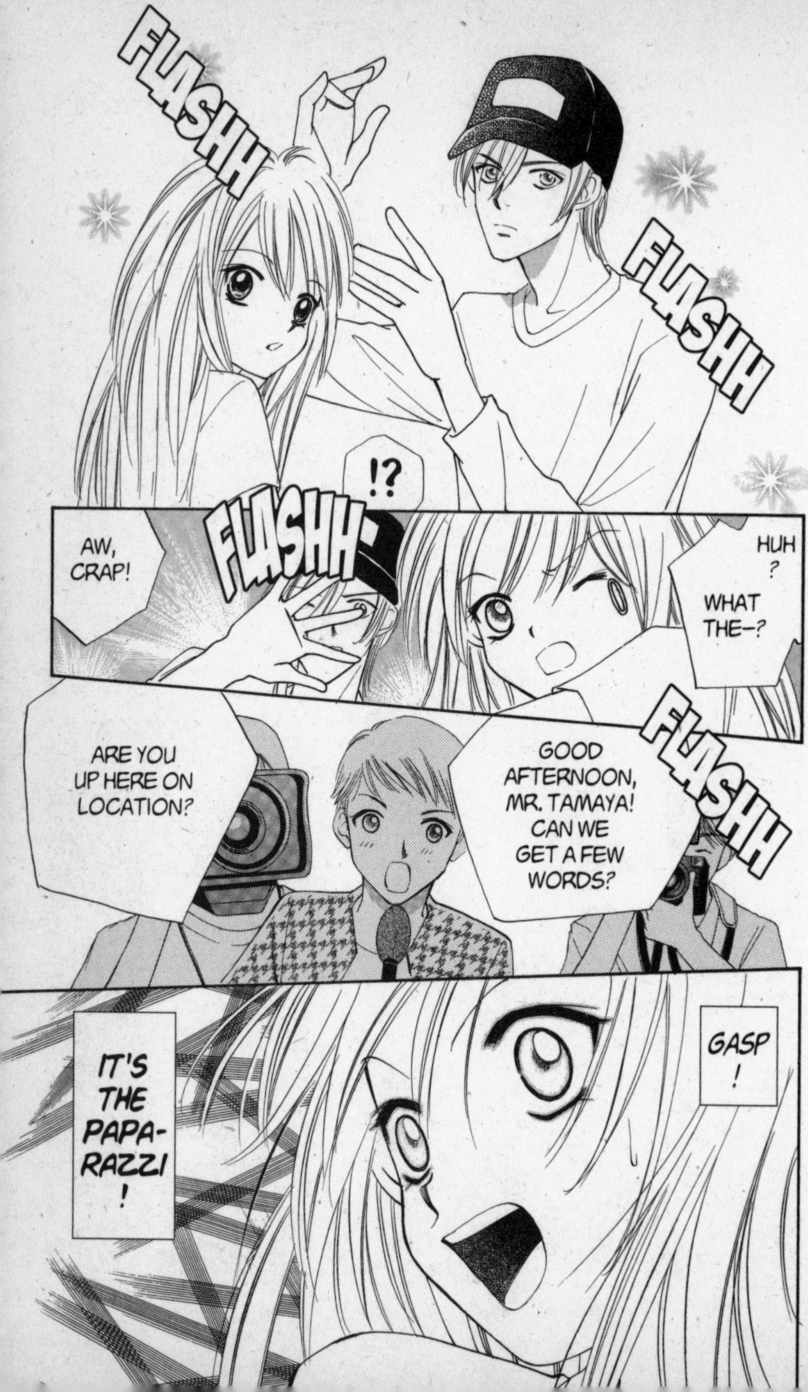
FLASHH
FLASHH
!?
HUH? WHAT THE-?
FLASHH
AW, CRAP!
FLASHH
GOOD AFTERNOON, MR. TAMAYA! CAN WE GET A FEW WORDS?
ARE YOU UP HERE ON LOCATION?
GASP!
IT'S THE PAPARAZZI!

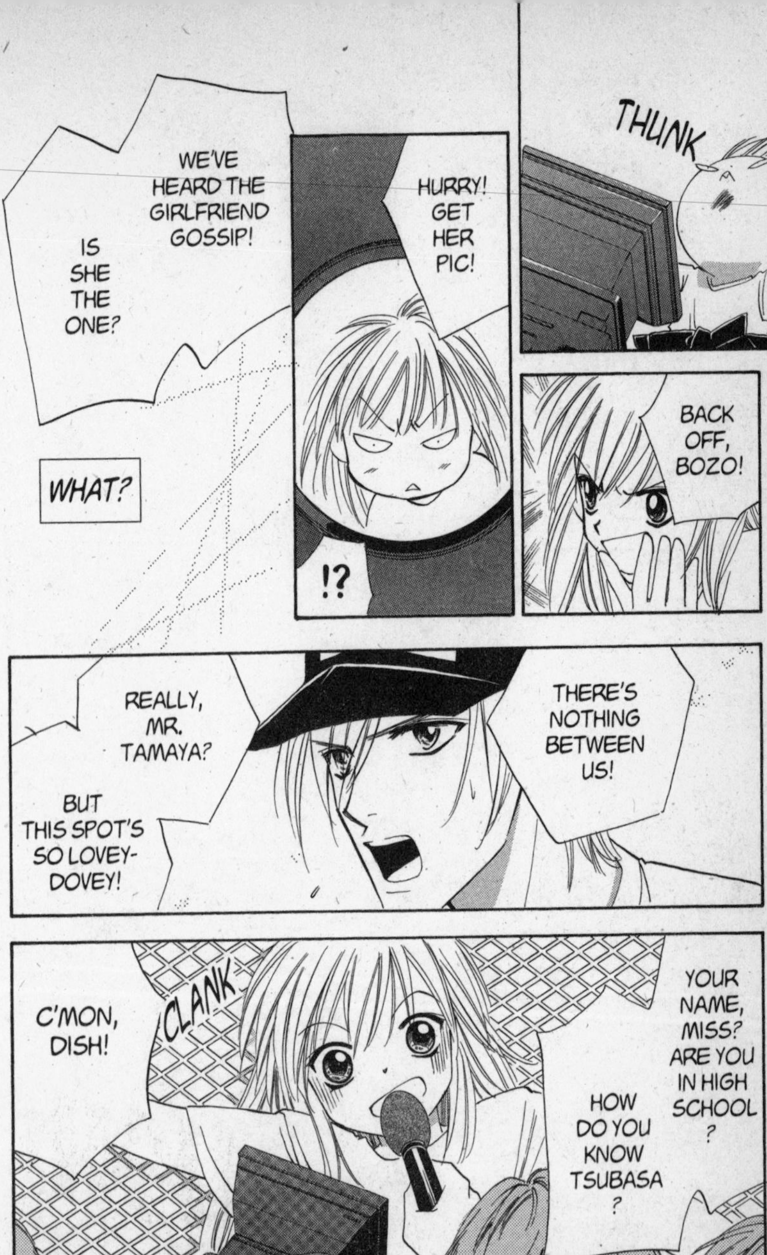

THUNK
BACK OFF, BOZO!
HURRY! GET HER PIC!
!?
WE'VE HEARD THE GIRLFRIEND GOSSIP!
IS SHE THE ONE?
WHAT?
THERE'S NOTHING BETWEEN US!
REALLY, MR. TAMAYA?
BUT THIS SPOT'S SO LOVEY-DOVEY!
YOUR NAME, MISS? ARE YOU IN HIGH SCHOOL?
HOW DO YOU KNOW TSUBASA?
CLANK
C'MON, DISH!

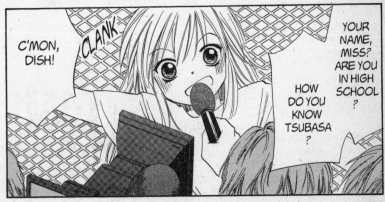

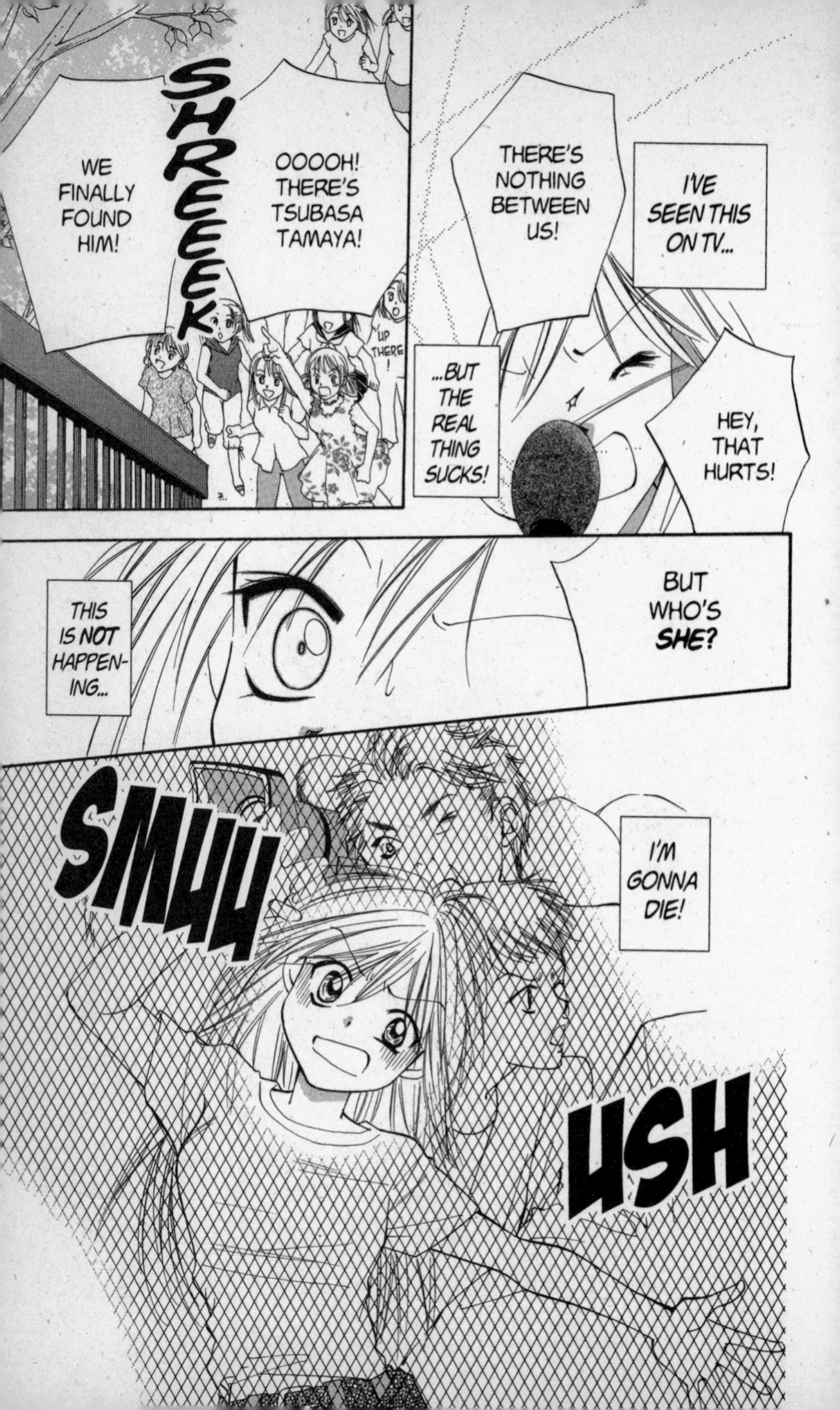
I'VE SEEN THIS ON TV...
THERE'S NOTHING BETWEEN US!
HEY, THAT HURTS!
...BUT THE REAL THING SUCKS!
OOOOH! THERE'S TSUBASA TAMAYA!
SHREEEK
WE FINALLY FOUND HIM!
UP THERE!
BUT WHO'S **SHE?**
THIS IS **NOT** HAPPENING...
I'M GONNA DIE!
SMUU
USH

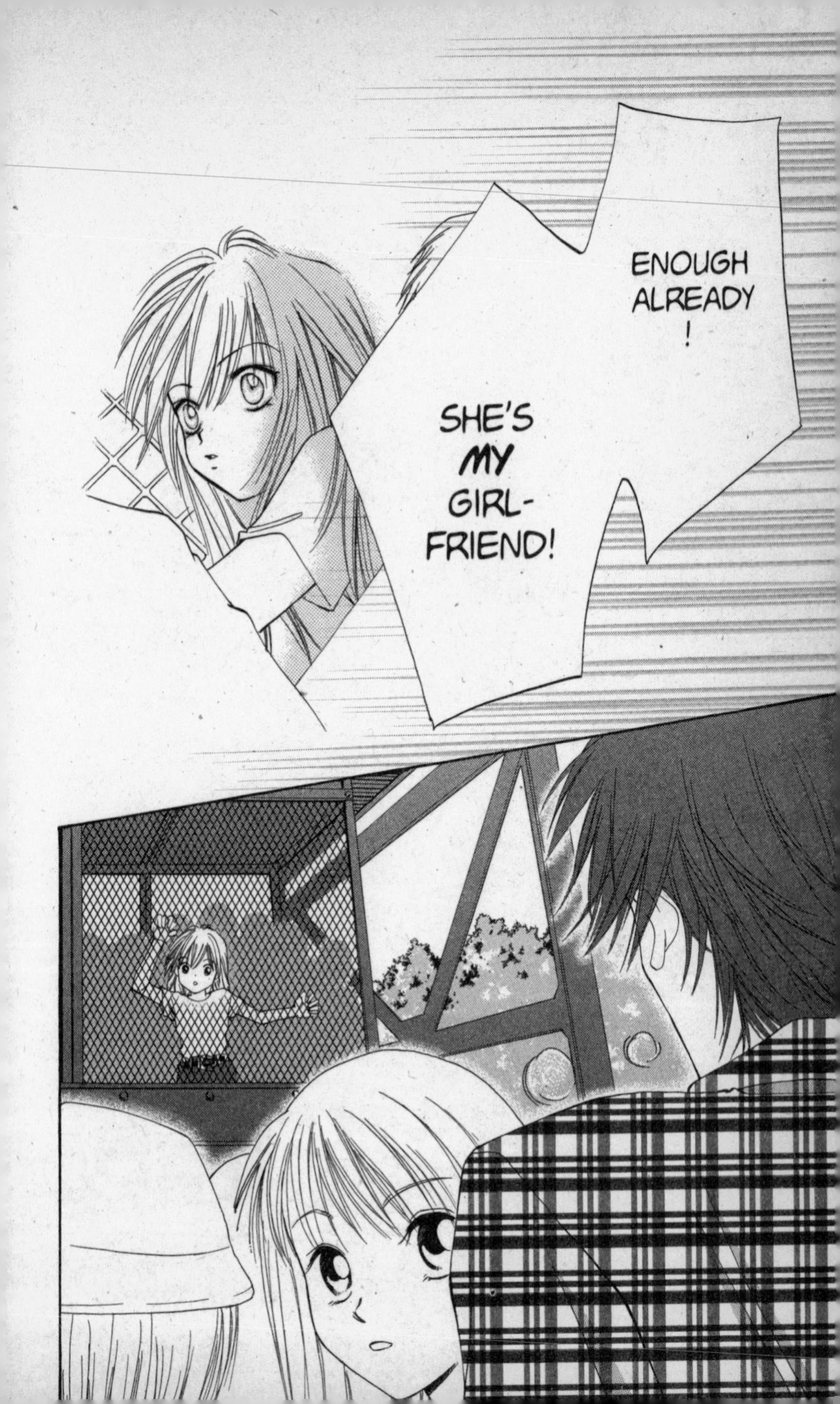
ENOUGH ALREADY !
SHE'S MY GIRL-FRIEND!

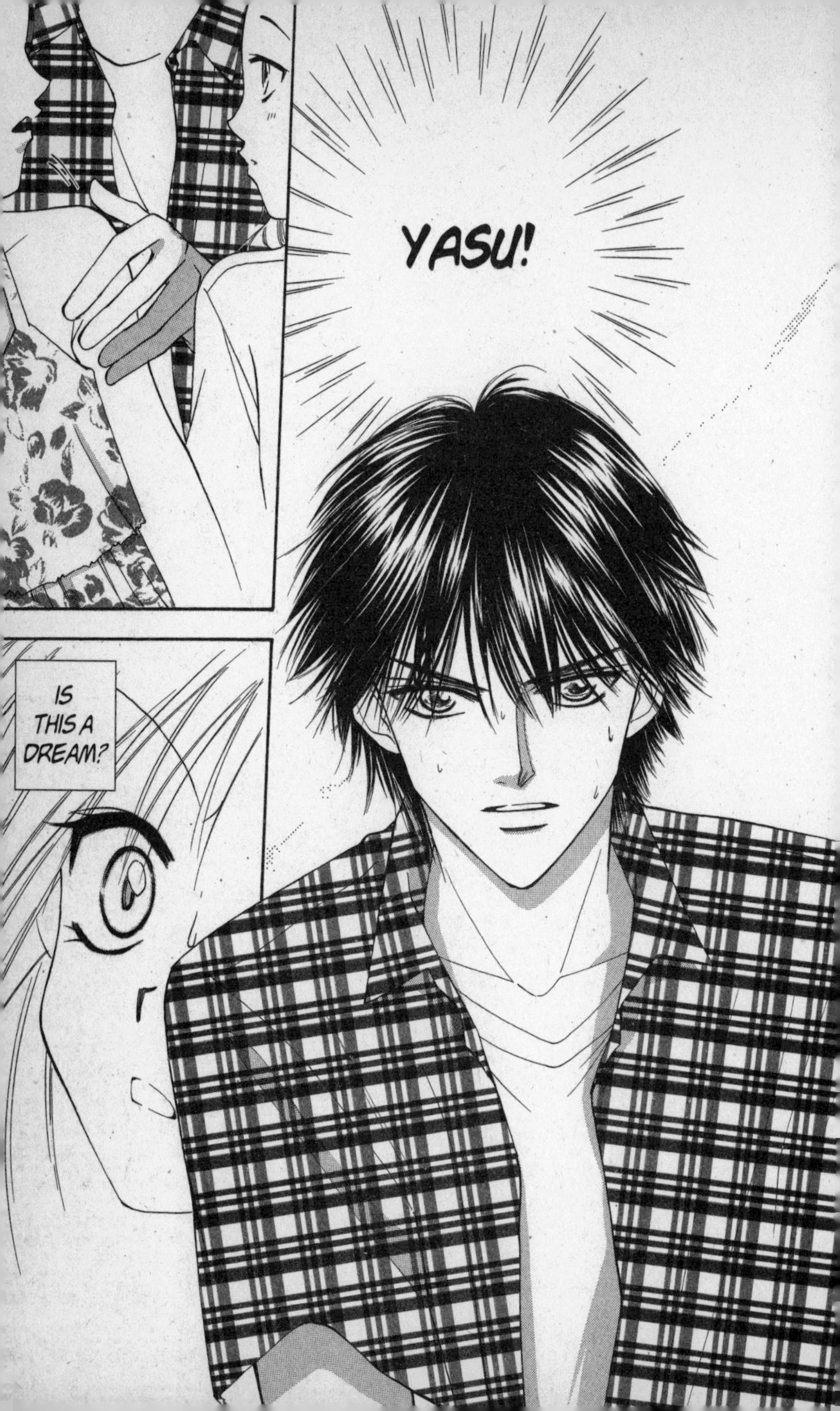
YASU!
IS THIS A DREAM?

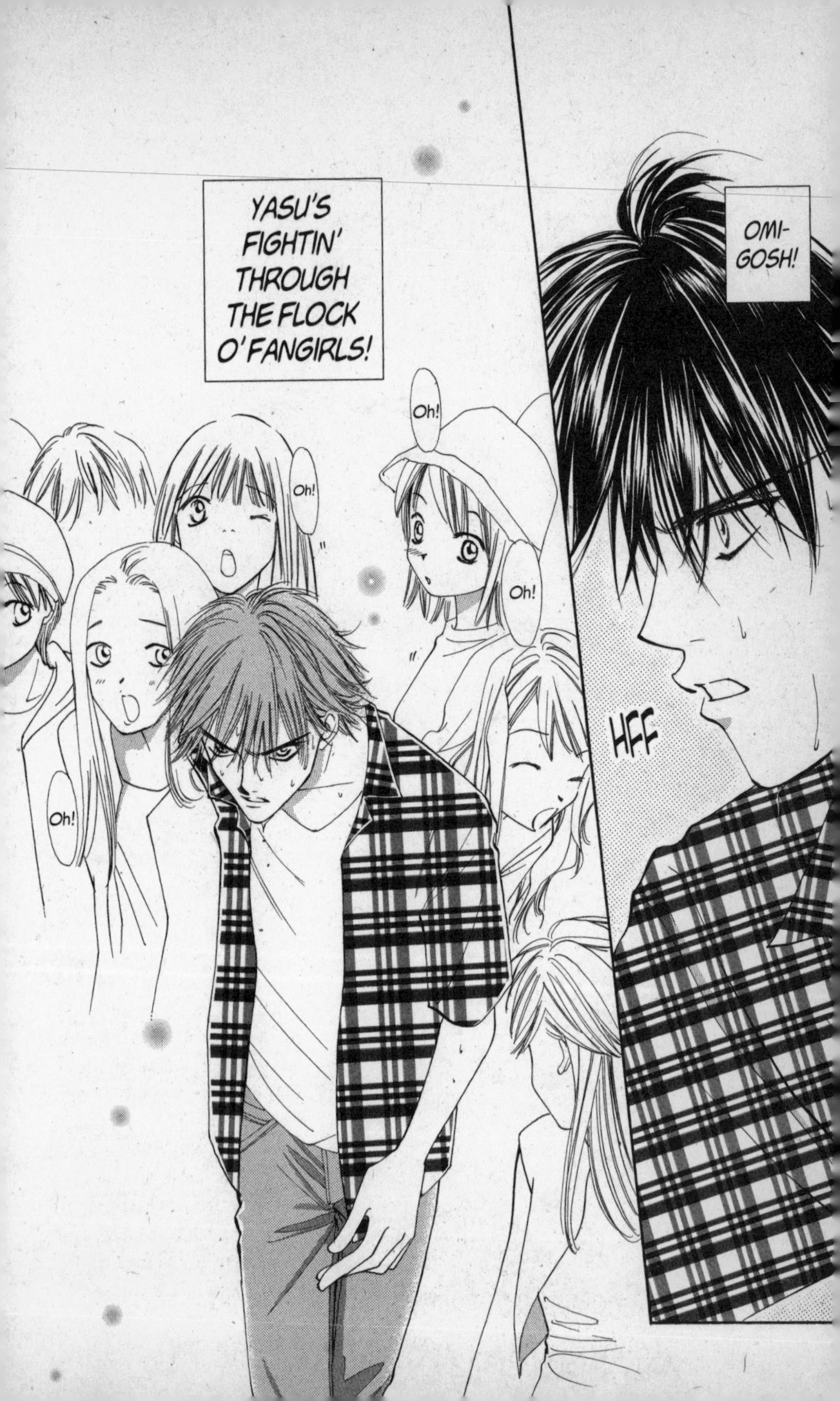
OMI-GOSH!
HFF
YASU'S FIGHTIN' THROUGH THE FLOCK O' FANGIRLS!
Oh!
Oh!
Oh!
Oh!

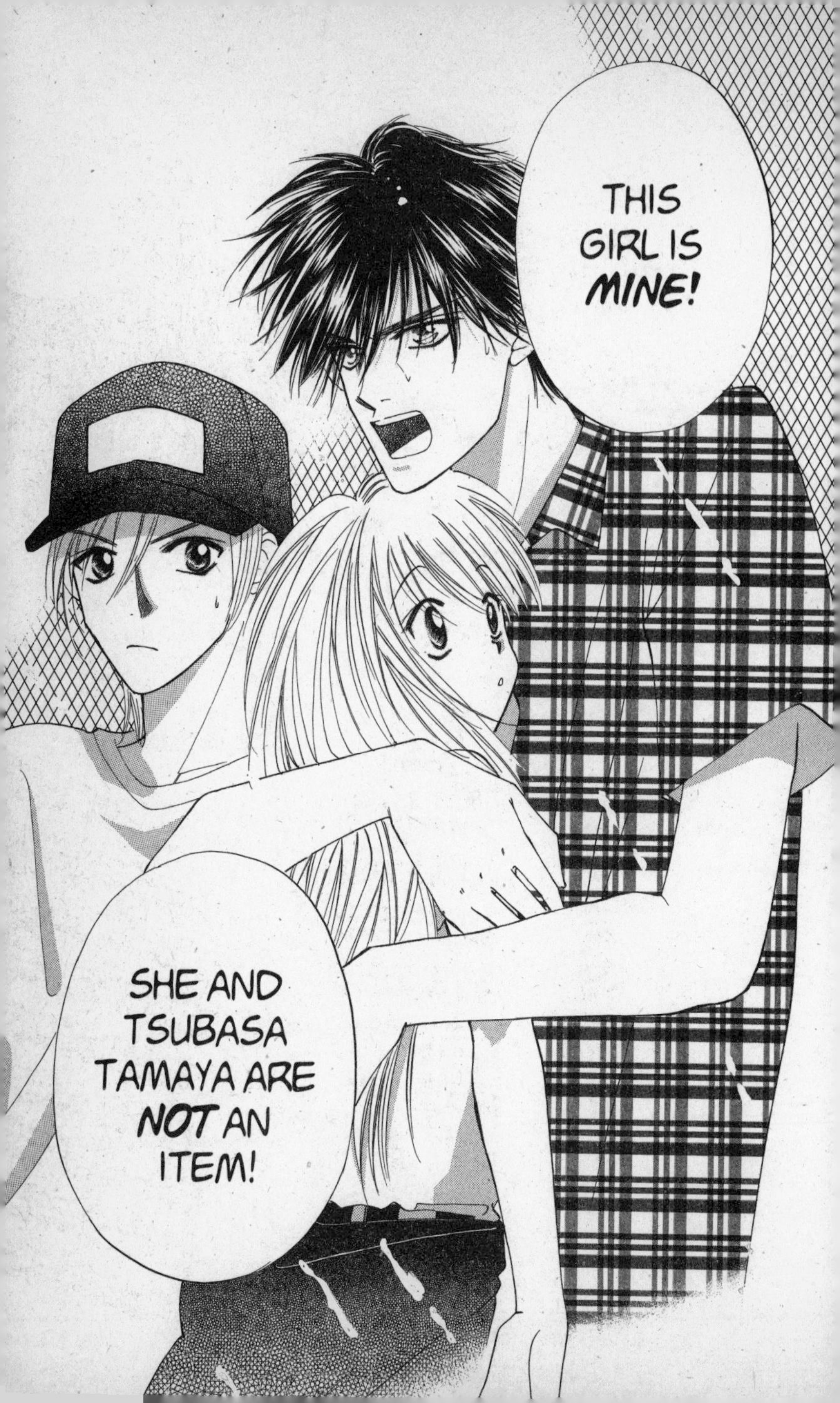
THIS GIRL IS MINE!
SHE AND TSUBASA TAMAYA ARE NOT AN ITEM!

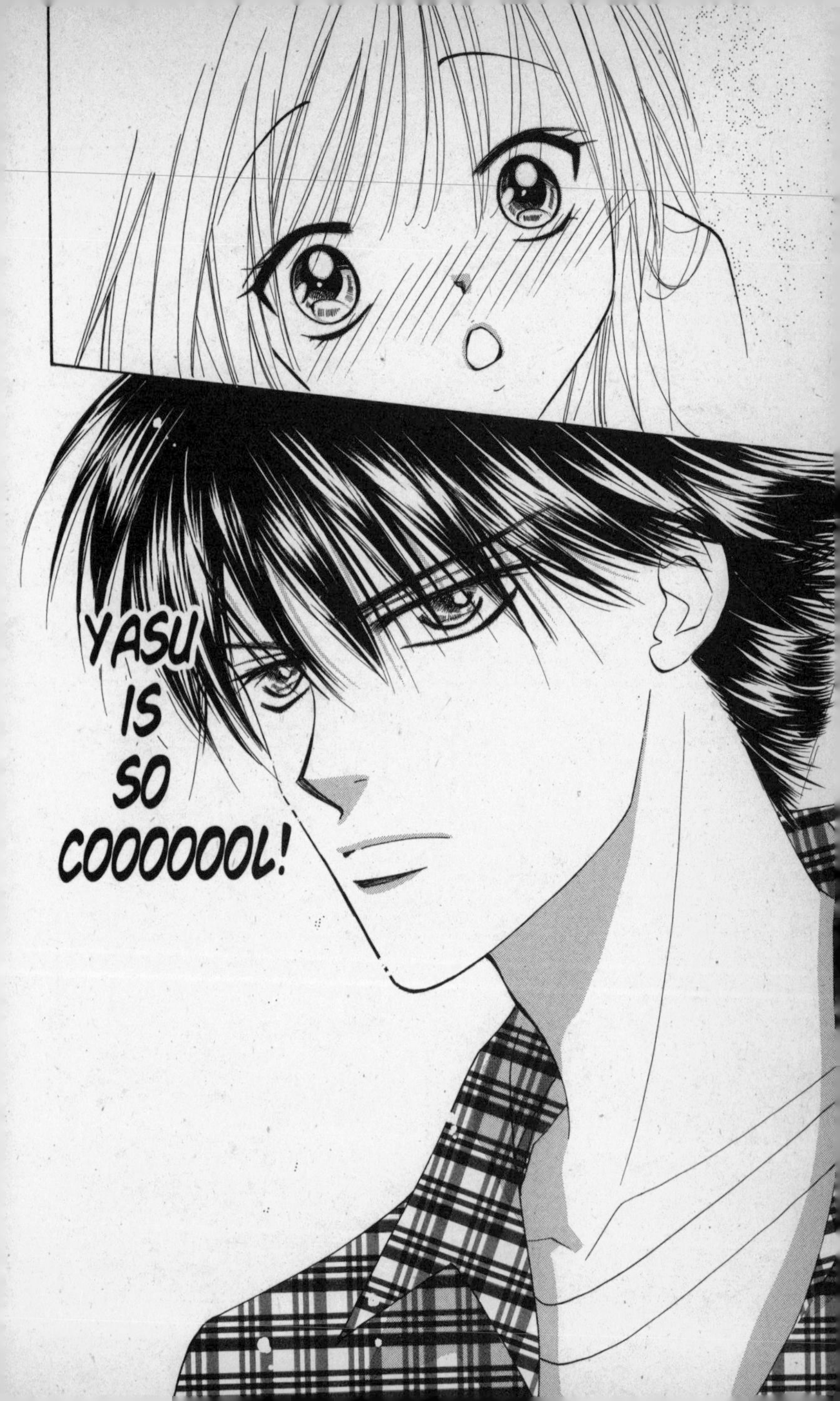
YASU IS SO COOOOOOL!

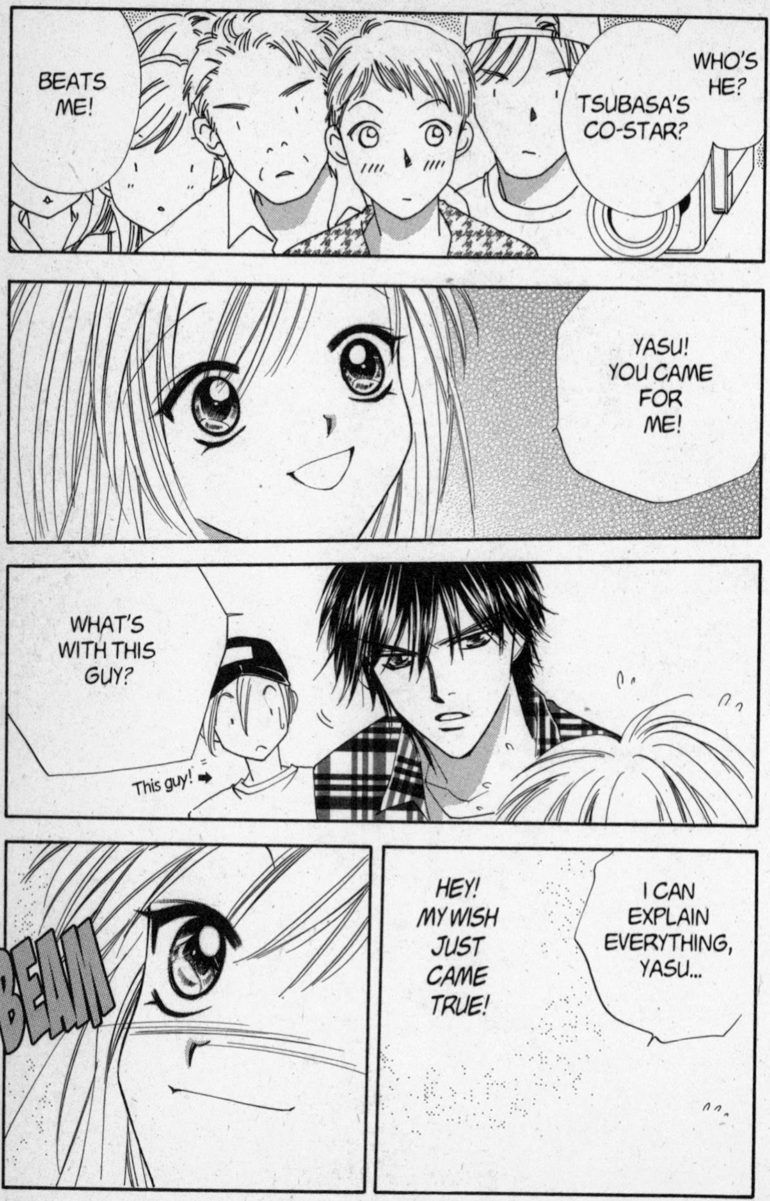
WHO'S HE? TSUBASA'S CO-STAR?
BEATS ME!
YASU! YOU CAME FOR ME!
WHAT'S WITH THIS GUY?
This guy!
I CAN EXPLAIN EVERYTHING, YASU...
HEY! MY WISH JUST CAME TRUE!
BEAM

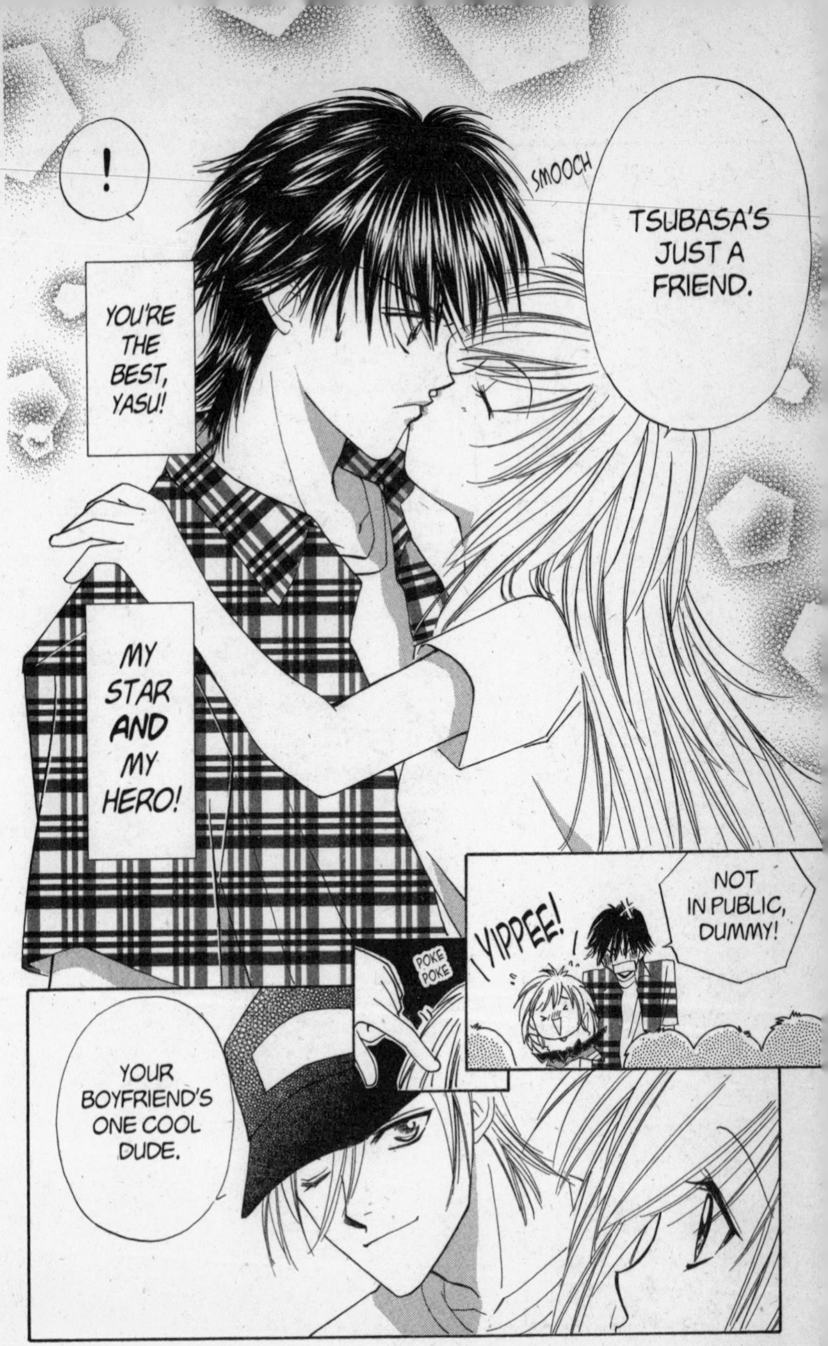
TSUBASA'S JUST A FRIEND.
SMOOCH
!
YOU'RE THE BEST, YASU!
MY STAR AND MY HERO!
NOT IN PUBLIC, DUMMY!
YIPPEE!
POKE POKE
YOUR BOYFRIEND'S ONE COOL DUDE.

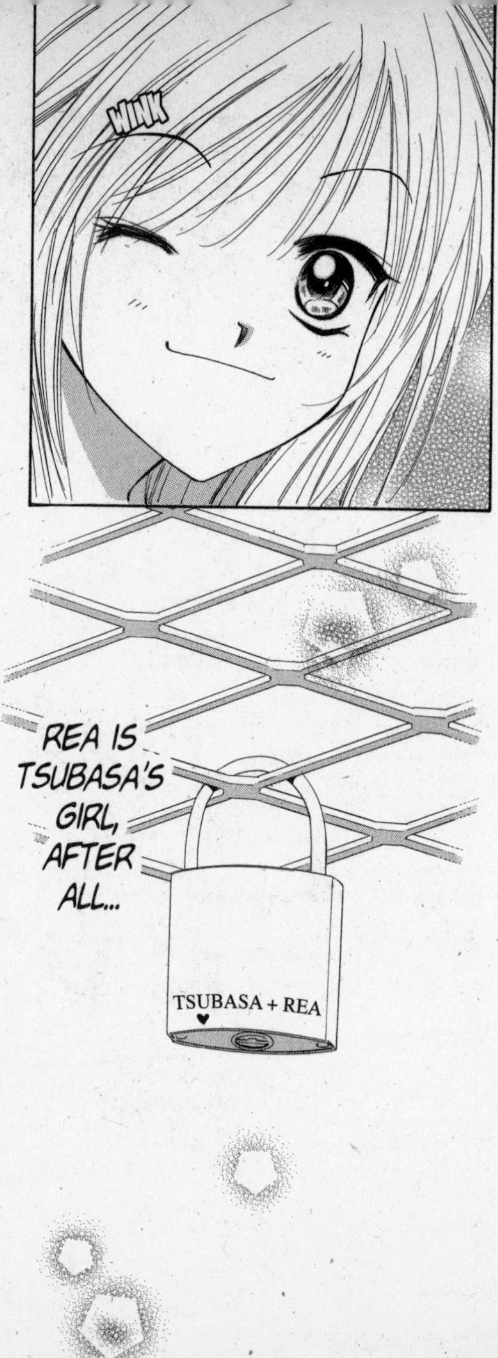
WINK
REA IS TSUBASA'S GIRL, AFTER ALL...
TSUBASA + REA

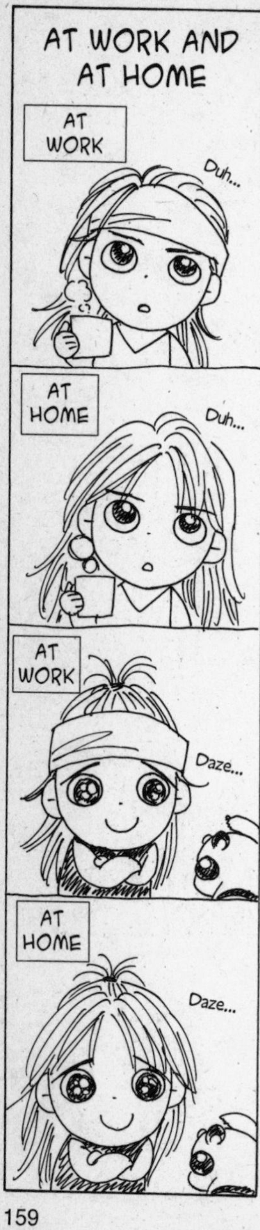
AT WORK AND AT HOME
AT WORK
Duh...
AT HOME
Duh...
AT WORK
Daze...
AT HOME
Daze...

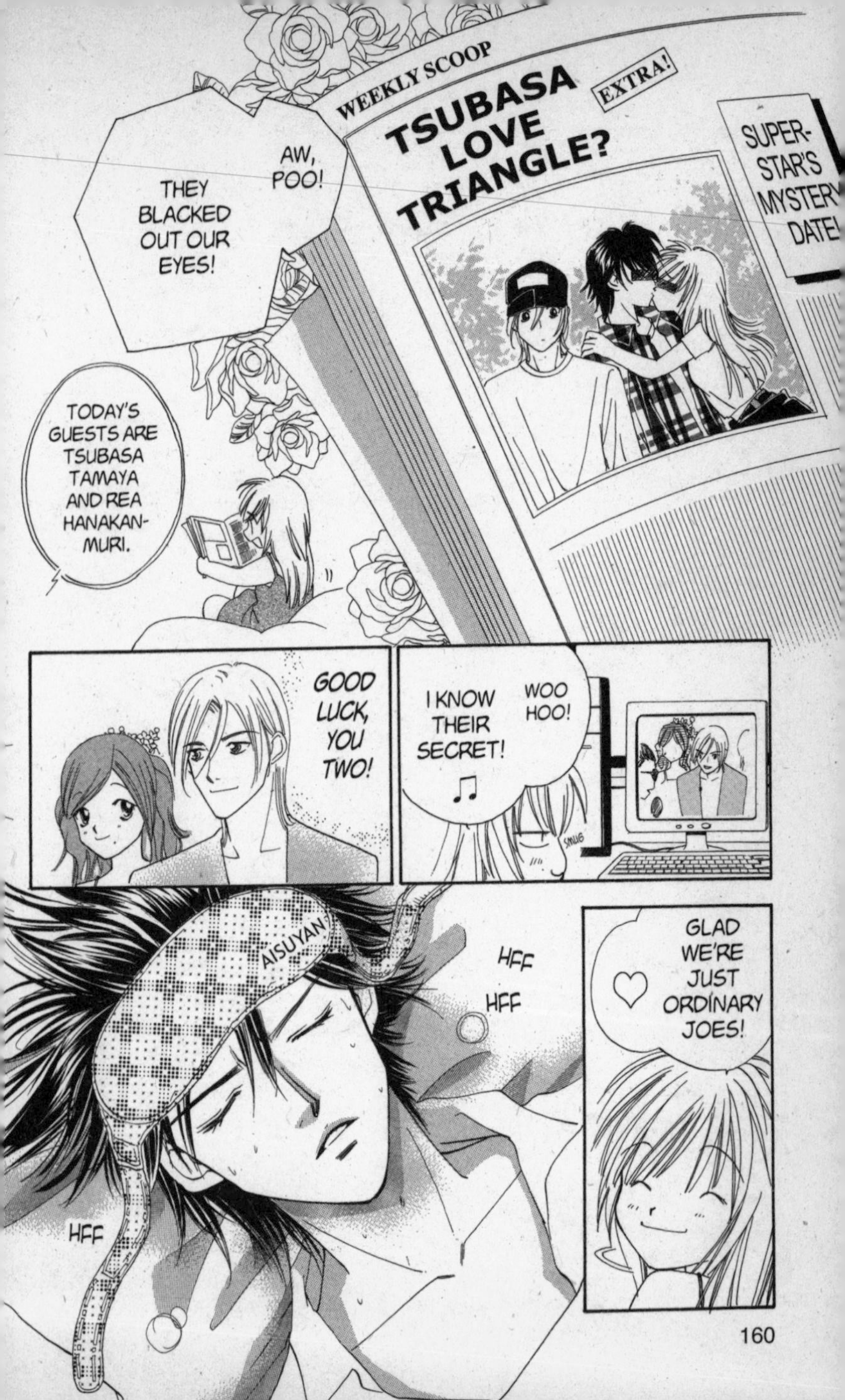
WEEKLY SCOOP
TSUBASA LOVE TRIANGLE?
EXTRA!
SUPER-STAR'S MYSTERY DATE!
AW, POO!
THEY BLACKED OUT OUR EYES!
TODAY'S GUESTS ARE TSUBASA TAMAYA AND REA HANAKAN-MURI.
WOO HOO!
I KNOW THEIR SECRET!
SMUG
GOOD LUCK, YOU TWO!
GLAD WE'RE JUST ORDINARY JOES!
HFF
HFF
AISUYAN
HFF

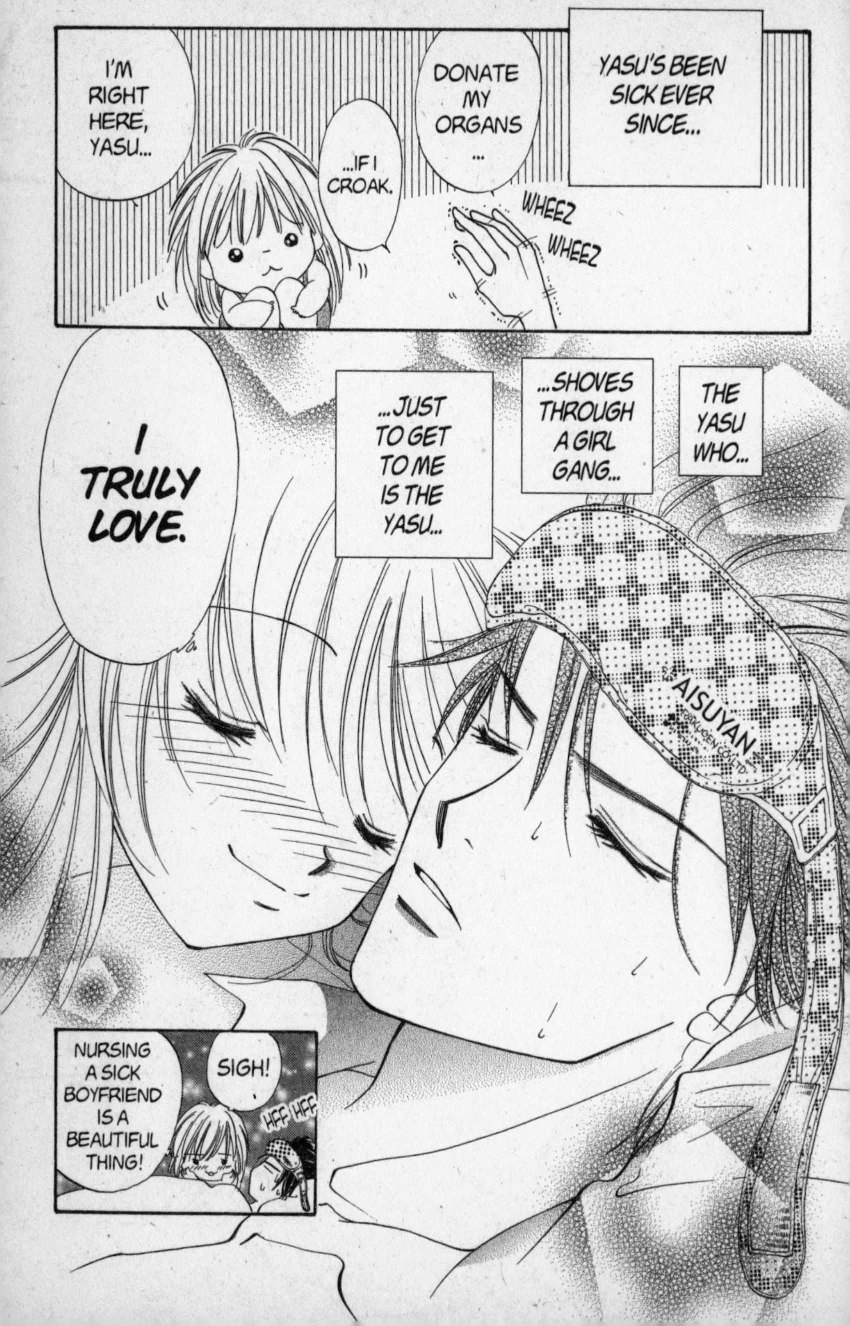

YASU'S BEEN SICK EVER SINCE...
DONATE MY ORGANS ...
...IF I CROAK.
I'M RIGHT HERE, YASU...
WHEEZ
WHEEZ
THE YASU WHO...
...SHOVES THROUGH A GIRL GANG...
...JUST TO GET TO ME IS THE YASU...
I TRULY LOVE.
AISUYAN
SIGH!
HFF HFF
NURSING A SICK BOYFRIEND IS A BEAUTIFUL THING!

HAPPY HUSTLE HIGH

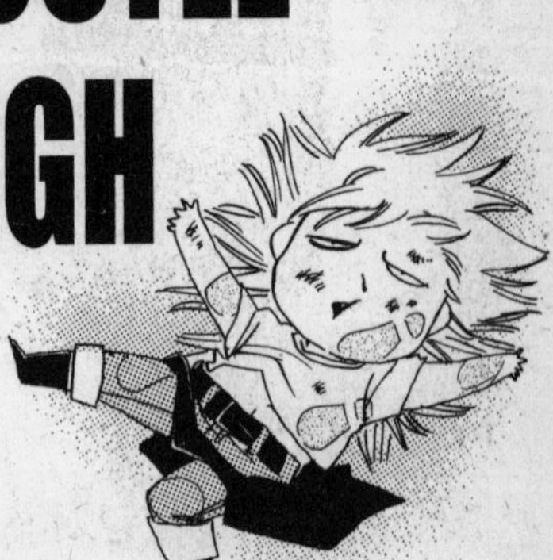

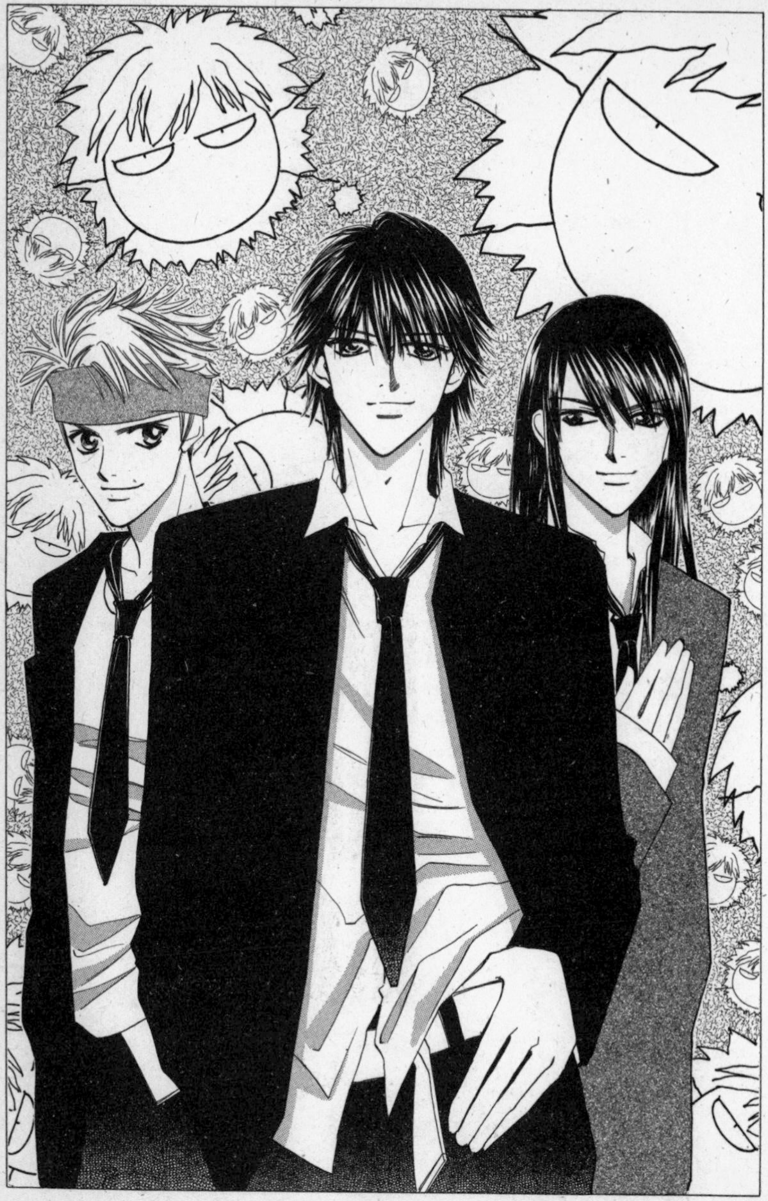

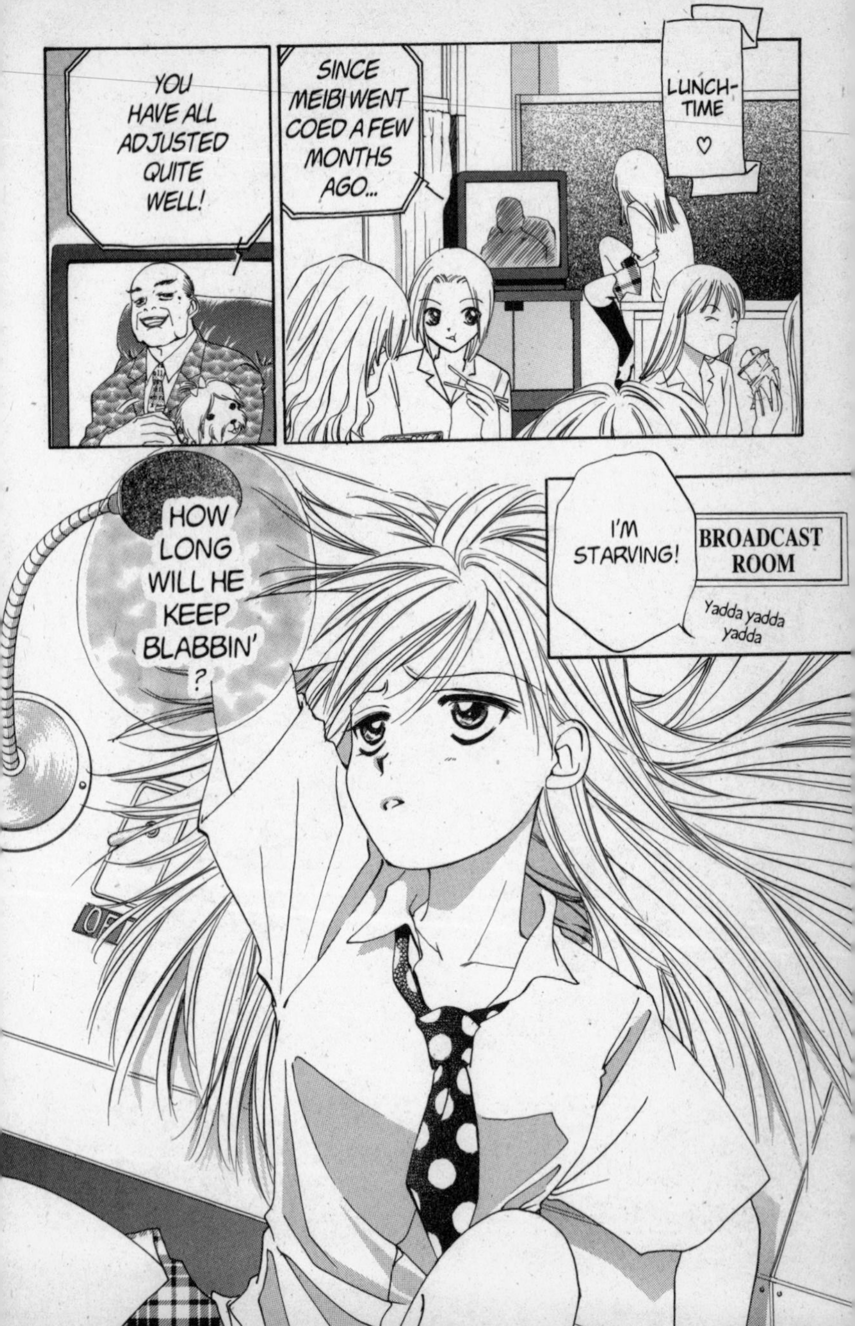
LUNCH-TIME ♡
SINCE MEIBI WENT COED A FEW MONTHS AGO...
YOU HAVE ALL ADJUSTED QUITE WELL!
BROADCAST ROOM
I'M STARVING!
Yadda yadda yadda
HOW LONG WILL HE KEEP BLABBIN'?

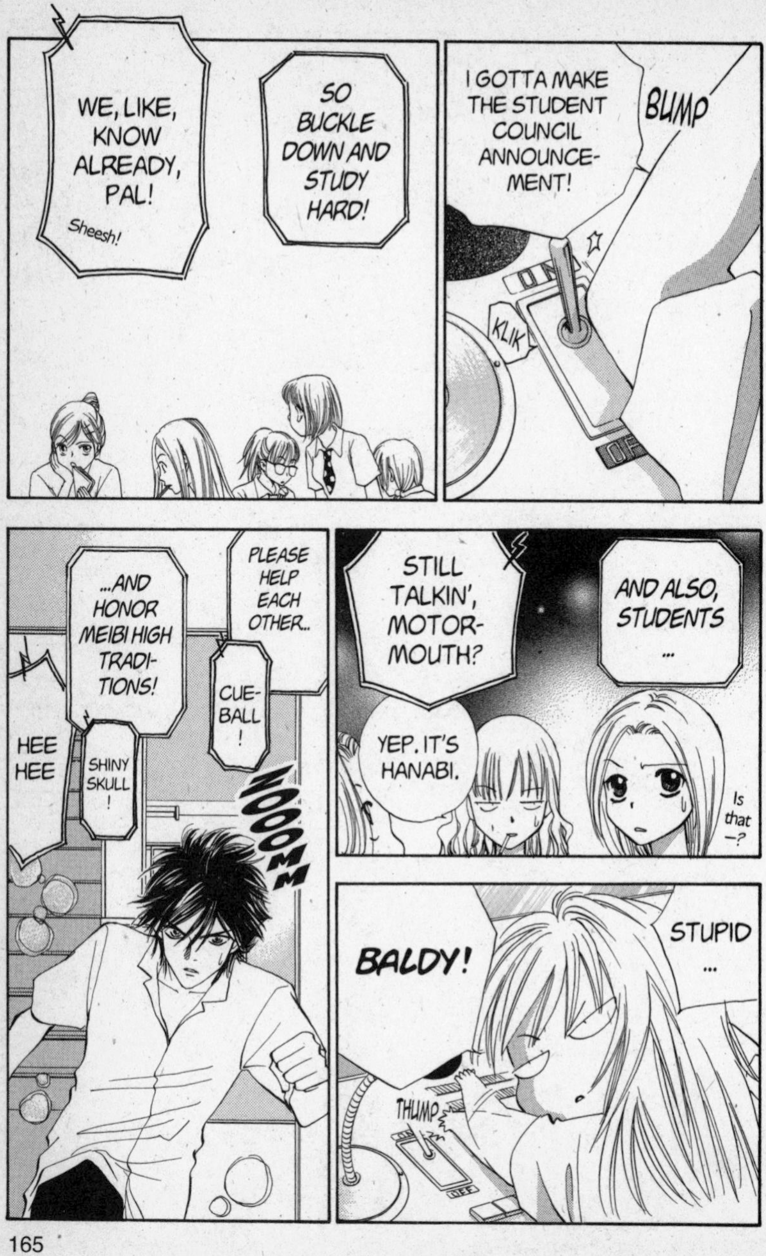
I GOTTA MAKE THE STUDENT COUNCIL ANNOUNCEMENT!
BUMP
KLIK
SO BUCKLE DOWN AND STUDY HARD!
WE, LIKE, KNOW ALREADY, PAL!
Sheesh!
AND ALSO, STUDENTS ...
STILL TALKIN', MOTOR-MOUTH?
Is that —?
YEP. IT'S HANABI.
STUPID ...
BALDY!
THUMP
PLEASE HELP EACH OTHER..
...AND HONOR MEIBI HIGH TRADITIONS!
CUE-BALL!
SHINY SKULL!
HEE HEE
NOOOOMM

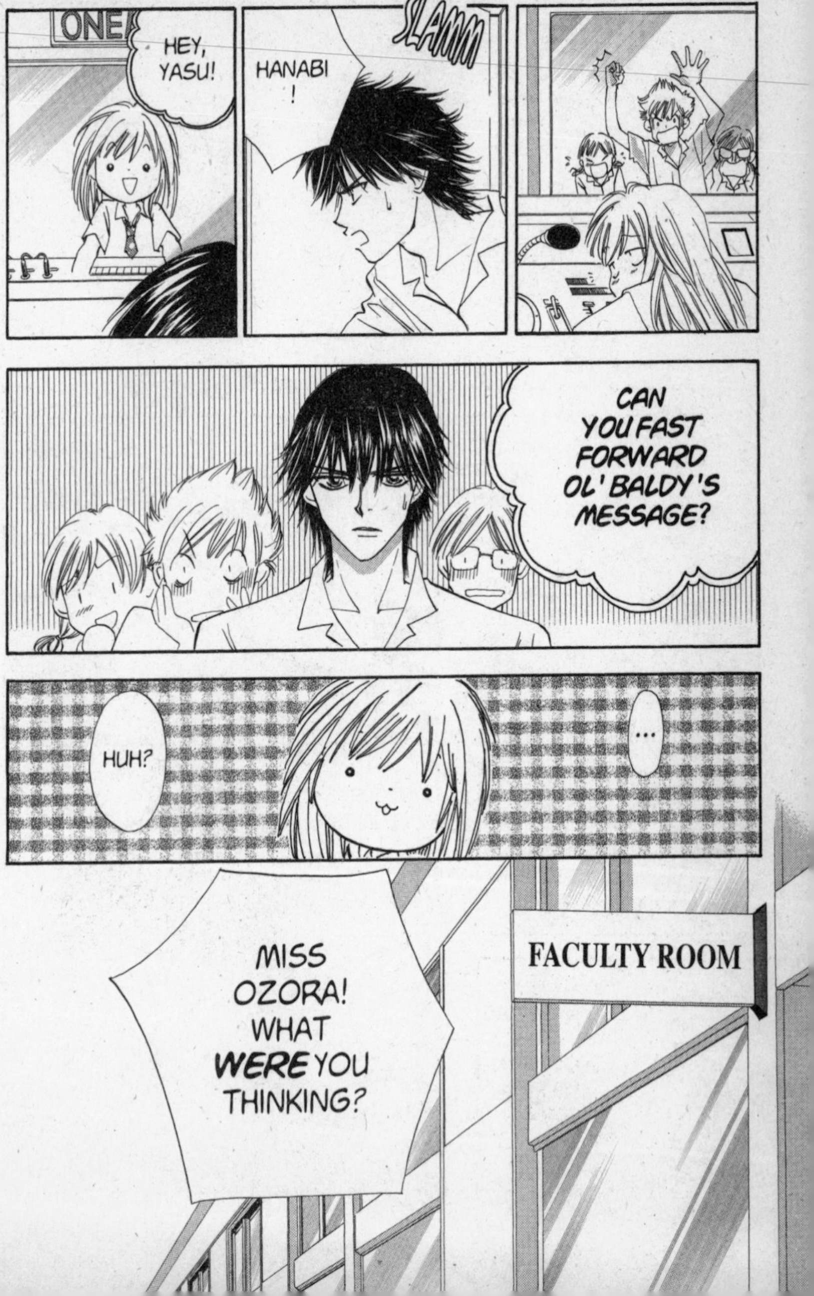
SLAMM
HANABI!
HEY, YASU!
CAN YOU FAST FORWARD OL' BALDY'S MESSAGE?
...
HUH?
FACULTY ROOM
MISS OZORA! WHAT **WERE** YOU THINKING?

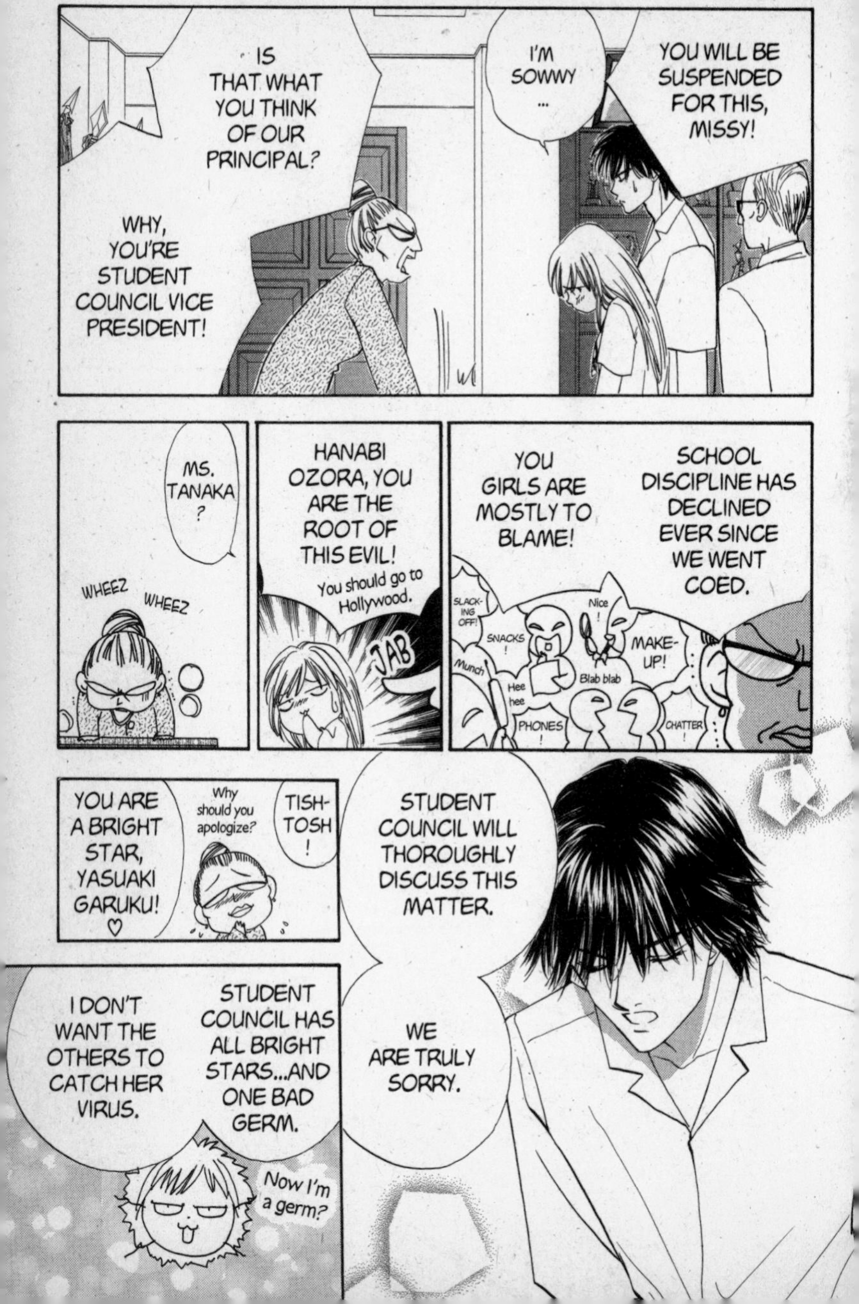
YOU WILL BE SUSPENDED FOR THIS, MISSY!
I'M SOWWY ...
IS THAT WHAT YOU THINK OF OUR PRINCIPAL?
WHY, YOU'RE STUDENT COUNCIL VICE PRESIDENT!
SCHOOL DISCIPLINE HAS DECLINED EVER SINCE WE WENT COED.
YOU GIRLS ARE MOSTLY TO BLAME!
Nice!
MAKE-UP!
SLACKING OFF!
SNACKS!
Munch
Blab blab
Hee hee
PHONES!
CHATTER!
HANABI OZORA, YOU ARE THE ROOT OF THIS EVIL!
You should go to Hollywood.
JAB
MS. TANAKA?
WHEEZ
WHEEZ
STUDENT COUNCIL WILL THOROUGHLY DISCUSS THIS MATTER.
WE ARE TRULY SORRY.
TISH-TOSH!
Why should you apologize?
YOU ARE A BRIGHT STAR, YASUAKI GARUKU! ♡
STUDENT COUNCIL HAS ALL BRIGHT STARS...AND ONE BAD GERM.
I DON'T WANT THE OTHERS TO CATCH HER VIRUS.
Now I'm a germ?

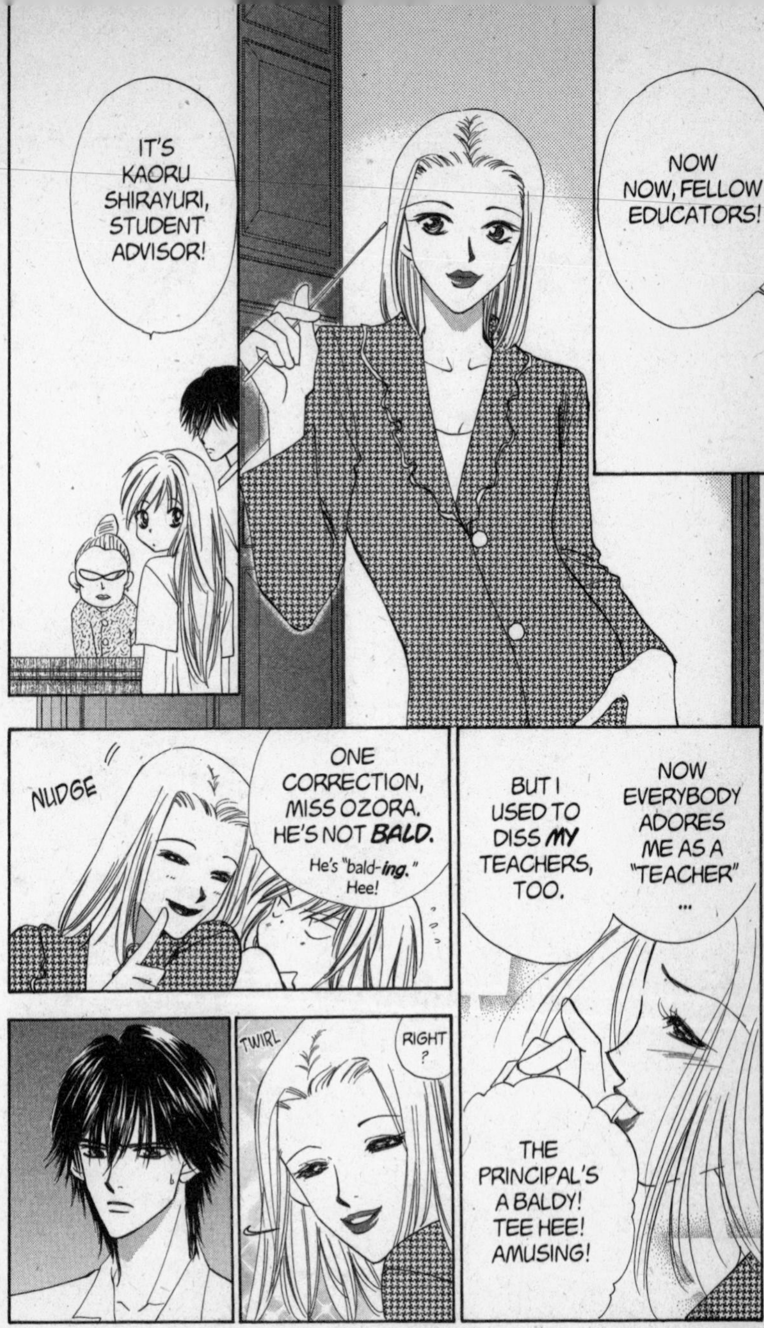
NOW NOW, FELLOW EDUCATORS!
IT'S KAORU SHIRAYURI, STUDENT ADVISOR!
NOW EVERYBODY ADORES ME AS A "TEACHER" ...
BUT I USED TO DISS MY TEACHERS, TOO.
THE PRINCIPAL'S A BALDY! TEE HEE! AMUSING!
ONE CORRECTION, MISS OZORA. HE'S NOT BALD.
He's "bald-ing." Hee!
NUDGE
RIGHT?
TWIRL

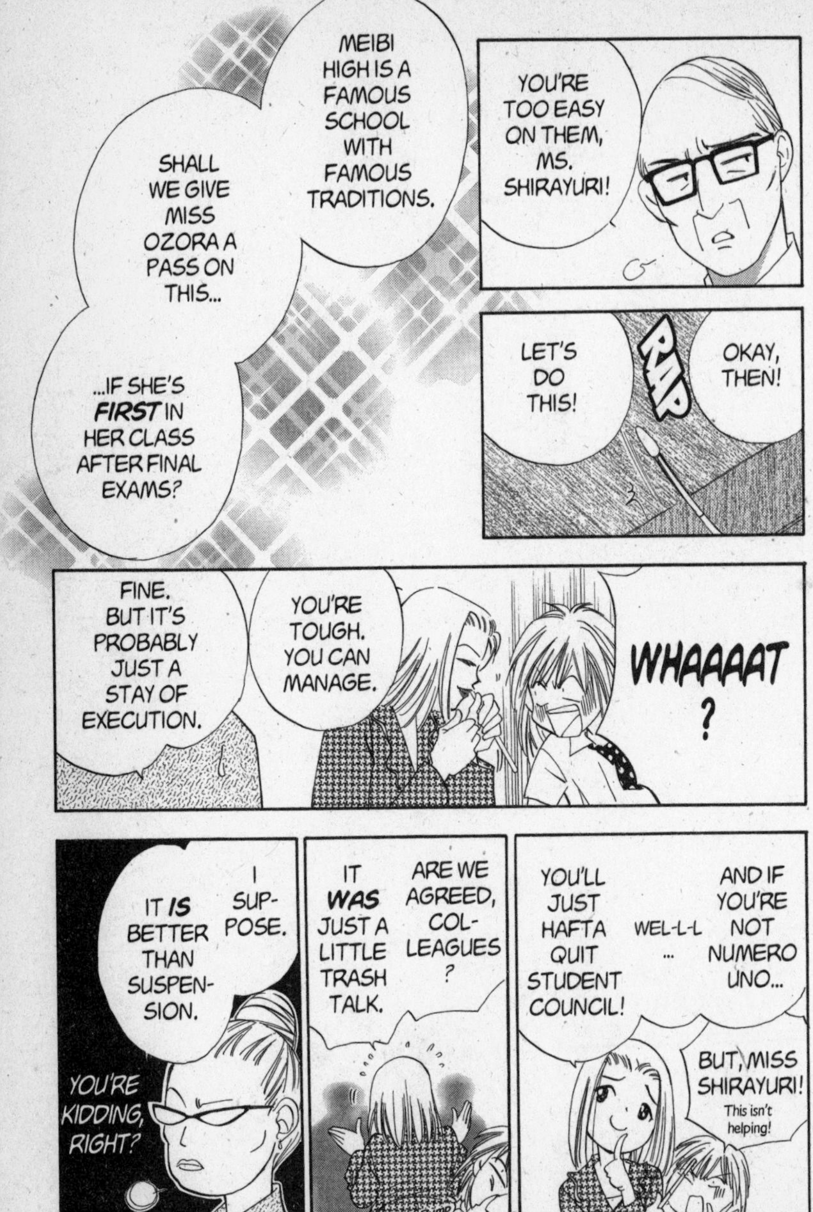
YOU'RE TOO EASY ON THEM, MS. SHIRAYURI!
OKAY, THEN!
RAP
LET'S DO THIS!
MEIBI HIGH IS A FAMOUS SCHOOL WITH FAMOUS TRADITIONS.
SHALL WE GIVE MISS OZORA A PASS ON THIS...
...IF SHE'S FIRST IN HER CLASS AFTER FINAL EXAMS?
WHAAAAT?
YOU'RE TOUGH. YOU CAN MANAGE.
FINE. BUT IT'S PROBABLY JUST A STAY OF EXECUTION.
AND IF YOU'RE NOT NUMERO UNO...
WEL-L-L...
YOU'LL JUST HAFTA QUIT STUDENT COUNCIL!
BUT, MISS SHIRAYURI!
This isn't helping!
ARE WE AGREED, COL-LEAGUES?
IT WAS JUST A LITTLE TRASH TALK.
Bump
I SUP-POSE.
IT IS BETTER THAN SUSPEN-SION.
YOU'RE KIDDING, RIGHT?

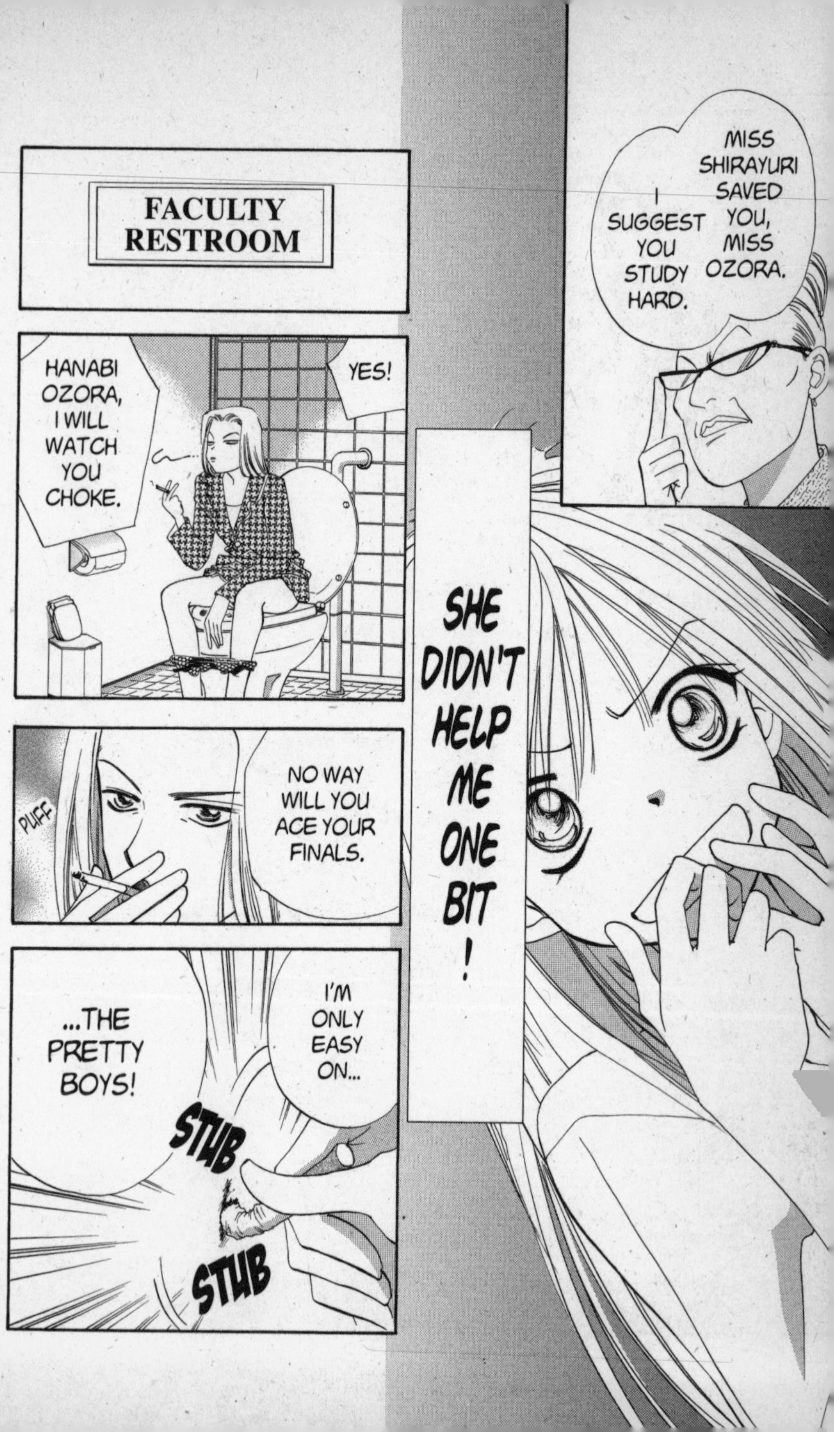
MISS SHIRAYURI SAVED YOU, MISS OZORA.
I SUGGEST YOU STUDY HARD.
SHE DIDN'T HELP ME ONE BIT!
FACULTY RESTROOM
YES!
HANABI OZORA, I WILL WATCH YOU CHOKE.
NO WAY WILL YOU ACE YOUR FINALS.
PUFF
I'M ONLY EASY ON...
...THE PRETTY BOYS!
STUB
STUB

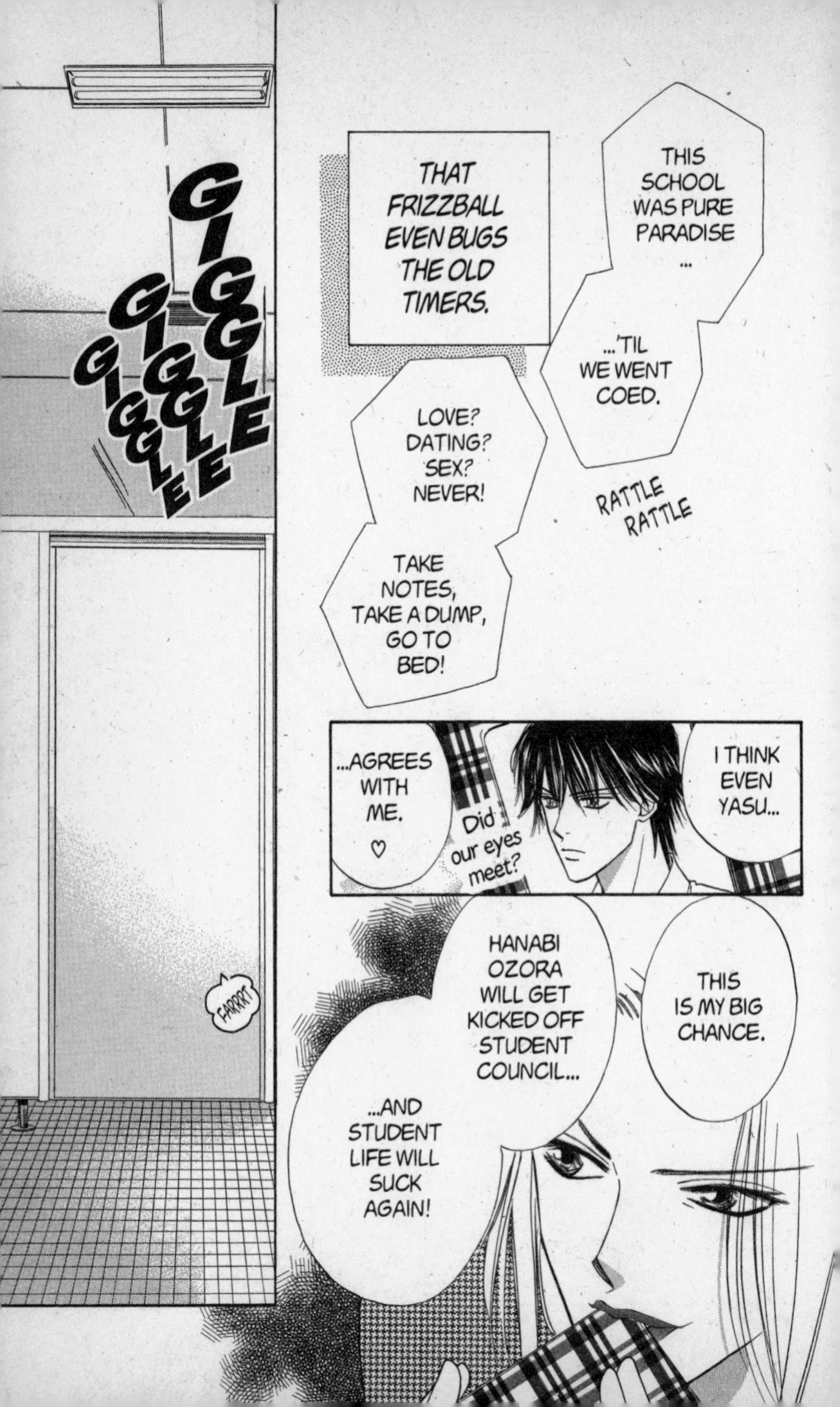
THIS SCHOOL WAS PURE PARADISE ...
...'TIL WE WENT COED.
THAT FRIZZBALL EVEN BUGS THE OLD TIMERS.
LOVE? DATING? SEX? NEVER!
TAKE NOTES, TAKE A DUMP, GO TO BED!
RATTLE RATTLE
I THINK EVEN YASU...
Did our eyes meet?
...AGREES WITH ME. ♡
THIS IS MY BIG CHANCE.
HANABI OZORA WILL GET KICKED OFF STUDENT COUNCIL...
...AND STUDENT LIFE WILL SUCK AGAIN!
GIGGLE
GIGGLE
GIGGLE
FARRRT

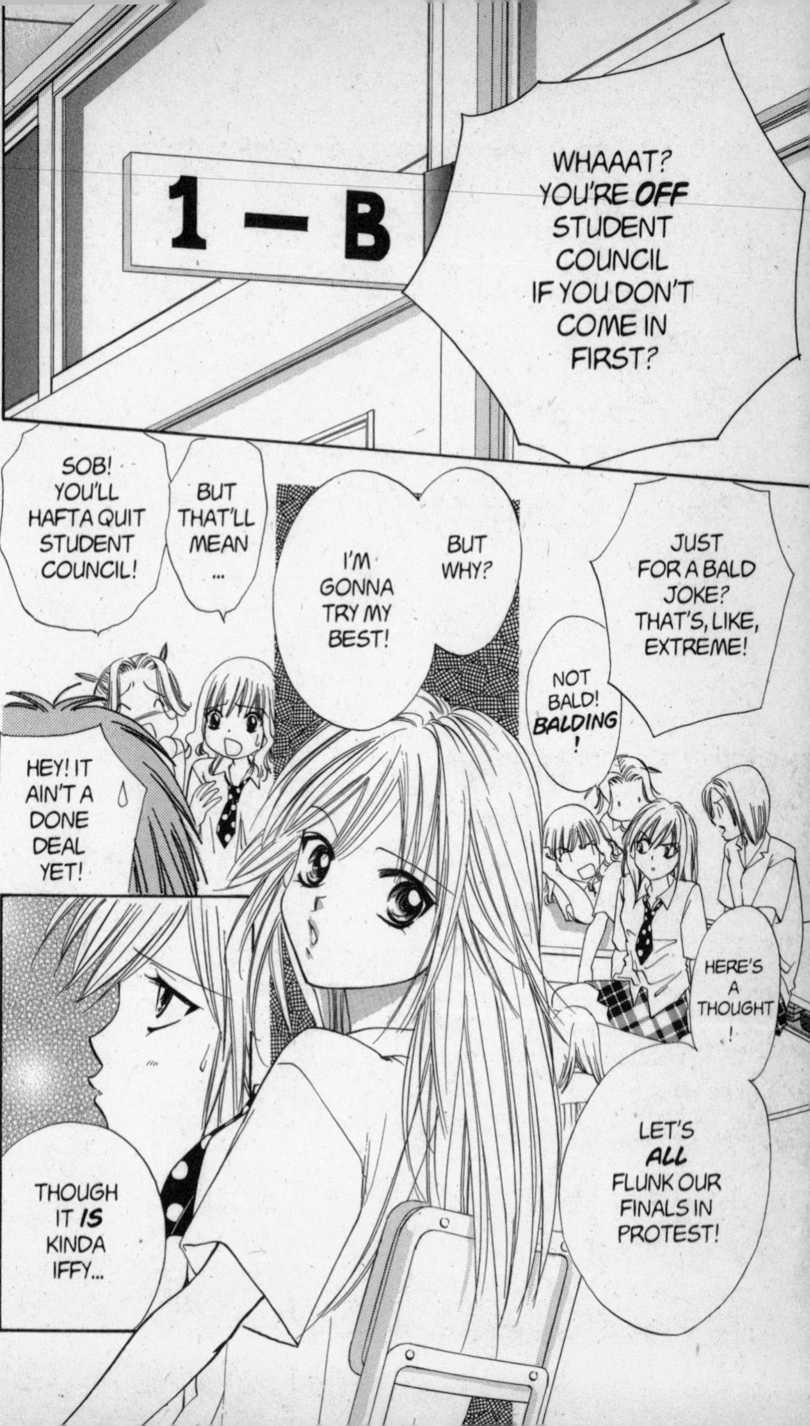

1 — B
WHAAAT? YOU'RE **OFF** STUDENT COUNCIL IF YOU DON'T COME IN FIRST?
JUST FOR A BALD JOKE? THAT'S, LIKE, EXTREME!
NOT BALD! **BALDING**!
BUT WHY?
I'M GONNA TRY MY BEST!
BUT THAT'LL MEAN ...
SOB! YOU'LL HAFTA QUIT STUDENT COUNCIL!
HEY! IT AIN'T A DONE DEAL YET!
HERE'S A THOUGHT!
LET'S **ALL** FLUNK OUR FINALS IN PROTEST!
THOUGH IT **IS** KINDA IFFY...

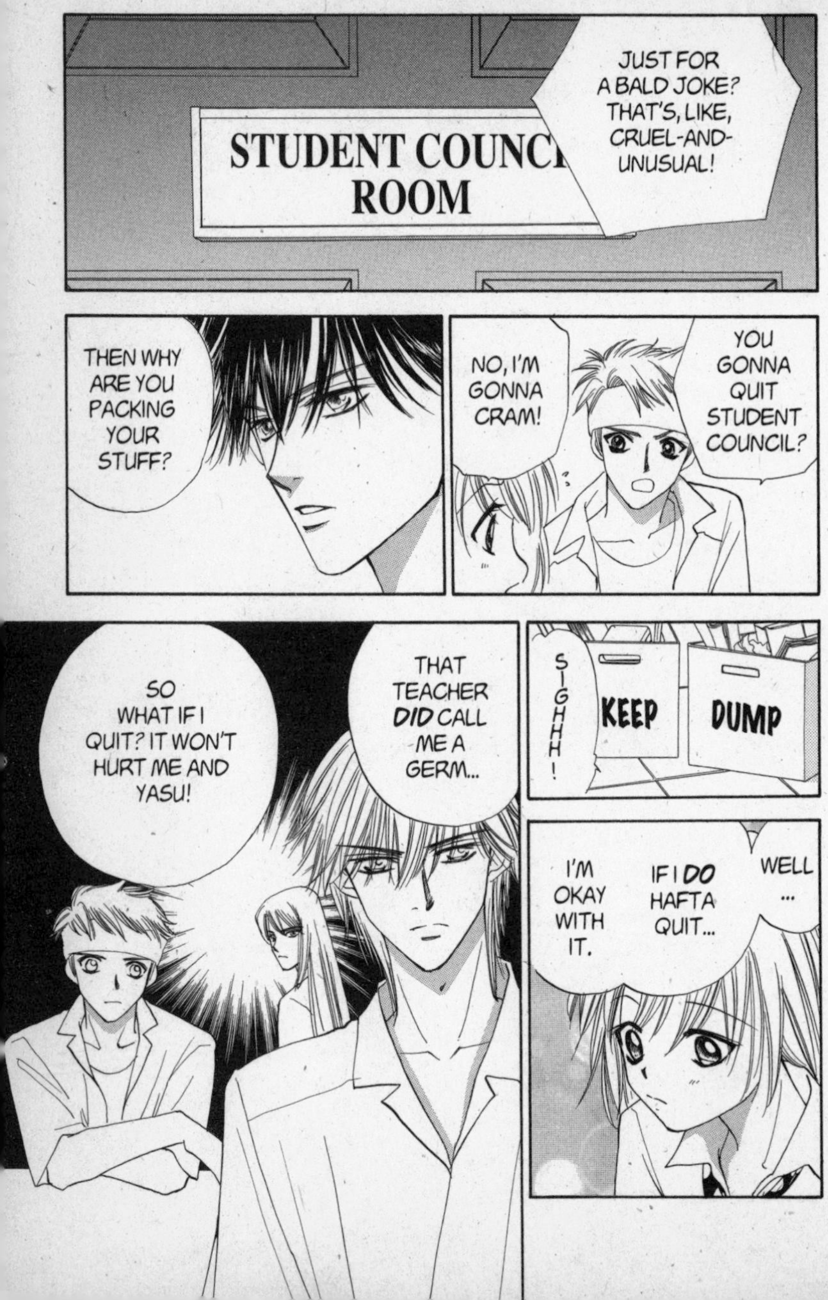
STUDENT COUNC
ROOM
JUST FOR A BALD JOKE? THAT'S, LIKE, CRUEL-AND-UNUSUAL!
YOU GONNA QUIT STUDENT COUNCIL?
NO, I'M GONNA CRAM!
THEN WHY ARE YOU PACKING YOUR STUFF?
SIGHHH!
KEEP
DUMP
WELL...
IF I DO HAFTA QUIT...
I'M OKAY WITH IT.
THAT TEACHER DID CALL ME A GERM...
SO WHAT IF I QUIT? IT WON'T HURT ME AND YASU!

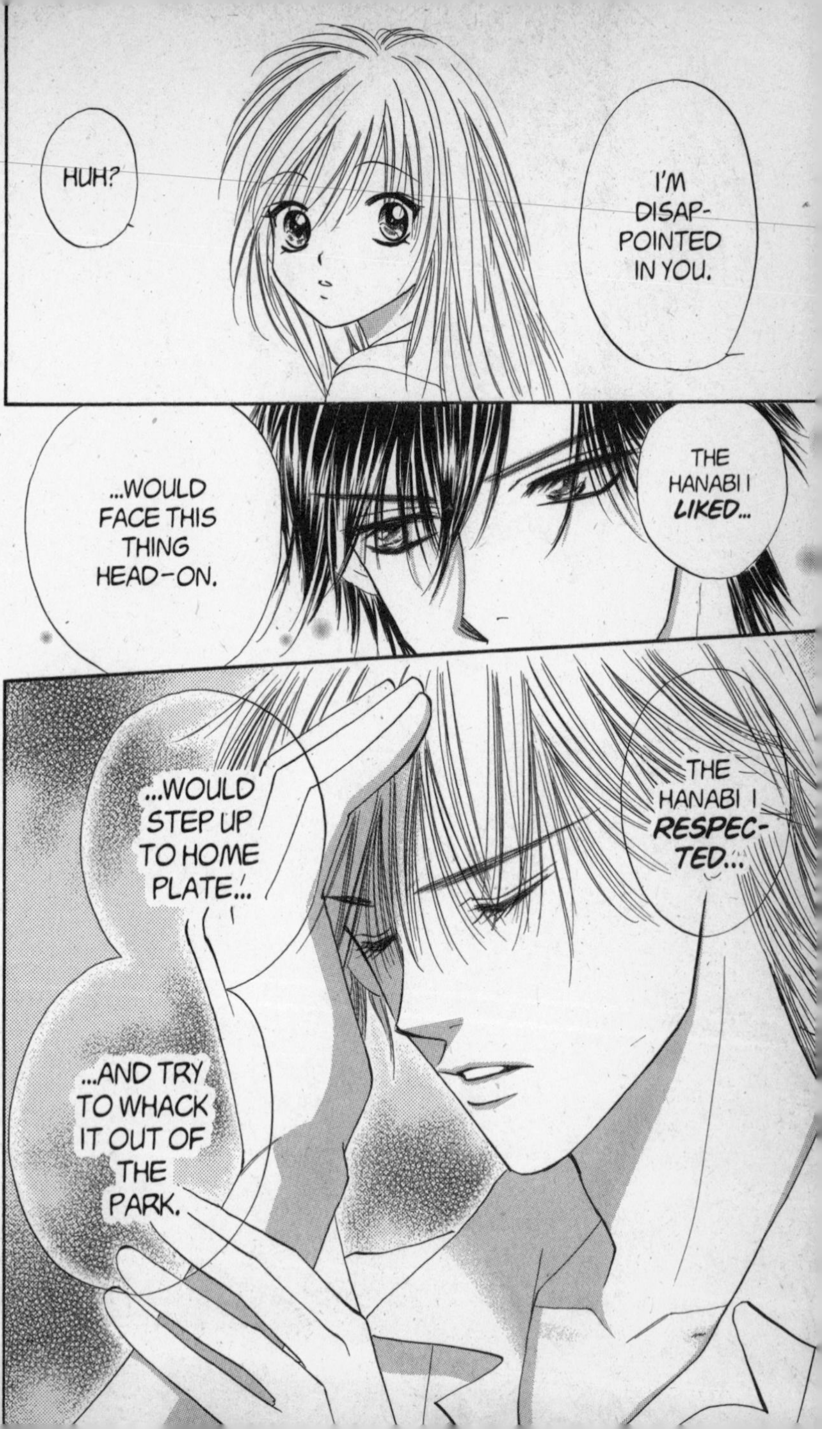
I'M DISAP-POINTED IN YOU.
HUH?
THE HANABI I **LIKED**...
...WOULD FACE THIS THING HEAD-ON.
THE HANABI I **RESPEC-TED**...
...WOULD STEP UP TO HOME PLATE...
...AND TRY TO WHACK IT OUT OF THE PARK.

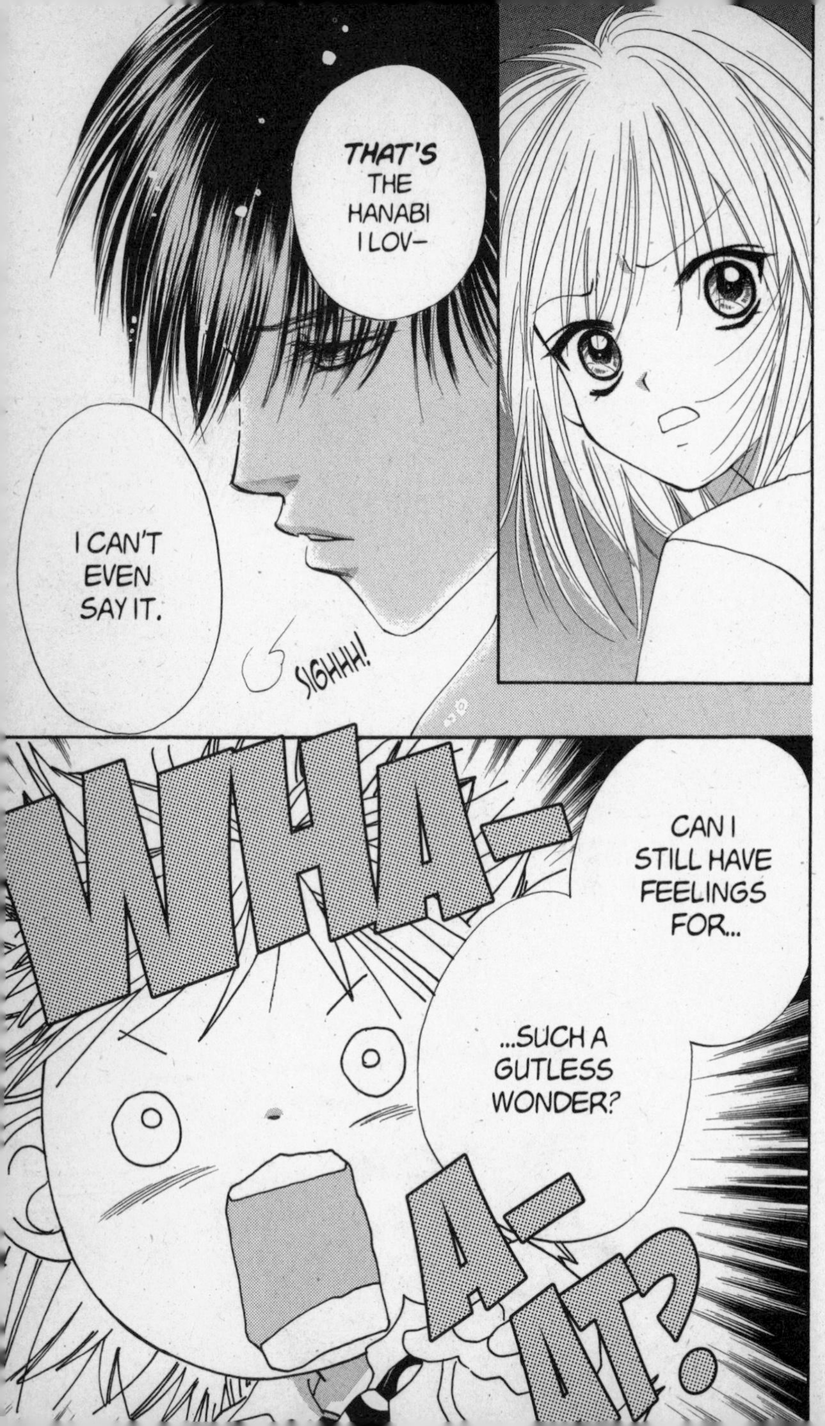
THAT'S THE HANABI I LOV—
I CAN'T EVEN SAY IT.
SIGHHH!
CAN I STILL HAVE FEELINGS FOR...
...SUCH A GUTLESS WONDER?
WHA-A-AT?

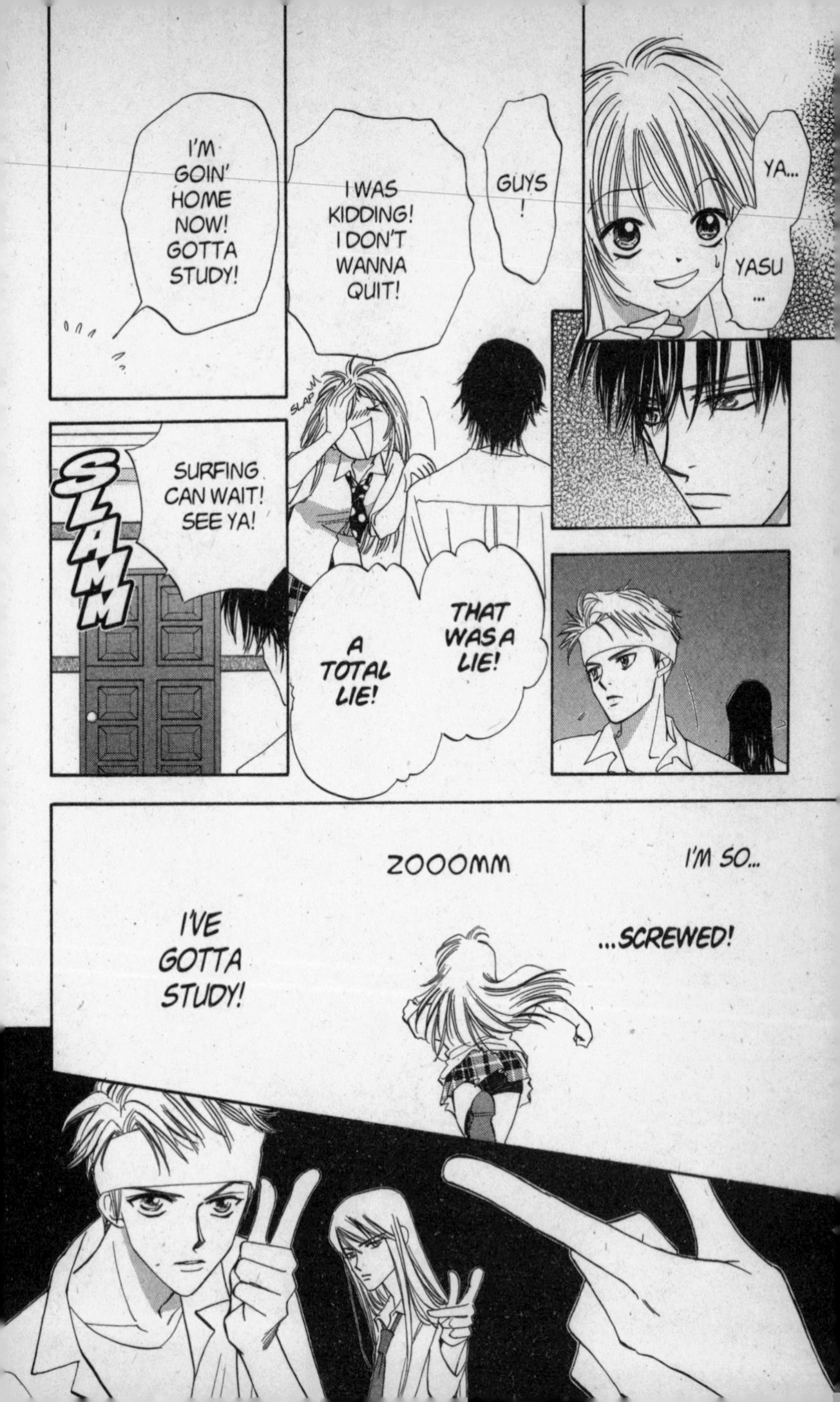

YA...
YASU ...
GUYS !
I WAS KIDDING! I DON'T WANNA QUIT!
I'M GOIN' HOME NOW! GOTTA STUDY!
SLAP
THAT WAS A LIE!
A TOTAL LIE!
SURFING CAN WAIT! SEE YA!
SLAMM
I'M SO...
...SCREWED!
ZOOOMM
I'VE GOTTA STUDY!

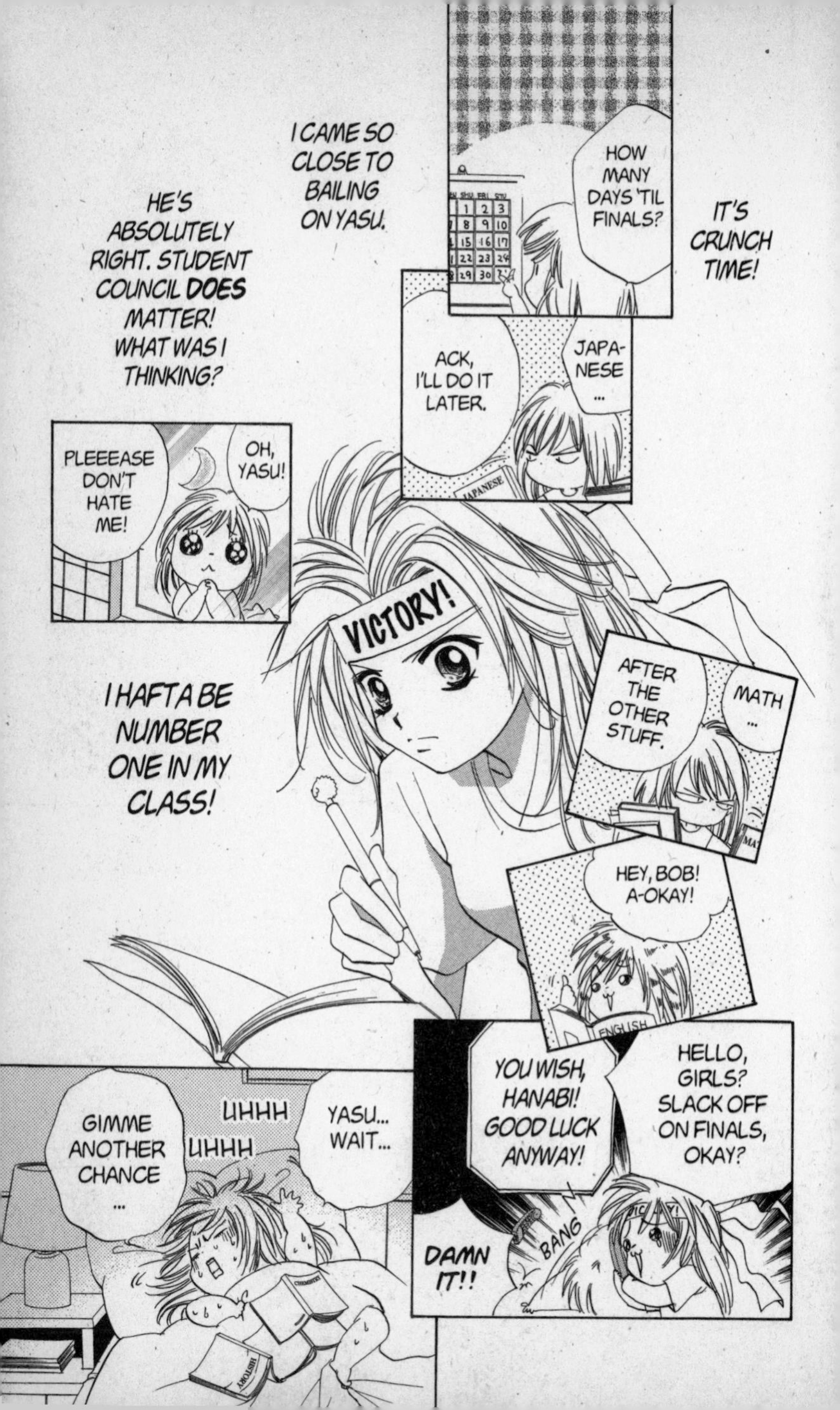
IT'S CRUNCH TIME!
HOW MANY DAYS 'TIL FINALS?
I CAME SO CLOSE TO BAILING ON YASU.
HE'S ABSOLUTELY RIGHT. STUDENT COUNCIL **DOES** MATTER! WHAT WAS I THINKING?
JAPA-NESE ...
ACK, I'LL DO IT LATER.
JAPANESE
OH, YASU!
PLEEEASE DON'T HATE ME!
VICTORY!
I HAFTA BE NUMBER ONE IN MY CLASS!
MATH ...
AFTER THE OTHER STUFF.
HEY, BOB! A-OKAY!
ENGLISH
HELLO, GIRLS? SLACK OFF ON FINALS, OKAY?
YOU WISH, HANABI! GOOD LUCK ANYWAY!
BANG
DAMN IT!!
YASU... WAIT...
UHHH
UHHH
GIMME ANOTHER CHANCE ...
HISTORY

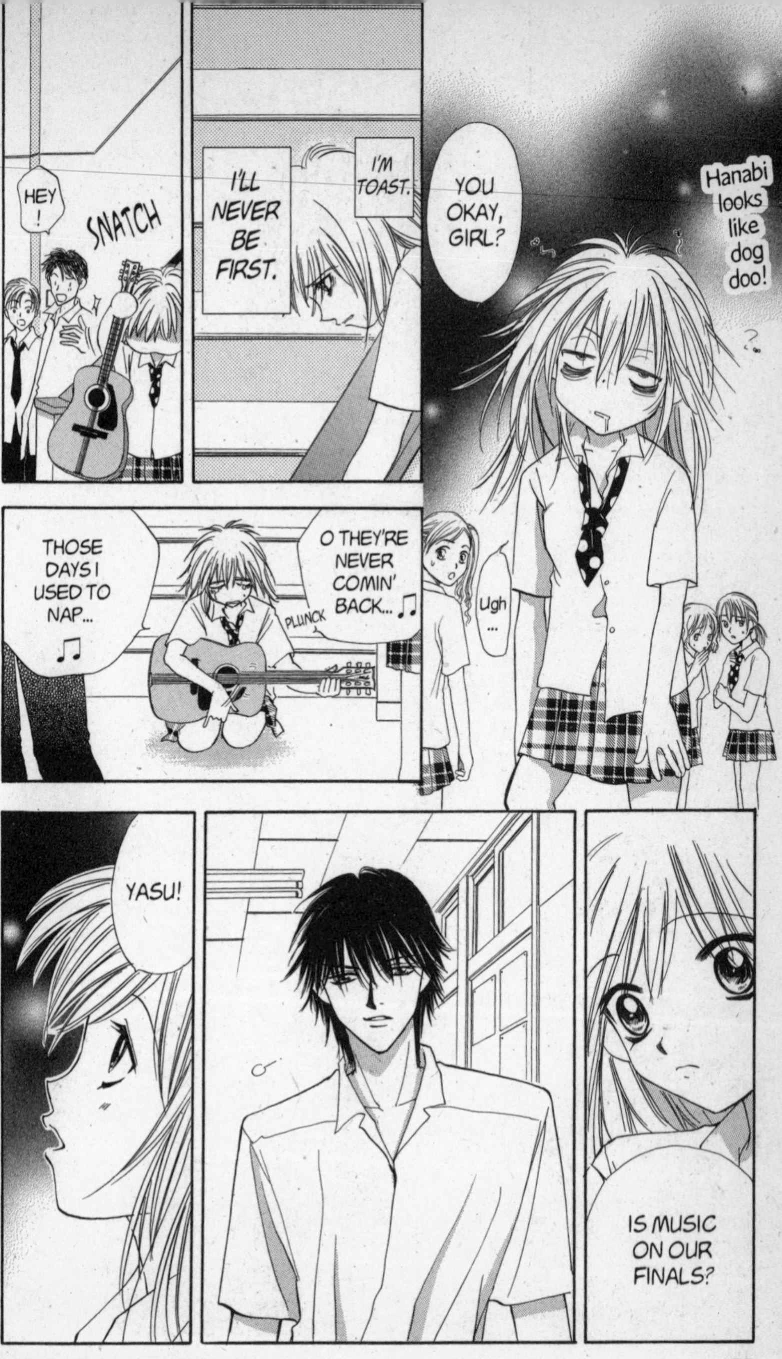
Hanabi looks like dog doo!
YOU OKAY, GIRL?
Ugh...
I'M TOAST.
I'LL NEVER BE FIRST.
SNATCH
HEY!
O THEY'RE NEVER COMIN' BACK... ♫
PLUNCK
THOSE DAYS I USED TO NAP... ♫
IS MUSIC ON OUR FINALS?
YASU!

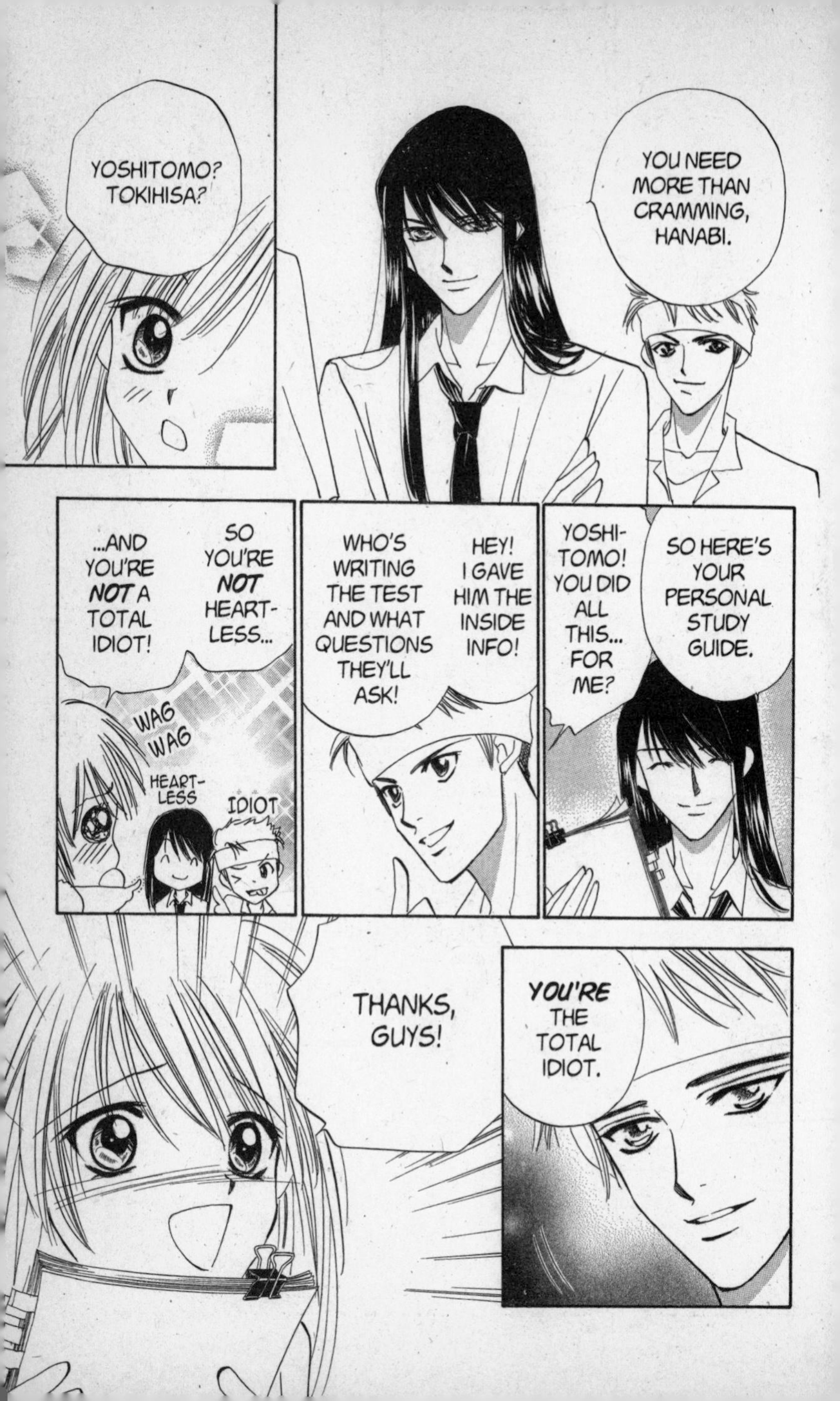
YOU NEED MORE THAN CRAMMING, HANABI.
YOSHITOMO? TOKIHISA?
SO HERE'S YOUR PERSONAL STUDY GUIDE.
YOSHITOMO! YOU DID ALL THIS... FOR ME?
HEY! I GAVE HIM THE INSIDE INFO!
WHO'S WRITING THE TEST AND WHAT QUESTIONS THEY'LL ASK!
SO YOU'RE NOT HEARTLESS...
...AND YOU'RE NOT A TOTAL IDIOT!
WAG WAG
HEARTLESS
IDIOT
YOU'RE THE TOTAL IDIOT.
THANKS, GUYS!

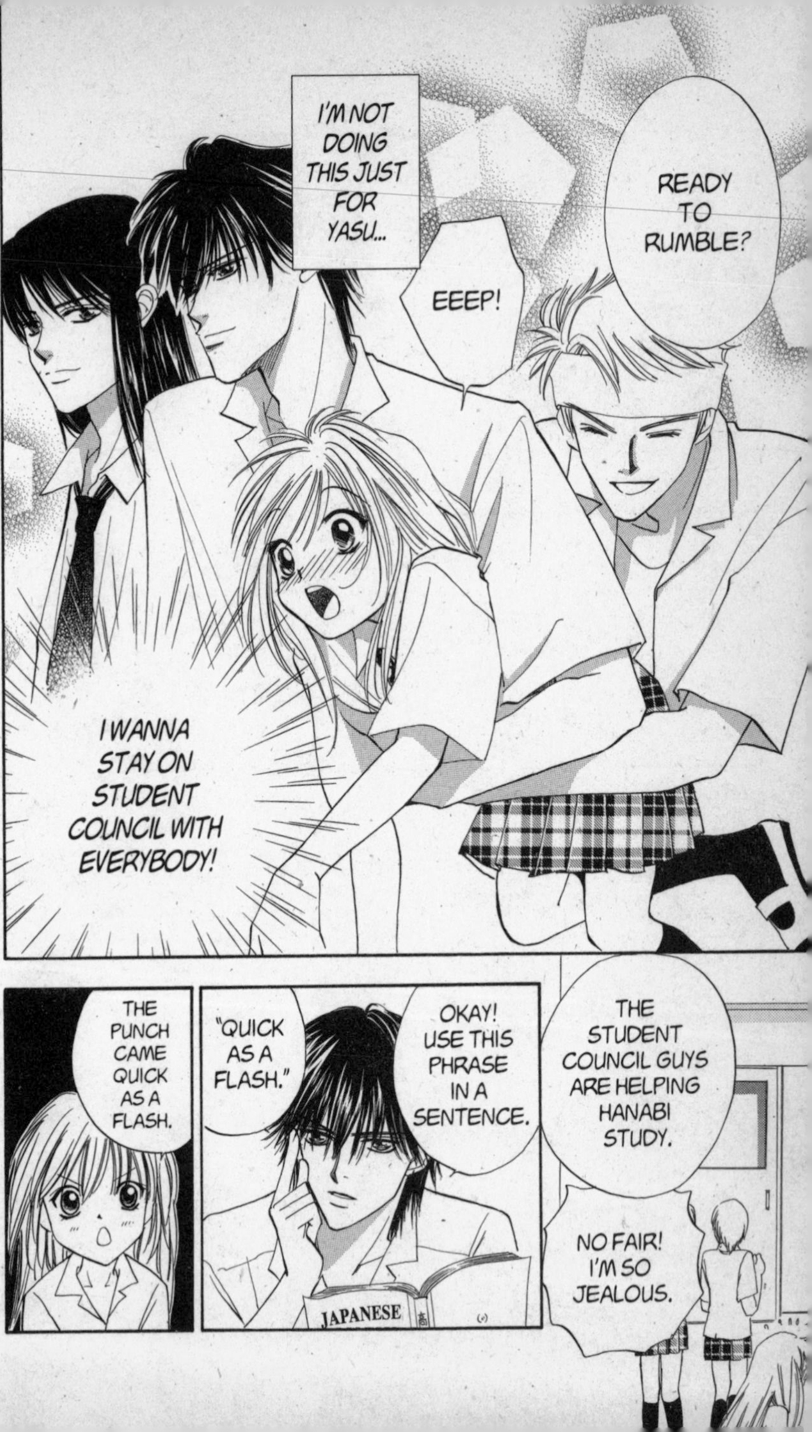
READY TO RUMBLE?
I'M NOT DOING THIS JUST FOR YASU...
EEEP!
I WANNA STAY ON STUDENT COUNCIL WITH EVERYBODY!
THE STUDENT COUNCIL GUYS ARE HELPING HANABI STUDY.
NO FAIR! I'M SO JEALOUS.
OKAY! USE THIS PHRASE IN A SENTENCE.
"QUICK AS A FLASH."
JAPANESE
THE PUNCH CAME QUICK AS A FLASH.

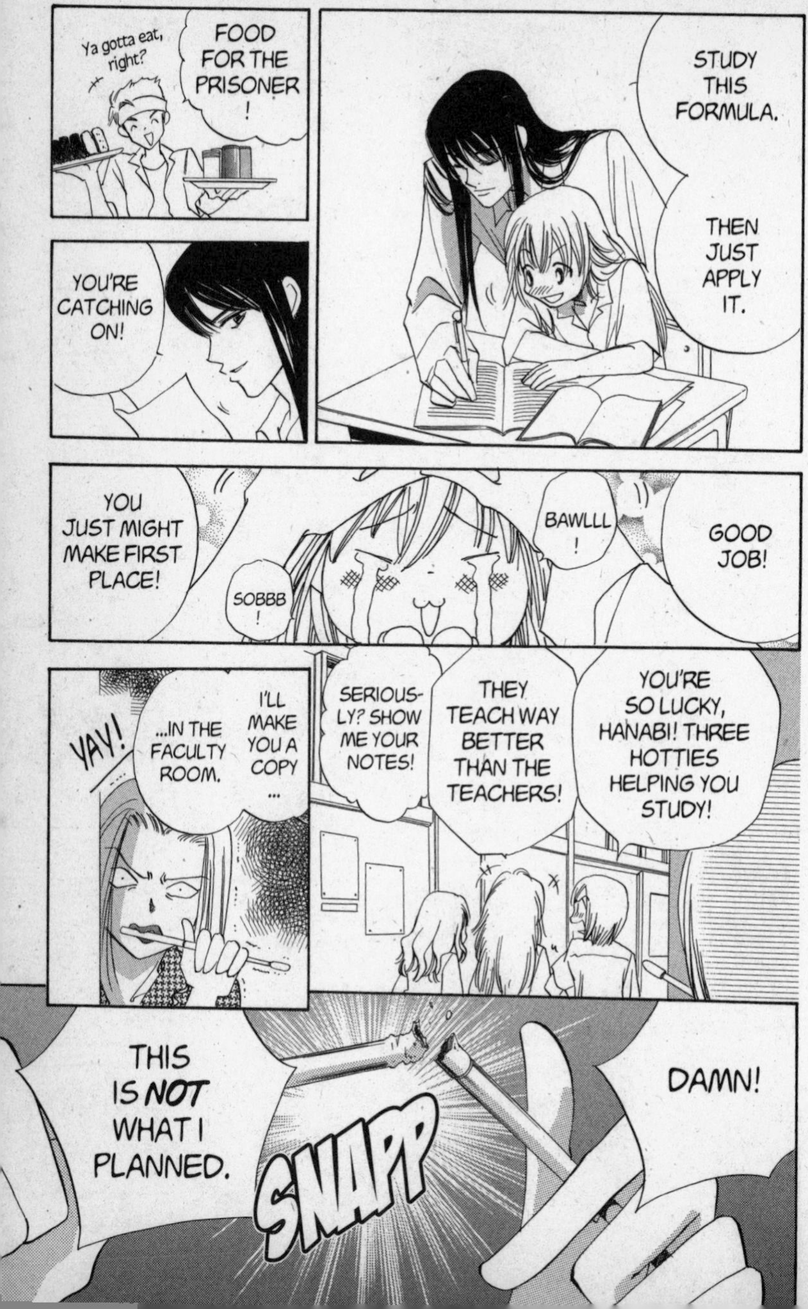

STUDY THIS FORMULA.
THEN JUST APPLY IT.
FOOD FOR THE PRISONER!
Ya gotta eat, right?
YOU'RE CATCHING ON!
GOOD JOB!
BAWLLL!
YOU JUST MIGHT MAKE FIRST PLACE!
SOBBB!
YOU'RE SO LUCKY, HANABI! THREE HOTTIES HELPING YOU STUDY!
THEY TEACH WAY BETTER THAN THE TEACHERS!
SERIOUS-LY? SHOW ME YOUR NOTES!
I'LL MAKE YOU A COPY...
...IN THE FACULTY ROOM.
YAY!
DAMN!
SNAPP
THIS IS **NOT** WHAT I PLANNED.

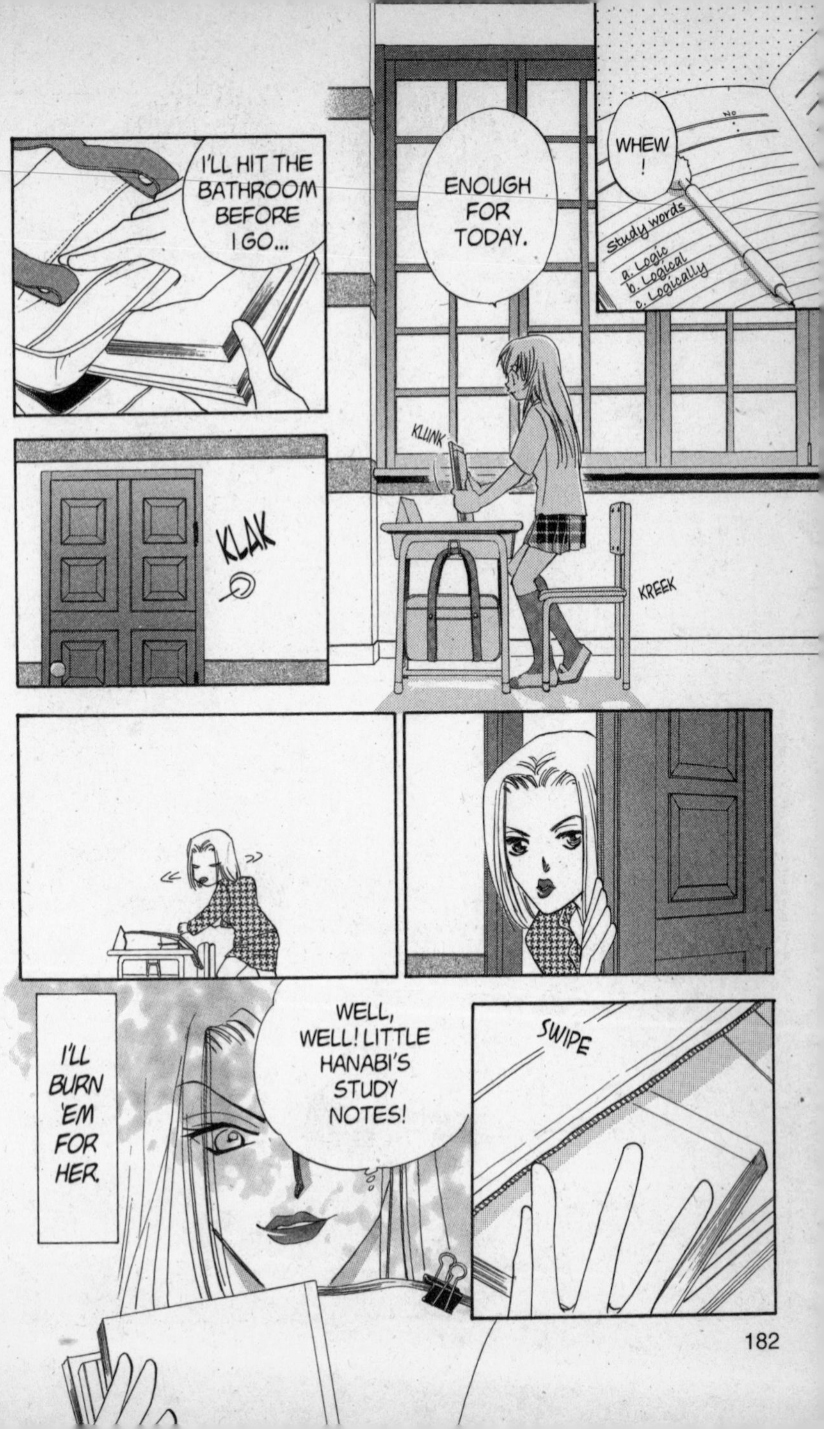
WHEW!
No
Study words
a. Logic
b. Logical
c. Logically
ENOUGH FOR TODAY.
KLUNK
KREEK
I'LL HIT THE BATHROOM BEFORE I GO...
KLAK
SWIPE
WELL, WELL! LITTLE HANABI'S STUDY NOTES!
I'LL BURN 'EM FOR HER.

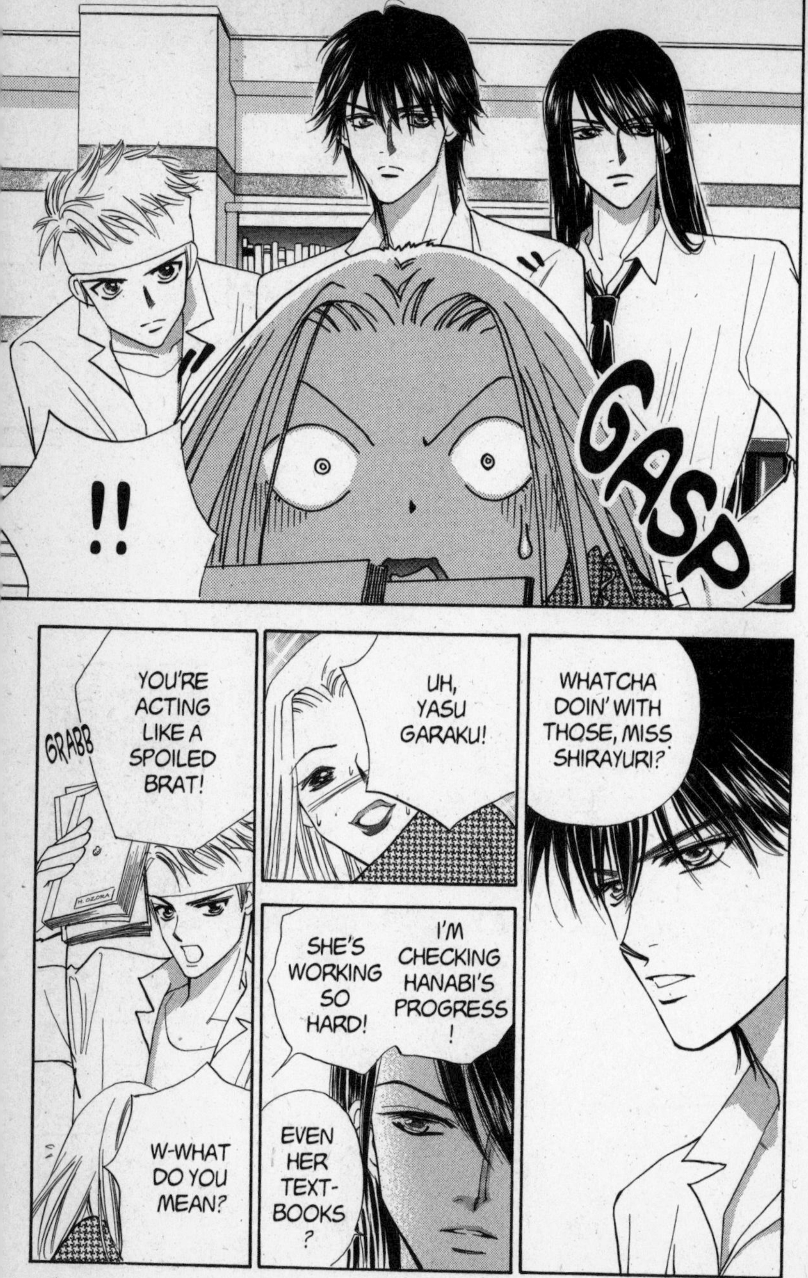
GASP
!!
WHATCHA DOIN' WITH THOSE, MISS SHIRAYURI?
UH, YASU GARAKU!
I'M CHECKING HANABI'S PROGRESS!
SHE'S WORKING SO HARD!
EVEN HER TEXT-BOOKS?
YOU'RE ACTING LIKE A SPOILED BRAT!
GRABB
H. OZORA
W-WHAT DO YOU MEAN?

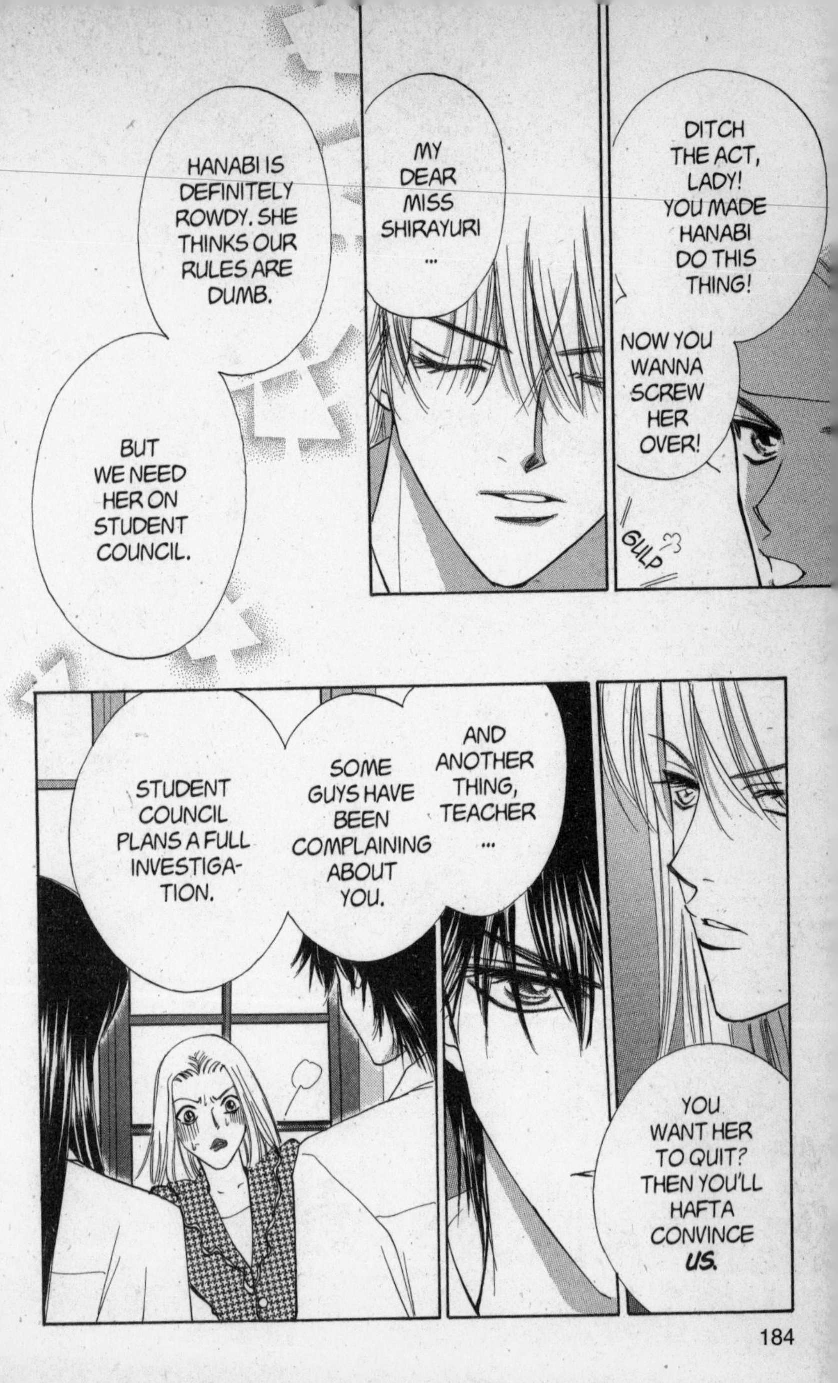
DITCH THE ACT, LADY! YOU MADE HANABI DO THIS THING!
NOW YOU WANNA SCREW HER OVER!
GULP
MY DEAR MISS SHIRAYURI ...
HANABI IS DEFINITELY ROWDY. SHE THINKS OUR RULES ARE DUMB.
BUT WE NEED HER ON STUDENT COUNCIL.
YOU WANT HER TO QUIT? THEN YOU'LL HAFTA CONVINCE **US.**
AND ANOTHER THING, TEACHER ...
SOME GUYS HAVE BEEN COMPLAINING ABOUT YOU.
STUDENT COUNCIL PLANS A FULL INVESTIGA-TION.

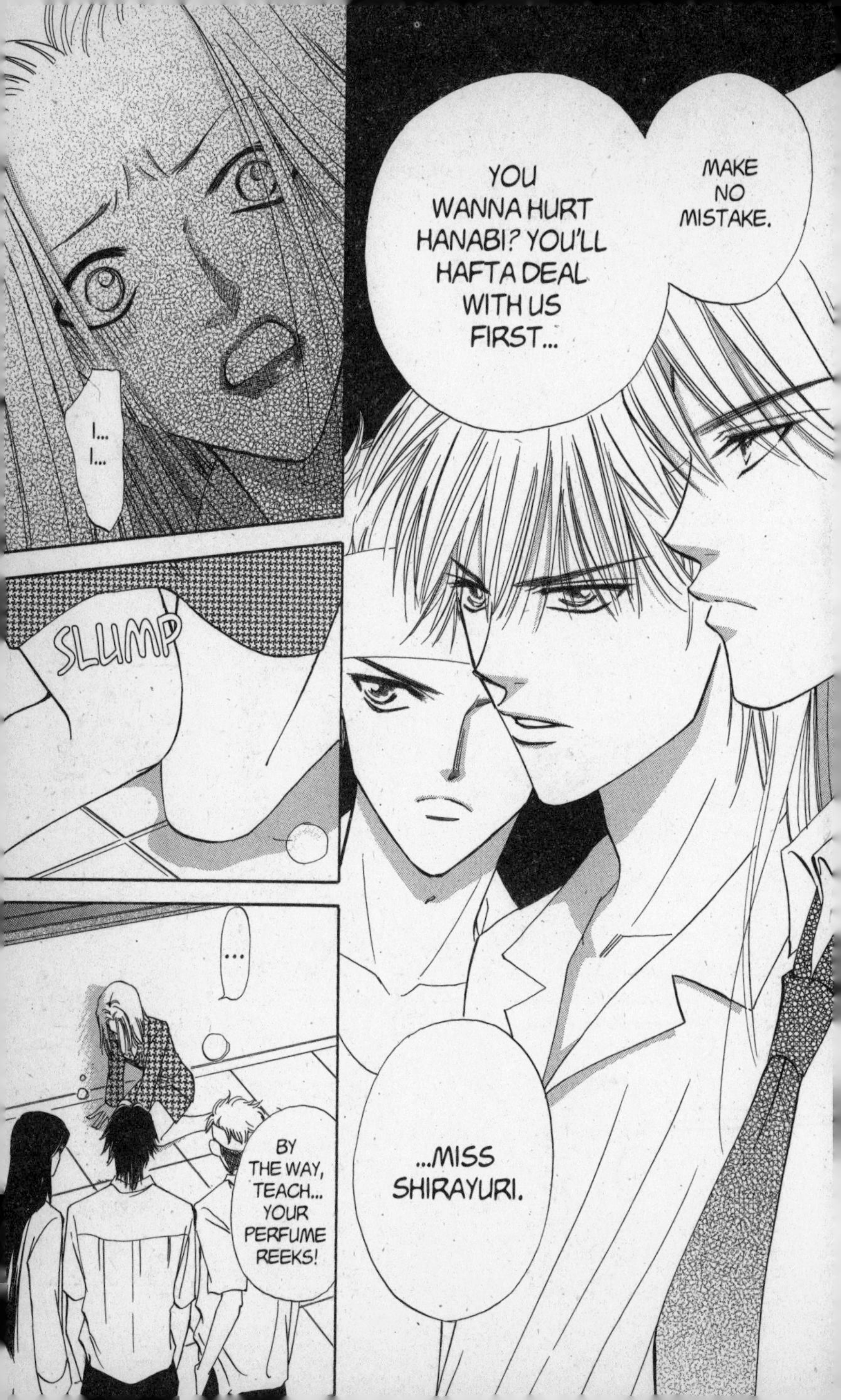
MAKE NO MISTAKE.
YOU WANNA HURT HANABI? YOU'LL HAFTA DEAL WITH US FIRST...
...MISS SHIRAYURI.
I... I...
SLUMP
...
BY THE WAY, TEACH... YOUR PERFUME REEKS!

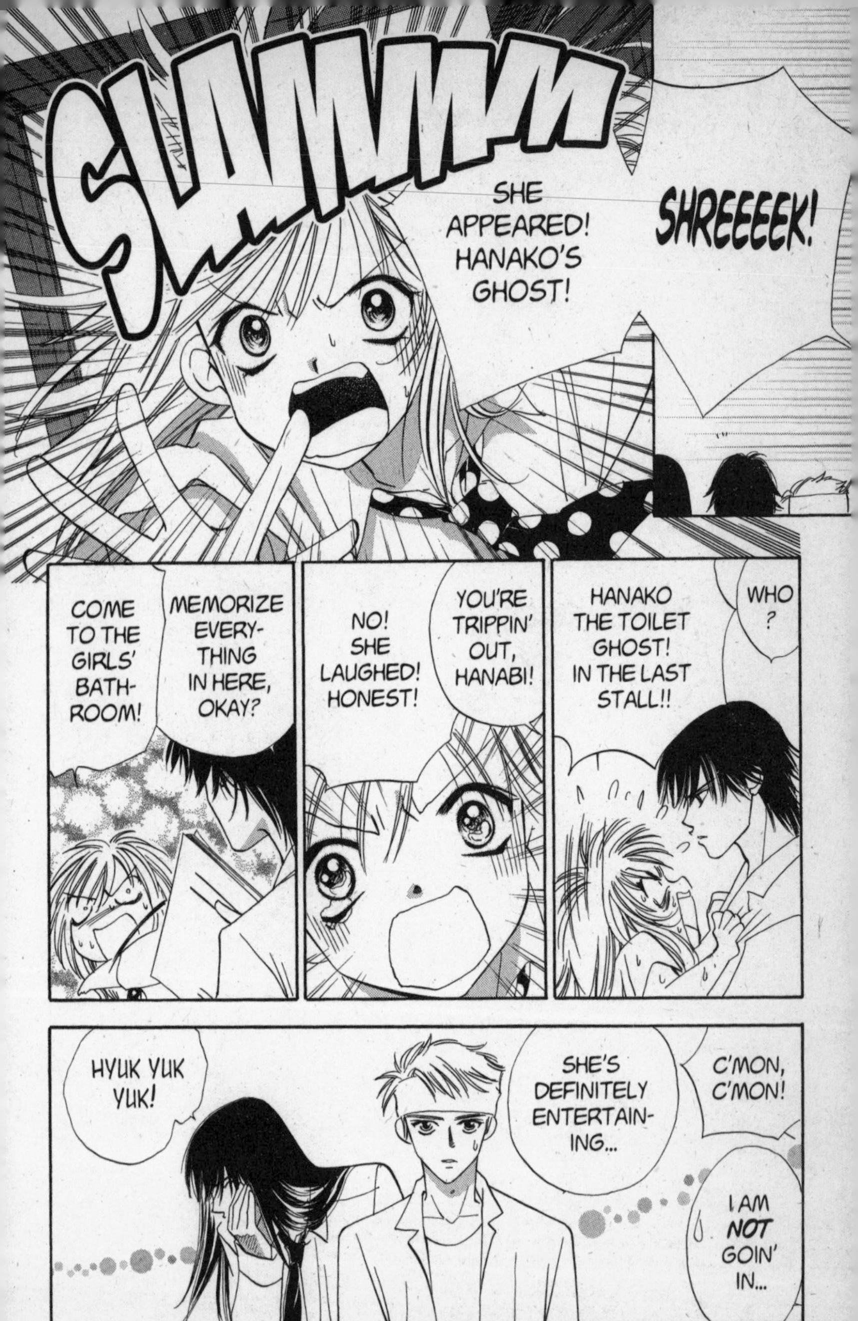
SHREEEEK!
SHE APPEARED! HANAKO'S GHOST!
SLAMMMM
WHO?
HANAKO THE TOILET GHOST! IN THE LAST STALL!!
YOU'RE TRIPPIN' OUT, HANABI!
NO! SHE LAUGHED! HONEST!
MEMORIZE EVERY-THING IN HERE, OKAY?
COME TO THE GIRLS' BATH-ROOM!
C'MON, C'MON!
I AM ***NOT*** GOIN' IN...
SHE'S DEFINITELY ENTERTAIN-ING...
HYUK YUK YUK!

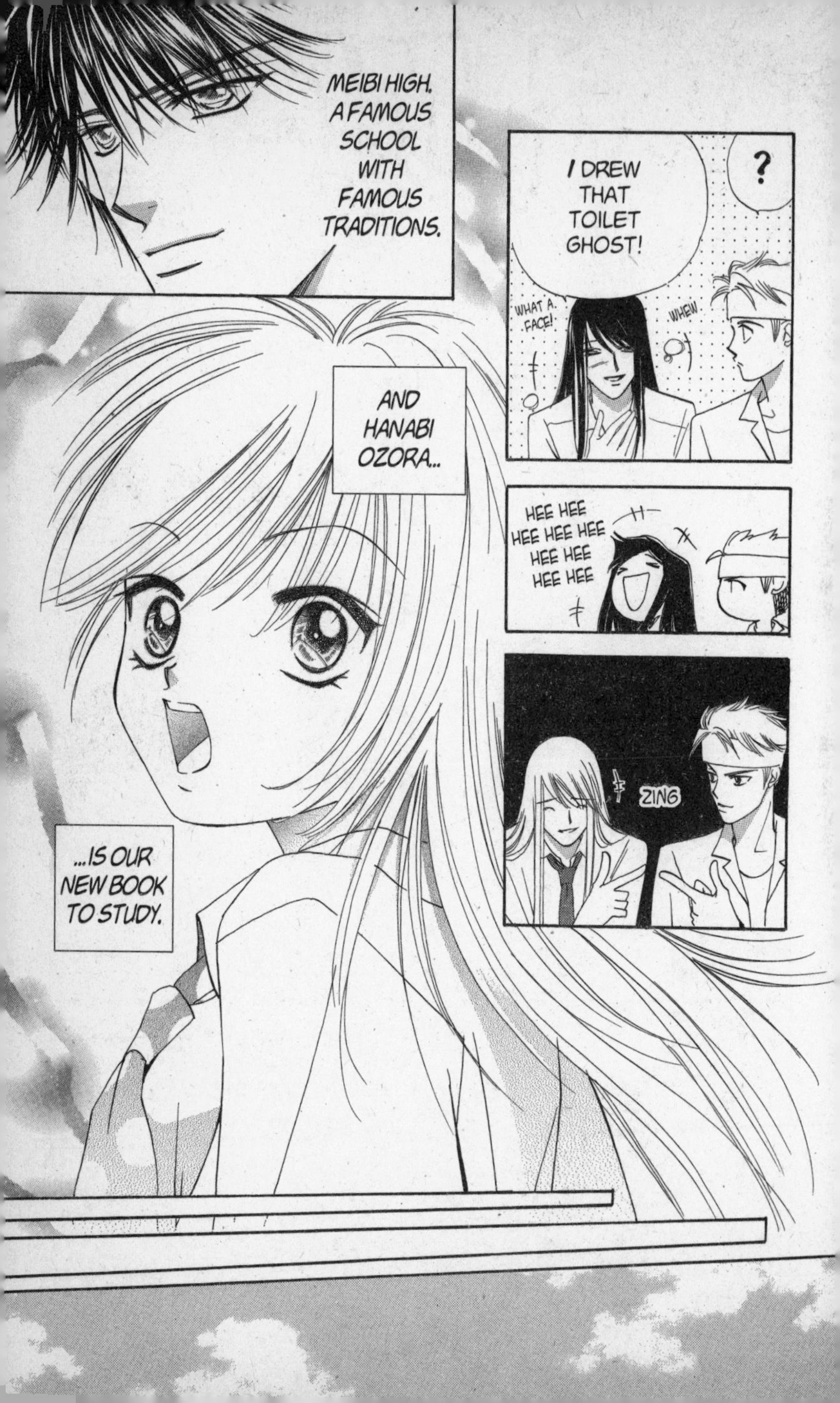

?
I DREW THAT TOILET GHOST!
WHEW
WHAT A. FACE!
HEE HEE HEE HEE HEE HEE HEE HEE HEE
ZING
MEIBI HIGH. A FAMOUS SCHOOL WITH FAMOUS TRADITIONS.
AND HANABI OZORA...
...IS OUR NEW BOOK TO STUDY.

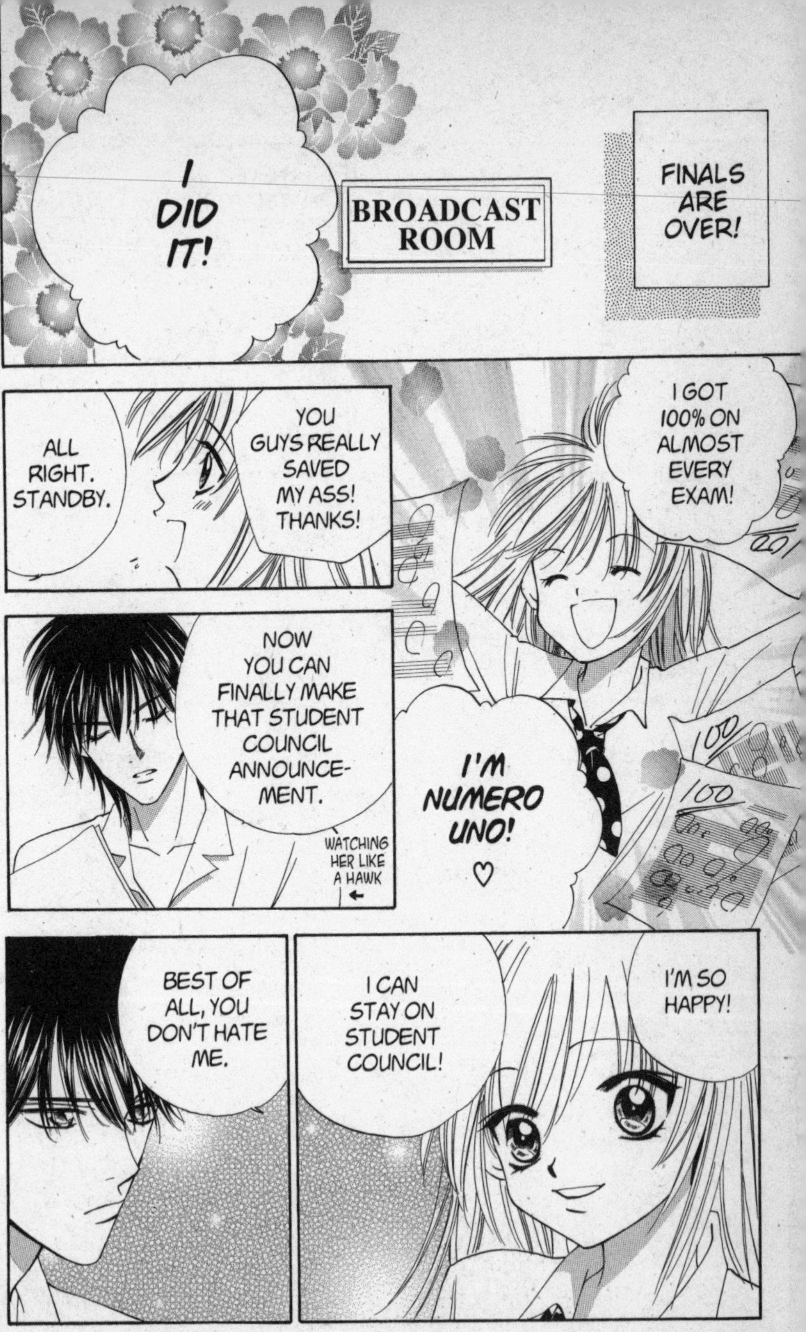
FINALS ARE OVER!
BROADCAST ROOM
I DID IT!
I GOT 100% ON ALMOST EVERY EXAM!
I'M NUMERO UNO! ♡
YOU GUYS REALLY SAVED MY ASS! THANKS!
ALL RIGHT. STANDBY.
NOW YOU CAN FINALLY MAKE THAT STUDENT COUNCIL ANNOUNCE-MENT.
WATCHING HER LIKE A HAWK ←
I'M SO HAPPY!
I CAN STAY ON STUDENT COUNCIL!
BEST OF ALL, YOU DON'T HATE ME.

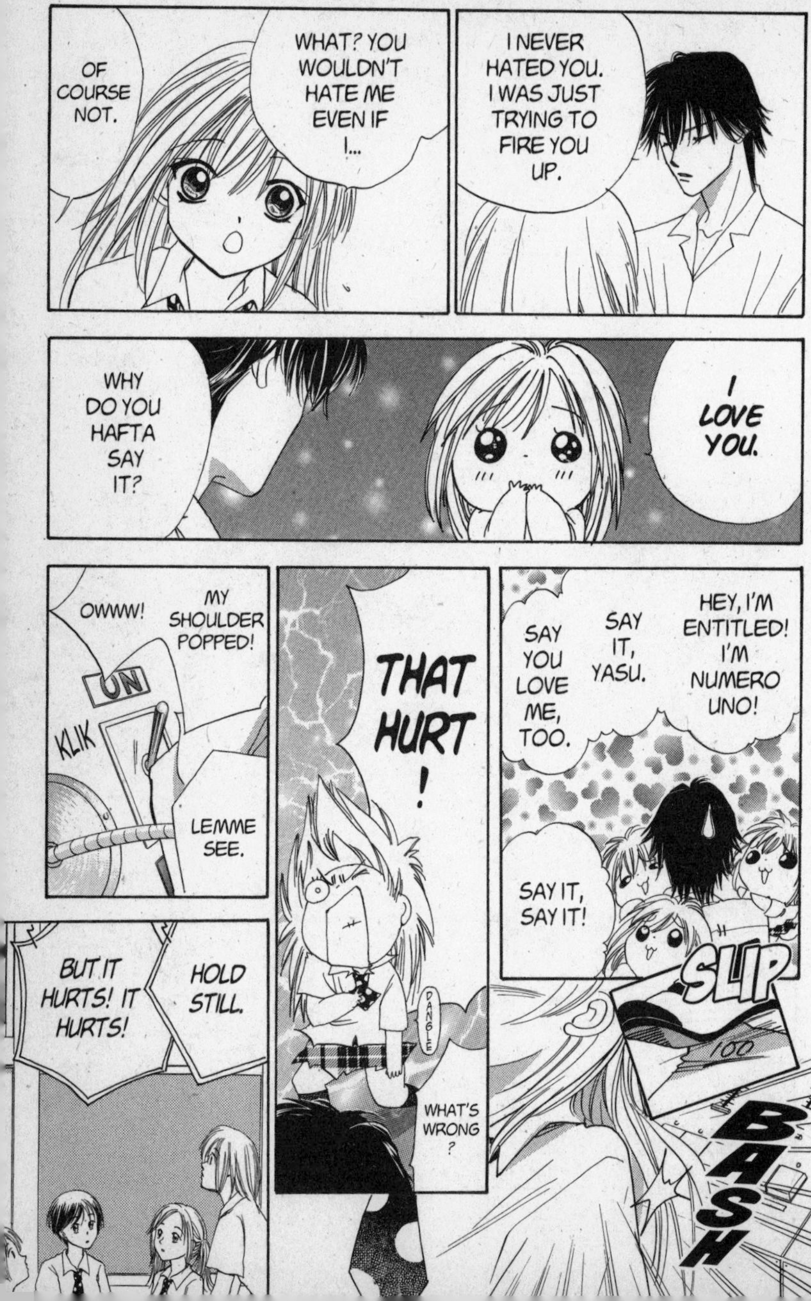
I NEVER HATED YOU. I WAS JUST TRYING TO FIRE YOU UP.
WHAT? YOU WOULDN'T HATE ME EVEN IF I...
OF COURSE NOT.
I LOVE YOU.
WHY DO YOU HAFTA SAY IT?
HEY, I'M ENTITLED! I'M NUMERO UNO!
SAY IT, YASU.
SAY YOU LOVE ME, TOO.
SAY IT, SAY IT!
SLIP
100
BASH
THAT HURT!
DANGLE
WHAT'S WRONG?
MY SHOULDER POPPED!
OWWW!
UN
KLIK
LEMME SEE.
HOLD STILL.
BUT IT HURTS! IT HURTS!

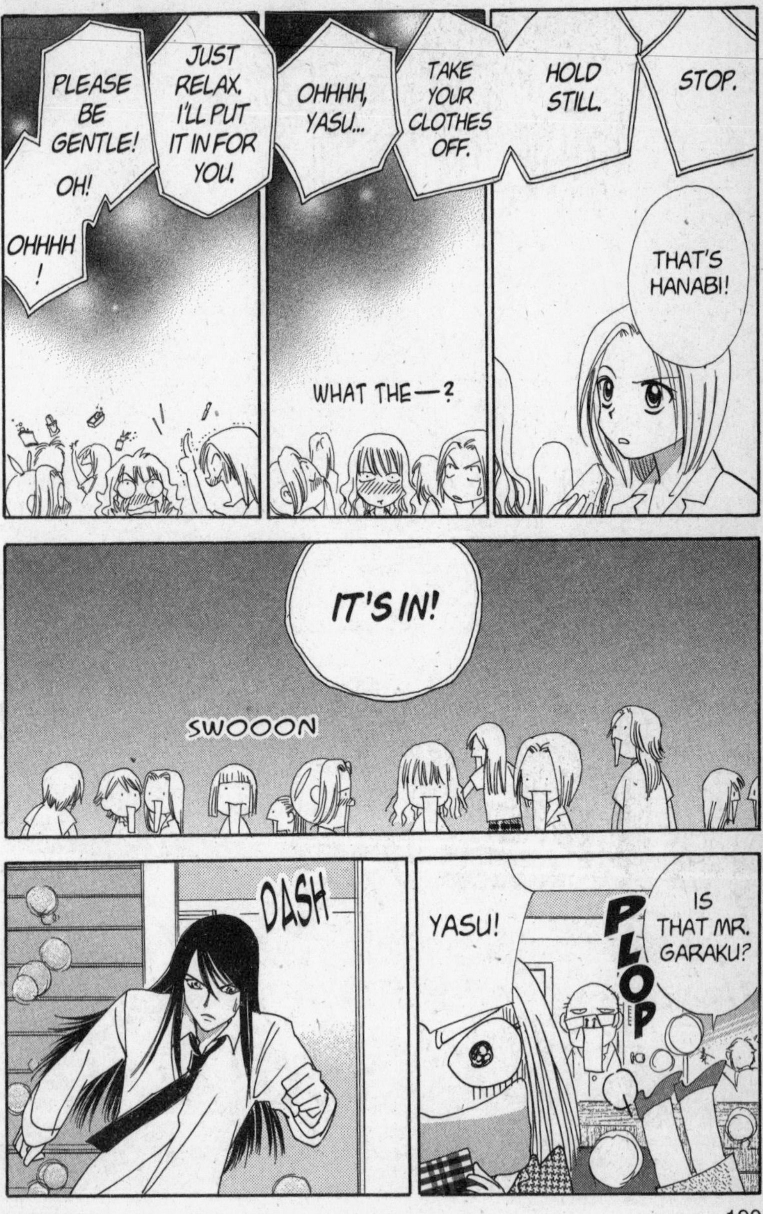
STOP.
HOLD STILL.
THAT'S HANABI!
TAKE YOUR CLOTHES OFF.
OHHHH, YASU...
WHAT THE—?
JUST RELAX. I'LL PUT IT IN FOR YOU.
PLEASE BE GENTLE!
OH!
OHHHH!
IT'S IN!
SWOOON
IS THAT MR. GARAKU?
PLOP
YASU!
DASH

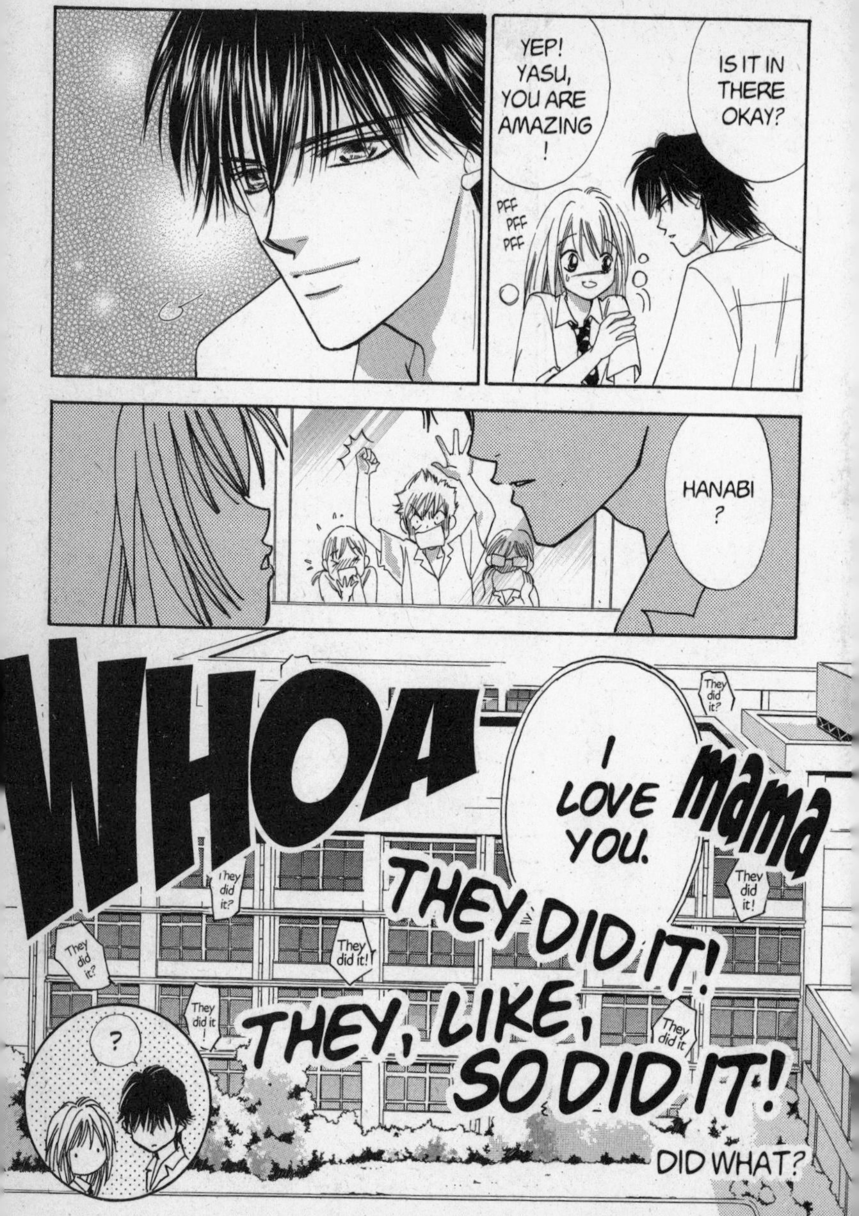
IS IT IN THERE OKAY?
YEP! YASU, YOU ARE AMAZING!
PFF PFF PFF
HANABI?
They did it?
mama
I LOVE YOU.
WHOA
They did it!
They did it?
THEY DID IT!
They did it!
They did it?
They did it
They did it!
THEY, LIKE, SO DID IT!
?
DID WHAT?

TO BE CONTINUED!

HAPPY HUSTLE HIGH
Vol. 4

Story and Art by Rie Takada

Translation/June Honma
Touch-up Art & Lettering/Rina Mapa
Design/Izumi Evers
Editor/Janet Gilbert

Supervising Editor/Kit Fox
Managing Editor/Annette Roman
Director of Production/Noboru Watanabe
Vice President of Publishing/Alvin Lu
Sr. Director of Acquisitions/Rika Inouye
Vice President of Sales & Marketing/Liza Coppola
Publisher/Hyoe Narita

Printed in the U.S.A.

Published by VIZ Media, LLC
P.O. Box 77010
San Francisco, CA 94107

10 9 8 7 6 5 4 3 2 1
First printing, November 2005

www.viz.com
store.viz.com

EDITOR'S RECOMMENDATIONS

If you enjoyed this volume of

HAPPY HUSTLE HIGH

then here's some more manga you might be interested in.

© 2000 Kaneyoshi IZUMI/
Shogakukan Inc.

Doubt!! by Kaneyoshi Izumi: What happens when an ugly duckling decides to fight back? What happens when a self-described wallflower declares all-out war on her school's popularity structure? What happens when the heroine of a *shojo* manga realizes that to overcome her doubt, and her own self-image, she must become the most gorgeous girl in Japan? Kaneyoshi Izumi's *DOUBT!!* is what happens, and you've got to check it out.

© 2002 Kaho MIYASAKA/
Shogakukan Inc.

Kare First Love by Kaho Miyasaka: Karin's fairy-tale love affair with her dishy photographer boyfriend Kiriya is almost too much for her heart to handle. Now that she and Kiriya are going on a vacation to sunny Okinawa, will they finally, um, consummate their relationship? Or, will Kiriya's past tear their love to shreds?

© 2001 Miki AIHARA/
Shogakukan Inc.

Hot Gimmick by Miki Aihara: While hapless heroine Hatsumi's romantic misadventures have kept *HOT GIMMICK* fans on the edge of their seats for months on end, what's been going on with her coquettish little sister Akane? An avouched man-killer, Akane has set her sights on her dorky (yet surprisingly cute—in a really dorky kind of way) neighbor Subaru. Not one used to being rejected by boys, what's Akane to do when Subaru doesn't jump at the chance to be her boyfriend?

LOVE SHOJO? LET US KNOW!

☐ Please do NOT send me information about VIZ Media products, news and events, special offers, or other information.

☐ Please do NOT send me information from VIZ' trusted business partners.

Name: _____

Address: _____

City:_____ State:_____ Zip:_____

E-mail: _____

☐ Male ☐ Female Date of Birth (mm/dd/yyyy): ___/___/_____ (Under 13? Parental consent required)

What race/ethnicity do you consider yourself? (check all that apply)

☐ White/Caucasian ☐ Black/African American ☐ Hispanic/Latino

☐ Asian/Pacific Islander ☐ Native American/Alaskan Native ☐ Other: _____

What VIZ shojo title(s) did you purchase? (indicate title(s) purchased)

_____

What other shojo titles from other publishers do you own? _____

_____

Reason for purchase: (check all that apply)

☐ Special offer ☐ Favorite title / author / artist / genre

☐ Gift ☐ Recommendation ☐ Collection

☐ Read excerpt in VIZ manga sampler ☐ Other _____

Where did you make your purchase? (please check one)

☐ Comic store ☐ Bookstore ☐ Mass/Grocery Store

☐ Newsstand ☐ Video/Video Game Store

☐ Online (site:_____) ☐ Other _____

How many shojo titles have you purchased in the last year? How many were VIZ shojo titles?
(please check one from each column)

SHOJO MANGA	VIZ SHOJO MANGA
☐ None	☐ None
☐ 1 – 4	☐ 1 – 4
☐ 5 – 10	☐ 5 – 10
☐ 11+	☐ 11+

What do you like most about shojo graphic novels? **(check all that apply)**

☐ Romance	☐ Drama / conflict	☐ Fantasy
☐ Comedy	☐ Real-life storylines	☐ Relatable characters

☐ Other ______________________________

Do you purchase every volume of your favorite shojo series?

☐ Yes! Gotta have 'em as my own

☐ No. Please explain: ______________________________

Who are your favorite shojo authors / artists? ______________________________

____

What shojo titles would like you translated and sold in English? ______________________________

____

THANK YOU! Please send the completed form to:

NJW Research
ATTN: VIZ Media Shojo Survey
42 Catharine Street
Poughkeepsie, NY 12601

Your privacy is very important to us. All information provided will be used for internal purposes only and will not be sold or otherwise divulged.